A FIRST NATIONS VOICE IN THE AUSTRALIAN CONSTITUTION

This book makes the legal and political case for Indigenous constitutional recognition through a constitutionally guaranteed First Nations voice, as advocated by the historic Uluru Statement from the Heart. It argues that a constitutional amendment to empower Indigenous peoples with a fairer say in laws and policies made about them and their rights, is both constitutionally congruent and politically achievable. A First Nations voice is deeply in keeping with the culture, design and philosophy of Australia's federal Constitution, as well as the long history of Indigenous advocacy for greater empowerment and self-determination in their affairs.

Morris explores the historical, political, theoretical and international contexts underpinning the contemporary debate, before delving into the constitutional detail to craft a compelling case for change.

A First Nations Voice in the Australian Constitution

Shireen Morris

•HART•
OXFORD • LONDON • NEW YORK • NEW DELHI • SYDNEY

HART PUBLISHING
Bloomsbury Publishing Plc
Kemp House, Chawley Park, Cumnor Hill, Oxford, OX2 9PH, UK
1385 Broadway, New York, NY 10018, USA

First published in Great Britain 2020

A catalogue record for this book is available from the British Library.

Library of Congress Cataloging-in-Publication data

Names: Morris, Shireen, author.

Title: A first nations voice in the Australian constitution / Shireen Morris.

Description: Oxford ; New York : Hart, 2020. | Based on author's thesis (doctoral – Monash University, 2017) issued under title: Recognition through representation : the case for an Indigenous representative body in the Constitution | Includes bibliographical references and index.

Identifiers: LCCN 2020012041 (print) | LCCN 2020012042 (ebook) | ISBN 9781509928927 (hardcover) | ISBN 9781509928934 (Epub)

Subjects: LCSH: Aboriginal Australians—Legal status, laws, etc. | Constitutional law—Australia. | Representative government and representation—Australia.

Classification: LCC KU2107.M56 M67 2020 (print) | LCC KU2107.M56 (ebook) | DDC 342.9408/72—dc23

LC record available at https://lccn.loc.gov/2020012041

LC ebook record available at https://lccn.loc.gov/2020012042

ISBN: HB: 978-1-50992-892-7
ePDF: 978-1-50992-894-1
ePub: 978-1-50992-893-4

Typeset by Compuscript Ltd, Shannon

Acknowledgements

THIS BOOK IS the product of an intellectual journey undertaken over the last nine years. In 2011, I began working at Cape York Institute (CYI) with the Aboriginal leader and lawyer, Noel Pearson, exploring reform solutions in the debate about Indigenous constitutional recognition. For seven years I worked at the Institute, during which time I completed my PhD thesis making the case for a First Nations constitutional body to ensure Indigenous peoples a fairer voice in laws and policies made about them. In 2018, I began work at the University of Melbourne Law School (MLS) as a McKenzie Postdoctoral Fellow, which enabled me to turn my thesis into this book. I am grateful to CYI and MLS for supporting this work, which afforded me the opportunity for genuine intellectual exploration and collaboration across intellectual, political, ideological and cultural divides. A personal account of this journey is detailed in my 2018 book, *Radical Heart: Three Stories Make Us One* (Melbourne University Press 2018).

In 2014, under Pearson's leadership, this exploration and collaboration gave rise to a new conception of a very old idea, which built on decades of Indigenous advocacy: a constitutionally enshrined Indigenous representative body, to guarantee Indigenous people a voice in the governance of their affairs. Might this proposal present a model for constitutionally recognising Indigenous peoples and rights in a way that enlivens the kind of coalition of political support necessary for a successful 'double majority' referendum? In this book, I make the case for a First Nations voice in the *Constitution*, as advocated by the historic Uluru Statement from the Heart in 2017. Through the chapters I seek to share steps I took in my own reasoning as I searched for workable solutions to the legal and political challenges being faced in this debate.

My first step is to explore the historical, political and theoretical context in which the conversation about Indigenous constitutional recognition takes place, to elucidate the fundamental problem of purpose: what problem does constitutional recognition seek to fix? I suggest that constitutional recognition seeks much more than just symbolism: it seeks to reform the power relationship between Indigenous peoples and the Australian state, to ensure that it is fairer than in the past. I discuss how best to achieve this, given the legal and political parameters involved in successful constitutional reform. As I did in my own journey of discoveries and dead ends, the book grapples with, explores and eliminates particular reform solutions. Is a racial non-discrimination guarantee the answer? History and politics tell us this may not attract the bipartisan support arguably necessary for referendum success. I then seek inspiration from overseas, before considering non-litigious, political and procedural constitutional reform alternatives. Could reserved Indigenous seats in Parliament present a way forward, like in New Zealand? Given Australia's *Constitution* and politics this may not be the best answer either. What about a constitutionally guaranteed Indigenous body, to ensure the First Nations a voice in laws and policies made about them? My hope is that readers will come to the same conclusion I did: a First Nations voice in the *Constitution*, as advocated by the Uluru Statement, properly drafted and implemented, fits with the culture, history and philosophy of *Australian Constitution*. A First Nations constitutional voice offers the best chance at winning an Indigenous recognition referendum.

Writing an academic book is in many ways a collective effort. I thank my parents, my brother and my husband, Sam, for being supportive throughout the process. I thank Kirsty Gover for her useful comments on the comparative chapter and Cheryl Saunders and Adrienne Stone for their leadership at the Centre for Comparative Constitutional Studies at MLS. I thank Melissa Castan and Patrick Emerton at Monash University for supervising my PhD thesis. I thank Damien Freeman for his ongoing guidance. I am grateful to Greg Craven, Anne Twomey and Julian Leeser for their collaboration and expertise. I appreciate, too, to the MLS Academic Research team and the support of Ken Kiat and Cate Read in converting the footnotes in the manuscript.

I want to particularly thank Noel Pearson for his mentorship, leadership and continued intellectual challenges over the years – it has been through my work with Pearson that the original thinking that gave rise to the concept of a First Nations constitutional voice was able to flourish. Pearson, and the other Indigenous leaders who worked so hard to achieve the Uluru Statement, remain a source of inspiration. While this book is the product of ongoing collaboration and conversation and my thinking has been shaped by many, any errors in fact or interpretation are my own.

I write this book from the perspective of an Australian constitutional lawyer of Indian and Fijian-Indian heritage. I do not speak for Indigenous Australians. I write as an academic and advocate for sensible and achievable constitutional recognition of the kind Indigenous people say they want, and as an Australian who wants to see justice and reconciliation in my lifetime.

Dr Shireen Morris
Melbourne Law School

Contents

Table of Cases

Table of Legislation

Legislation

Treaties

1

Introduction

All the black man wants is representation in federal parliament … One hundred and fifty years ago, the Aboriginals owned Australia, and today he demands more than the white man's charity. He wants the right to live.

King Burraga (Joe Anderson), chief of the Thurawal tribe near Sydney, in 1933.[1]

[T]he procedures of the excision of this land and the fate of the people on it were never explained to them beforehand, and were kept secret from them.

… when Welfare Officers and Government officials came to inform them of decisions taken without them and against them, they did not undertake to convey to the Government in Canberra the views and feelings of the Yirrkala aboriginal people.

… the people of this area fear that their needs and interests will be completely ignored as they have been ignored in the past, and they fear that the fate which has overtaken the Larrakeah tribe will overtake them.

And they humbly pray that the Honourable the House of Representatives will appoint a Committee, accompanied by competent interpreters, to hear the views of the people of Yirrkala before permitting the excision of this land.

The Yirrkala Bark Petitions in 1963.[2]

Our Yolgnu law is more like your Balanda Constitution than Balanda legislation or statutory law. It doesn't change at the whim of short-term political expediency. It protects the principles which go to make up the very essence of who we are and how we should manage the most precious things about our culture and our society. Changing it is a very serious business … If our Indigenous rights were recognised in the Constitution, it would not be so easy for Governments to change the laws all the time, and wipe out our rights.

Yolngu elder, Galarrwuy Yunupingu in 1998.[3]

[1] Heather Goodall, Invasion to Embassy: Land in Aboriginal Politics in New South Wales, 1770–1972 (Sydney University Press 2008) 204. See also Bain Attwood and Andrew Markus, Thinking Black: William Cooper and the Australian Aborigines' League (Aboriginal Studies Press 2004) 36.

[2] 'Documenting a Democracy, Yirrkala Bark Petitions 1963 (Cth)' <http://www.foundingdocs.gov.au/item-did-104.html> accessed 1 October 2019.

[3] Galarrwuy Yunupingu, 'The Third Vincent Lingiari Memorial Lecture' (20 August 1998). ('Balanda' means European or Western).

> These dimensions of our crisis tell plainly the structural nature of our problem. This is the torment of our powerlessness.
>
> We seek constitutional reforms to empower our people and take a rightful place in our own country. When we have power over our destiny our children will flourish. They will walk in two worlds and their culture will be a gift to their country.
>
> We call for the establishment of a First Nations Voice enshrined in the Constitution …
>
> In 1967 we were counted, in 2017 we seek to be heard.
>
> Uluru Statement from the Heart in 2017.

I. BACKGROUND

INDIGENOUS CONSTITUTIONAL RECOGNITION is an area of Australian scholarship that simmers sporadically with political opportunity. Political leadership on the issue waxes and wanes. Both sides of politics maintain support for the idea of recognising Indigenous peoples in the *Australian Constitution*. But what does this mean? The debate challenges constitutional experts and reform advocates to ask and answer some of the nation's toughest yet most fundamental legal and political questions – questions that go to the heart of who we are as a country and who we want to be. What is the purpose of Indigenous constitutional recognition? What problem does it seek to fix? How might Australia reform and reset its constitutional relationship between Indigenous peoples and the Australian state, to ensure it is fairer than in the past? What is the best and most legally sound way to recognise and protect Indigenous rights and interests in Australia's *Constitution*? And how do the various solutions measure up against considerations of political viability? Constitutional reform cannot be separated from constitutional politics: the two are inextricably entwined. It is the people and the Parliament who hold the keys to changing the *Constitution*, with Parliament often acting as gatekeeper to structural progress that the Australian people may otherwise find attractive. Will the nation ever find a way through this maze, to take the steps to meaningfully recognise Indigenous peoples within the nation's constitutional arrangements – steps that other comparable democracies seem to have taken with greater ease?

The politics are complex and can make the *Australian Constitution* seem frozen in its intransigence: only 8 out of 44 attempted referenda have succeeded and the last successful constitutional reform was in 1977.[4] Former Prime Minister John Howard attempted to symbolically recognise Indigenous peoples in 1999 with a new preamble to the *Constitution*, alongside the Republic referendum. Many

[4] For the track record, see Australian Electoral Commission, Referendum Dates and Results, <http://www.aec.gov.au/Elections/referendums/Referendum_Dates_and_Results.htm> accessed 18 October 2019.

Indigenous leaders opposed the change[5] and the Australian people voted 'no' to both reforms – only 39.34 per cent voted 'yes' to the new preamble.[6] Troublingly, some politicians seem to want to re-run the 1999 failure. Australian governments thus far have not implemented Indigenous calls for substantive constitutional reform, instead tending to prefer a merely symbolic constitutional mention that entails no structural or operational reform.[7] But the government preference for pure symbolism is contrary to the long history of Indigenous advocacy for substantive constitutional reform and Indigenous aspirations as expressed in the historic Uluru Statement from the Heart. It is also strategically unwise. As this book will argue, the minimalist route will lead to a repeated referendum defeat.[8] Cracking the difficult formula for winning a constitutional referendum requires innovative thinking and hard work. There are no lazy ways through.

The Uluru Statement calls for one constitutional reform: a constitutionally guaranteed First Nations voice in their affairs.[9] I argue this is the right approach to Indigenous constitutional recognition. A constitutional voice is a balanced reform solution that is at once constitutionally innovative and constitutionally conservative: it is substantive and empowering, yet in keeping with Australian constitutional history, culture and design. This is a 'modest yet profound',[10] 'radical centre'[11] reform which, with leadership, perseverance and determination, can navigate the political blockages to meaningful constitutional reform in Australia. The Uluru Statement offers a breakthrough way forward that, in my view, provides the only way to win a recognition referendum.

The call for a First Nations constitutional voice builds on decades of Indigenous advocacy for greater representation, participation and self-determination in their affairs; however, the convergence of such calls for First Nations political empowerment with the push for Indigenous constitutional recognition

[5] See Mark McKenna, 'First words: A Brief History of Public Debate on a New Preamble to the Australian Constitution 1991-99', Parliament of Australia, Research Paper No 16, 1999–2000 <https://www.aph.gov.au/About_Parliament/Parliamentary_Departments/Parliamentary_Library/pubs/rp/rp9900/2000RP16> accessed on 31 December 2019.

[6] Australian Electoral Commission, '1999 Referendum Report and Statistics' (24 January 2011) <https://www.aec.gov.au/Elections/referendums/1999_Referendum_Reports_Statistics/Key_Results.htm> accessed 1 October 2019.

[7] See Megan Davis, 'Political timetables Trump Workable Timetables: Indigenous Constitutional Recognition and the Temptation of Symbolism over Substance' in Simon Young, Jennifer Nielsen and Jeremy Patrick (eds), *Constitutional Recognition of First Peoples in Australia* (Federation Press 2016) 81, 88.

[8] Shireen Morris and Noel Pearson, 'Indigenous Constitutional Recognition: Paths to Failure and Possible Paths to Success' (2017) 91(5) *Australian Law Journal* 350.

[9] It also called for a Makarrata Commission, set up in legislation, to oversee agreement-making and truth telling.

[10] Greg Craven, 'Noel Pearson's Indigenous Recognition Plan Profound and Practical', *The Australian* (23 May 2015) <https://www.theaustralian.com.au/nation/politics/noel-pearsons-indigenous-recognition-plan-profound-and-practical/news-story/472ff0238ad4f48cd423fdd9f74a9363> accessed 1 October 2019.

[11] Shireen Morris, 'The Radical Centre: Constitutional Conservatism and Indigenous Recognition', *ABC Religion & Ethics* (17 April 2018): <http://www.abc.net.au/religion/articles/2018/04/17/4831438.htm> accessed 1 October 2019.

represents a decisive shift in the recent debate. For the first part of the last decade, the debate on Indigenous constitutional recognition tended to focus on judicially adjudicated constitutional avenues for Indigenous rights protection. Particularly, it focused on the possibility of a new racial non-discrimination clause in the *Constitution*, as proposed by the Expert Panel in 2012.[12] The Uluru Statement changed the conversation. It offered a new way of thinking about the challenge of Indigenous constitutional recognition.

This shift in thinking presents fresh possibilities for consensus. Where proposals for additional constitutional rights guarantees have tended to create an intellectual and political impasse beyond which consensus has struggled to progress, discussion of political, procedural and participatory mechanisms for Indigenous recognition can illuminate more viable, alternative pathways forward in the national debate. A First Nations voice fits neatly with the philosophy, history and culture of Australia's *Constitution*. The *Constitution* is a power-sharing compact that is all about voices. It recognises and constitutionally guarantees representation of even the smallest historic political communities – the former colonies – ensuring their concerns will always be heard by more populous powers. It is but a small step to also recognise and guarantee that the voices of the First Nations – the historic political community wrongfully omitted from the constitutional compact of 1901 – are also heard in their affairs.

Australian constitutional culture, design and history support the argument that Indigenous constitutional recognition can best occur through political participation, representation and dialogue, rather than through a judicially adjudicated limitation on parliamentary power. This is the crux of the proposal for a First Nations constitutional voice: it presents a mechanism for Indigenous empowerment through political processes, not through the courts. The proposal thus upholds Australia's *Constitution* and respects parliamentary supremacy. It is a constitutionally congruent reform, revolutionary in its modesty. Properly conceived and drafted, the concept can address the relevant aspirations and concerns of divergent stakeholders in this debate: the aspirations of Indigenous peoples who have repeatedly made clear they want substantive, empowering constitutional reform – not mere symbolism; the concerns of constitutional conservatives, who want to uphold the *Constitution* and minimise legal uncertainty; and the concerns of Australian politicians, many of whom may not want to give up power to the High Court. Appropriately formulated, this is a workable 'noble compromise' solution.[13]

[12] Expert Panel on Constitution Recognition of Indigenous Australians, *Recognising Aboriginal and Torres Strait Islander Peoples in the Constitution: Report of the Expert Panel* (2012) <https://antar.org.au/sites/default/files/expert_panel_report_.pdf>.

[13] Noel Pearson and Shireen Morris, 'Indigenous Voice Ideal Option for Constitutional Change', *The Australian* (22 July 2017) <https://www.theaustralian.com.au/nation/inquirer/indigenous-voice-ideal-option-for-constitutional-change/news-story/8d318fd0a596dfd963e151c3c1fabccc> accessed 1 October 2019.

Addressing all rational concerns in this debate is important. As a matter of political strategy, a successful referendum can only be achieved by developing wide political consensus. Indigenous constitutional recognition must therefore forge three layers of consensus, each building upon the other. The first requirement is Indigenous consensus. A majority of Indigenous Australians should agree that the model of constitutional recognition is acceptable to them. This is a morally necessary precondition: it would be unconscionable to go ahead with a form of recognition that Indigenous people do not want. Indigenous national consensus has now been achieved through the Uluru Statement.

Indigenous consensus alone is not enough, however. The second requirement is winning widespread support from representatives in the Commonwealth Parliament – for Parliament will need to initiate any proposed referendum to make the constitutional reform a reality. Here, bipartisan support is usually considered important. Parliamentarians across the political spectrum will need to explain and advocate the proposed reform to the wider public. It is therefore not enough if reform-eager progressives support the change; success will likely require reform-cautious conservatives to champion the reform as well.[14] With political leadership across left and right, Australians across the political spectrum will be more inclined to vote 'yes'.

The Australian people will pose the final test through a referendum to change the *Constitution*. Section 128 of the *Constitution* requires a 'double majority' referendum: a majority of voters in a majority of States, as well as a majority nationally, must vote 'yes' to approve any constitutional change. Australians so far seem amenable to the proposal for a First Nations voice in the *Constitution*. A 2017 Omnipoll showed 61 per cent would vote 'yes' to the proposal,[15] and a February 2018 Newspoll demonstrated 57 per cent support.[16] In July 2019, research showed support at 66 per cent[17] – even in the face of sustained

[14] See also Noel Pearson, 'Indigenous People Need a Lot More than Just Symbolism', *The Australian* (4 July 2015) <https://www.theaustralian.com.au/commentary/opinion/indigenous-people-need-a-lot-more-than-just-symbolism/news-story/5db4aa54cbb26969420b4ff141d85aed> accessed 18 October 2019.

[15] Calla Wahlquist, 'Most Australians Would Support Indigenous Voice to Parliament Plan that Turnbull Rejected', *The Guardian* (30 October 2017) <https://www.theguardian.com/australia-news/2017/oct/30/most-australians-support-indigenous-voice-to-parliament-plan-that-turnbull-rejected> accessed 1 October 2019.

[16] Simon Benson, 'Shorten Raising Voice a Winner with Voters: Newspoll', *The Australian* (20 February 2018) <https://www.theaustralian.com.au/nation/bill-shorten-raising-voice-a-winner-with-voters-newspoll/news-story/3d6ee299780b7ac6901df9ccdfa16cc5> accessed 1 October 2019.

[17] Katherine Murphy, 'Essential Poll: Majority of Australians Want Indigenous Recognition and Voice to Parliament', *The Guardian* (12 July 2019) <https://www.theguardian.com/australia-news/2019/jul/12/essential-poll-majority-of-australians-want-indigenous-recognition-and-voice-to-parliament> accessed 1 October 2019. See also Isabella Higgins and Sarah Collard, 'Federal Election 2019: Vote Compass Finds Australians Are Ready to Back Indigenous "Voice to Parliament"', *ABC News* (3 May 2019) <https://www.abc.net.au/news/2019-05-03/vote-compass-federal-election-voice-to-parliament/11071384> accessed 1 October 2019.

government opposition. But a majority national vote is insufficient: at least four out of six States must achieve majority 'yes' votes as well. This is a high threshold for success.

This book argues that a First Nations constitutional voice is capable of winning support across voters of the left and right, and across a majority of States and nationally. Through the Uluru Statement, the idea of an Indigenous constitutional voice has won Indigenous consensus. I argue it can and should also win widespread political consensus and the popular support necessary for success.

II. STRUCTURE OF THIS BOOK

Chapter two contextualises the constitutional recognition question. It explores the historical, political and theoretical context underpinning the argument for a First Nations constitutional voice, weaving in observations from the international context (which will be explored in greater depth in Chapter four).

Chapter three grapples with objections to the Expert Panel's 2012 proposal for a racial non-discrimination guarantee in the *Constitution*.[18] It seeks to understand those objections, in order to form a principled basis for exploring alternative reform solutions. This chapter also contrasts and compares the commonly proposed alternative – a qualified Indigenous power – but concludes that judicially adjudicated qualifications to a new Indigenous power are susceptible to all the same criticisms as a racial non-discrimination clause; such avenues are no more conducive to political consensus. Rather than judicially adjudicated solutions, the chapter suggests that political and procedural constitutional mechanisms should be considered as alternative constitutional avenues for empowering Indigenous peoples and safeguarding their rights.

In search of alternative approaches, Chapter four seeks inspiration from the international context, with a focus on mechanisms that empower Indigenous peoples to be heard in their affairs. It discusses the political and institutional mechanisms for Māori recognition in New Zealand's constitutional arrangements,[19] and the contrastingly judicialised approach taken in Canada under section 35 of the *Canadian Constitution*, particularly the court-adjudicated duty to consult. My analysis observes that judicial adjudication may not always lead to robust protection of Indigenous rights or fulsome empowerment of Indigenous voices in their affairs: constitutional litigation comes with its own risks. The chapter then briefly discusses arrangements in the Scandinavian countries of Norway,

[18] See also Shireen Morris, 'Undemocratic, Uncertain and Politically Unviable? An Analysis of and Response to Objections to a Proposed Racial Non-Discrimination Clause as Part of Constitutional Reforms for Indigenous Recognition' (2014) 40(2) *Monash Law Review* 488.

[19] See also Shireen Morris, 'Lessons from New Zealand: Towards a Better Working Relationship between Indigenous Peoples and the State' (2014/2015) 18 *Australian Indigenous Law Review* 67.

Sweden and Finland, where Sámi parliaments operate as Indigenous representative and advisory bodies that can engage with the state on Sámi matters.

Prompted by discussion of reserved Māori seats in New Zealand, Chapter five explores the idea of legislated reserved Indigenous seats under Australia's constitutional arrangements,[20] with a particular focus on the High Court's evolving approach to electoral law and voting rights. The chapter suggests there may be some legal uncertainty with respect to the legislative possibility of reserved Indigenous seats. While reserved seats would obviously be possible through constitutional amendment, this would be a complex change. I therefore suggest that a constitutionally guaranteed Indigenous body, to ensure the First Nations a voice in their affairs, would be a more constitutionally congruent and politically viable reform solution for Australia.

Chapter six makes the case for a constitutionally enshrined First Nations voice, as advocated by the Uluru Statement and the Referendum Council.[21] It recaps the case for change by distilling seven key arguments for this constitutional reform. The chapter draws insights from the Inter-State Commission and the Aboriginal and Torres Strait Islander Commission, and then delves into ideas for execution and implementation. It shows how a properly drafted constitutional amendment guaranteeing a First Nations voice, together with appropriate legislative design, can achieve the aspirations of the Uluru Statement while addressing concerns to uphold the *Constitution*, respect parliamentary supremacy and eliminate legal uncertainty. The chapter also responds to common objections to a First Nations constitutional voice.

Chapter seven concludes by urging the parties to work together in good faith to achieve the aims of the Uluru Statement. A First Nations voice would give effect to longstanding Indigenous aspirations for meaningful and empowering constitutional recognition and would also address common concerns related to constitutional reform in Australia. The proposed reform would empower Indigenous peoples with a voice in their affairs, in a way that is fundamentally constitutionally congruent. This would be a political and participatory approach to Indigenous constitutional recognition, in keeping with the *Australian Constitution*. A First Nations constitutional voice would make the constitutional relationship between Indigenous peoples and the Australian state fairer, both procedurally and thus hopefully in outcomes.

[20] As advocated, for example, by Michael Mansell, *Treaty and Statehood: Aboriginal Self-Determination* (Federation Press 2016) 35–41.

[21] See also Shireen Morris, 'The Argument for a Constitutional Procedure for Parliament to Consult with Indigenous Peoples When Making Laws for Indigenous Affairs' (2015) 26 *Public Law Review* 166; Shireen Morris, 'The Torment of Our Powerlessness: Indigenous Constitutional Vulnerability and the Uluru Statement's Call for a First Nations Voice' (2018) 41 *University of New South Wales Law Journal* 1; Shireen Morris, 'Parliamentary Scrutiny and Insights for a First Nations Voice to Parliament' in Julie Debeljak and Laura Grenfell (eds), *Law Making and Human Rights* (Thomson Reuters 2020).

2

The Historical, Political and Theoretical Context

I. THE PROBLEM OF PURPOSE

Any discussion about Indigenous constitutional recognition must first grapple with the problem of purpose. Sensible dialogue about appropriate reform tends to remain elusive unless the parties can first agree on the problem constitutional recognition seeks to fix. Confusion about purpose has been evident in the Australian debate. Some believe constitutional recognition seeks only to make a symbolic statement. Others argue it must implement practical and substantive reform. Which answer is correct?

As will be shown below, an examination of the historical context – the history of Indigenous peoples in the development of the constitutional arrangements of Australia, the treatment of Indigenous peoples under those arrangements, and the related history of Indigenous advocacy for constitutional reform – contextualises Indigenous constitutional recognition as primarily seeking to solve a practical and structural problem. While the historic moment created by the act of Indigenous constitutional recognition may indeed carry symbolic meaning for the nation, the potential for a moving symbolic moment of national reconciliation should not obscure fundamental purpose or confuse the appropriate substance of the reform – yet often it does. Articulating a better answer to the problem of purpose requires an examination of what Indigenous advocates have been arguing for in their advocacy for constitutional recognition and reform, and an understanding of the historical, legal and political factors driving this advocacy for change. It calls for an appreciation of the legal and political power relationships that give rise to Indigenous feelings of powerlessness, and thus advocacy for constitutional empowerment.

The contemporary project of Indigenous constitutional recognition seeks to more fairly resolve some of the injustices perpetuated in the colonisation of Australia, through constitutional and structural reform. It arises because of the deeply unbalanced power relationship between Indigenous peoples and the state that was forged through colonisation and perpetuated in the making of the *Constitution*, as well as subsequently under it. Indigenous constitutional recognition seeks to reform and reset this constitutional power relationship to ensure it is fairer than in the past. It seeks to find a more just and inclusive place for Indigenous peoples in the constitutional arrangements of Australia. The aim is not just a feel-good moment implementing a symbolic statement of no operational effect. Rather, the aim is to operationally reform structures and relationships so they work more fairly, produce better and fairer policies and laws, and thus improved outcomes for Indigenous Australians and the nation.[1]

The concept of fairness is used as a starting point because it speaks to the need for a practical shift in the way power is distributed and operationalised in this constitutional relationship, but also acknowledges that there are multiple ways to achieve this: there are judicially adjudicated non-discrimination guarantees and rights protections, and there are political, participatory and self-determinative mechanisms which could also be adopted. Fairness is an inherently subjective and amorphous concept.[2] Everyone has a different view on what is fair or not in a given set of circumstances. Fairness is defined by the Cambridge English Dictionary as 'the quality of treating people equally or in a way that is right or reasonable'.[3] It is clear the *Constitution* did not and does not treat Indigenous people equally: they were explicitly excluded by the *Constitution*[4] and there are still constitutional clauses demonstrating and promoting racial discrimination.[5] The *Constitution* has presided over discriminatory laws and policies directed particularly at Indigenous people. As will be shown, equality before the law is not a value protected by the *Australian Constitution*.

Before the Uluru Statement in 2017, the solution most commonly canvassed in recent official recommendations for Indigenous constitutional recognition was to guarantee fairness through constitutionally guaranteeing equality. A racial non-discrimination guarantee, as proposed by the Expert Panel on Constitutional Recognition of Indigenous Australians (the Expert Panel) in 2012, would largely position courts as the determiners of what is equal, reasonable and fair in the circumstances: it would give the judiciary authority to strike down

[1] The structural reform sought through Indigenous constitutional recognition therefore cannot be separated from the desire to 'close the gap' in social and economic outcomes, because Indigenous disparity has a structural and historical dimension. Present disadvantage is connected to a history of structural oppression and exclusion. This will be discussed further below.

[2] As discussed below, my understanding of fairness draws from John Rawls' conception of justice as fairness, as well as many other authors who discuss fairness in contexts of liberalism, constitutionalism, federalism, pluralism and postcolonialism. But see eg John Rawls, 'Justice as Fairness' in John Rawls (ed), *A Theory of Justice* (Harvard University Press 1971); John Rawls, *Justice as Fairness: A Restatement*, Erin Kelly (ed) (Harvard University Press 2001); John Rawls, *Political Liberalism* (Columbia University Press 2005); John Rawls, *A Theory of Justice* (Harvard University Press 1971).

[3] 'Cambridge Dictionary' <https://dictionary.cambridge.org/dictionary/english/fairness> accessed 18 October 2019.

[4] Prior to the 1967 referendum, Indigenous people were excluded from equal participation in the constitutional system under s 127 and from the ambit of the Commonwealth law-making power under s 51(xxvi).

[5] See *Australian Constitution* ss 25, 51(xxvi).

Parliament's laws found in breach of the clause. This is a solution conceptually anchored in the idea of fairness as equality, and operationally and procedurally reliant on litigation as the main means of achieving fairness and equality.

Given the legal and political objections to a racial non-discrimination clause, explored briefly in this chapter and in detail in Chapter three, this book examines other ways – particularly political and non-litigious ways – in which the relationship between Indigenous peoples and the Australian state might be made constitutionally fairer, including constitutional mechanisms which could encourage the making of more reasoned, more reasonable and thus fairer, political decisions with respect to Indigenous peoples, affairs and rights. My concept of fairness in this discussion therefore also draws on notions of mutual respect, civility, reciprocity, consultation, dialogue and participation as ways of achieving reasonableness in dealings, processes and decisions. I argue that ensuring Indigenous peoples a distinctive opportunity to be heard in political decision-making about them and their rights, as the Uluru Statement requests, provides a sound way of improving constitutional fairness in Australia. Whereas the colonial relationship tends to be top-down, imposed, oppressive and discriminatory, and thus can appropriately be characterised as unfair to Indigenous peoples, a fairer relationship should strive for mutually respectful communication.[6] Australia, as a nation aspiring towards reconciliation, should work towards notions of consent and consultation, rather than force and imposition.[7] A sense of procedural fairness is important in this respect, because the way political decisions and laws are made can be as crucial an indicator of fairness as the outcomes of the decisions themselves.[8] Fairness in decision-making procedures can improve the quality of decisions arising from those procedures. The idea that a party should be heard before decisions about their rights and affairs are made is thus central to ideas developed in this book.

Australia's *Constitution* protects citizens' rights predominantly through institutional, democratic and federal power-sharing mechanisms, rather than through judicially adjudicated 'Bill of rights' style clauses. A constitutionally guaranteed First Nations voice would be in keeping with this constitutional culture. While litigation under new constitutional rights clauses is one way to give Indigenous peoples a platform and process via which to be heard, through

[6] See discussion of reciprocity and deliberative democracy in Duncan Ivison, *Postcolonial Liberalism* (Cambridge University Press 2002) 18–23.

[7] The importance of free, prior and informed consent, consultation and political participation is emphasised in the UN Declaration on the Rights of Indigenous Peoples (DRIP), Arts 3, 18, 19.

[8] I use the term 'procedural fairness' in a non-technical way here, as a moral and political principle of natural justice that requires a fair hearing and fair participation in political decision-making. This is particularly relevant to protecting Indigenous rights. For example, the requirement in Article 19 of DRIP that 'Indigenous peoples have the right to participate in decision-making in matters which would affect their rights' entails procedural involvement by Indigenous people in the making of political decisions affecting their interests, and is essentially requiring a form of procedural fairness. See also Ivison (n 6 above) 23.

the courts, it is not the only way. The *Constitution* could empower Indigenous peoples to more actively participate in the political and policy decisions made about them. A constitutional amendment guaranteeing the Indigenous voice in Indigenous affairs would achieve recognition through increased representation and participation.

The next sections will discuss the historical, political and theoretical context that informs and underpins the debate about Indigenous constitutional recognition and my argument for a First Nations voice in their affairs.

II. HISTORICAL CONTEXT

A. *Terra Nullius*

Indigenous peoples inhabited the Australian continent for approximately 60,000 years or more, before the arrival of the British.[9] The interactions between Indigenous peoples and the British colonisers share some similarities with, and also certain differences from, the stories of colonisation in other comparable former British colonies, like New Zealand,[10] Canada,[11] and the USA.[12] Like the Indigenous peoples in those countries, Indigenous peoples in Australia suffered discrimination and dispossession.[13] There was warfare over land[14] and in some areas there was arguably attempted genocide of Indigenous peoples.[15]

[9] See eg Helen Davidson and Calla Wahlquist, 'Australian Dig Finds Evidence of Aboriginal Habitation up to 80,000 Years Ago', *The Guardian* (20 July 2017): <https://www.theguardian.com/australia-news/2017/jul/19/dig-finds-evidence-of-aboriginal-habitation-up-to-80000-years-ago> accessed 18 October 2019; Sean Brennan and Megan Davis, 'First Peoples' in Cheryl Saunders and Adrienne Stone (eds), *The Oxford Handbook of the Australian Constitution* (Oxford University Press 2018) 27; Geoffrey Blainey, *The Story of Australia's People: The Rise and Fall of Ancient Australia* (Penguin Australia 2015); Scott Cane, *First Footprints: The Epic Story of the First Australians* (Allen and Unwin 2013).

[10] See eg Ian Pool, *Colonisation and Development in New Zealand between 1769 and 1900* (Springer International Publishing 2015).

[11] See eg Sarah Carter, *Aboriginal People and the Colonizers of Western Canada to 1900* (University of Toronto Press 1999).

[12] See eg Francis Jennings, *The Invasion of America: Indians, Colonialism, and the Cant of Conquest* (University of North Carolina Press 2010).

[13] See Henry Reynolds, *Frontier: Aborigines, Settlers and Land* (Allen and Unwin 1987); Henry Reynolds, *Dispossession: Black Australians and White Invaders* (Allen and Unwin 1989); Bain Attwood, *Telling the Truth about Aboriginal History* (Allen and Unwin 2005).

[14] Henry Reynolds, *The Other Side of the Frontier* (UNSW Press 2006); John Connor, *The Australian Frontier Wars 1788–1838* (UNSW Press 2005); Henry Reynolds, *Forgotten War* (NewSouth Publishing 2012); Maurice French, *Conflict on the Condamine: Aborigines and the European Invasion* (University of Southern Queensland Press 1989).

[15] See A Dirk Moses (ed), *Genocide and Settler Society: Frontier Violence and Stolen Indigenous Children in Australian History* (Berghahn Books 2004); Rosalind Kidd, *The Way We Civilize: Aboriginal Affairs – the Untold Story* (University of Queensland Press 2005). Noel Pearson also writes of the attempted genocide of Indigenous Tasmanians in Noel Pearson, 'A Rightful Place: Race, Recognition and a More Complete Commonwealth' (2014) 55 *Quarterly Essay* 16–23.

The colonisers tended to view Indigenous peoples as inferior races.[16] Such attitudes worked to justify the assertion of Crown sovereignty and ownership of the land, at the expense of Indigenous rights.[17]

Assumptions of Indigenous inferiority were evident in the erroneous application of the international doctrine of *terra nullius* to inhabited land: the idea that the land belonged to nobody before the British arrived.[18] The 'common law cousin' to *terra nullius*, the English doctrine of 'desert and uncultivated' land, was also applied.[19] It held that practically uninhabited, uncultivated and undeveloped land could be acquired by settlement.[20] In *Cooper v Stuart* in 1889, the Privy Council characterised Australia as a 'colony which consisted of a tract of territory practically unoccupied, without settled inhabitants or settled law, [acquired by] settlement'.[21]

The related doctrines of *terra nullius* and 'desert and uncultivated' land were factually incorrect[22] and discriminatory in their application to Australian land that was inhabited by Indigenous peoples.[23] The doctrines were based on the assumption that Indigenous peoples were racially, culturally and socially inferior to whites. The explanation offered in the *Southern Rhodesia* case of

For essays exploring colonial interactions, see Marcia Langton and Rachel Perkins (eds), *The First Australians* (The Meigunyah Press 2010).

[16] See Pearson, 'A Rightful Place' (n 15 above) 16–23; Bain Attwood and Andrew Markus, *The 1967 Referendum: Race, Power and the Australian Constitution* (2nd edn, Aboriginal Studies Press 2007) 1; Noel Pearson, 'The Reward for Public Life Is Public Progress: An Appreciation of the Public Life of the Hon EG Whitlam AC QC, Prime Minister 1972–1975' (*Whitlam Oration*, Whitlam Institute, University of Western Sydney, 13 November 2013) <https://www.whitlam.org/publications/2013/11/13/the-reward-of-public-life-is-public-progress>.

[17] Henry Reynolds, *The Law of the Land* (3rd edn, Penguin 2003) 159. For alternative views of this history see Keith Windschuttle, *Fabrication of Aboriginal History: Van Dieman's Land 1803–1847* (Macleay 2003).

[18] See Patrick Macklem, 'Indigenous Recognition in International Law: Theoretical Observations' (2008) 30 *Michigan Journal of International Law* 177, 184; Ulla Secher, 'The High Court and Recognition of Native Title: Distinguishing between the Doctrines of *Terra Nullius* and "Desert and Uncultivated"' (2007) 11 *University of Western Sydney Law Review* 1.

[19] Secher (n 18 above).

[20] William Blackstone, *Commentaries on the Laws of England*, vol 1 (3rd edn, Clarendon Press 1768) 107. Note also that Blackstone questioned the morality of the dispossession of the Indigenous peoples of the Americas.

[21] *Cooper v Stuart* (1889) 14 App Cas 286, 291.

[22] Even the assumption that the land was uncultivated may have been incorrect: see Bill Gammage, *The Biggest Estate on Earth: How Aborigines Made Australia* (Allen and Unwin 2011); Bruce Pascoe, *Dark Emu: Aboriginal Australia and the Birth of Agriculture* (Magabala Books 2016).

[23] As Secher explains, '[a]lthough both doctrines classified inhabited land as uninhabited land, crucially, the two doctrines did so for different purposes: the doctrine of *terra nullius* served the purpose of legitimising the acquisition of sovereignty in international law and the "desert and uncultivated" doctrine served the purpose of ascertaining the law which is to govern a territory on colonisation at common law.': Secher (n 18 above) 3. See also Ulla Secher, 'The Reception of Land Law into the Australian Colonies Post-*Mabo*: The Continuity and Recognition Doctrines Revisited and the Emergence of the Doctrine of "*Continuity Pro-Tempore*"' (2004) 27 UNSWLJ 703, 707–8.

1919 for the non-recognition of Indigenous property rights demonstrates the thinking of the era:

> Some tribes are so low in the scale of social organization that their usages and conceptions of rights and duties are not to be reconciled with the institutions or the legal ideas of civilized society. Such a gulf cannot be bridged. It would be idle to impute to such people some shadow of the rights known to our law and then to transmute it into the substance of transferable rights of property as we know them.[24]

Under such logic, the colonisers were able to disregard Indigenous property and sovereignty rights in their quest for territorial expansion. As Brennan J explains in *Mabo*, the landmark case which eventually overturned the misapplied doctrine of *terra nullius* in Australia, treating the Indigenous inhabitants as 'barbarous', 'backwards peoples', 'without settled law', helped the colonisers justify the acquisition of sovereignty over inhabited land:

> The great voyages of European discovery opened to European nations the prospect of occupying new and valuable territories that were already inhabited. As among themselves, the European nations parcelled out the territories newly discovered to the sovereigns of the respective discoverers, provided the discovery was confirmed by occupation and provided the indigenous inhabitants were not organized in a society that was united permanently for political action. To these territories the European colonial nations applied the doctrines relating to acquisition of territory that was terra nullius. They recognized the sovereignty of the respective European nations over the territory of 'backward peoples' and, by State practice, permitted the acquisition of sovereignty of such territory by occupation rather than by conquest ...[25]

Both *terra nullius* and the 'desert and uncultivated' doctrine embodied a discriminatory attitude towards Indigenous people that denied Indigenous sovereignty and property rights, but also denied Indigenous human rights in general – including rights to be treated equally before the law. The principles embodied, in essence, a denial of Indigenous equal humanity.[26] Yet even under Britain's own law (had the British law been non-discriminatorily applied in Australia), Indigenous peoples should have been treated equally.[27] As Brennan J explained in *Mabo*, 'in a settled colony in inhabited territory, the law of England was not merely the personal law of the English colonists; it became the law of the land, protecting and binding colonists and indigenous inhabitants alike

[24] *In re Southern Rhodesia* [1919] AC 211, 233–34.

[25] *Mabo v Queensland (No 2)* (1992) 175 CLR 1, 32. See also at 37–40.

[26] See Pearson, 'The Reward for Public Life is Public Progress' (n 16 above). Assumptions of Indigenous inferiority are evident in the writings and observations of the era. See eg Sigmund Freud, *Totem and Taboo*, Abraham A Brill (tr) (Cosimo Classics 2009), who wrote about Indigenous Australians in his 1918 analysis: '[f]or outer as well as for inner reasons, I am choosing for this comparison those tribes which have been described by ethnographists as being most backward and wretched: the aborigines of the youngest continent, namely Australia, whose fauna has also preserved for us so much that is archaic and no longer to be found elsewhere.' (at 4).

[27] Shireen Morris, 'Re-Evaluating *Mabo*: The Case for Native Title Reform to Remove Discrimination and Promote Economic Opportunity' (2012) 5 *Land, Rights, Laws: Issues of Native Title* 1, 8.

and equally'.[28] Toohey J suggested in the same case that, had the British law been applied equally, the colonisers should have recognised that the Indigenous peoples, being in possession of the land, owned a title under the British common law that should have been 'good against all the world'.[29] The colonisers often failed to apply their own principles of equality and justice to the Indigenous peoples they sought to colonise.

Equal application of the imported law was not the case in practice. From the unofficial policies of frontier killing of Indigenous people,[30] to official policies which included forced removal of Indigenous people into protective 'missions',[31] as well as laws and policies denying Indigenous people equal voting rights in some jurisdictions,[32] denying them equal wages,[33] dictating who they could marry and controlling where they could live,[34] and of course denying their property rights[35] – Indigenous people in practice were treated in a deeply discriminatory way under the imported law. Such discrimination facilitated dispossession. The prosperity and success of the modern Australian nation in a real sense was built on historical Indigenous losses. As Brennan J described, Indigenous dispossession 'underwrote the development of the nation'.[36]

The 1992 *Mabo* decision overturned some of this discrimination in relation to land rights by legally recognising that Indigenous people held native title under their traditional laws and customs, where that title was not extinguished by the Crown. The Commonwealth subsequently enacted the *Native Title Act 1993* (Cth) to recognise native title rights in legislation. But legislated recognition

[28] *Mabo* (n 25 above) 37. For a contrary interpretation contending that Indigenous peoples retained their own legal autonomy, see the much earlier case of *R v Ballard* [1829] NSWSupC 26.

[29] *Mabo* (n 25 above) 206 (Toohey J). See also Morris, 'Re-Evaluating *Mabo*' (n 27 above) 8.

[30] See Kidd (n 15 above); Pearson, 'A Rightful Place' (n 15 above) 16–23.

[31] Australian Human Rights Commission, 'Bringing Them Home: The Stolen Children Report' (1997); Pearson, 'A Rightful Place' (n 15 above), 24–28.

[32] See eg *Elections Act 1885* (Qld) s 6 provided that '[n]o aboriginal native of Australia, India, China or of the South Sea Islands shall be entitled to be entered on the roll except in respect of a freehold qualification'. The *Constitution Act Amendment Act 1899* (WA) s 26 provided that 'no aboriginal native of Australia, Asia, or Africa, or person of the half-blood, shall be entitled to be registered, except in respect of a freehold qualification.' The *Electoral Code 1896* (SA), s 16 provided that 'in the Northern Territory immigrants under the *Indian Immigration Act 1882* and all persons except natural-born British subjects and Europeans or Americans naturalized as British subjects, are disqualified from voting.'

[33] See Australian Associated Press, 'Indigenous Workers Receive $190m Stolen Wages Settlement from Queensland Government', *The Guardian* (9 July 2018) <https://www.theguardian.com/australia-news/2019/jul/09/indigenous-workers-receive-190m-stolen-wages-settlement-from-queensland-government> accessed 18 October 2019; Commonwealth of Australia, *Unfinished Business: Indigenous Stolen Wages* (Standing Committee on Legal and Constitutional Affairs 2006); *Bligh v Queensland* [1996] HREOCA 28.

[34] The Protection Acts empowered appointed protectors and boards to control many day-to-day aspects of Indigenous people's lives. See eg *Aborigines Protection Act 1886* (WA), *Aborigines Protection Act 1869* (Vic), *Aboriginals Preservation and Protection Act 1939* (Qld). See also John Chesterman and Brian Galligan, *Citizens without Rights: Aborigines and Australian Citizenship* (Cambridge University Press 1997) 12.

[35] See full discussion in *Mabo* (n 25 above).

[36] ibid 69.

of rights can be legislated away, as shown when former Prime Minister John Howard weakened native title rights under his Wik Ten-Point Plan in 1998.[37] The vulnerability of Indigenous rights in Australia's legal and political system is underpinned by the fact that Australia's *Constitution* provides no recognition or protection of Indigenous rights and interests. Indeed, the *Constitution* can be understood as creating a framework still predicated on the now defunct fiction of *terra nullius*. Ironically, after the 1967 amendments (discussed further below), the *Constitution* now makes no mention of Indigenous peoples: it reads as if Indigenous people do not exist and still provides means for continued discrimination and exclusion.[38]

B. The Royal Instructions

There was no negotiated agreement with Indigenous peoples when the British colonised Australia. There was no consent. This appears contrary to initial Imperial intentions and instructions. Lieutenant James Cook on his exploration voyages carried with him secret instructions from the British King, authorising Cook to 'take possession of convenient situations in the country in the name of the King of Great Britain', but 'with the consent of the natives'.[39] On 22 August 1770, Cook declared possession of the east coast at Possession Island. Cook had noted that the land was inhabited, but no documented negotiation occurred and there was no consent.[40] Then in 1787, King George III issued further instructions to Arthur Phillip. The instructions this time did not mention 'consent',[41] but instructed as follows:

> You are to endeavour, by every possible means, to open an intercourse with the natives, and to conciliate their affections, enjoining all our subjects to live in amity and kindness with them.[42]

[37] This was subsequent to the 1996 *Wik* case, which held that native title rights could coexist with the rights of pastoralist leaseholders: see *Wik Peoples v Queensland* (1996) 187 CLR 1; Wik Ten-Point Plan: *Native Title Amendment Act 1998* (Cth). See Paul Keating, 'The 10-Point Plan that Undid the Good Done on Native Title', *Sydney Morning Herald* (1 June 2011) <https://www.smh.com.au/politics/federal/the-10-point-plan-that-undid-the-good-done-on-native-title-20110531-1feec.html> accessed 18 October 2019.

[38] Discriminatory clauses still remain: see *Australian Constitution* ss 25, 51(xxvi), which apply to 'races' in general. See also Jennifer Nielsen, 'Breaking the Silence: the Importance of Constitutional Change' in Simon Young, Jennifer Nielsen and Jeremy Patrick (eds), *Constitutional Recognition of First Peoples in Australia* (Federation Press 2016).

[39] Secret Instructions to Captain Cook (30 June 1768): <http://foundingdocs.gov.au/resources/transcripts/nsw1_doc_1768.pdf> accessed 18 October 2019.

[40] Pearson, 'A Rightful Place' (n 15 above) 40.

[41] The Expert Panel argue that these instructions perpetuate the notion of *terra nullius*, that the land belonged to no one. See Expert Panel on Constitution Recognition of Indigenous Australians, *Recognising Aboriginal and Torres Strait Islander Peoples in the Constitution: Report of the Expert Panel* (2012) 205 (Expert Panel Report).

[42] Governor Phillip's Instructions 25 April 1787 (UK): <www.foundingdocs.gov.au/resources/transcripts/nsw2_doc_1787.rtf> accessed 18 October 2019.

As the process of dispossession played out, these instructions were also not followed. Edward Wilson lamented in an 1856 newspaper that:

> In less than twenty years we have nearly swept them off the face of the earth. We have shot them down like dogs. In the guise of friendship we have issued corrosive sublimate in their damper and consigned whole tribes to the agonies of an excruciating death. We have made them drunkards, and infected them with diseases which have rotted the bones of their adults, and made such few children as are born amongst them a sorrow and a torture from the very instant of their birth. We have made them outcasts on their own land, and are rapidly consigning them to entire annihilation.[43]

The force and violence of colonisation in Australian history cannot accurately be described as fostering 'amity and kindness'. No 'intercourse' or dialogue was officially opened, and 'conciliation' or peaceful negotiation did not in any formal sense occur.[44] The British took control and asserted their sovereignty without Indigenous agreement.[45]

The issue of consent and surviving Indigenous sovereignty was sometimes kept alive by the colonial courts. Justice Dowling's judgment in *R v Ballard* in 1829 suggested that the Indigenous peoples retained their own legal authority in certain circumstances, until formal consent occurred:

> Until the aboriginal natives of this Country shall consent, either actually or by implication, to the interposition of our laws in the administration of justice for acts committed by themselves upon themselves, I know of no reason human, or divine, which ought to justify us interfering with their institutions even if such interference were practicable.[46]

Justice Willis, in *R v Bonjon* in 1841, perhaps inspired by the American cases establishing 'domestic dependent sovereignty' for the Native American tribes,[47] also observed that the colony was not 'obtained by right of conquest and driving out the natives, nor by treaties'.[48] Willis J argued that because no terms had been defined for the 'internal government, civilisation and protection' of Indigenous peoples, Indigenous peoples remained 'unconquered and free' as 'independent tribes' and 'self-governing communities'. Willis J thus urged that treaties should be made with the Indigenous peoples.[49]

[43] Edward Wilson, 'The Aborigines', *The Argus* (Melbourne, 16 March 1856) <https://trove.nla.gov.au/newspaper/article/4833244> accessed 18 October 2019.

[44] Though it was informally attempted, as discussed below.

[45] See also Attwood (n 13 above) 124.

[46] *R v Ballard* [1829] NSWSC 26, quoted in Expert Panel Report (n 41 above) 205; Larissa Behrendt, Chris Cunneen and Terri Libesman, *Indigenous Legal Relations in Australia* (Oxford University Press 2009) 13. See also Bruce Kercher, 'Recognition of Indigenous Legal Autonomy in Nineteenth Century New South Wales' (1998) 4(13) *Indigenous Law Bulletin* 7.

[47] See eg *Cherokee Nation v Georgia*, 30 US (5 Pet) 1 (1831).

[48] Expert Panel Report (n 41 above) 206.

[49] See 'Supreme Court: Criminal Side', *The Port Phillip and Melbourne Advertiser* (Vol IV, No 243, 20 September 1841) <http://nla.gov.au/nla.news-article226510616> accessed 18 October

Despite such urgings, there was no formal treaty, agreement or mutually established terms of engagement in the relationship between Indigenous peoples and the Crown. Though consent was never obtained, the *Mabo* decision held that the issue of surviving Indigenous sovereignty is not justiciable in an Australian court.[50] This confirmed the principle stated in the *Sea and Submerged Lands case* that 'the acquisition of territory by a sovereign state for the first time is an act of state which cannot be challenged, controlled or interfered with by the courts of that state'.[51] The principle was again confirmed in 1993 in *Coe*.[52]

The unfulfilled royal instructions can be seen as broken promises of liberal justice in relation to Indigenous peoples. As Ivison puts it, '[t]he history of settler colonialism demonstrates how indigenous peoples have experienced the promise of liberal legitimacy as perpetually deferred, if not a matter of colossal bad faith.'[53] When it came to Indigenous peoples, the colonisers seemed to abandon their professed ideals.[54]

C. Unrealised Attempts at Indigenous-Settler Negotiations

There were, however, unfulfilled, unrealised or unreciprocated attempts at Indigenous-settler negotiation and agreement-making. John Batman's attempted treaty with the Indigenous peoples near Port Phillip in 1835[55] is seen by some as a sham and an attempt at fraud: a tricky exchange of trinkets and supplies for vast

2019 for Justice Willis' judgment in the trial of *Bonjon*. See also Expert Panel Report (n 41 above) 206; Behrendt, Cunneen and Libesman (n 46 above) 15; Julie Cassidy, 'The Impact of the Conquered/Settled Distinction Regarding the Acquisition of Sovereignty in Australia' (2004) 8 *Southern Cross University Law Review* 1, 8–9; Ann Hunter, 'The Boundaries of Colonial Criminal Law in Relation to Inter-Aboriginal Conflict ("Inter Se Offences") in Western Australia in the 1830–1840s' (2004) 8(2) *Australian Journal of Legal History* 215.

[50] *Mabo* (n 25 above) 31–32.

[51] *New South Wales v Commonwealth* (1975) 135 CLR 337, 388.

[52] *Coe v Commonwealth (No 2)* (1993) 214 CLR 422.

[53] Duncan Ivison, 'Pluralising Political Legitimacy' (2017) 2(1) *Postcolonial Studies* 118, 128.

[54] In Frantz Fanon, *The Wretched of the Earth* (Grove Press, 1963) 309–12, Fanon poetically observes this apparent incongruence between principle and practice: '[l]eave this Europe where they are never done talking of Man, yet murder men everywhere they find them, at the corner of every one of their own streets, in all the corners of the globe … That same Europe where they were never done talking of Man, and where they never stopped proclaiming that they were only anxious for the welfare of Man: today we know with what sufferings humanity has paid for every one of their triumphs of the mind.' For more on the discrepancy between stated intentions and colonisation in practice, see Attwood (n 13 above) 128–30. See also Dylan Lino, 'The Rule of Law and the Rule of Empire: A.V. Dicey in Imperial Context' (2018) 81(5) *Modern Law Review* 73.

[55] James Boyce, *1835: The Founding of Melbourne and the Conquest of Australia* (Black Inc 2008). See also Malcolm Turnbull, 'Beneath the Boulevards' *The Monthly* (July 2011) <https://www.themonthly.com.au/issue/2011/june/1309412782/malcolm-turnbull/beneath-boulevards> accessed 18 October 2019.

swathes of traditional Kulin land.[56] On another view, it was a genuine bargain struck out of political and practical necessity on both sides.[57] In any case, the treaty was soon declared invalid by the colonial authorities.[58] Henry Reynolds explains the reasoning of the colonial lawyers of the time: because the colonisers had 'gained ultimate dominion in and sovereignty over the soil', the Indigenous people only retained a 'right of occupancy' – not ownership. The colonisers asserted that they were sovereign, so allowing Indigenous people rights to sell the land directly to the settlers would have been inconsistent with the rights of the Crown to retain 'sovereignty and dominion' over that land.[59] The concept of the inalienability of native land thus later emerged, not from colonial goodwill, but as a restraint on Indigenous choice and control of their land for the purpose of reserving power and control of land for the new sovereign.[60] This approach allowed the Imperial government to control how land was alienated, instead of allowing Indigenous people to strike bargains with the settlers for themselves.[61] One can see the fictitious logic of *terra nullius* at work here: by denying Indigenous sovereignty or ownership of the land, the Crown denied them their right to negotiate with respect to their rights, thus relegating Indigenous peoples to positions of passivity and powerlessness.

[56] See eg Stuart Macintyre, *A Concise History of Australia* (2nd edn, Cambridge University Press 2004) 66, 76; David Day, *Claiming a Continent: A New History of Australia* (Angus & Robertson 1997) 96–97; Alistair Campbell, *John Batman and the Aborigines* (Kibble Books 1987) 99–106.

[57] Robert Kenny, 'Tricks or Treats?: A case for Kulin Knowing in Batman's Treaty' (2008) 5(2) *History Australia* 38.1. For nuanced discussions see the history in Boyce, *1835* (n 55 above); Geoffrey Blainey, *A History of Victoria* (Cambridge University Press 2006); Bain Attwood, *Possession: Batman's Treaty and the Matter of History* (Miegunyah Press 2009); Joanna Cruickshank, 'Treating history: New approaches to Batman's treaty and indigenous dispossession in Colonial Victoria' (2013) 48(1) *Agora* 11.

[58] 'Whereas, it has been represented to me, that divers of His Majesty's Subjects have taken possession of vacant Lands of the Crown, within the limits of this Colony, under the pretence of a treaty, bargain, or contract, for the purchase thereof, with the Aboriginal Natives; Now therefore, I, the Governor, in virtue and in exercise of the power and authority in me vested, do hereby proclaim and notify to all His Majesty's Subjects, and others whom it may concern, that every such treaty, bargain, and contract with the Aboriginal Natives, as aforesaid, for the possession, title, or claim to any Lands lying and being within the limits of the Government of the Colony of New South Wales … is void and of no effect against the rights of the Crown; and that all persons who shall be found in possession of any such Lands as aforesaid, without the license or authority of His Majesty's Government, for such purpose, first had and obtained, will be considered as trespassers, and liable to be dealt with in like manner as other intruders upon the vacant Lands of the Crown within the said Colony.': Governor Bourke's Proclamation, 1835 (UK): <http://www.foundingdocs.gov.au/resources/transcripts/nsw7_doc_1835.pdf> accessed 18 October 2019.

[59] Henry Reynolds, *The Law of the Land* (Penguin 2003) 159.

[60] Morris, 'Re-Evaluating *Mabo*' (n 27 above) 5.

[61] This was also consistent with early jurisprudence from the US concerning Indian title: see *Johnson v M'Intosh*, 21 US 543 (1823); *United States v Paine Lumber Co*, 206 US 467 (1907). See also discussion of the confusion surrounding private purchases of Indian land in the USA in Kent McNeil, *Common Law Aboriginal Title* (Clarendon Press 1989) 221–35. In the USA, the Crown issued similar kinds of instructions to forbid bargains struck between settlers: see historical resources listed in Kent McNeil, 'Self-Government and the Inalienability of Aboriginal Title' (Osgoode Hall Law School 2001) <http://fngovernance.org/ncfng_research/inalienability.pdf> accessed 18 October 2019.

Yet historical records show Indigenous people exercising agency and attempting to negotiate deals that might ensure their survival in the face of creeping dispossession. The *Mabo* judgment quotes Governor King's account of early negotiations with Aboriginal people in 1804:

> They very ingenuously answered that they did not like to be driven from the few places that were left on the banks of the river, where alone they could procure food ... that if they could retain some places from the lower part of the river they should be satisfied and would not trouble the white men. The observation and request appear to be so just and equitable that I assured them no more settlements should be made lower down the river.[62]

The account again suggests that an informal deal was struck; a promise was made by the Governor. Like previous Crown promises, however, the assurance was dishonoured and '[w]hile the wrongs involved in the dispossession of the Aboriginals were acknowledged, the underlying problems were left unaddressed.'[63] This good intention, like the royal instructions, went unfulfilled in the face of the political imperatives of the colonial era.

D. Indigenous Omission from Constitutional Negotiations

A similar insight is applicable to the constitutional negotiations that preceded Australia's Federation. Discriminatory attitudes meant Indigenous peoples were seen neither as sovereign entities nor as owners of the land. They were accordingly not included as negotiating parties to the constitutional compact. Professor Mick Dodson explains:

> Indigenous peoples were not included in the self-governing peoples that came together in the lead-up to 1901 to negotiate Australia's Constitution and to form a 'federated Australia'. We were excluded from that act of nation-building. We had no delegates at the constitutional conventions in the 1890s. We were not asked to send representatives to engage in the negotiations of how power would be distributed and order maintained.[64]

Nearby in New Zealand, Māori prior sovereignty was initially recognised through the Treaty of Waitangi (even if it was later denied) and the key promises of equal citizenship and respect for property were made (even if they were later ignored).[65] By contrast, the Indigenous peoples of Australia were by and

[62] *Mabo* (n 25 above) 104–5.

[63] ibid 105.

[64] Mick Dodson, 'The Continuing Relevance of the Constitution for Indigenous Peoples', speech delivered at the National Archives of Australia, Canberra, 13 July 2008 <http://hdl.handle.net/1885/10693> accessed 18 October 2019.

[65] Shireen Morris, 'Lessons from New Zealand: Towards a Better Working Relationship between Indigenous Peoples and the State' (2014–15) 18(2) *Australian Indigenous Law Review* 67. See Chapter 4 of this volume for full discussion of New Zealand.

large not dealt with as prior sovereign rulers. The pragmatic imperatives of settlement meant that the liberal democratic principles of equality before the law and respect for property rights were ignored in respect of the Indigenous people whom the British sought to colonise. Discriminatory attitudes which saw Indigenous peoples as 'backward' and 'low in the scale of social organization' still prevailed during the several years of constitutional negotiations, or constitutional conventions, preceding the establishment of Australia's *Constitution*. During this time, Indigenous peoples were largely regarded as a 'dying race' and an inferior people.[66] As Professor Patrick Dodson observed, the *Constitution* of 1901 was drafted 'in the spirit of *terra nullius*'.[67]

E. A Union of the Colonies, but No Union with the Colonised

The lack of Indigenous agreement to the establishment of the Australian nation under the *Constitution* stands in direct contrast to the reciprocal and power-sharing principles (if non-discriminatorily applied) on which Australia's *Constitution* is based. The *Commonwealth of Australia Constitution Act 1900* (UK), enacted by the UK Parliament to establish the *Constitution* of Australia, was an agreement to which the colonial parties consented. As Professor James Stellios describes, it was 'an agreement between sovereign powers to give up some of their powers to a new central body, but preserving their sovereignty over what they retained'.[68] The *Constitution* set up a power-sharing and sovereignty-sharing arrangement between the Commonwealth and the States.

Having negotiated the terms of their inclusion in the new nation and the rules by which the parties would be governed, the preamble to the UK Act proclaimed that the colonies had 'agreed to unite in one indissoluble Federal Commonwealth under the Crown', thereby forming the new Commonwealth of Australia. The *Constitution* can thus be understood as a compact, the terms of which ensured that the most vulnerable former colonies would survive as dynamic political entities in the federal union: the most minimally populated States are guaranteed an equal voice in the Senate under section 7. These distinct historical, political and geographical collective identities were constitutionally recognised, and their dynamic longevity was thereby guaranteed – their continued political survival as distinct political identities was a condition of

[66] Attwood and Markus, *The 1967 Referendum* (n 16 above) 1; Attwood (n 13 above) 136. On the race power as a 'relic of colonial thinking', see Michael Kirby, 'Constitutional Law and Indigenous Australians: Challenge for a Parched Continent' (2012) 15 *Southern Cross University Law Review* 3, 16; Justin Malbon, 'The Race Power under the *Australian Constitution*: Altered Meanings' (1999) 21(1) *Sydney Law Review* 80, 91; Geoffrey Sawer, 'The *Australian Constitution* and the Australian Aborigine' (1966) 2(1) *Federal Law Review* 17, 18.

[67] Patrick Dodson, 'Welcoming Speech', Position of Indigenous People in National Constitutions Conference, Canberra, 4 June 1993, quoted in Attwood and Markus, *The 1967 Referendum* (n 16 above) 146–47.

[68] James Stellios, *Zines's The High Court and the Constitution* (6th edn, Federation Press 2015) 1.

their inclusion. Australia's federal *Constitution* in these respects is like a treaty, balancing independence with unity.[69] As Professor Nicholas Aroney explains,

> the 'primary and fundamental' meaning of federalism … is the idea of a federal compact between the states … the focus is on the *foedus*, treaty or covenant by which several independent states agree to form a common political system while retaining their separate identities.[70]

Importantly, the compact affords these historic political communities *constitutional recognition* through collective representation.[71] In this sense, the *Australian Constitution* does not adhere to individualistic equality or strict majoritarianism in its approach to political representation. As Aroney explains:

> [F]ederations posit the continuing existence of their constituent states as partially independent political societies – which have agreed to form, for certain purposes, a larger political society of which they will each become a part. The constituent units of a federation are not a gathering of individuals wishing to unite for the better preservation of their natural rights, but a collection of political societies wishing to unite for the better preservation of their pre-existing powers of local self-government. Federations are thus non-majoritarian …[72]

Indigenous peoples, however, were not treated as sovereigns or the owners of the land on which the new nation was being established. They were not recognised as self-governing political societies entitled to a place in power-sharing negotiations and the resulting constitutional compact. In respect of Indigenous peoples, the drafting of the *Australian Constitution* was informed by the attitudes of the era. Thus, while the *Constitution* embodied a negotiated and agreed union of the colonies, there was no such agreed union with the colonised. Accordingly, there were no constitutional clauses drafted to protect Indigenous rights or guarantee them equality before the law. There was no provision for specific Indigenous representation or political participation within the constitutional compact, nor any structural accommodation establishing the appropriate level of Indigenous authority over Indigenous affairs. There was the opposite.

Insofar as Indigenous people were mentioned in the *Constitution*, it was to exclude them. Section 127 excluded Indigenous people from being counted

[69] See also John Quick and Robert Randolph Garran, *The Annotated Constitution of the Australian Commonwealth* (Legal Books 1995) 332–42.

[70] Nicholas Aroney, *The Constitution of a Federal Commonwealth: The Making and Meaning of the Australian Constitution* (Cambridge University Press 2009) 4. See also Paul Chen, 'Federalism and Rights: A Neglected Relationship' (1999) 40 *South Texas Law Review* 845, 859; Barbara Thomas-Woolley and Edmond J. Keller, 'Majority Rule and Minority Rights: American Federalism and African Experience' (1994) 32(3) *Journal of Modern African Studies* 411, 414.

[71] Thanks to Dylan Lino for articulating the point that Indigenous peoples were a pre-existing political community wrongfully excluded from the constitutional compact. See Dylan Lino, 'Towards Indigenous Settler Federalism' (2017) 28 *Public Law Review* 118; see also Dylan Lino, *Constitutional Recognition: The First Peoples and the Australian Settler State* (Federation Press 2018) 244–49.

[72] Nicholas Aroney, 'Reasonable Disagreement, Democracy and the Judicial Safeguards of Federalism' (2008) 27(1) *University of Queensland Law Journal* 129, 139.

as part of the population. It provided that, '[i]n reckoning the numbers of the people of the Commonwealth, or of a State or other part of the Commonwealth, aboriginal natives shall not be counted.' Indigenous people were also excluded from the operation of section 51(xxvi), the 'Race Power', either because it was widely believed that Indigenous people were a 'dying race whose future was unimportant', or because their welfare was considered the responsibility of the States.[73] Similarly, section 25 contemplates, though also deters, the possibility of barring races from voting. It provides that:

> For the purposes of the last section, if by the law of any State all persons of any race are disqualified from voting at elections for the more numerous House of the Parliament of the State, then, in reckoning the number of the people of the State or of the Commonwealth, persons of that race resident in that State shall not be counted.

The discriminatory attitudes embedded in the *Constitution* and reflected in these clauses flowed on into the legal and political system through which decisions about Indigenous rights are made. The structures created for Indigenous people a position of long-term powerlessness, with clear practical consequences. An apt example is the *Racial Discrimination Act 1975* (Cth) (RDA), which is supposed to ensure all Australians are treated equally before the law with respect to race, except in justified circumstances. But the RDA has been suspended or displaced several times in recent decades – each time only in relation to Indigenous people.[74] That this is able to occur is a direct result of the constitutional vulnerability of Indigenous peoples and rights.

F. The 1967 Referendum did Not Fix the Problem

The 1967 'Aboriginals' referendum was Australia's most successful referendum, passing with a 90.77 per cent 'yes' vote.[75] The referendum removed the

[73] See regarding the 'race power'. Henry Reynolds, *Frontier* (Allen and Unwin 1996) 108–30; Sawer (n 66 above) 18; Attwood and Markus, *The 1967 Referendum* (n 16 above) 1; Kirby, 'Constitutional Law and Indigenous Australians' (n 66 above) 15; Paul Kildea, 'The Bill of Rights Debate in Australian Political Culture' (2003) 9(1) *Australian Journal of Human Rights* 65, 97; Malbon (n 66 above) 91; Martin CJ, 'Passing the Buck – Has the Diffusion of Responsibility for Aboriginal People in our Federation Impeded Closing the Gap?' (2017) 44 *Brief* 28, 31. But see also Greg Taylor, 'Why Were Aborigines Originally Excluded from the Races Power?' (2018) 37 *University of Queensland Law Journal* 237.

[74] The *Hindmarsh Island Bridge Act 1997* (Cth) displaced the application of the RDA; *Native Title Amendment Act 1998* (Cth); *Northern Territory Emergency Response Act 2007* (Cth) s 132. See Dylan Lino, 'Thinking Outside the Constitution on Indigenous Constitutional Recognition: Entrenching the Racial Discrimination Act' (2017) 91 *Australian Law Journal* 381, 382; Lino, *Constitutional Recognition* (n 71 above) 177–90, 204–8. For more on the fragility of the RDA, see Jennifer Nielsen, 'Breaking the Silence: the Importance of Constitutional Change' in Simon Young, Jennifer Nielsen and Jeremy Patrick (eds), *Constitutional Recognition of First Peoples in Australia* (Federation Press 2016) 21–23.

[75] *Constitution Alteration (Aboriginals)*, 1967; George Williams and David Hume, *People Power: The History and Future of the Referendum in Australia* (UNSW Press 2010) 141–54.

explicit exclusions of Indigenous people from the *Constitution*. It deleted the exclusion of Indigenous people from the Race Power, section 51(xxvi), thus conferring upon the Commonwealth the power and discretion to legislate for the management and recognition of Indigenous rights and interests.[76] This eventually enabled the Commonwealth to enact legislation like the *World Heritage Properties Conservation Act 1983* (Cth), the *Aboriginal and Torres Strait Islander Heritage Protection Act 1984* (Cth), the *Native Title Act 1993* (Cth) and the *Corporations (Aboriginal and Torres Strait Islander) Act 2006* (Cth), which gave legislative recognition to some Indigenous rights.[77] The referendum also deleted section 127, which meant Indigenous people could be counted as part of the population for voting purposes.

The 1967 reforms did not, however, implement any positive constitutional protection of Indigenous rights or interests, thus leaving open the possibility that the Commonwealth could still enact discriminatory laws and legislation winding back protections of Indigenous rights. This was a problem anticipated by Liberal MP, Bill Wentworth, who proposed a racial non-discrimination guarantee to read as follows:

> Neither the commonwealth nor any state shall make or maintain any law which subjects any person who has been born or naturalised within the Commonwealth of Australia to any discrimination or disability within the commonwealth by reason of his racial origin.[78]

A qualified Indigenous power was also discussed;[79] however neither form of constitutional guarantee was adopted. Though the Labor Party was supportive, the government rejected the idea on the basis that, although such a guarantee would 'provide evidence of the Australian people's desire to outlaw discrimination', it would also 'provide a fertile source of attack on the constitutional validity of legislation'.[80] The political difficulties of constitutional change and the Australian attachment to parliamentary supremacy were evidently as influential then as they remain today. No form of equality guarantee was adopted. The question of the appropriate form of constitutional protection of Indigenous rights remained unanswered.

[76] See Sarah Pritchard, 'The Race Power in Section 51(xxvi) of the Constitution' (2011) 15(2) *Australian Indigenous Law Review* 44.

[77] Expert Panel Report (n 41 above) 33. Brennan and Davis, 'First Peoples' (n 9 above) 49.

[78] Expert Panel Report (n 41 above) 30. See also Attwood and Markus, *The 1967 Referendum* (n 16 above) 114–15; Michael Kirby, 'First Australians, Law and the High Court of Australia' (Wentworth Lecture, AIATSIS 2010) 4–5.

[79] Expert Panel Report (n 41 above) 30.

[80] See John Gardiner-Garden, 'The Origin of Commonwealth Involvement in Indigenous Affairs and the 1967 Referendum' (1996–97) Social Policy Group, Background Paper No 11 <https://www.aph.gov.au/About_Parliament/Parliamentary_Departments/Parliamentary_Library/Publications_Archive/Background_Papers/bp9697/97bp11> accessed 18 October 2019; Kirby, 'First Australians, Law and the High Court of Australia' (n 78 above) 5.

The 1967 vote was a historic referendum win, but according to Kirby J, the 'dregs of the cup of that victory' were not properly understood.[81] The 1967 constitutional amendments failed to solve the key problem that the *Constitution* still allowed for adverse discrimination against Indigenous peoples. This was confirmed in the 1998 case of *Kartinyeri*.[82] This decision dealt with whether the *Hindmarsh Island Bridge Act 1997* (Cth) validly repealed provisions of the earlier *Aboriginal and Torres Strait Islander Heritage Protection Act 1984* (Cth), which had been enacted under section 51(xxvi) to protect Indigenous sacred sites. The High Court majority held that the subsequent Act was valid and repealed the previous legislative protections of the relevant Indigenous heritage rights. This was because the plenary power conferred under section 51(xxvi) included the power to repeal laws enacted,[83] despite the 1967 amendment.[84] The decision demonstrated that the Race Power can probably be used to enact adversely racially discriminatory laws[85] as well as laws positively recognising Indigenous rights. It confirmed that the 1967 reform of the Race Power to include Indigenous peoples within its ambit did not alter the power's discriminatory capacity.[86]

The Race Power is not the only problem in this respect. Other Commonwealth powers can also be used to discriminate. The Northern Territory

[81] Kirby, 'Constitutional Law and Indigenous Australians' (n 66 above) 5. For more on the incompleteness of the 1967 constitutional reform, see Lino, *Constitutional Recognition* (n 71 above) 148-56. For the positive symbolism that attended the 1967 referendum, see Brennan and Davis, 'First Peoples' (n 9 above) 48–50; Larissa Behrendt, 'The 1967 Referendum: 40 Years On' (2007) 11 *Australian Indigenous Law Review* 12, 14, 15; Lael K Weis, 'Constituting 'the People': The Paradoxical Place of the Formal Amendment Procedure in Australian Constitutionalism' in R Albert, X Contiades, and A Fontiadou (eds), *The Foundations and Traditions of Constitutional Amendment* (Hart 2017) 267.

[82] *Kartinyeri v The Commonwealth* (1998) 195 CLR 337.

[83] See Robert French, 'The Race Power: A Constitutional Chimera' in HP Lee and George Winterton (eds), *Australian Constitutional Landmarks* (Cambridge University Press 2003) 199–208.

[84] Justice Kirby dissented, positing that the 1967 amendments meant that the Race Power only empowered the Commonwealth to enact laws of benefit to a particular race. For a reflection on why Kirby understood the 1967 amendments as limiting the Race Power, see Kirby, 'First Australians, Law and the High Court of Australia' (n 78 above) 3–6.

[85] *Kartinyeri* (n 82 above) 376; See also George Williams, 'Thawing the Frozen Continent' (2007) *Griffith Review* 11, 27; Rosalind Dixon and George Williams, 'Drafting a Replacement to the Races Power in the Australian Constitution' (2014) 25 *Public Law Review* 83, 83–84.

[86] Malcolm Mackerras argues that Indigenous incorporation into the discriminatory Race Power was a fundamental strategic error. For a detailed history of the lead up to 1967, see Malcolm Mackerras, 'How Many Times Do We Need To Say Sorry?' in Damien Freeman and Shireen Morris (eds), *The Forgotten People: Liberal and Conservative Approaches to Recognising Indigenous Peoples* (Melbourne University Press 2016) 128–37. See also Brennan and Davis, 'First Peoples' (n 9 above) 50. For more on the thwarted aspirations of the 1967 referendum, see Ambelin Kwaymullina, 'Recognition, Referendums and Relationships: Indigenous Worldviews, Constitutional Change, and the Spirit of the 1967 Referendum' in Simon Young, Jennifer Nielsen and Jeremy Patrick (eds), *Constitutional Recognition of First Peoples in Australia* (Federation Press 2016).

Intervention,[87] which many felt was discriminatory and predominantly affected Indigenous people, was also reliant on section 122 of the *Constitution.*[88] Further, the 1967 referendum did not remove section 25. Together with the Race Power, and absent any constitutional protection against racial discrimination, the existence of section 25 arguably demonstrates a continuing possibility that Indigenous people and other groups could be prevented from voting – though equal voting rights have over time been achieved, they could be wound back.[89] Parliament can still enact discriminatory laws and policies, particularly in relation to Indigenous people.[90] Thus, even after the 1967 referendum, Indigenous advocacy for constitutional reform continues – because the nation today is grappling with the same legal and political issues it failed to adequately resolve in 1967.

In the lead up to 1967, despite support from Labor, the idea of a racial non-discrimination guarantee in the *Constitution* was rejected by the government due to concerns about empowering the High Court and creating legal uncertainty – but no alternative, non-litigious constitutional solution to the problem of unjust political decision-making in relation to Indigenous peoples was offered. As will be discussed later, history repeated itself in 2012: the same objections arose against the Expert Panel's proposed racial non-discrimination clause.[91] Australia's strong attachment to parliamentary supremacy and related suspicion of judicial review has been a recurring blockage to meaningful constitutional recognition. As Noel Pearson lamented, '[h]ad 1967 achieved rightful constitutional recognition and protection of indigenous interests, in a form acceptable by both Left and Right, we would not still be seeking a meaningful solution.'[92]

[87] *Northern Territory National Emergency Response Act 2007*; *Social Security and Other Legislation Amendment (Welfare Payment Reform) Bill 2007*; *Families, Community Services and Indigenous Affairs and Other Legislation Amendment; (Northern Territory National Emergency Response and Other Measures) Act 2007*; *Appropriation (Northern Territory National Emergency Response) Bill (No 1) 2007–2008*; *Appropriation (Northern Territory National Emergency Response) Bill (No 2) 2007–2008*.

[88] *Wurridjal v Commonwealth* (2009) 237 CLR 309, 387, 435. See also Sean Brennan, 'Wurridjal v Commonwealth: The Northern Territory Intervention and Just Terms for the Acquisition of Property' (2009) 33(3) *Melbourne University Law Review* 957; Brooke Greenwood, 'The Commonwealth Government's Northern Territory Emergency Response Act: Some Constitutional Issues' (2009) V *Cross Sections* 21, 22.

[89] The complexities of this assertion will be discussed further in Chapter 5.

[90] Kirby, 'Constitutional Law and Indigenous Australians' (n 66 above) 15–16; Kirby, 'First Australians, Law and the High Court of Australia' (n 78 above) 21–24.

[91] See Shireen Morris, 'Undemocratic, Uncertain and Politically Unviable? An Analysis of and Response to Objections to a Proposed Racial Non-Discrimination Clause as Part of Constitutional Reforms for Indigenous Recognition' (2014) 40(2) *Monash Law Review* 488; Brennan and Davis, 'First Peoples' (n 9 above) 52.

[92] Noel Pearson, 'Indigenous People Need a Lot More than Just Symbolism', *The Australian* (4 July 2015) <https://www.theaustralian.com.au/commentary/opinion/indigenous-people-need-a-lot-more-than-just-symbolism/news-story/5db4aa54cbb26969420b4ff141d85aed> accessed 18 October 2019.

G. The Constitutional Vulnerability of Indigenous Rights

In relation to Indigenous rights, parliamentary supremacy prevails in Australia. The Commonwealth Parliament is limited in its powers only by the *Constitution*, which allows racial discrimination. The Parliament is therefore not bound by the *Racial Discrimination Act 1975* (Cth),[93] which can be suspended or amended at any time.[94] Similarly, absent constitutional protection, legislated protections of rights can be impliedly repealed or amended by later inconsistent Acts.[95]

The *Constitution* provides Indigenous people with no specific rights protections to which they can appeal through the courts when their rights are breached by Parliament. Nor does it provide specific mechanisms for Indigenous people to influence the making of laws and policies which affect their rights – apart from through normal election processes. As a three per cent minority,[96] Indigenous Australians have a limited capacity to influence political decisions and law-making through ordinary processes.[97] While the *Constitution* guarantees even the smallest of the former colonies an equal voice in the Senate, despite wide variations in population, the Indigenous minority is guaranteed no specific say in the laws that Parliament makes specifically about them, whether under the Race Power or any other constitutional head of power.

Lack of constitutional recognition in this respect is an omission with tangible consequences for Indigenous survival as peoples, in a nation in which they are an extreme and highly disadvantaged minority. While the *Constitution* recognises and guarantees the political existence of the former colonies as distinct, self-governing political communities within Australia, the *Constitution* can equally be said to encourage the Indigenous polity to quietly disappear. The only constitutional articulation of the relationship between Indigenous people and

[93] See George Winterton, 'Can the Commonwealth Enact Manner and Form Legislation?' (1980) 11(2) *Federal Law Review* 167, 168.

[94] This was demonstrated in the initial version of the Northern Territory Intervention. The *Northern Territory Emergency Response Act 2007* (Cth) provided in s 132: '(1) The provisions of this Act, and any acts done under or for the purposes of those provisions, are, for the purposes of the Racial Discrimination Act 1975, special measures. (2) The provisions of this Act, and any acts done under or for the purposes of those provisions, are excluded from the operation of Part II of the Racial Discrimination Act 1975. (3) In this section, a reference to any acts done includes a reference to any failure to do an act.'

[95] See Julie Taylor, 'Human Rights Protection in Australia and Parliamentary Supremacy' (2004) 32(1) *Federal Law Review* 61; Jeffrey Goldsworthy, *Parliamentary Sovereignty: Contemporary Debates* (Cambridge University Press 2010). For mechanisms aimed at tempering this legislative vulnerability, see discussions of manner and form restrictions on amendment and repeal: Jeffrey Goldsworthy, 'Manner and Form in the Australian States' (1987) 16(2) *Melbourne University Law Review* 403; Gerard Carney, 'An Overview of Manner and Form in Australia' (1989) 5 *Queensland University of Technology Law Journal* 69; Anne Twomey, 'Manner and Form', speech given at Gilbert + Tobin Public Law Conference, 2.

[96] Australian Bureau of Statistics, *Estimates of Aboriginal and Torres Strait Islander Australians, June 2016* (Catalogue No 3238.0.55.001, 31 August 2018).

[97] Michael Mansell, *Treaty and Statehood: Aboriginal Self-Determination* (Federation Press 2016) 15.

government is now made by implication, via discriminatory references to race – implying a relationship of exclusion and subordination.[98] The *Constitution* sets up an unfair power relationship between Indigenous peoples and the Australian state. This is the problem Indigenous constitutional recognition seeks to fix.

H. The Implications of Australia's Lack of a Founding Treaty

The lack of a treaty or treaties between Indigenous peoples and the colonising state in Australia, in addition to the lack of constitutionally entrenched protection of their rights, has similarly had longstanding implications for the extent to which Indigenous peoples have been able to prosecute and defend their rights. Indigenous advocacy for a treaty continues.

While the founding treaties in New Zealand, Canada and the USA[99] were not always respected by the much more powerful Crown, and their content was informed by the imbalanced power relations inherent in colonial interactions, such treaties nonetheless set in place agreed terms for formal ongoing relationships between Indigenous peoples and colonising states. They created a sense of nation-to-nation relationships. While the terms of those treaties were often breached and their promises abandoned, the enactment of treaties over time and with the changing of attitudes tended to create circumstances in which Indigenous peoples were able to exercise varying degrees of self-determination within the state.[100] Treaties can help carve out space within a nation's constitutional arrangements for Indigenous peoples to survive as distinct peoples and exercise varying levels of agency in their affairs.

For example, in the USA some treaties set out spheres of practical autonomy for Indigenous peoples through 'domestic dependent sovereignty', which over time enabled increasing levels of Indigenous legal authority in their affairs.[101] In New Zealand, the relationship established under the Treaty of Waitangi in

[98] 'Race' in the Race Power carries connotations of the inferiority and passivity of the dark-skinned so-called 'races', referred to as 'inferior' 'coloured' peoples and 'undesirable immigrants' in the 19th century constitutional convention debates. See *Official Record of the Debates of the Australasian Federal Convention*, Third Session, Melbourne, 20 January–17 March 1898, at 227–43. See also Pritchard (n 76 above) 50–51; Marcia Langton, 'Why "Race" Is a Central Idea in Australia's Construction of the Idea of a Nation' (1999) 18 *Australian Cultural History* 22, 26.

[99] Indigenous recognition in New Zealand, Canada and Scandinavia will be discussed in Chapter 4 of this volume. See discussion in Sean Brennan and others, *Treaty* (Federation Press 2005) 82–101.

[100] ibid.

[101] *Cherokee Nation v Georgia*, 30 US (5 Pet) 1 (1831). Note, however, that in an inherently imbalanced power relationship, Indigenous people had to fight for legal recognition of their treaty rights, which were always vulnerable to being ignored or reneged on by the US government. The important thing, however, was that the existence of treaties meant that there was something which established the relationship, and to which Indigenous people could appeal. See ibid, 83–87. See also Lance F Sorenson, 'Tribal Sovereignty and the Recognition Power' (2017) 42 *American Indian Law Review* 69.

time led to institutional arrangements in which Māori peoples have a specific representative voice in the nation's constitutional arrangements, as well as measures for language and cultural recognition and settlement processes for treaty breaches.[102] In Canada, Indigenous treaty rights were constitutionally recognised in the *Constitution of Canada* of 1982.[103] This led to a court-implied 'duty to consult' Indigenous people in government actions detrimentally affecting their rights.[104] Treaties in Canada helped create a framework for ongoing agreement-making as well as a contemporary Truth and Reconciliation process.[105] In 2015, the Canadian government committed to revitalising its Indigenous relationships:

> Because it is both the right thing to do and a certain path to economic growth, the Government will undertake to renew, nation-to-nation, the relationship between Canada and Indigenous peoples, one based on recognition of rights, respect, co-operation and partnership.[106]

Despite breaches, in comparable liberal democratic nations, treaties have helped create 'nation-to-nation' or 'sovereign-to-sovereign' relationships, which have enabled Indigenous peoples to fight for increased autonomy and political power. Treaties can establish the terms for ongoing engagement and partnership which can be revisited and revitalised over time.[107]

Establishment of these kinds of formal relationships between Indigenous peoples and colonising states can also be seen as recognition and affirmation of Indigenous peoples as distinct and continuing political entities within the nation's future – an important recognition in the colonial context where the existential threat to Indigenous peoples has been palpable. Formal recognition of the relationship, including through agreements and treaties, is important because it establishes that there is an autonomous, surviving party (or parties)

[102] International examples will be discussed in detail in Chapter 4 of this volume. See also Morris, 'Lessons from New Zealand' (n 65 above).

[103] *Constitution Act 1982* (Can) s 35.

[104] Discussed further in Chapter 4 of this volume.

[105] See Kirsten Anker, 'Symptoms of Sovereignty? Apologies, Indigenous Rights and Reconciliation in Canada and Australia' in Ruth Buchanan and Peter Zumbansen, *Law in Transition: Human Rights, Development and Transitional Justice* (Hart Publishing 2014) 253–54; James 'Youngblood' Henderson, 'Constitutional Vision and Judicial Commitment: Aboriginal Treaty Rights in Canada' (2010) 14(2) *Australian Indigenous Law Review* 24.

[106] House of Commons, Canada, Official Hansard Vol 142(2), 4 December 2015. Prime Minister Justin Trudeau similarly promised 'a total renewal of the relationship between Canada and Indigenous peoples. We have a plan to move toward a nation-to-nation relationship based on recognition, rights, respect, cooperation and partnership'. Canada, 'Statement by Prime Minister on Release of the Final Report of the Truth and Reconciliation Commission' (15 December 2015) <pm.gc.ca> accessed 18 October 2019.

[107] The UN Declaration on the Rights of Indigenous Peoples (DRIP) in its preamble recognises that 'the rights affirmed in treaties, agreements and constructive arrangements between States and indigenous peoples are, in some situations, matters of international concern, interest, responsibility and character' and that 'treaties, agreements and other constructive arrangements, and the relationship they represent, are the basis for a strengthened partnership between indigenous peoples and States'.

to be dealt with in an ongoing way. It establishes an expectation of Indigenous dynamic survival. It indicates, ostensibly at least if not always in practice, an intention not to completely eradicate or assimilate Indigenous peoples. Constitutional recognition of Indigenous peoples, particularly if the reforms include measures for increased Indigenous autonomy, agency and representation in their affairs, can be similarly viewed – such reforms help establish an expectation of Indigenous survival as distinct and dynamic peoples within the nation. Practically, too, the fact of reaching agreement is important. The agreements, once made, can be recalled in future conflict, providing a documented collection of mutual promises to which the parties can return.

As noted, Australia's historical relationship between Indigenous peoples and the colonising state stands in contrast to other British former colonies because there was no founding treaty in the settlement of Australia.[108] Achieving recognition of Indigenous rights and interests in Australia is therefore all the more challenging: there is no treaty to which Indigenous peoples can appeal in advocating for reformed constitutional arrangements. The challenge for Australia will be to embark upon a process of genuine negotiations between Indigenous peoples and the state to settle the terms for a fairer future relationship, which can then be enacted through constitutional and legislative reform.

I. Indigenous Advocacy for Constitutional Reform and Empowerment

Indigenous advocacy for constitutional recognition and reform can be characterised as continued attempts at instigating and completing the constitutional negotiation that did not occur before 1901. Such advocacy has tended to centre on the need for increased Indigenous self-determination, agency and authority in their affairs.

In human rights language, self-determination means the right to freely pursue personal and community development: especially political, economic, social and cultural development.[109] In the context of Indigenous peoples, self-determination often refers to the right to self-govern and exercise autonomy and political agency within colonising states.[110] The UN Declaration on the Rights of Indigenous Peoples, which Australia signed in 2009, asserts in its preamble that 'indigenous peoples are equal to all other peoples, while recognizing the right of all peoples to be different, to consider themselves different, and to be

[108] Not including the Batman treaty which, as discussed in Section II.C above, was invalidated by the Crown. See also Brennan and Davis, 'First Peoples' (n 9 above) 41; Paul McHugh, *Aboriginal Societies and the Common Law* (Oxford University Press 2004) 277.

[109] See Art 1 of both the International Covenant on Civil and Political Rights and the International Covenant on Economic, Social and Cultural Rights, and Arts 3 and 4 of the UN DRIP.

[110] S James Anaya, *Indigenous Peoples in International Law* (2nd edn, Oxford University Press 2004) 150–53. See Arts 18 and 19 of the UN DRIP.

respected as such'. The Indigenous right to self-determination can similarly be understood as the right to be equal yet different;[111] it is the right to prosper, thrive and develop in the way they wish to prosper, thrive and develop. Further, the Indigenous right to self-determination is generally understood as a group right. While Indigenous individuals have an equal right to equal citizenship, collectively, Indigenous *peoples* have a right to freely choose to pursue their development as peoples.

The practical realisation of Indigenous self-determination usually depends on the state being willing to make room, share power and relinquish some control over Indigenous peoples and affairs. Self-determination cannot be achieved in isolation – it is necessarily relational. Though the goal is increased Indigenous autonomy and empowerment, practically this requires state co-operation and partnership. That is why Indigenous calls for increased self-determination are usually directed at government: because achieving Indigenous empowerment does not occur in a vacuum. It requires structural reform to the relationship between Indigenous peoples and the state: reform that makes room for active and empowered Indigenous participation.

Indigenous Australian advocacy for increased self-determination within the Australian state has generally taken three overlapping forms: advocacy for an Indigenous representative body, advocacy for reserved Indigenous parliamentary seats, and advocacy for a treaty or treaties. Indigenous people have also advocated for guarantees of equality and non-discrimination, alongside measures for increased self-determination. In 1927, Fred Maynard wrote a letter to the New South Wales Premier asking for equal citizenship rights and for the control of Indigenous affairs to be transferred to an Indigenous board. 'Our request to supervise our affairs is no innovation', he stated in his letter. But while arguing eloquently for Indigenous self-determination, Maynard also maintained that Indigenous people should be treated equally:

> I wish to make it perfectly clear on behalf of our people that we accept no condition of inferiority as compared with European people ... We are therefore striving to obtain full citizenship rights on terms of absolute equality with all other people in our land.[112]

Indigenous advocacy throughout the decades has viewed the need for Indigenous self-determination as compatible with the need for Indigenous equality and equal citizenship. As will be discussed later, the two principles are complementary.

[111] For more on the interplay between equality and difference, see Lino, *Constitutional Recognition* (n 71 above) 73.

[112] A history of Aboriginal Sydney, 'Australian Aboriginal Progressive Association Writes a Letter of Protest to the NSW Premier' <http://www.historyofaboriginalsydney.edu.au/north-west/australian-aboriginal-progressive-association-writes-letter-protest-nsw-premier> accessed 18 October 2019.

In 1933, Joe Anderson, otherwise known as King Burraga, Chief of the Thurawal tribe near Sydney, also argued for self-determination and sought Indigenous representation in Parliament. Burraga petitioned the Prime Minister as follows:

> All the black man wants is representation in federal parliament. There is also plenty of fish in the river for us all, and land to grow all we want. One hundred and fifty years ago, the Aboriginals owned Australia, and today he demands more than the white man's charity. He wants the right to live.[113]

Yorta Yorta leader William Cooper's letter to King George V in 1937 echoed that call and also sought Indigenous representation in federal Parliament.[114] This petition was not delivered to the King because the Australian government felt that reserved seats were constitutionally impossible – an assertion I will further explore in Chapter five.[115] In 1949, Pastor Sir Doug Nicholls wrote to then Prime Minister, Ben Chifley, also arguing for Indigenous representation in federal Parliament.[116] Indigenous people have never stopped asking for specific representation and a voice in Parliament. Notably, the advocacy continued even after Indigenous people were fully enfranchised in the 1960s.[117]

The need for increased consultation and participation in the political decisions made about their affairs has also been a prominent aspect of Indigenous advocacy for self-determination. In 1963, the Yirrkala Bark Petitions pleaded for

[113] See Bain Attwood and Andrew Markus, *Thinking Black: William Cooper and the Australian Aborigines' League* (Aboriginal Studies Press 2004) 36; Heather Goodall, *Invasion to Embassy: Aboriginal Politics in NSW 1770–1972* (Sydney University Press 2006) 204; Heather Goodall and Alison Cadzow, *Rivers and Resilience: Aboriginal People on Sydney's Georges River* (University of New South Wales Press 2009) 155; Natasha Robinson, 'Aborigines Want to Be Responsible for Themselves', *The Australian* (27 March 2015) <https://www.theaustralian.com.au/nation/aborigines-want-to-be-responsible-for-themselves/news-story/e33f9aaaf6fceb38b4e1372e8889a407> accessed 18 October 2019.

[114] Alexander Reilley, 'Dedicated Seats in the Federal Parliament for Indigenous Australians' (2001) 2(1) *Balayi: Culture, Law and Colonialism* 73, 82; Attwood and Markus, *Thinking Black* (n 113 above).

[115] However, in 2014 the petition was finally delivered to Queen Elizabeth II by Cooper's descendants. Timna Jacks, 'Queen Accepts Petition for Aboriginal Rights, 80 Years On', *Sydney Morning Herald* (4 October 2014) <https://www.smh.com.au/politics/federal/queen-accepts-petition-for-aboriginal-rights-80-years-on-20141003-10ksh6.html> accessed 18 October 2019.

[116] Reilley (n 114 above) 82–83.

[117] See eg Geoff Bagnall, 'A Seventh State: Of First Peoples', *The Stringer Independent News* (11 June 2014) <https://thestringer.com.au/a-seventh-state-of-first-peoples-7865> accessed 18 October 2019; Michael Mansell, 'Self-Determination through an Aboriginal 7th State of Australia: An Australian Provisional Government Model', *First Nations Telegraph* (30 July 2014), Issuu.com; Rosie Lewis, 'Reserved Seats for Aboriginal MPs, Says Jacquie Lambie', *The Australian* (14 September 2014) <https://www.theaustralian.com.au/nation/reserve-seats-for-aboriginal-mps-says-pup-senator-jacqui-lambie/news-story/640efa5cbecfff698c4fc2e6e60a12c8> accessed 18 October 2019; Misha Schubert, 'Indigenous Want Reserved Seats in Parliament: Congress', *Sydney Morning Herald* (31 July 2011) <https://www.smh.com.au/national/indigenous-want-seats-reserved-20110730-1i5l0.html> accessed 18 October 2019.

the government to listen to Yolngu people before making decisions about their land and their lives:

> [T]he procedures of the excision of this land and the fate of the people on it were never explained to them beforehand, and were kept secret from them.
>
> ... when Welfare Officers and Government officials came to inform them of decisions taken without them and against them, they did not undertake to convey to the Government in Canberra the views and feelings of the Yirrkala aboriginal people.
>
> ... the people of this area fear that their needs and interests will be completely ignored as they have been ignored in the past, and they fear that the fate which has overtaken the Larrakeah tribe will overtake them.
>
> And they humbly pray that the Honourable the House of Representatives will appoint a Committee, accompanied by competent interpreters, to hear the views of the people of Yirrkala before permitting the excision of this land.[118]

The Yolngu asked then, as they have asked since, to be properly heard before government decisions about them are made.[119]

Indigenous claims for self-determination and representation also often manifest through advocacy for a treaty. In 1972 the Aboriginal Tent Embassy argued for Aboriginal control of Aboriginal affairs, which included a demand that the Northern Territory Parliament be made up predominantly of Indigenous representatives.[120] In 1975, the Aboriginal Treaty Commission recommended a national agreement on the 'right of Indigenous Australians to control their own affairs and to establish their own associations for this purpose.'[121] In 1979, the National Aboriginal Conference's Sub-Committee on a Makarrata, after consulting widely with Indigenous people, argued for Aboriginal 'management of their own affairs' and asked for 'the reservation of several seats in the Commonwealth, State and local governments', among other reforms.[122]

In 1988, Yolngu leader Galarrwuy Yunupingu presented the Barunga Statement to then Prime Minister, Bob Hawke. In this Statement, Yunupingu and the leaders of the clans and tribes of Northern and Central Australia called for the enactment of a treaty to recognise Indigenous rights to self-determination

[118] Documenting Democracy, Yirrkala Bark Petitions 1963 (Cth): <http://www.foundingdocs.gov.au/item-did-104.html> accessed 18 October 2019.

[119] See also Damien Freeman, 'Introduction' in Damien Freeman and Shireen Morris (eds), *The Forgotten People: Liberal and Conservative Approaches to Recognising Indigenous Peoples* (Melbourne University Press 2016) 4–6.

[120] J Newfong, The Aboriginal Embassy – Its purpose and aims: <https://www.nma.gov.au/__data/assets/pdf_file/0003/384384/f63.pdf> accessed 18 October 2019.

[121] W Jonas, 'Reflections on the History of Indigenous People's Struggle for Human Rights in Australia: What Role Could a Treaty Play?' speech at Murdoch University, 27 June 2002, 45.

[122] National Aboriginal Conference, Sub-Committee on the Makarrata, 'Makarrata Report', 1979. Calls for reserved seats continued through the 1980s: Reilley (n 114 above) 82–83. See also Julie Fenley, 'The National Aboriginal Conference and the Makarrata: Sovereignty and Treaty Discussions, 1979–1981' (2011) 42(3) *Australian Historical Studies* 372. For a history of the Indigenous movement from 1979-2018, see Lino, *Constitutional Recognition* (n 71 above) 11–68.

and self-management. The Barunga Statement called for Aboriginal control, freedom and respect, and for a national elected Aboriginal and Islander organisation to oversee Aboriginal and Islander affairs.[123] Hawke responded at the time that a treaty with Indigenous peoples was desirable, though the promise was never fulfilled. However, the Barunga Statement's call for an Indigenous-elected Indigenous body probably helped drive momentum for the establishment of the Aboriginal and Torres Strait Islander Commission (ATSIC) in 1990.[124] ATSIC was established by legislation but was abolished by the Howard government in 2005.

Also in 1988, the Constitutional Commission recommended a new constitutional clause guaranteeing all people freedom from discrimination on the grounds of race, as well as on other grounds.[125] The Council for Aboriginal Reconciliation (CAR) similarly advocated such a protection in its final report in 2000,[126] a call which would be echoed years later by the Expert Panel in 2012 and a Joint Select Committee in 2015. But even in the 1990s and beyond, a large proportion of the Indigenous advocacy focused on the need for democratic participation, leadership and representation in their affairs.[127] A 1995 ATSIC report highlighted the vulnerability of the Indigenous minority within the democratic process as a key reason for seeking this kind of politically empowering reform:

> Indigenous Australians are particularly susceptible to shifts in Government policies and funding priorities because of powerlessness. Political participation would foster greater equity in the provision of services and accountability by Governments. It would enable articulation of indigenous policy perspectives, broader participation in policy development and promote a wider understanding of indigenous issues in the broader community.[128]

ATSIC suggested its chairperson be granted observer status in Parliament and the ability to speak to both houses on bills affecting Indigenous interests,

[123] Council for Aboriginal Reconciliation, Documents of Reconciliation, Attachment A, <http://www.austlii.edu.au/au/orgs/car/docrec/policy/brief/attach.htm> accessed 18 October 2019.

[124] Other advocacy included the work of Lois O'Donoghue, *Proposal for an Aboriginal and Islander Consultative Organisation: Discussion Paper*, Department of Aboriginal Affairs, 1985; Lois O'Donoghue, *An Aboriginal and Islander Consultative Organisation: Report of Consultations* (Australian Government Publishing Service 1986).

[125] Constitutional Commission, *Final Report of the Constitutional Commission* (Australian Government Publishing Service 1988) vol 1 at [10.372].

[126] Council for Aboriginal Reconciliation, *Reconciliation: Australia's Challenge – Final report of the Council for Aboriginal Reconciliation to the Prime Minister and the Commonwealth Parliament*, 2000.

[127] See eg Council for Aboriginal Reconciliation, *Going Forward: Social Justice for the First Australians, a Submission to the Commonwealth Government*, 1995, 41.

[128] Aboriginal and Torres Strait Islander Commission (ATSIC), *Rights, Recognition and Reform: A Report to Government on Native Title Social Justice Measures*, 1995, [4.25].

while also calling for further investigation into reserved parliamentary seats.[129] In the same year, CAR also called for 'recognition and empowerment' through incorporation of the ATSIC chairperson as a 'full member of the Ministerial Council' on Indigenous affairs, noting a widespread view amongst Indigenous Australians that 'the structures of governments … do not provide adequately for Indigenous peoples to exercise legal powers over matters that were of concern to them nor influence major decision-making processes'.[130] As noted, however, ATSIC was an institution set up only by legislation. It was short-lived.

In years to come, there were inquiries into reserved Indigenous parliamentary seats in NSW and Queensland.[131] In 2007, Noel Pearson urged mechanisms to better manage the interface between government and Indigenous people,[132] such as the reinstatement of a national representative body to enable Indigenous people to take more responsibility and control of their affairs.[133] In 2008, the Yolngu people petitioned the Commonwealth through a presentation from their senior Dilak, led again by Galarrwuy Yunupingu, to then Prime Minister, Kevin Rudd. They asked again for constitutional recognition of their Indigenous rights:

> We, the united clans of East Arnhem land, through our most senior Dilak, do humbly petition you, the 26th Prime Minister of Australia, in your capacity as the first amongst equals in the Australian Parliament, and as the chief adviser to Her Majesty Queen Elizabeth the Second, to secure within the Australian Constitution the recognition and protection of our full and complete right to:
>
> – Our way of life in all its diversity;
> – Our property, being the lands and waters of East Arnhem land;
> – Economic independence, through the proper use of the riches of our land and waters in all their abundance and wealth;
> – Control of our lives and responsibility for our children's future.
>
> These rights are self-evident.

[129] 'Representatives of indigenous peoples, including ATSIC, should have legally enforceable speaking rights in legislatures and in Local Government councils on issues relating to indigenous peoples. The Chairperson of ATSIC should be entitled to address the Parliament annually to report on the state of indigenous affairs.': ibid [4.31].

[130] Council for Aboriginal Reconciliation, *Going Forward: Social Justice for the First Australians, a Submission to the Commonwealth Government*, 1995, Recommendation 18, 35–45.

[131] See K Struthers, 'Hands on Parliament: A Parliamentary Committee Inquiry into Aboriginal and Torres Strait Islander Peoples' Participation in Queensland's Democratic Process' (2003) 5(22) *Indigenous Law Bulletin* 6; Queensland Constitutional Review Commission, *Report on the Possible Reform of and Changes to the Acts and Laws that Relate to the Queensland Constitution* (2000); Reilley (n 114 above) 83.

[132] Noel Pearson, 'A Structure for Empowerment', *The Australian* (16–17 June 2007) <https://www.theaustralian.com.au/opinion/columnists/a-structure-for-empowerment/news-story/d39847a9916b4d80d88646bb6b608c02> accessed 18 October 2019.

[133] Pearson argued, '[t]here's got to be some kind of structure in which we interface with government'. *Lateline*, 'Noel Pearson discusses the issues faced by Indigenous communities', 26 June 2007, <http://www.abc.net.au/lateline/content/2007/s1962844.htm>.

> These rights are fundamental to our place within the Australian nation.
>
> We ask for your leadership to have the Commonwealth Parliament start the process of recognition of these rights through serious constitutional reform.[134]

An examination of the Indigenous advocacy for constitutional recognition and reform reveals what is meant by 'serious constitutional reform'. 'Serious constitutional reform' means substantive, structural reform to the way Indigenous affairs are governed at the national and constitutional level. An integral characteristic of Indigenous advocacy for constitutional recognition is that the reform being sought is practical, empowering and substantive, rather than merely decorative or symbolic. What is meant by 'recognition' is not recognition in a purely static, symbolic sense, but recognition and accommodation of Indigenous rights and interests in the operational constitutional framework of the nation.[135]

Importantly, Indigenous leaders have articulated the need for *constitutional* recognition and reform, because only the *Constitution* is capable of providing enduring and stable protection of rights. Yunupingu in 1998 explained the importance of the legal and political stability provided by the *Australian Constitution* in relation to Indigenous rights:

> Our Yolgnu law is more like your Balanda Constitution than Balanda legislation or statutory law. It doesn't change at the whim of short-term political expediency. It protects the principles which go to make up the very essence of who we are and how we should manage the most precious things about our culture and our society. Changing it is a very serious business … If our Indigenous rights were recognised in the Constitution, it would not be so easy for Governments to change the laws all the time, and wipe out our rights.[136]

The comments demonstrate that the search for a stable and enduring guarantee is at the heart of advocacy for Indigenous constitutional recognition. Professor Patrick Dodson articulated similar reasoning in 1999:

> It may be a harsh thing to say, but many actions of Australian Governments have given Aboriginal people little faith in the promises Governments make in relation to protecting and defending the rights of Indigenous Australians. That is why we need a formal Agreement that recognises and guarantees the rights of Indigenous Australians within the Australian Constitution.[137]

[134] Galarrwuy Yunupingu, 'Tradition, Truth and Tomorrow', *The Monthly* (December 2008) <https://www.themonthly.com.au/issue/2008/december/1268179150/galarrwuy-yunupingu/tradition-truth-tomorrow> accessed 18 October 2019.

[135] See also Shireen Morris and Noel Pearson, 'Indigenous Constitutional Recognition: Paths to Failure and Possible Paths to Success' (2017) 91(5) *Australian Law Journal* 350; Megan Davis, 'Political Timetables Trump Workable Timetables: Indigenous Constitutional Recognition and the Temptation of Symbolism over Substance' in Simon Young, Jennifer Nielsen and Jeremy Patrick (eds), *Constitutional Recognition of First Peoples in Australia* (Federation Press 2016) 62, 81, 88.

[136] See Galarrwuy Yunupingu, *Vincent Lingiari Memorial Lecture*, Darwin, 20 August 1998. ('Balanda' means European/Western).

[137] Patrick Dodson, 'Until the Chains are Broken', *Vincent Lingiari Memorial Lecture*, Darwin, 8 September 1999.

Noel Pearson in 2013 similarly called for a national 'promise', in the form of a constitutional guarantee that the discrimination of the past will not be repeated.[138] Indigenous advocacy for 'serious constitution reform' has not softened over time or yielded to political pressures.

J. The Last Decade: From the Expert Panel to the Uluru Statement from the Heart

As demonstrated, Indigenous Australians have been calling for a stronger political voice and increased representation and participation in their affairs for decades. More recently, this advocacy has converged decisively with the movement for Indigenous constitutional recognition: the debate has grappled with whether judicially adjudicated constitutional guarantees should be adopted to enhance Indigenous rights protections, or whether political and procedural constitutional mechanisms are to be preferred.

In 2010, an Expert Panel was established by Julia Gillard's Labor Government to advise on Indigenous constitutional recognition. The Expert Panel conducted consultations in Indigenous communities. The message was clear: Indigenous people want substantive constitutional reform. In 2012, the Expert Panel proposed a judicially adjudicated racial non-discrimination clause as the key means for protecting Indigenous rights.[139] Then history began to repeat itself. Just like in 1967, there were concerns about empowering the High Court, creating legal uncertainty and undermining parliamentary supremacy.[140] The proposal did not win bipartisan support.

Indigenous advocates, however, did not want to settle for a merely symbolic, minimalistic constitutional amendment. This was confirmed at a meeting with political leaders in July 2015 at Kirribilli House, where Indigenous leaders again emphasised that they sought a form of constitutional recognition that has substance and propels positive practical change, and that provides an answer to the history of racial discrimination Indigenous peoples have suffered under the *Constitution*.[141] Indigenous advocacy for practical and empowering constitutional change should rule out proposals for minimalistic, purely symbolic recognition. None of the Indigenous letters or petitions to kings or prime

[138] Noel Pearson, 'Next Step for the Nation is to Leave Race Behind', *The Australian* (25 May 2013) <https://www.theaustralian.com.au/national-affairs/in-depth/next-step-is-for-australia-to-leave-race-behind/news-story/f9acee8f859d79f8f3fac2b374d1300a> accessed 18 October 2019.

[139] Expert Panel Report (n 41 above) xviii.

[140] For an exploration of these objections, see Morris, 'Undemocratic, Uncertain and Politically Unviable?' (n 91 above).

[141] See Natasha Robinson, 'Indigenous Recognition "Must Be Real": Aboriginal Leaders', *The Australian* (6 July 2015) <https://www.theaustralian.com.au/nation/indigenous-recognition-must-be-real-aboriginal-leaders/news-story/38109c55d83277a5dae4f0e91fa11203> accessed 18 October 2019.

ministers asked for a symbolic mention in a preamble. All asked for substantive, empowering reform. There would be no point in proceeding with an Indigenous recognition proposal that Indigenous people do not want, and it is unlikely that Australians would vote 'yes' to such a proposal.

Grappling with the negative political responses to the Expert Panel's key recommendation, and understanding the importance of bipartisan support for referendum success, Indigenous leaders like Noel Pearson (who was also an Expert Panel member) went in search of alternative solutions that would address objections to a racial non-discrimination guarantee, while realising Indigenous aspirations for substantive constitutional change over constitutional minimalism (a mere symbolic mention in the *Constitution* or cosmetic amendments to the 'race' clauses).[142] In 2013, Cape York Institute began engaging with constitutional conservatives – those who opposed the insertion of new judicially adjudicated constitutional guarantees – to try to find common ground in the Indigenous constitutional recognition debate.[143] The collaboration produced an alternative proposal, in keeping with decades of Indigenous advocacy for greater participation and representation: a constitutionally guaranteed Indigenous voice in their affairs. This was a political and procedural approach to Indigenous constitutional recognition.[144]

In 2015, Professor Anne Twomey published a draft constitutional clause that would establish a constitutionally enshrined Indigenous advisory body[145] to provide advice on laws and policies with respect to Indigenous affairs.[146] The draft provisions explicitly addressed the concerns raised with respect to the Expert Panel's racial non-discrimination clause: the body would have no veto power, it would eliminate any risk of laws being struck down by the High Court for being unconstitutional, and parliamentary supremacy would be totally upheld. The proposed amendment would transfer no power to

[142] See Morris and Pearson, 'Indigenous Constitutional Recognition' (n 135 above).

[143] The author was working with Pearson driving Cape York Institute's Indigenous constitutional recognition policy during this time. For more on this engagement, see Shireen Morris, *Radical Heart: Three Stories Make Us One* (Melbourne University Press 2018); Pearson, 'A Rightful Place' (n 15 above) 65-66; Noel Pearson, 'Foreword' in Damien Freeman and Shireen Morris (eds), *The Forgotten People: Liberal and Conservative Approaches to Recognising Indigenous Peoples* (Melbourne University Press 2016).

[144] Shireen Morris, 'The Argument for a Constitutional Procedure for Parliament to Consult with Indigenous Peoples When Making Laws for Indigenous Affairs' (2015) 26(3) *Public Law Review* 1; Shireen Morris, 'The Torment of Our Powerlessness: Indigenous Constitutional Vulnerability and the Uluru Statement's Call for a First Nations Voice' (2018) 41(3) *University of New South Wales Law Journal* 629; Shireen Morris, 'Parliamentary Scrutiny and Insights for a First Nations Voice to Parliament' in Laura Grenfell and Julie Debeljak, *Law Making and Human Rights* (Thomson Reuters 2020); see also Davis, 'Political Timetables' (n 135 above) 76–79.

[145] Anne Twomey, 'Putting Words to the Tune of Indigenous Constitutional Recognition', *The Conversation* (20 May 2015) <https://theconversation.com/putting-words-to-the-tune-of-indigenous-constitutional-recognition-42038> accessed 18 October 2019.

[146] See Anne Twomey, 'An Indigenous Advisory Body: Addressing Concerns about Justiciability and Parliamentary Sovereignty' (2015) 8(19) *Indigenous Law Bulletin* 6.

the High Court: it was specifically designed to be non-justiciable. Instead of empowering the judiciary, the proposal would constitutionally empower Indigenous peoples *themselves* to have a fairer say in political decisions made about them.

In May 2017, following a series of First Nations regional dialogues, Indigenous Australians formed a national consensus on how they want to be constitutionally recognised. After assessing the various constitutional recognition options (a minimalistic mention, a racial non-discrimination clause, a constitutionally enshrined Indigenous voice, treaty-making), their consensus was articulated in the historic Uluru Statement from the Heart, which called for a singular constitutional reform: a First Nations voice to be enshrined in the *Constitution*.[147] This was an unprecedented moment in Indigenous peoples' struggle for constitutional recognition. Most of the Indigenous advocacy of the past tended to emanate from particular regions: never before had a *national* Indigenous consensus position been realised. Although seven of the 250 delegates dissented and walked out of the Uluru convention, citing a preference for 'sovereign treaties',[148] the majority position was powerful, and reflected views expressed at every dialogue calling for a constitutional voice.[149] Notably, a First Nations voice was also the preferred reform articulated in submissions from the broader public.[150]

The Uluru Statement confirmed that Indigenous people seek practical and empowering constitutional reform, not symbolism alone, and that increased self-determination remains a key aspiration. The Referendum Council's final report, delivered in June 2017, supported the Uluru Statement's call for a constitutionally guaranteed Indigenous representative body to provide input into laws and policies with respect to Indigenous affairs as the only recommended constitutional reform. This represented a decisive shift in thinking about Indigenous constitutional recognition. It was an important breakthrough, both politically and constitutionally. The proposal for a First Nations voice is deeply in keeping not only with the history of Indigenous advocacy for political empowerment, but also with Australian constitutional culture, history and design – arguably more so than the insertion of poetic statements into what is fundamentally a rulebook, and more so than introducing a racial non-discrimination guarantee into Australia's 'Bill of rights' free *Constitution*. The proposal aligns with

[147] It also called for a Makarrata Commission, set up in legislation, to oversee agreement-making or treaty-making. The Referendum Council recommended a constitutionally guaranteed Indigenous advisory body, with legislated processes and functions, such as advising on the operation ss 51(xxvi) and 122 of the *Constitution* – powers that have been used to enact Indigenous-specific laws: see *Final Report of the Referendum Council*, Report (30 June 2017) Recommendation 1.

[148] Laudiana Blanco, '"We Won't Sell Out Our Mob": Delegates Walk Out of Constitutional Recognition Forum in Protest', *NITV News* (25 May 2017) <https://www.sbs.com.au/nitv/nitv-news/article/2017/05/25/breaking-delegates-walk-out-constitutional-recognition-forum-protest> accessed 18 October 2019.

[149] *Final Report of the Referendum Council* (n 147 above), 9–16.

[150] ibid 33–35.

the ideas underpinning the Australian federal compact, which guarantees the historic political communities fair representation in their affairs.[151]

Australia's *Constitution* is all about voices: it provides mechanisms for the historic political communities – even the very small ones, like Tasmania – to have their voices heard by the might of the majority.[152] The First Nations, however, were not at the negotiating table during the constitutional conventions of the 1800s, and the Indigenous historic constituency was omitted from the compact of 1901. There is thus no constitutional mechanism for the First Nations to be specifically heard in their affairs, even in laws and policies made directly about them – notwithstanding that there are more Indigenous Australians than Tasmanians.[153] If Tasmanians should be constitutionally guaranteed a voice in their affairs, Indigenous peoples should be constitutionally guaranteed a voice in their affairs too. The race power has only ever been used to make laws in relation to Indigenous peoples: it is thus logical that Indigenous peoples should have a fair say in the exercise of this power, as well as other relevant powers when used in a way that especially or uniquely impacts Indigenous peoples, to ensure such powers are wielded in a fairer way. In asking for a constitutionally enshrined voice in their affairs, the Uluru Statement makes a reasonable and constitutionally congruent request.

Despite its reasonableness, in 2017 former Prime Minister Malcolm Turnbull rejected the call for a First Nations constitutional voice, misleadingly suggesting it would breach principles of equality,[154] and erroneously describing it as a 'third chamber of Parliament'[155] that Australians would reject at referendum.

[151] See also Dylan Lino, 'Towards Indigenous-Settler Federalism' (2017) 28(2) *Public Law Review* 118, 134–37.

[152] Chen (n 70 above) 865–66; Thomas-Woolley and Keller (n 70 above); see also Malcolm M Feeley and Edward L Rubin, *Federalism: Political Identity and Tragic Compromise* (University of Michigan Press 2009) 18–20.

[153] In 2017, the Tasmanian population was 519,166: *Population Australia*, 'Population of Tasmania 2019' (Web Page) <http://www.population.net.au/population-of-tasmania/> accessed 18 October 2019. The 2016 Census reported the Indigenous population as 649,200: Australian Bureau of Statistics, 'Census: Aboriginal and Torres Strait Islander population' (Web Page, 27 June 2017) <https://www.abs.gov.au/ausstats/abs@.nsf/MediaRealesesByCatalogue/02D50FAA9987D6B7CA25814800087E03?OpenDocument> accessed 18 October 2019.

[154] Prime Minister, Attorney-General, Minister for Indigenous Affairs, 'Response to Referendum Council's Report on Constitutional Recognition' (Media Release, 26 October 2017) <https://ministers.pmc.gov.au/scullion/2017/response-referendum-councils-report-constitutional-recognition> accessed 18 October 2019. This claim is incorrect. There is no principle of equality in Australia's constitutional arrangements. The High Court has declined to read in a principle of equality from Australia's Constitution because of discriminatory provisions within the Constitution and its history: see *Leeth v The Commonwealth* (1992) 174 CLR 455; *Kruger v Commonwealth* (1997) 190 CLR 1; Sarah Joseph, 'Kruger v Commonwealth: Constitutional Rights and the Stolen Generation' (1998) 24(2) *Monash Law Review* 486, 491–92. Nor is there equality of individual voting power; for example, Tasmanians get a greater proportional say in the Senate than Victorians, due to the operation of s 7 of the *Constitution* which guarantees the States equal representation in the Senate.

[155] This claim was also incorrect because no 'third chamber of Parliament' was proposed by the Referendum Council. The proposed Indigenous advisory body would be external to Parliament, would have no veto powers, no power to make laws, would be set up by Parliament, with powers and functions determined by Parliament. No reform to the Houses of Parliament was proposed.

Independent polling contradicts the latter claim. A 2017 Omnipoll showed 61 per cent of Australians would vote 'yes' to a First Nations voice in the *Constitution*[156] and a February 2018 Newspoll showed 57 per cent support.[157] By July 2019, research showed support at 66 per cent,[158] despite sustained government negativity about the proposal.

Both Indigenous and Non-Indigenous Australians continue to push for the Uluru Statement.[159] The 2018 Joint Select Committee on Constitutional Recognition relating to Aboriginal and Torres Strait Islander Peoples endorsed a First Nations constitutional voice as the only viable pathway forward for Indigenous constitutional recognition, and called for further consultation with Indigenous people to progress design details.[160] The Scott Morrison Liberal Government appears to have taken up this suggestion and intends to consult with Indigenous Australians to co-design the details of a First Nations voice.[161] However the Prime Minister has also indicated opposition to the idea of the body being constitutionalised,[162] while maintaining support for constitutional recognition. Attorney-General, Christian Porter, says he needs to see the 'precise words' of the constitutional amendment before it can be supported.[163]

[156] Calla Wahlquist, 'Most Australians Would Support Indigenous Voice to Parliament Plan that Turnbull Rejected', *The Guardian* (30 October 2017) <https://www.theguardian.com/australia-news/2017/oct/30/most-australians-support-indigenous-voice-to-parliament-plan-that-turnbull-rejected> accessed 18 October 2019.

[157] Simon Benson, 'Bill Shorten Raising Voice a Winner With Voters: Newspoll' *The Australian* (20 February 2018) <https://www.theaustralian.com.au/nation/bill-shorten-raising-voice-a-winner-with-voters-newspoll/news-story/3d6ee299780b7ac6901df9ccdfa16cc5> accessed 18 October 2019.

[158] Katherine Murphy, 'Essential Poll: Majority of Australians Want Indigenous Recognition and Voice to Parliament', *The Guardian* (12 July 2019) <https://www.theguardian.com/australia-news/2019/jul/12/essential-poll-majority-of-australians-want-indigenous-recognition-and-voice-to-parliament> accessed 18 October 2019. Earlier, in May 2019, research showed 64% support: Isabella Higgins and Sarah Collard, 'Federal Election 2019: Vote Compass Finds Australians Are Ready to Back Indigenous "Voice to Parliament"', *ABC News* (3 May 2019) <https://www.abc.net.au/news/2019-05-03/vote-compass-federal-election-voice-to-parliament/11071384> accessed 18 October 2019.

[159] For example, a petition run by Professor Fiona Stanley has gathered thousands of signatures ('Joint Statement: A Call to the Prime Minister and Australian Parliament' <https://www.acoss.org.au/supportfirstnations/>) and the proposal is gathering support across the political spectrum. Even right-wing radio host, Alan Jones, agreed with former Labor Prime Minister, Kevin Rudd, on the merits of the proposed Indigenous voice: see Neil McMahon, 'Q&A Recap: Old Foes Alan Jones and Kevin Rudd Finally Find Common Ground', *Sydney Morning Herald* (31 October 2017) <https://www.smh.com.au/entertainment/tv-and-radio/qa-recap-old-foes-alan-jones-and-kevin-rudd-finally-find-common-ground-20171031-gzbew1.html> accessed 18 October 2019.

[160] Joint Select Committee on Constitutional Recognition Relating to Aboriginal and Torres Strait Islander Peoples, *Final Report* (November 2018).

[161] Deborah Snow, 'Morrison Pledges Recognition but Will Take "As Long As Needed"', *Sydney Morning Herald* (26 May 2019) <https://www.smh.com.au/politics/federal/morrison-pledges-recognition-but-will-take-as-long-as-needed-20190526-p51r80.html> accessed 18 October 2019.

[162] Greg Brown, 'Morrison to Veto Voice as Part of the Constitution', *The Australian* (12 July 2019) <https://www.theaustralian.com.au/nation/politics/morrison-to-veto-voice-as-part-of-constitution/news-story/c9753bbe3595470032ac7fa95636931e> accessed 18 October 2019.

[163] Michael Pelley, 'Public Won't "Buy" Uluru Statement, Claims AG', *Financial Review* (21 June 2019) <https://www.afr.com/politics/federal/public-won-t-buy-uluru-statement-claims-ag-20190620-p51zf6> accessed 18 October 2019. Yet, the 2018 Joint Select Committee complained there were

Meanwhile National Party member, Barnaby Joyce, who initially coined the misleading 'third chamber of Parliament' phrase, more recently admitted this was a mischaracterisation and apologised unreservedly.[164]

The recurring disagreement about the fundamental purpose of Indigenous constitutional recognition remains evident in the contemporary debate. By maintaining support for constitutional recognition while rejecting the idea of a constitutionally guaranteed First Nations voice, the government seems to demonstrate a preference for the merely symbolic recognition that Indigenous people have consistently rejected. Whereas Indigenous people have shifted their advocacy to accommodate political concerns with respect to judicial review – instead of advocating a racial non-discrimination guarantee the Uluru Statement advocates a First Nations voice – the government is yet to truly shift its understanding of what Indigenous constitutional recognition requires in light of Indigenous concerns. Political leaders, strangely, seem to be veering towards a re-run of the 1999 symbolic preamble, which failed when put to the people.[165] At the time of writing, it is unclear how or when this debate will be resolved. It is to be hoped, however, that Australian political leaders might in time be persuaded by the arguments for modest and constitutionally congruent reform that Indigenous advocates have put forward in the Uluru Statement.

The stakes are high and the political challenge remains immense. While the Uluru Statement was a historic, national articulation of how Indigenous people want to be constitutionally recognised, Indigenous consensus on the constitutional reform model (though crucial) does not ensure referendum success. How Australian politicians, and the Australian polity at large, ultimately respond to this Indigenous consensus remains to be seen.

III. POLITICAL CONTEXT

Achieving Indigenous constitutional recognition is politically difficult in three overlapping ways: first, because it involves constitutional reform, which in Australia is particularly challenging due to the requirements of section 128 mandating a double majority referendum for any constitutional amendment; second, because it involves discussion of Indigenous issues, which

too many ('no fewer than 18 different versions') examples of precise words being offered up to government. Many constitutional experts have drafted versions of how this amendment could be worded. Joint Select Committee on Constitutional Recognition relating to Aboriginal and Torres Strait Islander Peoples, *Final Report* (November 2018) ix.

[164] Amy Remeikis, 'Barnaby Joyce 'Apologises' for Calling Indigenous Voice a Third Chamber of Parliament' *The Guardian* (18 July 2019) <https://www.theguardian.com/australia-news/2019/jul/18/barnaby-joyce-apologises-for-calling-indigenous-voice-a-third-chamber-of-parliament> accessed 18 October 2019.

[165] For an argument on why a minimalist approach would not succeed, see Morris and Pearson, 'Indigenous Constitutional Recognition' (n 135 above).

can be an emotional and contested area of Australian politics and policy; and third, because it involves discussion of constitutional rights, which in Australia generally tends to prompt particular attachment to the constitutional status quo.

Australian politics in relation to constitutional change can be vicious, no matter what the reform initiative. The machinery of Australian referenda, with the requirements for presentation of 'yes' and 'no' cases[166] and the referendum process itself, can prompt divisive debate, characteristically unconstrained by measured adherence to fact.[167] As journalist Paul Kelly observed during the 1988 constitutional reform discussions, the 'technique of scaremongering reaches its highest political art form in the field of constitutional alteration'.[168] Australia's *Constitution* is notoriously difficult to reform and referenda are thus a fertile political environment for fear campaigns. Add to this the reality that Indigenous affairs in Australia are a politically fraught area which can impel polarised debate and bring latent prejudice and unresolved historical tensions to the fore.

The sense of political friction surrounding Indigenous issues has its roots in the unresolved aspects of Australia's history. As noted, unlike other British former colonies, Australia lacks a founding agreement or treaty with its Indigenous peoples. Similarly, other countries have pursued contemporary Truth and Reconciliation Commissions and formal settlements of their domestic Indigenous relationships.[169] Australia has not formally dealt with the uncomfortable aspects of its colonial past – though this may be changing through the push for Indigenous constitutional recognition itself and other cultural shifts that have begun to occur in recent years. Former Prime Minister Kevin Rudd's National Apology to the Stolen Generations in 2007, for example, was a moment of public acknowledgement for past discriminatory policies which removed Indigenous children from their families, though it was not accompanied by compensation.[170] More recently, the extensive public discussion about the on-field treatment of

[166] The *Referendum (Machinery Provisions) Act 1984* (Cth) s 11 requires that a pamphlet presenting both the 'yes' and a 'no' case arguments be distributed to the public in the lead up to a constitutional referendum. Often, these 'yes' and 'no' cases involve exaggeration and fear campaigns, despite the criminal prohibition on the making of misleading or deceptive statements in s 122 of the Act.

[167] See the discussion of referendum tactics and exaggerated claims, in Scott Bennett, 'The Politics of Constitutional Amendment', Parliament of Australia, Research Paper No 11, 2002–03 <https://www.aph.gov.au/About_Parliament/Parliamentary_Departments/Parliamentary_Library/pubs/rp/rp0203/03rp11> accessed 18 October 2019.

[168] Paul Kelly, 'The Referendums: Myths and Bogeys', *The Australian* (2 September 1988) quoted in Williams and Hume (n 75 above) 82. See also Enid Campbell, 'Southey Memorial Lecture 1988: Changing the Constitution: Past and Future' (1989) 17(1) *Melbourne University Law Review* 1, 12.

[169] For example, the Truth and Reconciliation settlement processes in Canada and South Africa and the Waitangi Tribunal settlement process in New Zealand.

[170] See Noel Pearson, 'When Words Aren't Enough', *The Australian* (12 February 2008); Chiara Lawry, 'Beyond the Apology: Achieving Full and Effective Reparations for the Stolen Generations' (2010) 18(2) *Australian Indigenous Law Review* 83.

Indigenous footballer Adam Goodes by opposition fans[171] and Indigenous journalist Stan Grant's popular speech on the problem of racism in Australia[172] have brought the nation's unresolved colonial history to the fore of public discourse. Likewise, State treaty processes have begun in Victoria,[173] and more recently in Queensland,[174] with discussion percolating in other States.[175] There is a sense in which the nation may increasingly be open to discussing and dealing with its complex past.[176]

The discourse remains largely polarised, however. Lacking a founding treaty, Australia also lacks a baseline of agreed principles by reference to which we might be better able to conduct coherent conversations about reconciliation and Indigenous affairs. Absent this kind of principled frame of reference, the politics of Indigenous affairs tends to swing between extremes, with little agreement on the values towards which Australia should be striving in the relationship between Indigenous peoples and the state.[177] Blockages of shame and denial with respect to past wrongdoing can hinder productive discussion. A sense of guilt may make issues involving Indigenous history and national reconciliation emotionally difficult, leading to a denial that there is any problem to solve. As Waleed Aly argues, some commentators may prefer to retain a mythologised view of Australian history as morally faultless.[178] Viewed defensively, suggestions for

[171] See Sean Kelly, 'The Adam Goodes Debate is All about Race: What the Right-Wing Commentariat Gets Wrong', *The Monthly* (15 April 2016) <https://www.themonthly.com.au/today/sean-kelly/2015/30/2015/1438240711/adam-goodes-debate-all-about-race> accessed 18 October 2019.

[172] See Stan Grant, 'Racism Is Destroying the Australian Dream', *IQ2 debate*, Ethics Centre, Sydney, 27 October 2015.

[173] *Advancing the Treaty Process with Aboriginal Victorians Act 2018* (Vic).

[174] Talissa Siganto, 'Queensland Government Announces "Conversation" to Formalise Indigenous Treaty', *ABC News* (14 July 2019) <https://www.abc.net.au/news/2019-07-14/queensland-government-indigenous-treaty-process-promise/11307682> accessed 18 October 2019.

[175] Michael Graham and Alice Petrie, 'Treaty Discussions in Australia: An Overview', Parliament of Victoria, Research Papers: <https://www.parliament.vic.gov.au/publications/research-papers/download/36-research-papers/13862-treaty-discussions-in-australia-an-overview> accessed 18 October 2019.

[176] Though, notably, treaty discussions only tend to be fostered in States where there is a Labor government in power. There is not, in that sense, bipartisan interest in treaties.

[177] Noel Pearson has described Indigenous affairs in Australia as a pendulum, swinging from one political extreme to the other: Noel Pearson, 'Next Step For the Nation is to Leave Race Behind', *The Australian* (25 May 2013) <https://www.theaustralian.com.au/national-affairs/in-depth/next-step-is-for-australia-to-leave-race-behind/news-story/f9acee8f859d79f8f3fac2b374d1300a> accessed 18 October 2019.

[178] Aly compares the American political culture as one that acknowledges its past wrongs and strives for perfection. This is reflected, Aly argues, in the American constitutional quest to 'perfect their union', a sentiment which references the words of the preamble to the US Constitution. Australian political culture, by contrast, in Aly's view may struggle to admit historical imperfection and may thus deny or downplay past wrongs. Note, however, that the *Australian Constitution* also contains rhetoric about unifying the colonies as an 'indissoluble Commonwealth', and there is a significant section of the population that does want to improve upon history. See Waleed Aly, 'Why Australia Lies to Itself about Its Indigenous History', *Sydney Morning Herald* (31 March 2016) <https://www.smh.com.au/opinion/why-australia-lies-to-itself-about-its-indigenous-history-20160331-gnuo4t.html> accessed 18 October 2019.

constitutional reform can be interpreted as an aggressive moral critique and thus may meet resistance. There is a sense in which the nation is still not comfortable discussing historical injustice, perhaps due to the incorrect assumption that such admission would imply contemporary individual wrongdoing. Lacking agreement on the problem to be solved, discussion about potential reform solutions remains fraught.

The added dimension that Indigenous peoples generally seek constitutional recognition to improve protection of their Indigenous rights and interests under the *Constitution* heightens the political difficulty. Rights clauses and bills of rights, whether constitutional or legislated, have often generated opposition in Australia, rather than consensus. Previous attempts at extending constitutional rights protections or implementing a legislated federal Bill of rights have failed.[179] There are therefore three combined aspects to the challenge at hand: the challenge of constitutional reform, the challenge of Indigenous affairs, and the challenge of constitutional rights. The combined political difficulty entailed in achieving Indigenous constitutional recognition is significant.

A. The Challenge of Constitutional Reform in Australia

Section 128 of the Constitution sets out special manner and form requirements for any constitutional amendment. It requires, first, that any legislation proposing a change to the *Constitution* must pass by 'an absolute majority of each House of the Parliament'. An 'absolute majority' means a majority of the total number of members of each House must approve the Bill.[180] Secondly, section 128 requires a 'double majority' popular referendum to approve any constitutional change. That is, the proposed alteration may only be presented to the Governor-General for the Queen's Assent if: 'in a majority of the States a majority of the electors voting approve the proposed law, and if a majority of all the

[179] For a history and discussion of Australian bill of rights campaigns and failures see George Williams, 'The Future of the Australian Bill of Rights Debate', *Alice Tay Lecture on Law and Human Rights*, Freilich Foundation, ANU, 16 September 2010; Kildea (n 73 above); George Williams, 'The Federal Parliament and the Protection of Human Rights', Parliamentary Library, Research Paper No 20, 1998–99.

[180] Section 128 provides: '[t]his Constitution shall not be altered except in the following manner: The proposed law for the alteration thereof must be passed by an absolute majority of each House of the Parliament, and not less than two nor more than six months after its passage through both Houses the proposed law shall be submitted in each State and Territory to the electors qualified to vote for the election of members of the House of Representatives'. As the Australian Electoral Commission explains: '[i]f passed by one House but rejected, or altered in the other (and the alterations are unacceptable to the first House) and this is repeated in the next session of the Parliament, the Governor-General may put the proposal to the electors as last proposed by the first House with or without any amendments agreed by both Houses.': Australian Electoral Commission, *Referendums Overview*, <http://www.aec.gov.au/elections/referendums/Referendums_Overview.htm> accessed 18 October 2019. See also Williams and Hume (n 75 above) 36.

electors voting also approve the proposed law'. A successful referendum therefore must satisfy two requirements: first that a majority of electors nationally support the amendment, and secondly, that a majority of electors in a majority of States support it. Since the 'Referendum – Territories' referendum was carried in 1977, voters in the Territories also have their votes counted towards the national tally, but not towards any State total.[181]

Now that Indigenous consensus has been achieved through the Uluru Statement, a successful Indigenous recognition referendum must overcome three further political hurdles. The first is getting the Commonwealth government of the day to initiate the constitutional amendment Bill.[182] The second is achieving an absolute majority approval in both Houses of Parliament.[183] The third is winning the approval of the Australian people via a double majority referendum.[184] These requirements, combined with a political culture resistant to structural change, make constitutional reform in Australia difficult. As noted, only 8 out of 44 attempted referenda have succeeded.[185]

Given the difficulty of constitutional reform, bipartisan support is usually considered a pre-condition for success. Professor Cheryl Saunders in 1994 explained that the '[b]elief in political bipartisanship as a mechanism for securing constitutional change stems from the observation that referendums have failed in the past when they are opposed by one side of politics.' Saunders observed that

> As the Australian Labor Party can be relied upon to support most proposals for constitutional change which achieve passage through the Commonwealth Parliament, an ironic consequence is that most textual amendment has taken place when non-Labor parties are in government.[186]

Because the conservative right of Australian politics is traditionally more cautious about constitutional change, constitutional reform may be more likely to succeed under a Liberal-National government: conservative political

[181] See Campbell (n 168 above) 1; Williams and Hume (n 75 above) 52.

[182] Noel Pearson separates this first hurdle into two: '[t]here are four hurdles that need to be crossed. First, the Prime Minister. Second, his partyroom. Third, the parliament. And fourth, the Australian people.' Pearson, 'Indigenous People Need a Lot More than Just Symbolism' (n 92 above).

[183] Williams and Hume explain: '[p]roposals to change Australia's Constitution are often made, but very few are ever put to the people at a referendum. One bottleneck has been the difficulty of first securing the support of the federal Parliament … only one in 17 of the Bills introduced to Parliament have ended up changing the Constitution.': Williams and Hume (n 75 above) 89.

[184] Williams and Hume (n 75 above) 37.

[185] For the track record, see Australian Electoral Commission, Referendum Dates and Results, <http://www.aec.gov.au/Elections/referendums/Referendum_Dates_and_Results.htm> accessed 18 October 2019.

[186] Cheryl Saunders, 'The Australian Experience with Constitutional Review' (1994) 66(3) *Australian Quarterly* 49, 53. See also, John Macmillan, 'Constitutional Reform in Australia', Papers on Parliament No 13, November 1991: <https://www.aph.gov.au/~/~/link.aspx?_id=042958A33D7D4CD985246D0974B643AA&_z=z> accessed 18 October 2019. The 'Labor urge to reform' and the Liberal tendency to protect the *Constitution* is also discussed in Bennett (n 167 above).

leadership may be required to persuade Australians across the political spectrum to vote 'yes' to constitutional change.

Such political realities led Pearson to calculate that, for Indigenous constitutional recognition, 'Nixon must go to China'.[187] This is because constitutional change, with its requirement of a 'double majority' referendum, poses a very particular political challenge. Whereas simple legislative reform is a 51 per cent battle, constitutional reform is more like a 90 per cent battle, ideally requiring conservative political endorsement to help muster the support of Australians across the political spectrum. As Pearson explains:

> The *Native Title Act 1993* was a classic example of the 51% battle. Others – such as constitutional amendment requiring 'a majority of voters in a majority of the states' – are 90% battles. These require bipartisanship … on some issues Nixon has to go to China.
>
> Aboriginal reconciliation (to use the omnibus if ambiguous term) was a progressive, leftist issue, by definition anathema to the right, which would need a leader of the right to go to China, so to speak.[188]

But while bipartisan support is evidently important for referendum success, Campbell, upon assessing the history, observes that bipartisanship is nonetheless not a 'guarantee of success at the polls'. Five proposals have failed at referendum in spite of bipartisan support. Bipartisanship might therefore be understood as a necessary, but not a sufficient condition of success.[189] Given initial reluctance from the Liberal-National government in relation to the Uluru Statement, however, some argue the strategic orthodoxy in relation to bipartisanship needs re-thinking.[190] Whether a referendum on a First Nations voice can succeed without bipartisan support is a strategic question that Indigenous advocates may need to consider. It is to be hoped, however, that leaders on the political right as well as on the left will take the time to carefully consider the arguments. As will be shown, the call for a First Nations constitutional voice is inherently constitutionally conservative, as well as constitutionally innovative and practically empowering. Properly understood, it is a reform which conservatives and progressives alike should champion. This is what could be termed a 'radical centre' reform.[191]

[187] Pearson, 'Indigenous People Need a Lot More than Just Symbolism' (n 92 above).

[188] Noel Pearson, 'Betrayal', *The Monthly* (December 2017) <https://www.themonthly.com.au/issue/2017/december/1512046800/noel-pearson/betrayal> accessed 18 October 2019.

[189] Campbell (n 168 above) 5.

[190] See Paul Kildea's comments in Stephen Fitzpatrick, 'A Fresh Canvas for Indigenous Politics', *The Monthly* (May 2019) <https://www.themonthly.com.au/issue/2019/may/1556632800/stephen-fitzpatrick/fresh-canvas-indigenous-politics> accessed 18 October 2019.

[191] Shireen Morris, 'The Radical Centre: Constitutional Conservatism and Indigenous Recognition', *ABC Regligion and Ethics* (17 April 2018) <https://www.abc.net.au/religion/the-radical-centre-constitutional-conservatism-and-indigenous-re/10094802>.

B. Parliament Tends to Preserve its Own Supremacy

A First Nations voice fits with the history and culture of Australian constitutional reform because it upholds parliamentary supremacy. The procedural requirement of parliamentary supremacy in all Australian constitutional reform under section 128 creates an important political parameter that cannot be overlooked. The *Constitution* establishes the Commonwealth Parliament as the initiator of any proposed law for constitutional change. As a result, the constitutional reform proposals put forward are usually proposals to *increase* Commonwealth power rather than to provide restraints or checks on power.[192] As former Chief Justice of the High Court, Murray Gleeson explains:

> Only the Federal Parliament can initiate a referendum. The Federal Parliament has shown little appetite for proposals to limit its own power; and rightly so. Parliamentary supremacy … is one of the essential safeguards of our liberal democracy. It is unlikely that Parliament will propose a change to the Constitution in aid of Indigenous recognition if the effect of the change will be to curtail its own legislative power.[193]

This assessment accords with the history of constitutional change. While most of the proposals to increase Commonwealth power have been unsuccessful when put to the people,[194] of the eight successful referenda in Australia's history, two increased the legislative power of the Commonwealth. No successful referendum has restrained Parliament's power. The 1946 'social services' referendum conferred upon the Commonwealth a broad power to legislate for welfare and social matters.[195] The 1967 'Aboriginals' referendum conferred upon the Commonwealth the power to legislate for Indigenous affairs, a governance area previously left to the States, and removed section 127.[196]

The remaining six successful referenda varied in nature but all of them proposed reforms to resolve practical issues of government: the timing of Senate elections in 1906,[197] State debts in 1909[198] and the further management of State debts in 1928,[199] and the management of Senate vacancies,[200] the allowance of

[192] 'Of the 44 referendum proposals put to the Australian people, 24 have sought to increase federal power, while only 4 have reduced or checked that power.': Williams and Hume (n 75 above) 38. See also Cheryl Saunders, *It's Your Constitution* (2nd edn, Federation Press 2003) 89.

[193] Murray Gleeson, 'Recognition in Keeping with the Constitution: A Worthwhile Project', speech at Gilbert + Tobin, Sydney, 18 July 2019, 12.

[194] Bennett (n 167 above).

[195] *Constitution Alteration (Social Services) 1946* (Cth). Note, however, the civil conscription qualification in s 51(xxiiiA).

[196] *Constitution Alteration (Aboriginals) 1967* (Cth).

[197] *Constitution Alteration (Senate Elections) 1906* (Cth).

[198] *Constitution Alteration (State Debts) 1909* (Cth).

[199] *Constitution Alteration (State Debts) 1928* (Cth).

[200] *Constitution Alteration (Senate Casual Vacancies) 1977* (Cth).

Territory voting in referenda[201] and the retirement age of judges in 1977.[202] These constitutional amendments are sometimes called 'machinery' amendments.[203] They are practical and technical in nature – reforms to resolve practical problems of government.

Bennett notes that the two successful referenda which specifically increased the Commonwealth's legislative authority[204] can be characterised as dealing with 'social' issues:

> The only amendments seeking to increase Commonwealth power that have been passed were not typical of such questions. If we classify the *Social Services* (1946) and *Aboriginals* (1967) referenda as 'social', then we note that, together with the *Judges* (1977) example that dealt with retirement ages, three of five such 'social' referenda have been carried. The two that missed out were *Communism* (1951) and *Rights and Freedoms* (1988).[205]

This is an interesting observation. The 'social' nature of the 1946 and the 1967 referenda means they could be understood as being driven by ideals of government social responsibility and benevolence – they were referenda authorising governments to take legislative action to protect the vulnerable in society and ensure their wellbeing. From a human rights perspective, they might be understood as reforms conferring upon the Commonwealth the power to take legislative action to protect citizens' rights: citizens' social, economic but also specific Indigenous rights. The 1946 'social services' referendum enabled the Commonwealth to legislate for a variety of public benefits and welfare entitlements; the 'yes' case focused on the need to pursue social progress and the government's desire to provide free medical care.[206] Similarly, the 1967 referendum was promoted as conferring upon the Commonwealth the power to remedy Indigenous disadvantage and protect Indigenous interests.[207] The media promoted a 'yes' vote as a positive matter of Indigenous humanity;[208] thus the reform was sold like an argument about human rights. Bennett's analysis of the successful referenda leads him to observe that

> amendments perceived to weaken the federal system such as perceived attacks on the Senate are likely to receive short shrift, whereas attempts to repair the

[201] *Constitution Alteration (Referendums) 1977* (Cth).

[202] *Constitution Alteration (Retirement of Judges) 1977* (Cth).

[203] Enid Campbell defines 'government machinery' referendum questions as 'questions to do with the structure and composition of, and interrelationships between institutions of government, both state and federal, and also questions concerning electors' rights.': Campbell (n 168 above) 4. See also Bennett (n 167 above).

[204] See also Campbell (n 168 above) 3.

[205] Bennett (n 167 above).

[206] Williams and Hume (n 75 above) 119–23.

[207] ibid 141–42.

[208] ibid. On the positive symbolism of the 1967 referendum see Brennan and Davis, 'First Peoples' (n 9 above) 48–50.

> perennially-flawed finance chapter have been received sympathetically. Questions dealing with societal relations are considered closely.[209]

An Indigenous recognition referendum would in a broad sense deal with 'societal relations' – it seeks to reform the relationship between Indigenous peoples and the state. It is an attempt to repair a 'perennially flawed' constitutional relationship. Thus, on Bennett's logic, it may be hoped that an Indigenous recognition referendum will be considered closely and received with sympathy by the Australian public.[210] But *how* the proposal reforms the relationship – the specific model of Indigenous recognition and perhaps rights protection – will impact whether the proposal is widely politically acceptable.

The constitutional referenda successfully conferring on Parliament legislative powers that may be used to protect rights have not included any constitutional compulsion that the Commonwealth exercise its powers in a way that actually protects rights, nor constitutional restraints to prevent the Commonwealth from using its new powers (or other existing powers) to undermine those rights ostensibly intended to be protected.[211] This observation is relevant to the ideas for Indigenous constitutional recognition developed in this book. For example, the 1946 referendum implemented a new section 51(xxiiiA) which empowers the Commonwealth to legislate with respect to the provision of medical services, if it chooses to do so, but it does not create any right to which citizens can appeal if those services are not provided.[212] Similarly, as the High Court acknowledged in *Kartinyeri*, post-1967, section 51(xxvi) can be used to create positive laws protecting and enhancing Indigenous rights, but it can also probably be used to enact adversely discriminatory laws, curtailing Indigenous rights.[213] The history of constitutional reform in Australia indicates a preference for constitutionally

[209] Bennett (n 167 above).

[210] Australians demonstrate high levels of goodwill with respect to Indigenous constitutional recognition, with 70% supporting the cause. See Katherine Murphy, 'Essential Poll: Majority of Australians Want Indigenous Recognition and Voice to Parliament', *The Guardian* (12 July 2019) <https://www.theguardian.com/australia-news/2019/jul/12/essential-poll-majority-of-australians-want-indigenous-recognition-and-voice-to-parliament> accessed 18 October 2019.

[211] This was also true of the failed 1942 proposal, which did not make it to a referendum. It sought to give the Commonwealth the power to make laws with respect to guaranteeing freedom of speech and expression, religious freedom, 'freedom from want', and 'freedom from fear', but did not impose any constitutional restraints to protect those rights: George Williams, 'The Federal Parliament and the Protection of Human Rights' (n 179 above).

[212] Note, however, the civil conscription restraint in s 51(xxiiiA). See Chief Justice Robert French, 'The Constitution and the Protection of Human Rights', *Edith Cowan University Vice Chancellor's Oration*, Perth, 20 November 2009, 10–11. The unsuccessful 'Essential Services' referendum of 1926 was another attempted power-expanding 'social' referendum. It sought to allow the Commonwealth to take measures to protect the public against interruption of essential services but did not seek to declare a right to essential services in the Constitution. See Scott Bennett, 'Constitutional Referenda in Australia', Parliamentary Library, Research Paper 2, 1999–2000, <https://www.aph.gov.au/About_Parliament/Parliamentary_Departments/Parliamentary_Library/pubs/rp/rp9900/2000RP02> accessed 18 October 2019.

[213] *Kartinyeri* (n 82 above).

conferring upon Parliament the power and discretion to protect citizens' rights, rather than imposing judicially adjudicated constitutional restraints on parliamentary power in order to protect citizens' rights. This history confirms the embedded respect for parliamentary supremacy in Australian constitutional culture.

C. Failed Attempts at Implementing Constitutional Rights Guarantees

The Australian resistance to new constitutional rights guarantees is notable.[214] The 'post-war reconstruction and democratic rights' referendum in 1944 sought to create a constitutional protection of freedom of speech and expression and to extend the freedom of religion restraint imposed by section 116 so that it also applied to also the States, but only as temporary provisions.[215] That referendum failed. The 1988 'rights and freedoms' referendum sought to extend the right to trial by jury, extend freedom of religion, and ensure just terms for persons whose property is acquired by any government, rather than just the Commonwealth.[216] The reforms were proposed by Labor but were robustly attacked by the Opposition. All failed.[217] The proposals were defeated nationally and in each State.[218]

Thus far in Australia's history there have been no successful referenda to implement new constitutional rights protections or restraints to protect citizens from the abusive use of parliamentary power. The two 'social' referenda, which can be interpreted as being driven by the desire to enhance citizens' rights, sought to do so through *increasing* Commonwealth power and discretion rather than restraining such power and discretion. This choice of method for rights protection may reflect the fact that the Parliament is the initiator[219] and thus the gatekeeper of constitutional reform proposals, but it may also reflect what might be described as the trusting attitude of the majority of Australians towards government, which is related to an ongoing political preference for parliamentary supremacy in the protection of rights.

[214] Williams, 'The Federal Parliament and the Protection of Human Rights' (n 179 above).

[215] *Constitution Alteration (Post-war Reconstruction and Democratic Rights) 1944*. See ibid. See also WJ Waters, 'The Opposition and the "Powers" Referendum, 1944' (1969) 4(1) *Australian Journal of Political Science* 42; Charlie Fox, 'The Fourteen Powers Referendum of 1944 and the Federalisation of Aboriginal Affairs' (2008) 32 *Aboriginal History* 27.

[216] *Constitution Alteration (Rights and Freedoms) 1988*; George Williams, 'The Federal Parliament and the Protection of Human Rights' (n 180 above).

[217] Campbell (n 168 above) 7–9.

[218] ibid 10.

[219] Parliament has also been described as the 'sponsor' of constitutional reform proposals. See John MacMillan, 'Constitutional Reform or Constitutional Delusion?' (2003) 14(1) *Public Law Review* 5, 5. See also Glenn Patmore, *Choosing the Republic* (UNSW Press 2009) 33.

D. Australian Constitutional Culture: Majoritarian Trust and Indigenous Mistrust

The preceding discussion reveals an Australian preference for constitutionally authorised legislative intervention as the preferred mechanism for rights protection, over explicit constitutional protections from government intervention. Parliament has been trusted to be the protector of rights and the appropriate balancer of conflicting rights, more than the judiciary is trusted to interpret, balance and enforce constitutional rights protections which restrain parliamentary power.[220] As Dawson J observed,

> Those responsible for drafting the Constitution saw constitutional guarantees of freedom as exhibiting a distrust of the democratic process. They preferred to place their trust in Parliament to preserve the nature of our society and regarded as undemocratic guarantees which fettered its powers.[221]

This apparent trust in Parliament is related to what Kildea describes as Australia's 'political culture', which is characterised by utilitarianism and majoritarianism, but also to what Goldsworthy describes as Australia's 'constitutional culture',[222] which is heavily influenced by Australian political culture – since the *Constitution* requires parliamentary action and popular assent for any amendment.

Leading political philosopher and Bill of rights critic, Jeremy Waldron, would defend this constitutional culture as sensibly trusting of elected parliamentarians making contentious decisions about citizens' rights through legislative action and sensibly mistrustful of unelected courts making such decisions through litigation and adjudication.[223] The failure of campaigns for a national Bill of rights in Australia[224] may support the proposition that

[220] The view began with the founding fathers and has continued on today. See also Jeffrey Goldsworthy, 'Constitutional Cultures, Democracy, and Unwritten Principles' [2012] *University of Illinois Law Review* 683; Kildea (n 73 above). Though founding father, Andrew Inglis Clark, advocated for the inclusion of constitutional rights to counter the 'tyranny of the majority': see Andrew Inglis Clark, *Studies in Australian Constitutional Law* (1997 edn, Legal Books [first published 1901]) 386. See also Chief Justice Robert French, 'The Constitution and the Protection of Human Rights', *Edith Cowan University Vice Chancellor's Oration*, Perth, 20 November 2009, 1–2.

[221] *Australian Capital Television Pty Ltd v Commonwealth* (1992) 177 CLR 1, 71 (fn 25) quoted in Matthew Groves, Janina Boughey and Dan Meagher, 'Rights, Rhetoric and Reality: an Overview of Rights Protection in Australia' in Matthew Groves, Janina Boughey and Dan Meagher (eds), *The Legal Protection of Rights in Australia* (Hart Publishing 2019) 4. See also Helen Irving, *To Constitute a Nation: A Cultural History of Australia's Constitution* (Cambridge University Press 1999) 168–69; Chief Justice Robert French, 'The Constitution and the Protection of Human Rights', Edith Cowan University Vice Chancellor's Oration, Perth, 20 November 2009, 8–10.

[222] Kildea (n 73 above) 65–66; Goldsworthy, 'Constitutional Cultures' (n 220 above).

[223] See the arguments put forward in Jeremy Waldron, *Law and Disagreement* (Oxford University Press 1999); Jeremy Waldron, 'A Right-Based Critique of Constitutional Rights' (1993) 13(1) *Oxford Journal of Legal Studies* 18; Jeremy Waldron, 'The Core of the Case Against Judicial Review' (2006) 115(6) *Yale Law Journal* 1346.

[224] There are, however, a variety of legislative protections of rights in Commonwealth and State law and the *Constitution* does provide some limited protection of select rights (see eg *Constitution* ss 116 and 51(xxxi)).

the majority of Australians trust parliaments to use their powers to protect, rather than abuse, citizens' rights and freedoms. This trust may be historically understandable: in comparison to nations like the USA or South Africa, where Bills of rights are in constitutional operation, Australia has been mostly free of civil war or revolution (not including the frontier wars). Most Australians may thus have a historical basis for their trust in governments generally respecting their rights. If governments do not, then Australians can vote them out at the next election. Alternatively, given that citizens cannot independently initiate a constitutional reform referendum, this may reflect the tendency of Parliament, as the gatekeeper of constitutional reform, to tightly guard its own power.

Whatever the main driver, the preference for politically-driven rights protection has persisted over time. As noted, previous attempts at inserting judicially adjudicated rights guarantees into the *Constitution* have failed,[225] but even recommendations for a non-binding, legislated federal Bill of rights were rejected.[226] Instead, a federal human rights scrutiny process, omitting any role for the judiciary, was implemented in 2011.[227] State and Territory jurisdictions that have legislated charters of rights[228] have similarly declined to give the judiciary a decisive enforcement role, opting instead for softer 'dialogue'-style mechanisms.[229] These models allow Parliament to override specific enumerated rights when enacting laws[230] and are designed to preserve parliamentary supremacy.[231]

[225] For a history and discussion of Australian Bill of rights campaigns and failures, see George Williams, 'The Future of the Australian Bill of Rights Debate' (n 179 above); Kildea (n 73 above); George Williams, 'The Federal Parliament and the Protection of Human Rights' (n 179 above).

[226] For reasons why, see Bruce Stone, 'Why Australia Has No Bill of Rights' (Conference Paper, Australasian Political Studies Association Conference, 30 September–2 October 2013). See also Groves, Boughey and Meagher (n 221 above) 7–10.

[227] *Human Rights (Parliamentary Scrutiny) Act 2011* (Cth). See also Morris, 'Parliamentary Scrutiny and Insights for a First Nations Voice to Parliament' (n 144 above).

[228] *Human Rights Act 2004* (ACT) (ACT HRA); *Charter of Human Rights and Responsibilities Act 2006* (Vic) (Victorian Charter). See also *Human Rights Bill 2018* (Qld) (Qld HRA).

[229] For an explanation of 'dialogue' models for rights protection, see Tom Campbell and Stephen Morris, 'Human Rights for Democracies: A Provisional Assessment of the Australian *Human Rights (Parliamentary Scrutiny) Act 2011*' (2015) 34(1) *University of Queensland Law Journal* 7. These instruments require parliamentarians to produce Statements of Compatibility (SOCs) when introducing proposed legislation into Parliament and establish human rights scrutiny committees within Parliament to review proposed and existing legislation for rights compatibility. Under such approaches, the courts are empowered only to interpret legislation to be rights-compatible where possible, and to issue non-binding Declarations of Incompatibility where not possible.

[230] The relevant provisions under the Victorian Charter are ss 28, 30, 31, 32 and 36.

[231] Campbell and Morris describe these as 'democratic models' of human rights protection: Campbell and Morris, 'Human Rights for Democracies' (n 229 above). See also Julie Debeljak, 'Rights Protection Without Judicial Supremacy: A Review of the Canadian and British Models of Bills of Rights' (2002) 26(2) *Melbourne University Law Review* 285; Julie Debeljak, 'Parliamentary Sovereignty and Dialogue under the Victorian *Charter on Human Rights and Responsibilities*: Drawing the Line Between Judicial Interpretation and Judicial Law-Making' (2007) 33(1) *Monash Law Review* 9.

This predominantly political system of rights protection – based on what some describe as a mix of political and legal constitutionalism[232] – has worked relatively well: most Australians enjoy political stability, economic prosperity and respect for their rights.[233] It is therefore perhaps understandable that reformist calls for new, court-enforced restraints on majoritarian power have generally been rejected by that same majority.[234] The constitutional status quo has evidently worked well for the majority of Australians and so the political representatives of the majority are not eager to reform it. Yet while the status quo has benefitted the many who are accustomed to having their rights respected, minorities historically subject to denial of rights by the elected majority may feel differently.[235] Indigenous people, as an extreme minority – the only dispossessed minority and the most disadvantaged minority in Australia – have had a different historical experience to the non-Indigenous majority. That is why many Indigenous Australians have for so many decades consistently sought constitutional protections of their rights: they have sought a guarantee that their rights will be better protected against potential tyrannies of the majority. A lack of trust in parliaments is apparent in Indigenous advocacy for constitutional recognition and reform, and for good reason. Majoritarian parliaments have historically not proved trustworthy in upholding Indigenous minority rights.[236]

Waldron, making the case against entrenched, judicially adjudicated rights guarantees, agrees that the rights reformer's attitude may be characterised as mistrustful. He does not, however, agree that such mistrust is justified:

> To embody a right in an entrenched constitutional document is to adopt a certain attitude towards one's fellow citizens. That attitude is best summed up as a combination

[232] Janina Boughey and others, *Public Law and Statutory Interpretation: Principle and Practice* (Federation Press 2017) 16.

[233] Professor Cheryl Saunders has explained that 'Australia is fortunate in the stability and efficiency of its democracy and the commitment of its institutions to the rule of law. The Australian legal and political system also stems from a tradition that accepts that the rights of individuals should be respected by the state. As a result, so far, the Australian approach to rights protection has worked reasonably well. By international standards, Australia has a good human rights record'.: Cheryl Saunders, 'The Australian Constitution and Our Rights' in Helen Sykes (ed), *Future Justice* (Future Leaders 2010) 118. See further Goldsworthy, 'Constitutional Cultures' (n 220 above) 687; Suri Ratnapala, 'Bills of Rights in Functioning Parliamentary Democracies: Kantian, Consequentialist and Institutionalist Scepticisms' (2010) 34(2) *Melbourne University Law Review* 592, 609.

[234] Kildea (n 73 above) 84.

[235] As former Chief Justice Murray Gleeson argues: '[a] democratic government seeks to represent the will of the majority … but majorities cannot always be relied upon to be sensitive to the interests and the legitimate concerns of minorities … How then does a democracy, which functions on the basis of majority rule, institutionalise protection of legitimate minority interests? This is the essential problem underlying debate about human rights'.: Murray Gleeson, *The Rule of Law and the Constitution* (ABC Books 2000) 68–69. See also Sir Anthony Mason, 'A Bill of Rights for Australia?' (1989) 5(1) *Australian Bar Review* 79, 83; Bernice Carrick, 'Freedom on the Wallaby: A Comparison of Arguments in the Australian Bill of Rights Debate' (2010) 1 *The Western Australian Jurist* 68, 98.

[236] See Sean Brennan, 'Constitutional Amendment and the Issue of Trust' in Simon Young, Jennifer Nielsen and Jeremy Patrick (eds), *Constitutional Recognition of First Peoples in Australia* (Federation Press 2016).

> of self-assurance and mistrust: self-assurance in the proponent's conviction that what she is putting forward really *is* a matter of fundamental right and that she has captured it adequately in the particular formulation she is propounding; and mistrust, implicit in her view that any alternative conception that might be concocted by elected legislators next year or the year after is so likely to be wrong-headed or ill-motivated that *her own* formulation is to be elevated immediately beyond the reach of ordinary legislative revision ...
>
> This attitude of mistrust of one's fellow citizens does not sit particularly well with the aura of respect for their autonomy and responsibility that is conveyed by the substance of the rights which are being entrenched in this way.[237]

Though the *Australian Constitution* contains few rights guarantees, the attitude of 'mistrustful self-assurance' could presumably be equally attributed to its founders, who opted to entrench their compact under section 128 to ensure that future generations could not easily change the system they had created: they were evidently mistrustful of future parliaments and assured that their own structural formulation should be changed only with extremely high levels of consensus.[238] Yet Waldron's view here does not adequately address why dispossessed and discriminated against peoples – especially those left out of initial constitutional negotiations – might sensibly seek constitutionally entrenched protection of their rights. If history has shown that the majority does not generally uphold and protect Indigenous minority rights and interests, then Indigenous mistrust of majoritarian decisions cannot be described as misplaced self-assurance but rather a justified attempt at self-preservation and survival in a situation of ongoing political and legal insecurity. Waldron counters that

> [i]f our only image of man is that of a self-seeking animal who is not to be trusted with a concern for the interests of others, we lack the conception of dignified moral autonomy on which such discriminations of interest might be based.[239]

Yet mistrust persists, Indigenous advocacy for constitutional change continues and reconciliation in Australia remains elusive. How, then, should a moral nation respond?

[237] Waldron, 'A Right-Based Critique of Constitutional Rights' (n 223 above) 27. Note that Waldron qualifies: '[t]hese are not intended as knock-down arguments against constitutionalization. All I have tried to show so far is that there is nothing obvious about combining a respect for rights with a profound mistrust of people in their democratic and representative capacities.': at 28.

[238] Note, however, Aroney's contention that Waldron's argument against judicial review should not apply to structural elements of Australia's Federation, because 'Waldron's core argument rests upon an account of the relationship between individual rights within a unitary democracy, a relationship which simply does not exist in the same way within a federal system.': Nicholas Aroney, 'Reasonable Disagreement, Democracy and the Judicial Safeguards of Federalism' (2008) 27(1) *University of Queensland Law Journal* 129, 132. As will be seen, however, Waldron's arguments in favour of political processes as the best means for resolving rights disputes do take positive account of structural features like bicameralism and federalism as mechanisms which allow a multiplicity of voices to be heard in deliberations.

[239] Waldron, 'A Right-Based Critique of Constitutional Rights' (n 223 above) 28; for Waldron's thinking on the case for redress of historic injustice with respect to Indigenous peoples, see Jeremy Waldron, 'Redressing Historic Injustice' (2002) 52(1) *University of Toronto Law Journal* 135.

As human beings, we have rights and we are moral agents, capable of making moral decisions, as Waldron observes. This is why democracy is important: because we should each get a say in the laws that govern us. But history also shows that we can be self-seeking. We are capable of behaving immorally and violating each other's rights – sometimes intergenerationally and for decades on end. The historical facts of colonisation demonstrate that human nature carries with it the propensity for deep, unethical injustice against our fellow human beings. This gives rise to understandable feelings of insecurity, anxiety and exclusion among historically oppressed and excluded Indigenous peoples who have suffered injustice. Arguably, the purpose of the law is to guard against and restrain the human propensity for immoral behaviour. Further, it is arguably the purpose of a constitutional law to guard against unethical behaviour in a long-term, intergenerational sense; or at least, a Constitution should ensure that political debates about what is ethical or not should occur in as ethical a way as possible. So how should Australian constitutional law respond to ongoing Indigenous calls for an entrenched guarantee of fairer treatment, when it has been shown that the current system does not work well to protect Indigenous minority rights or produce good outcomes in Indigenous affairs? If a judicially adjudicated rights guarantee is not a politically viable answer, then what is a more workable alternative?

Australian constitutional culture tends to adopt a Waldronian respect for political decision-making as the best mechanism for respecting rights, but it is important to note that in doing so, the Constitution does not give every individual a strictly equal share of decision-making power. As noted, Australian federalism means that citizens living in a less populated State like Tasmania have a greater share of political power, proportionately speaking, than individuals living in a more densely populated State like Victoria. This is because Australia's federal compact recognises the variously populated constitutional constituencies – the former colonies – and makes provision for them to be fairly heard in their affairs. In Australia's *Constitution*, the principle of individual equality is tempered to recognise the importance, and ensure the dynamic survival, of these historic political communities.[240]

The Uluru Statement asks for a constitutionally guaranteed voice for the First Nations because, given the history of exclusion and discrimination,

[240] Aroney notes that federations are therefore not strictly majoritarian: 'while they may incorporate democratic processes and majority rule in certain important respects', federations 'are obviously not unitary, and nor are they majoritarian in any simple sense of the word'. Thus, 'because of this qualification of majority-rule within federations, the equality of rights enjoyed by individual citizens is likewise qualified …'. Specifically, 'the special, and often equal, representation of [the people of] each state in at least one of the houses of the federal legislature means that individuals in different states do not, in that respect, have equality of voting power.' Nicholas Aroney, 'Reasonable Disagreement, Democracy and the Judicial Safeguards of Federalism' (2008) 27(1) *University of Queensland Law Journal* 129, 139–40.

Indigenous people want to be heard in their affairs too. They too are a historic political community and they too want to survive, be recognised and (belatedly) included in political debates about their rights. After all, individuals making rights-balancing decisions through their democratic vote, as well as the political decision-makers they elect, can only have proper 'concern for the interests of others', if they know who the relevant 'others' are and what their particular concerns are – decision-makers at least need to have heard those concerns. They might hear such concerns through the media, public debate and ordinary politics, but these mechanisms alone may be ineffective, given that the group whose rights are prone to being trampled is the three per cent historically dispossessed and disempowered minority that was wrongfully excluded from the original constitutional compact. In Australia, history has shown that ordinary democratic processes alone are not sufficient to protect Indigenous rights. This warrants a tailored solution that is respectful to all interests.

Any proposed solution will need to balance the concerns of the Indigenous minority with the concerns of the non-Indigenous majority. It must fairly balance all competing interests in society. This is stating the obvious: a referendum cannot succeed if it does not properly balance the rights of everyone; people would not vote for the reform. But it is also morally important. We are all living on this continent together and the constitutional system needs to be fair to all Australians. Waldron seems to suggest that the correct response to historical injustice is a practical focus on fair and balanced distribution of resources in the current day.[241] But a nation should also ensure that the decision-making processes that govern the distribution and re-distribution of material resources in society are fair and balanced. Those procedures should be trustworthy and trust-building. In a general sense, Australian constitutional culture may be characterised by majoritarian trust in the decision-making of elected governments, and Indigenous mistrust in such decision-making. Viewed in light of historical experiences, both attitudes are understandable. Here I contend that constitutionally mandated dialogue, consultation and conversation would be a constructive way to build ongoing understanding and trust across historical, political and cultural divides.[242]

E. Participatory and Power-Balancing Machinery Reforms

This kind of approach to constitutional recognition fits with Australian approaches to constitutional reform. While no successful referendum has

[241] Agreeing that present injustice and need must be addressed, Waldron critiques simplistic '[f]irst come, first served' or '[w]e were here first'-style arguments for redress of historical Indigenous dispossession and discrimination as ultimately unbalanced and therefore unpersuasive: Waldron, 'Redressing Historic Injustice' (n 239 above) 160; Waldron, 'Superseding Historic Injustice' (1992) 103(1) *Ethics* 4, 8.

[242] See Ivison, *Postcolonial Liberalism* (n 6 above) 72, 92–93.

implemented any new judicially adjudicated constitutional protection of citizens' rights, some of the proposed 'machinery' reforms have implemented, or attempted to implement, mechanisms for the better management of important national power relationships, particularly those between the Commonwealth and the States. Such machinery reforms, without constitutionalising explicit legal protections of State rights, can nonetheless be characterised as reforms that have a bearing on the effective protection of States' rights: they are reforms that sought to promote fairer federal power relationships. There are lessons here for Indigenous constitutional recognition.

'Machinery' amendment proposals can be understood as encouraging fairer political engagement between constitutional constituencies. For example, the 1928 'State debts' referendum, which inserted a new section 105A into the *Constitution*, sought to better manage the strained financial relationship between the Commonwealth and the States by enabling the Commonwealth to make agreements with the States regarding the takeover of State debts. An intergovernmental agreement, ratified by legislation, established the Australian Loan Council to control government borrowing and oversee financial conflicts.[243] Together, these reforms implemented a constitutionally authorised agreement-making mechanism to better manage Commonwealth-State financial relations. Reforms that seek to refine constitutional relationships through institutional and procedural means are particularly in keeping with Australia's constitutional culture and reform history.

Some of the failed attempts at constitutional reform to improve the protection and enjoyment of citizen's rights and wellbeing also adopted institutional, democratic and power-sharing mechanisms. The 1926 'industry and commerce' referendum unsuccessfully sought to authorise the creation of authorities to control the terms and conditions of industrial employment – it sought to give the Commonwealth the power to create such an authority, to help regulate industrial employment conditions; a similar approach to the Inter-State Commission or the Loan Council. The failed 1974 'democratic elections' referendum sought to make population, rather than the number of 'electors', the basis for determining the size of State electorates, to enhance voting fairness in the House of Representatives and protect democratic rights.[244] Likewise, the 1988 'fair elections' referendum tried to constitutionally enshrine the 'one vote one value' principle.[245] As Campbell describes, these proposals tried to impose 'limitations on governmental powers … in the name of protection of important individual interests against governments',[246] but they sought to do so through enhanced

[243] *Financial Agreement Act 1928* (Cth). See Parliament of the Commonwealth of Australia, *The Australian Loan Council* (2nd edn, Department of the Parliamentary Library 1993).
[244] *Constitution Alteration (Democratic Elections) 1974*.
[245] *Constitution Alteration (Fair Elections) 1988*.
[246] Campbell (n 168 above) 7.

political participation, rather than mandating or restraining the *outcome* of that participation through a rights guarantee. This is in keeping with Australia's embedded respect for the political process as the best mechanism for the defence and adjudication of rights.[247] The focus is on making sure machinery and systems work properly – procedural and political fairness.

The insight here is salient for Indigenous constitutional recognition. The difficulty of constitutional reform in Australia imposes onerous constraints on the types of reforms that are politically achievable. As a first step, the need for bipartisan political support is usually considered an important factor for referendum success.[248] But, as noted, some proposals fail even with bipartisan support. Bipartisanship aside, the resistance to judicially adjudicated constitutional restraints on parliamentary power is apparent upon analysis of Australia's constitutional reform history. Similarly, analysis of the referenda that have been carried demonstrates that social or 'human rights' issues have been successfully dealt with through the transfer of power to Parliament rather than through restraint on parliamentary power. Other reforms were machinery amendments which refined the institutional and procedural machinery of our federal democracy, or reforms which solved very practical problems.

Here I argue that Indigenous peoples and rights can be recognised and protected through modifying the practical machinery that governs Indigenous affairs under the *Constitution*, through institutional, procedural and political mechanisms – rather than through a judicially adjudicated constitutional restraint on parliamentary power. Indigenous rights could be recognised and protected through mechanisms for increased Indigenous political participation and representation in decision-making about Indigenous affairs.

F. Recognition Through Representation: A Way Through the Window of Constitutional Opportunity?

Reform advocates were reminded of the political difficulty of entrenching new constitutional rights guarantees in 2012. Given the history of constitutional reform discussed above, it is unsurprising the Expert Panel's proposed racial non-discrimination guarantee[249] proved controversial. The recommendation was criticised as a 'one-clause Bill of rights' that would improperly empower unelected judges to overturn the decisions of elected representatives.[250] Downplaying these criticisms, a Joint Select Committee in 2015 recommended

[247] Waldron makes the argument that political participation is the right of all rights. See Jeremy Waldron, 'Participation: The Right of Rights' (1998) 98 *Proceedings of the Aristotelian Society* 307.

[248] Williams and Hume (n 75 above) 244–46.

[249] Expert Panel Report (n 41 above) xviii.

[250] For a full analysis of these objections, see Chapter 3 of this volume. See also Morris, 'Undemocratic, Uncertain and Politically Unviable?' (n 91 above).

three versions of a racial non-discrimination clause in its final report, including two versions that would protect Indigenous people only.[251] But soon after the report's publication, Committee Chairman, Liberal MP Ken Wyatt, indicated that a racial non-discrimination clause would be unlikely to gain the necessary political support for a successful referendum, because it was already being opposed in his own party.[252] It became apparent that a racial non-discrimination clause, or a variation thereof, was politically unachievable – just as in 1967.

In 2013, Noel Pearson's challenge to opponents of the Expert Panel's approach was to ask: 'what is a better solution?' What other reform might ensure that '*things are done in a better way*'?[253] A racial non-discrimination clause in the *Constitution* represents one way of addressing the problem of a *Constitution* that has presided over discrimination in relation to Indigenous people. Had Australia's *Constitution* contained such a restraint, past discrimination might have been successfully challenged. The threat of legal action might have fostered a different parliamentary and political culture. As former Expert Panel member, Professor Megan Davis explains, it might have created

> an institutional tension or brake; a requirement to take time and consult; a requirement to go on country and talk to people before doing. That institutional pause is missing from our current political arrangements ... There is no compulsion for parliament to consult or take into account the views of the Aboriginal and Torres Strait Islander communities on any legislation or policy.[254]

Indigenous constitutional recognition is about forging a fairer relationship between Indigenous peoples and the state. This can also be achieved through processes for participation, consultation, dialogue and negotiation with Indigenous peoples. Such mechanisms can help prevent discrimination. As a member of the Expert Panel, Wyatt emphasised 'the need for public servants and parliamentarians to change their practices in dealing with ... communities'. He argued for an approach dealing with communities 'on a consensual basis.'[255] This sentiment is echoed in the history of Indigenous advocacy.

In 2014, Cape York Institute took up this approach and began to argue for a constitutional amendment to guarantee that Indigenous views are heard by Parliament and government in the making of laws and policies with respect to

[251] Joint Select Committee, *Final Report*, 2015, Recommendation 5.

[252] Natasha Robinson, 'Ken Wyatt: Time to Get a Move On with Constitutional Recognition', *The Australian* (10 July 2015) <https://www.theaustralian.com.au/nation/time-to-get-a-move-on-with-recognition-ken-wyatt/news-story/5af9387ecc0c3859374e9f2bd10a4963> accessed 18 October 2019.

[253] Pearson, 'A Rightful Place' (n 15 above) 65. See Chapter 3 of this volume for a full discussion of objections to judicially adjudicated rights clauses.

[254] Megan Davis, 'A Rightful Place: Correspondence. Response to Noel Pearson's *Quarterly Essay* "A Rightful Place: race, recognition and a more complete Commonwealth"' (2014) 56 *Quarterly Essay* 73–81.

[255] Expert Panel Report (n 41 above) 177–185. Wyatt's comment at 184.

Indigenous affairs.[256] In 2017, the Uluru Statement called for a First Nations voice to be enshrined in the *Constitution*, affirming a shift towards an institutional, political and procedural approach to Indigenous recognition and rights protection, fitting with the *Australian Constitution* and Australia's history of constitutional reform. This presents a potential way through the narrow window of constitutional opportunity.

G. Political Commitment to 'Closing the Gap'

The Uluru Statement's commitment to substantive and empowering constitutional reform to improve practical outcomes in Indigenous affairs should be the basis for political agreement with government. Since 2008, Australian governments have been committed to 'closing the gap' on Indigenous disadvantage.[257] Despite significant goodwill and public spending, however, the gap is not on track to close.[258] Australian policy approaches are failing to seriously address Indigenous social and economic disparity.

A key part of the problem is the incorrect assumption that one short-term policy or another can fix deep and ingrained Indigenous disadvantage that carries structural and historical dimensions. There appears to be limited political comprehension of the connection between long-term, structural reform to empower Indigenous peoples to have genuine input in and ownership of policies made about them, and improved policy outcomes.[259] Policy short-term-ism and a failure to see the links between constitutional reform and addressing Indigenous disadvantage were contributing factors in the former Prime Minister Malcolm Turnbull's 2017 rejection of the Uluru Statement's call for a First Nations constitutional voice in their affairs.[260] This lack of understanding of the necessity of

[256] This will be discussed in detail in Chapter 6 of this volume. Pearson, 'A Rightful Place' (n 15 above) 65–67. See also Morris, 'The Argument for a Constitutional Procedure for Parliament to Consult with Indigenous Peoples when Making Laws for Indigenous Affairs' (n 144 above); Shireen Morris, 'The Torment of Our Powerlessness' (n 144 above).

[257] John Gardiner-Garden, 'Closing the Gap' (*Parliament of Australia*, 28 September 2012) <https://www.aph.gov.au/About_Parliament/Parliamentary_Departments/Parliamentary_Library/pubs/BriefingBook44p/ClosingGap> accessed 18 October 2019.

[258] Only 2 out of 7 targets are on track to be met. See 'Closing the Gap' (Report 2019) 10 <https://ctgreport.niaa.gov.au/> accessed 18 October 2019.

[259] Research shows that when Indigenous peoples are empowered to make their own decisions about their communities, outcomes improve. The Harvard Project on Native American Economic Development found that '[w]hen Native nations make their own decisions about what development approaches to take, they consistently out-perform external decision makers on matters as diverse as governmental form, natural resource management, economic development, health care, and social service provision.': <https://hpaied.org/about> accessed 18 October 2019.

[260] Prime Minister, Attorney-General, Minister for Indigenous Affairs, 'Response to Referendum Council's Report on Constitutional Recognition' (Media Release, 26 October 2017) <https://ministers.pmc.gov.au/scullion/2017/response-referendum-councils-report-constitutional-recognition> accessed 18 October 2019.

structural reform for improved policy outcomes seemed to be perpetuated in 2019, when Prime Minister, Scott Morrison, suggested that while a First Nations voice may be important, he was more concerned with practical matters, like addressing Indigenous youth suicide.[261] Neither Prime Minister seemed to properly grasp the connection between the two objectives: the Uluru Statement seeks empowering structural reform through a guaranteed voice in Indigenous affairs *precisely because* Indigenous advocates want to see long-term practical improvement in policy areas like Indigenous suicide, incarceration, poverty and child removal. The intimate interplay between historic injustice, structural disempowerment and ongoing contemporary disadvantage seems little understood.

Though not the sole cause, it is clear that historic exclusion, discrimination and disempowerment can give rise to and exacerbate contemporary exclusion, disadvantage and disempowerment.[262] The intergenerational nature of the impacts of past injustice can be seen clearly in the example of stolen wages. In 2019, the Queensland government settled a class action and agreed to pay Au$190 million, to be shared by over 10,000 farm workers who had had their wages withheld by the Queensland government during the protection era from 1939 to 1972. The lead claimant, Hans Pearson, had £7000 of wages withheld by government, which meant he could not save up to buy a house.[263] The fact that Pearson could not build wealth and accumulate assets in the same way as other Australians also meant that this potential wealth could not be passed on to his descendants. Discrimination of this kind impacts not only the individuals suffering the injustice – it stymies the opportunities, choices and potential prosperity of future generations of Indigenous Australians.

Similarly, constitutional and institutional exclusion – denying a group a fair share of political and decision-making power – also has intergenerational and ongoing impacts. The fact that there were no First Nations representatives in initial power-sharing negotiations that gave rise to the *Australian Constitution*

[261] Lorena Allam, '"Unfinished Business": What the Parties Offer Indigenous Voters in the 2019 Election', *The Guardian* (20 April 2019) <https://www.theguardian.com/australia-news/2019/apr/20/unfinished-business-what-the-parties-offer-indigenous-voters-in-the-2019-election> accessed 18 October 2019. On the Indigenous youth suicide epidemic, see Brooke Fryer, 'Indigenous Youth Suicide at Crisis Point', *NITV News* (15 January 2019) <https://www.sbs.com.au/nitv/article/2019/01/15/indigenous-youth-suicide-crisis-point> accessed 18 October 2019.

[262] The relationship between systemic or structural vulnerability and day-to-day social and economic vulnerability is complex and multifaceted. As the Australian Human Rights Commission explained discussing inequality in health outcomes, 'Indigenous peoples are not merely "disadvantaged citizens". The poverty and inequality that they experience is a contemporary reflection of their historical treatment as peoples. The inequality in health status that they continue to experience can be linked to systemic discrimination.': Darren Dick on behalf of Tom Calma, 'Social Determinants and the Health of Indigenous Peoples in Australia: A Human Rights Based Approach', Workshop Paper, *International Symposium on the Social Determinants of Indigenous Health, Adelaide*, 29–30 April 2007.

[263] Jamie Walker, 'Uncle Hans' Stolen Wages Deal the New Mabo', *The Australian* (10 July 2019) <https://www.theaustralian.com.au/nation/politics/uncle-hans-stolen-wages-deal-the-new-mabo/news-story/b30435a9956cb7cd85ea738183735dc1> accessed 18 October 2019.

has led to ongoing Indigenous disempowerment in their affairs. As Ivison explains, historical injustice gives rise to 'enduring injustices … that continue to shape the conceptual, legal, political and institutional frameworks within which states and their citizens act'. The effect of such injustice 'continues through existing constitutional, legal and political frameworks, as well as in the attitudes, beliefs and practices of citizens that are shaped through these institutional arrangements'.[264] Institutional arrangements perpetuating power imbalances also perpetuate poor policy decisions and thus outcomes. Accordingly, past and perpetuated injustice help to create and exacerbate present disadvantage.[265] Because these historic and structural causes are entwined with more proximate causes of Indigenous disadvantage, short-term policy solutions that do not address fundamental structural problems are unlikely to be sufficient to effect real improvement in outcomes. Until underlying power imbalances are addressed through Indigenous structural empowerment, Indigenous disadvantage is unlikely to be rectified. Failure to reform structural power imbalances has arguably contributed to repeated failures to 'close the gap' on Indigenous disparity.[266]

The appropriate solution to this ongoing challenge not only requires good, targeted policy and fair distribution of material resources in society, as decided through the usual processes of democracy; it requires fairer distribution of *constitutional and decision-making power*, so that the parties can have the conversations and debates more fairly and so the historically wronged group may more effectively speak up and defend their interests in future, thus preventing the repeat of past wrongs and the creation of inadvertent new wrongs through poorly designed and implemented Indigenous policy.[267] In this sense, the struggle for Indigenous constitutional recognition cannot be separated from

[264] Ivison, 'Pluralising Political Legitimacy' (n 53 above) 119.

[265] For a nuanced discussion on the complexities in the relationship between Indigenous disempowerment and Indigenous disadvantage, see Don Weatherburn, 'Disadvantage, Disempowerment and Indigenous Over-Representation in Prison', Children's Court Section 16 Meeting, October 2014, 8–10. As Weatherburn explains, '[t]he problems facing Indigenous Australians were not and are not the result of blocked social opportunity. They are the aftermath of successive assaults (e.g. colonisation and dispossession, the spread of alcohol and drug abuse, the forced removal of Indigenous children, loss of employment in the rural economy) on their traditional way of life.': at 10. While historical discrimination and dispossession may not be proximate causes of Indigenous offending and incarceration, it is acknowledged that these are historical and contextual causes, whereby past discrimination helped lead to present disadvantage.

[266] See 'Closing the Gap' Report (n 258 above) 10.

[267] Note that Tarunabh Khaitan argues that 'under conditions of extreme material inequality, fair political opportunity cannot be satisfied by mere formal equality of votes. Because of the nature of social and economic power, disempowered groups sometimes need to be given a measure of political insurance by constitutions in order to prevent their being locked out of power. Because political lockout of a group is a constitutional rather than a (mere) policy problem, there is a strong case for liberal constitutions to afford a measure of political insurance to the poor.': Tarunabh Khaitan, 'Political Insurance for the (Relative) Poor: How Liberal Constitutionalism Could Resist Plutocracy' (2019) 8(3) *Global Constitutionalism* 536, 540.

the nation's struggles to close the gap on Indigenous disadvantage: productive reform to the constitutional relationship and to decision-making processes under the *Constitution* will help lead to improved policies and thus outcomes. Fairer Indigenous input and ownership of policies will increase the chances of producing fairer, better targeted and more effective Indigenous policies, because Indigenous people themselves are best placed to determine what works and what doesn't for their communities. As Noel Pearson argues:

> The only path to closing socio-economic gaps is for indigenous Australians to become active agents in our own development. Our poverty is a development problem that can only be solved by reversing our disenfranchisement … After all, indigenous people live the problems facing us. No one is better placed to solve the issues that confront us.[268]

The Uluru Statement calls for a First Nations constitutional voice in their affairs based on this conviction that fairer process will lead to fairer outcomes:

> Proportionally, we are the most incarcerated people on the planet. We are not an innately criminal people. Our children are aliened from their families at unprecedented rates. This cannot be because we have no love for them. And our youth languish in detention in obscene numbers. They should be our hope for the future.
>
> These dimensions of our crisis tell plainly the structural nature of our problem. *This is the torment of our powerlessness.*
>
> We seek constitutional reforms to empower our people and take a *rightful place* in our own country. When we have power over our destiny our children will flourish. They will walk in two worlds and their culture will be a gift to their country.
>
> We call for the establishment of a First Nations Voice enshrined in the Constitution.[269]

The call for an empowered voice is logical. It is well established that proper consultation with Indigenous people is key to effective Indigenous policy, and integral to closing the gap. There is widespread acknowledgement that without genuine Indigenous input and empowerment, government measures for Indigenous people will continue to be ineffective and inefficient at best and unjust and discriminatory at worst.[270] The importance of Indigenous consultation and

[268] Pearson, 'A Rightful Place' (n 15 above) 48.

[269] Uluru Statement from the Heart, 2017.

[270] See Bill Shorten, 'Closing the Gap' speech, House of Representatives, Parliament House, Canberra, 15 February 2015. In acknowledgement of the need to have Indigenous input into Indigenous affairs, Tony Abbott established an Indigenous Advisory Council to provide advice on Indigenous affairs and to engage with Indigenous communities <https://www.niaa.gov.au/indigenous-affairs/prime-ministers-indigenous-advisory-council> accessed 18 October 2019. See also *Gerhardy v Brown* (1985) 159 CLR 70, 135; Committee on the Elimination of Racial Discrimination, General Recommendation No 23, 'Indigenous Peoples', 18 August 1997 para 4(d); Australian Human Rights and Equal Opportunities Commission, *Social Justice Report 2007*, Recommendations 7, 14; Shireen Morris, 'Indigenous Constitutional Recognition, Non-Discrimination and Equality Before the Law: Why Reform Is Necessary' (2011) 7(26) *Indigenous Law Bulletin* 7, 10–11.

participation in the laws and policies directed at them was acknowledged by former Prime Minister Malcolm Turnbull in his 2016 'Closing the Gap' speech, in which Turnbull promised his government would do things 'with Indigenous people' rather than 'to them'.[271] In early 2017 Turnbull re-vamped former Prime Minister Tony Abbott's Indigenous Advisory Council in an effort to ensure this happens in practice; however the Council is made up of hand-picked government-appointed advisers and lacks legitimacy.[272] Opposition leader Bill Shorten, in his 'Closing the Gap' speech of 2017, also acknowledged the need for a formalised and representative Indigenous voice in Indigenous affairs:

> [F]rom now on, the first Australians must have the first say in the decisions that shape their lives … [We need] A new approach to extend ourselves beyond hand-picked sources of advice … Not treating local consultation as a box to be ticked – but applying the wisdom of the people who know …
>
> The first Australians want a way to be heard – in a voice they are in control of. And I want Aboriginal and Torres Strait Islander people to know – Labor hears you. We understand the need for a structure that isn't at the mercy of cuts, or seen as a gift of largesse. A voice that cannot be kicked to the kerb by a change of government or policy.[273]

There is only one way to create an institution that is enduring over time and protected from changes of government, legislation and policy: it must be an institution that is guaranteed by the *Constitution*.

H. A First Nations Constitutional Voice: The Only Path to Referendum Success

The Uluru Statement asserts that Indigenous constitutional recognition can be achieved through political participation and representation, by implementing a constitutional guarantee that Indigenous people will always be heard in political decisions about them and their rights. Such a reform will only be realised if there is political will and leadership. The political constraints and complexities canvassed in this section, including the objections to the Expert Panel recommendations (explored in detail in Chapter three below) are central to the

[271] Quoting Indigenous leader Chris Sarra, who urged governments to '[d]o things with us, not to us.' See Malcolm Turnbull, 'Speech to Parliament on the 2016 Closing the Gap Report', Parliament House, Canberra, 10 February 2016.

[272] Note that all the Indigenous dialogues on constitutional recognition expressed strong support for an Indigenous body, but specified that it should be representative, not 'hand-picked'. See Michael Gordon, 'Noel Pearson's Model for Recognition Wins Support', *Sydney Morning Herald* (14 February 2017) <https://www.smh.com.au/politics/federal/noel-pearsons-model-for-recognition-wins-support-20170213-guc0gc.html> accessed 18 October 2019.

[273] Bill Shorten, 'Closing the Gap Report Statement', 14 February 2017, Parliament House, Canberra.

argument built here that mechanisms for Indigenous representation and political participation are the best and most achievable form of Indigenous constitutional recognition for Australia. This was the approach ultimately adopted by Indigenous peoples in the Uluru Statement and the approach recommended in the Referendum Council's final report in 2017, which called for a constitutionally guaranteed First Nations voice.[274]

A minimalist, purely symbolic preamble failed in 1999. It would fail again today, because it does not accord with Indigenous wishes. Australians are unlikely to vote 'yes' to a form of Indigenous recognition that Indigenous people do not agree with. Further, as the history of Australian constitutional reform demonstrates, Australian voters appear to favour practical reform over symbolism. Not one successful constitutional change has been merely symbolic – all have fixed practical problems. A symbolic insertion would likely also attract opposition from constitutional conservatives who view the *Constitution* as a rulebook – not the place for poetic clauses that may enliven uncertain judicial interpretation.[275]

The 1999 republic referendum debate showed how habitual opponents can become unexpected allies to defeat a referendum proposal. During that campaign, the direct electionists joined forces with the monarchists to successfully oppose a republic.[276] People who might ordinarily disagree can unite against a common enemy in a referendum campaign. In the Indigenous recognition debate, constitutional symbolism would become the common enemy of Indigenous advocates, who have consistently favoured substantive and empowering constitutional reform over symbolism, and constitutional conservatives, who seek to uphold the *Constitution* and protect it from legal uncertainty. With resistance from Indigenous Australians and constitutional conservatives alike, a minimalist, merely symbolic, form of recognition cannot win a referendum.

A judicially adjudicated rights guarantee is also unlikely to succeed. As the history of constitutional reform has shown, no attempt to insert new rights guarantees into the *Constitution* has succeeded. Others fizzled out before they were put to the people. It would appear that such reforms do not adequately accord with Australian constitutional and political culture, which tends to favour Parliament as the best defender, balancer and adjudicator of rights. Lack of success on this front may also reflect the fact that Parliament is the gatekeeper of constitutional reform and thus unlikely to put forward and champion proposals that diminish its own power.

[274] *Final Report of the Referendum Council* (n 147 above) Recommendation 1.

[275] Julian Leeser, 'Uphold and Recognise' in Damien Freeman and Shireen Morris (eds), *The Forgotten People: Liberal and Conservative Approaches to Recognising Indigenous Peoples* (Melbourne University Press 2016).

[276] Patmore (n 219 above) 25. See also arguments in Morris and Pearson, 'Indigenous Constitutional Recognition' (n 135 above) 356.

A First Nations constitutional voice is the middle ground, 'radical centre' reform proposal that can succeed. A representative and participatory approach to constitutional recognition is the only approach that genuinely addresses Indigenous aspirations for substantive and empowering constitutional recognition, as well as genuinely addressing concerns to uphold parliamentary supremacy and minimise legal uncertainty. It is the only proposal for constitutional recognition that aligns with Australian constitutional culture and history as well as Indigenous aspirations for substantive constitutional reform. Assessing the political parameters and the lessons of the history of Australian constitutional reform, a First Nations constitutional voice is the only proposal that can win a recognition referendum.

IV. THEORETICAL CONTEXT

I turn now to theoretical arguments. The proposition that a fair liberal democracy should constitutionally recognise Indigenous peoples is not self-explanatory and needs to be unpacked. Theoretical justifications for Indigenous constitutional recognition propel us to revisit the fundamental question of purpose: what does constitutional recognition seek to achieve? Strangely, it is often in response to objections to Indigenous recognition that articulations of fundamental purpose are best elucidated. Discussion of objections can help tease out important theoretical tensions in the debate.

For example, some argue that recognition of Indigenous peoples is unfair and antithetical to equality before the law – a basic tenet of a liberal democracy.[277] However, a simplistic equality ideology is not reflective of Australia's constitutional reality, or of the realities of most settler states which do in fact recognise the existence of Indigenous group rights. In an environment in which there has been past discriminatory denial of rights and unequal treatment of a particular group, contemporary recognition of that group's rights can be justified as an acceptable deviation from, or more accurately a measure enhancing, equality. Recognition of Indigenous rights is best understood as being consistent with and promoting equality in practice.

Besides which, as noted, Australia's *Constitution* does not adopt an individualistic equality approach to its rights protection nor to its democratic political

[277] See Brian M Barry's critique of indentity politics and multiculturalism, in *Culture and Equality: An Egalitarian Critique of Multiculturalism* (Harvard University Press 2001) which argues for universal citizenship without distinctions on the basis of group membership. For populist contributions, see Andrew Bolt, 'I am, you are, we are Australian', *Herald Sun* (29 January 2014) <https://www.heraldsun.com.au/news/opinion/i-am-you-are-we-are-australian/news-story/63336ae43afb30a9fd04a2220b3d4cdc> accessed 18 October 2019; Greg Sheridan, 'Constitutional Change Will Divide Not Unite the Nation', *The Australian* (20 September 2014) <https://www.theaustralian.com.au/commentary/opinion/constitutional-change-will-divide-not-unite-the-nation/news-story/ed3fdd9de4d4b4fe0527993544f2f185>.

representation. There remain discriminatory clauses[278] and the constitutional compact recognises the existence of unique, variously populated, self-governing political collectives within the union – the States – guaranteeing these entities equal representation in the Senate. Individualistically speaking, this is inequality; however, it is justified and accepted on the basis that the even the very small historic political communities deserve a fair voice in the compact. The proposition that Indigenous peoples should also be constitutionally recognised, so that their voices can be more fairly heard in political debates about their rights, is in keeping with the *Constitution's* fundamental philosophy, nature and design. The *Constitution* recognises the equality of political communities more than the equality of individuals.

This section discusses constitutional purpose and the role of Australia's *Constitution* in particular. It then explores arguments for Indigenous recognition within a liberal democracy, the tensions between recognition and equality, race and Indigeneity, the relationship between recognition and sovereignty, the possibilities for Indigenous self-determination within domestic democratic arrangements, and the nuanced interaction between symbolism and practical reform. Drawing on Waldron's defence of the political process as the best means for protecting rights, I argue that Indigenous political representation and participation in their own affairs may be the Indigenous 'right of rights' in the Australian constitutional context, which should be protected through Indigenous constitutional recognition, as the Uluru Statement requests.

A. What is the Job of Australia's *Constitution*?

Constitutions bind governments to the rule of law[279] by restraining, qualifying, codifying, and thus legitimising[280] the exercise of government and parliamentary power over its citizens.[281] Constitutions set up institutions for government

[278] The High Court has declined to imply a principle of equality from Australia's Constitution because of discriminatory provisions within the Constitution and its history of unequal treatment: see *Leeth v Commonwealth* (1992) 174 CLR 455; *Kruger v Commonwealth* (1997) 190 CLR 1; Joseph (n 154 above) 491–92.

[279] See Joseph Raz, *The Authority of Law* (Oxford University Press 2009) ch 11; Joseph Raz, 'The Rule of Law and Its Virtue' (1977) 93 *Law Quarterly Review* 195; David Dyzenhaus, 'Hobbes' Constitutional Theory' in Ian Shapiro (ed), *Leviathan: Or The Matter, Forme, and Power of a Commonwealth Ecclesiasticall and Civil: Thomas Hobbes* (Yale University Press 2010) 461–64; AV Dicey, *The Law of the Constitution* (Oxford University Press 2013) 97, 225.

[280] As Gleeson CJ explains, '[a]s an idea about government, the essence of the rule of law is that all authority is subject to, and constrained by, law. The opposing idea is of a state of affairs in which the will of an individual, or a group, (such as a Party), is the governing force in a society. The contrasting concepts are legitimacy and arbitrariness. The word "legitimacy" implies an external legal rule or principle by reference to which authority is constituted, identified, and controlled.': Gleeson CJ, 'Courts and the Rule of Law', speech delivered at the University of Melbourne, 7 November 2001.

[281] 'Every legislative assembly existing under a federal constitution is merely a subordinate law-making body, whose laws are of the nature of by-laws, valid whilst within the authority conferred

and establish rules and procedures for government to follow.[282] By bestowing on government particular powers and restraining the arbitrary exercise of power,[283] constitutions protect citizens' rights and freedoms from government abuse.[284]

Australia's *Constitution* is embedded with British constitutional principles,[285] but was also drafted with inspiration from federal nations like the USA and Canada.[286] Unlike the USA, however, the *Australian Constitution* contains no full Bill of judicially adjudicated rights. Instead, Australia relies mostly on democratic, federal and institutional mechanisms for rights protection.[287] The power-sharing arrangements of federalism and representative democracy, required by the *Constitution*, operate as procedural restraints on the abuse of power. Federalism sets up a 'check and balance' system in which the Senate, as the house of review, tempers the power of the House of

upon it by the constitution, but invalid or unconstitutional if they go beyond the limits of such authority.' AV Dicey, *Introduction to the Study of the Law of the Constitution* (8th edn, MacMillan and Co 1926) 145–46.

[282] Waldron emphasises this as a primary role of constitutions. 'First and foremost, they empower: they establish institutions which allow people to cooperate and coordinate to pursue projects that they cannot achieve on their own … Besides actually establishing centres of public power, constitutions lay down procedures for their operation, often quite formalistic procedures limiting not so much what can be done but *how* it is done.': Jeremy Waldron, 'Constitutionalism: A Skeptical View', Georgetown University Law Centre, 2010, 20–21. See also Lord Dyson MR, *Speech at Magna Carta, Religion and The Rule of Law*, Temple, London, Saturday 7 June 2014.

[283] This idea of constitutionalism as a restraint on the arbitrary exercise of power formed part of the principles underlying the Magna Carta, which was described by Lord Denning as 'the greatest constitutional document of all times – the foundation of the freedom of the individual against the arbitrary authority of the despot.' The Magna Carta was an agreement that even monarchs and governments must be bound by the law. See Danny Danziger and John Gillingham, *1215: The Year of the Magna Carta* (Hodder and Stoughton 2003) quoted in Chapter 16.

[284] As Thomas Paine articulated in 1791 in his foundational work, *The Rights of Man and the Citizen*: '[a] constitution is not a thing in name only, but in fact. It has not an ideal, but a real existence; and wherever it cannot be produced in a visible form, there is none. A constitution is a thing antecedent to a government, and a government is only the creature of a constitution. The constitution of a country is not the act of its government, but of the people constituting its government. It is the body of elements, to which you can refer, and quote article by article; and which contains the principles on which the government shall be established, the manner in which it shall be organised, the powers it shall have, the mode of elections, the duration of Parliaments, or by what other name such bodies may be called; the powers which the executive part of the government shall have; and in fine, everything that relates to the complete organisation of a civil government, and the principles on which it shall act, and by which it shall be bound.': Thomas Paine, *The Rights of Man* (JS Jordan 1791) ch 1.

[285] 'The Constitution took effect in a society operating upon certain assumptions about the rule of law and basic freedoms reflected in the common law inherited from England.': Robert French, 'The Constitution and the Protection of Human Rights', *Edith Cowan University Vice Chancellor's Oration*, Perth, 20 November 2009, 7.

[286] ibid 2–3. See also Clark (n 220).

[287] Owen Dixon, 'Two Constitutions Compared' in *Jesting Pilate and Other Papers and Addresses* (Law Book Company, 1965) 101–2; Groves, Boughey and Meagher (n 221 above) 6–7; Saunders, 'The Australian Constitution and Our Rights' (n 233 above) 117.

Representatives.[288] Australia's federal *Constitution* is accordingly built on principles of reciprocity, power-sharing, dialogue and deliberation – dynamics which can help protect rights.[289] The checks and balances of federalism by their nature require mutual dependence, compromise and negotiation.[290] The mandated sharing of power under the *Australian Constitution* compels a culture of 'mutual respect' between the constituent parts of the Federation. In the words of Callinan J:

> The whole Constitution is founded upon notions of comity, comity between the States which replaced the former colonies, comity between the Commonwealth as a polity and each of the States as a polity, and comity between the Imperial power, the Commonwealth and the States … Federations compel comity, that is to say mutual respect and deference in allocated areas.[291]

The notions of comity and mutual respect derived from the way the Federation came about. As noted, Australia's *Constitution* was a 'treaty' or compact between self-governing political entities, the colonies.[292] The colonies consented to their inclusion in the federal union on the basis of equality and maintained independence.[293] The idea of the *Constitution* as a compact or treaty, compelling mutual respect, is useful in thinking about Indigenous constitutional recognition. It is particularly useful in envisaging forms of recognition that encourage mutual respect, negotiation, reciprocity and dialogue in the relationship between Indigenous peoples and the Australian state.

Australia's federal *Constitution* empowers diverse voices to be heard in respect of their own affairs. Waldron describes constitutional structures that share power as providing ways of 'structuring deliberation and allowing multiple voices to be heard and securing multiple points of access for citizen input'. Similarly, bicameralism is a way of 'empowering different voices in the community … sampled for the purposes of representation in different ways'.

[288] *Wilson v Minister for Aboriginal Affairs* (1996) 189 CLR 1, 11 (Brennan CJ, Dawson, Toohey, McHugh and Gummow JJ). See also Cheryl Saunders, 'The Constitutional, Legal and Institutional Foundations of Australian Federalism' in Robert Carling (ed), *Where To for Australian Federalism?* (Centre for Independent Studies 2008); Saunders (n 192 above) 150–55.

[289] Chen (n 70 above); Thomas-Woolley and Keller (n 70 above); Ron Levy, Neomal Silva and Benjamin S Saunders, 'Deliberation at the Founding: Deliberative Democracy as an Original Constitutional Value' (2017) 28 *Public Law Review* 41; Scott Stephenson, 'Federalism and Rights Deliberation' (2014) 38 *Melbourne University Law Review* 709; Robyn Hollander and Haig Patapan, 'Deliberative Federalism' in Ron Levy, Hoi Kong, Graeme Orr and Jeff Kind (eds), *Deliberating under Constitutions* (Cambridge University Press 2018); James F Blumstein, 'Federalism and Civil Rights: Complementary and Competing Paradigms' (1994) 47 *Vanderbilt Law Review* 1251.

[290] Aroney (n 70) 18. See also Michelle Evans, 'Re-Thinking the Federal Balance: How Federal Theory Supports States' Rights' (2010) 1 *The Western Australian Jurist* 14, 21; Larry Kramer, 'Understanding Federalism' (1994) 47 *Vanderbilt Law Review* 1485.

[291] *New South Wales v Commonwealth* (2006) 229 CLR 1, 322 (Work Choices). Quoted in Evans (n 290 above) 16. See also Herbert Barry, 'Comity' (1926) 12(3) *Vanderbilt Law Review* 353.

[292] Quick and Garran (n 69 above) 332–42; Aroney (n 70 above) 4.

[293] Evans (n 290 above) 16.

Constitutions thus provide procedures to order political discourse, constructing mechanisms and formalities whereby 'public deliberation becomes a structured enterprise … facilitating the formation of well-thought-through, responsible and politically effective opinions'. Understood in this light, constitutions exist not just to restrain government power, but to proactively foster deliberation and dialogue between people and parties who disagree, which is ultimately important for peace, stability and national unity – not to mention good policy. Constitutions create procedures for civil communication and decision-making 'out of what would otherwise be the loose and lurching and dangerous politics of the street'.[294] Constitutions can therefore be seen as instruments of peaceful reconciliation.

Scholars such as Jeffrey Goldsworthy[295] and Sir Anthony Mason[296] characterise the *Australian Constitution* as primarily a basic and structural rulebook. It is a practical and pragmatic charter of government.[297] It may not be the appropriate place for symbolic statements and expressions of values and aspirations,[298] but it is the place for rules and procedures. By setting out rules, including the federal and democratic procedures which governments must follow, the *Australian Constitution* protects rights. But if Australia's *Constitution* is best characterised as a structural rulebook, it is also a uniquely enduring rulebook. Constitutional rules are more entrenched than ordinary legislative rules; they are enduring rules to guide and manage government behaviour over time. The harder a constitution is to change, the more this is true. Australia's *Constitution* is one of the hardest to change in the world. Indeed, Australia's constitutional rules can thus be understood as intergenerational promises from the founders to the future – even if those promises are largely procedural, institutional and structural.

In an important sense, the Australian 'future' and the stability and prosperity most Australians tend to enjoy demonstrates the success of a well-designed rulebook for Australian government, which has mostly been successful in protecting the rights and freedoms of Australian citizens.[299] Equally, the rules in relation

[294] Waldron, 'Constitutionalism' (n 282 above) 22–23. For discussion of how the Australian constitutional founders envisioned deliberation as part of Parliament's procedures, see Levy, Silva and Saunders, 'Deliberation at the Founding' (n 289 above).

[295] Goldsworthy, 'Constitutional Cultures' (n 220 above) 687–88.

[296] Sir Anthony Mason, 'The Australian Constitution in Retrospect and Prospect' in Robert French, Geoffrey Lindell and Cheryl Saunders (eds), *Reflections on the Australian Constitution* (Federation Press 2003) 8.

[297] See generally Damien Freeman and Shireen Morris (eds), *The Forgotten People: Liberal and Conservative Approaches to Recognising Indigenous Peoples* (Melbourne University Press 2016). See also this phrase as used in Antonin Scalia, *A Matter of Interpretation: Federal Courts and the Law* (Princeton University Press 1997) 134.

[298] Justice Keane contrasts Australia's 'small brown bird' of a Constitution, with America's more inspirational 'eagle'. The Hon Patrick Keane, 'In Celebration of the Constitution', speech delivered at the National Archives Commission, Queensland, 12 June 2008. For more on these contrasts see Jeremy Webber, 'Constitutional Poetry: The Tension between Symbolic and Functional Aims in Constitutional Reform' (1999) 21 *Sydney Law Review* 260, 260–61.

[299] Saunders, 'The Australian Constitution and Our Rights' (n 233 above) 118.

to Indigenous peoples, or perhaps more accurately, the *lack* of fair rules and the *lack* of positive constitutional promises with respect to them, have yielded corresponding outcomes for that group. Indigenous constitutional recognition is not just about removing outdated references to 'race' or inserting a symbolic reference of no operational effect. It is about implementing fairer rules for the good governance of Indigenous affairs at the constitutional level. Indigenous constitutional recognition is about ascertaining the appropriate intergenerational promise that Australia as a nation should make to Indigenous Australians, to ensure the future is fairer than the past.[300]

B. Arguments for Indigenous Recognition within a Federal, Liberal Democracy

It can be said, then, that Australia's federal constitutional compact provides the long-term machinery for reconciliation and co-operation between competing interests. It balances independence with inclusion, in contrast to maintaining separateness and fragmentation, by empowering disparate voices to forever be in dialogue with one another. In doing so, it is more communitarian than individualistic. The *Constitution* recognises the historic political communities within the national majority, compromising individual equality in favour of equality of the former colonies. According to Gleeson, this demonstrates the weakness of simplistic equality objections to Indigenous recognition:

> To say that the Constitution treats all Australians equally sounds reassuring, but is it true? Consider the example of representation in Parliament. Under the Constitution, about half a million Tasmanians are represented by the same number of Senators as about seven and a half million people of New South Wales. Is that equality? Or is it inequality? It is both, but, more to the point, it is Federalism.[301]

A constitutionally guaranteed First Nations voice in Indigenous affairs is particularly suited to Australia's essential constitutional character, which ensures that the historic political communities – even the very small ones – are heard in their affairs. As Lino argues,

> [f]ramed in federal terms, Indigenous peoplehood claims appear not as foreign and threatening to Australian constitutional culture but as fundamentally consistent with

[300] See Shireen Morris, 'What Promise Will the Nation Make?' in Damien Freeman and Shireen Morris (eds), *The Forgotten People: Liberal and Conservative Approaches to Recognising Indigenous Peoples* (Melbourne University Press 2016). Note also that Martin Luther King Jnr in his advocacy for civil rights in the USA also characterised the *American Constitution* as a 'promissory note': '[w]hen the architects of our republic wrote the magnificent words of the Constitution and the Declaration of Independence, they were signing a promissory note to which every American was to fall heir. This note was a promise that all men, yes, black men as well as white men, would be guaranteed the unalienable rights of life, liberty, and the pursuit of happiness': Martin Luther King Jnr, 'I Have a Dream' speech, Washington DC, 28 August 1963.

[301] Gleeson, 'Recognition in Keeping with the Constitution' (n 193 above) 15.

> it in important respects … Indigenous peoplehood claims can be justified as a means of respectfully and consensually, if belatedly, bringing Australia's original political communities into that political association.[302]

Australia's federal structure is especially amenable to substantive recognition of Indigenous peoples.

A tailored understanding of Indigenous recognition within liberal democracies also accords with international practice. As a matter of practical reality, democracies established through colonisation in the contemporary era tend to implement through their constitutional arrangements an understanding of fairness that is more nuanced and pragmatic than an inflexible individual equality paradigm. Where there are colonised peoples surviving within liberal democracies, the theoretical and practical meaning of equality is complex. History and circumstances are taken into account. Indigenous historical difference is often recognised and accommodated within the liberal democratic regime.[303] Māori former judge Sir Eddie Durie observes, in the New Zealand context, that:

> Justice, in the broad sense of fairness, requires respect for all peoples … In many cases, therefore, a plural legal order may be necessary …
>
> Maori, in this context, are not simply a race or cultural group, but a people with constitutional status arising from prior occupancy … Maori are a domestic constitutional entity entitled to special recognition.[304]

The argument for Indigenous constitutional recognition proceeds from an understanding that Indigenous peoples are a legitimately distinct 'constitutional entity', or constitutional constituency, within a plural legal order.[305] In the colonisation of Australia, the sovereign status of Indigenous peoples was discriminatorily denied by the colonising forces, and Indigenous peoples' status as a legitimate constitutional constituency similarly went unrecognised. Had things been fairer, the *Constitution* might also have embodied a union with the original owners: Indigenous peoples might have been treated as equals and been allowed to negotiate the terms of their inclusion in the new nation,

[302] Dylan Lino, 'Towards Indigenous Settler Federalism' (2017) 28 *Public Law Review* 118, 134. For a discussion of Aboriginal sovereignty in the context of Canadian federalism, see Martin Papillon, 'Chapter 14: Canadian Federalism and the Emerging Mosaic of Aboriginal Multilevel Governance' in Herman Bakvis and Grace Skogstad (eds), *Canadian federalism: Performance, Effectiveness, and Legitimacy* (3rd edn, Oxford University Press 2012).

[303] See generally, Ivison, *Postcolonial Liberalism* (n 6 above).

[304] ET Durie, 'Justice, Biculturalism and the Politics of Law' in *Justice and Identity: Antipodean Practices* (Allen and Unwin 1995) 33–34.

[305] Benedict Kingsbury, 'Competing Conceptual Approaches to Indigenous Group Issues in New Zealand Law' (2002) 52(1) *University of Toronto Law Journal* 101, 106; Alexander Reilley, 'A Constitutional Framework for Indigenous Governance' (2006) 28(3) *Sydney Law Review* 403, 404. See also John Griffiths, 'What is Legal Pluralism?' (1986) 18(24) *Journal of Legal Pluralism* 1, 1; James Tully, *Strange Multiplicity: Constitutionalism in an Age of Diversity* (Cambridge University Press 1995). For a further discussion of the theories underpinning Indigenous constitutional recognition, see Lino, *Constitutional Recognition* (n 71 above) 71–84.

rather than having those terms oppressively imposed upon them. This liberal, consent-based argument for Indigenous constitutional recognition therefore seeks to remedy the unfair and illiberal treatment of Indigenous peoples prior to and at federation, as well as the injustices that have flowed from that initial discrimination, by setting in place fairer terms for Indigenous inclusion and participation in the future.[306] Such recognition proceeds on the basis that Indigenous Australians, as well as being equal citizens, are a historically, politically and legally distinct constitutional constituency within Australia. While this constitutional status is currently not positively recognised in the *Constitution*, it is nonetheless evident.

Indigenous peoples in Australia are the only group that was dispossessed by British settlement. They were the only group especially excluded from the constitutional arrangements of 1901, particularly as noted, through sections 127 and 51(xxvi). They are therefore the only group that has particular rights and interests arising out of this history. These rights and interests are recognised at common law[307] and in legislation – there is legislation recognising Indigenous native title rights[308] and Indigenous cultural heritage.[309] Further, Indigenous peoples are the only group for whom the Commonwealth makes such laws, and the only group for whom the Commonwealth requires a special legislative head of power to do so – notably section 51(xxvi) has only ever been used with respect to Indigenous peoples.[310] It is clear, therefore, that the Commonwealth Parliament makes laws recognising distinct Indigenous rights which necessarily apply to Indigenous people but not to other Australians. Indigenous peoples are a demonstrably distinct constitutional constituency with a special relationship with Australian governments under the *Constitution*.[311] This is a fact of

[306] Kingsbury (n 305 above) 123; Patrick Macklem, 'Distributing Sovereignty: Indian Nations and Equality of Peoples' (1993) 45(5) *Stanford Law Review* 1311, 1329. See also Ivison, *Postcolonial Liberalism* (n 6 above) 16–18. Note that Jeremy Waldron rejects this consent-based justification for Indigenous recognition. See Jeremy Waldron, 'Peoples Participating as Peoples: Interests, Ideas and Identity' in Claire Charters and Dean R Knight (eds), *We the People(s): Participation in Governance* (Victoria University Press 2011) 229–31.

[307] See eg *Mabo* (n 25 above).

[308] See eg *Native Title Act 1993* (Cth).

[309] See eg *Aboriginal and Torres Strait Islander Heritage Protection Act 1984* (Cth).

[310] See eg *World Heritage Properties Conservation Act 1983* (Cth), the *Aboriginal and Torres Strait Islander Heritage Protection Act 1984* (Cth), the *Native Title Act 1993* (Cth) and the *Corporations (Aboriginal and Torres Strait Islander) Act 2006* (Cth). Before the 1967 amendments, the Race Power was never used.

[311] In some other jurisdictions, like Canada and New Zealand, the special relationship between Indigenous peoples and the settler state has been characterised as akin to a fiduciary relationship, giving rise to principles of partnership. See *Te Runanga o Wharekauri Rekohu Inc v Attorney-General* [1993] 2 NZLR 301, 304, 306; *New Zealand Maori Council v Attorney-General* [1987] 1 NZLR 641, 664; *R v Sparrow* [1990] 1 SCR 1075, 1108. These fiduciary duties tend to arise out of the treaty relationships now recognised in the Canadian Constitution, and in legislative incorporation of the Treaty of Waitangi into New Zealand law. Such arguments have not been recognised in Australia, where there is no treaty and where Indigenous rights are not constitutionally recognised. Note, however, that Toohey J in *Mabo* (n 25 above) suggested that fiduciary duties may arise in state relationships with Indigenous peoples because of the vulnerable nature of native title rights and the

the history and the way Australia's constitutional system operates. Indigenous constitutional recognition seeks to reform and reset this relationship to make it fairer than in the past.

Will Kymlicka's understanding of minority group recognition within liberal democracies is grounded in his observation that Western democracies are often multinational – they can be home to distinct yet co-existing nations or peoples, while also developing into unified states with a shared sense of patriotism. Kymlicka observes that accommodation and recognition of co-existing domestic nations within states is often accepted as a necessary measure, 'above and beyond the common rights of citizenship', to ensure that these nations can exist in a way that is fair, moral and respectful to their common humanity.[312] Pearson, on a similar understanding, characterises recognition and accommodation as a middle way between absolute assimilation or total fragmentation of the state as alternative responses to the multinational or 'peoplehood' problem.[313]

Indeed, the middle way of recognition and accommodation, as demonstrated in comparable liberal democracies such as Canada,[314] New Zealand and the Scandinavian countries (discussed further in Chapter four of this volume), may be the most humanitarian way to reconcile colonised nations with colonising states. Frantz Fanon viscerally describes the resort to violence as a way of throwing off colonial oppression and counteracting colonial violence.[315] By contrast, advocates for constitutional recognition in Australia tend to articulate a peaceful and inclusive approach. Indeed, the Uluru Statement can be described as a 'peace offering' to the Australian people. Such inclusive accommodation measures stand as an appropriate recognition of historical difference and a justifiable deviation from strict, individualistic equality[316] – they are a way of more fairly distributing constitutional power[317] in a manner in keeping with Australia's

power of the Crown to extinguish such rights. See *Mabo* (n 25 above) 203–4. See also Kirsty Gover, 'The Honour of the Crowns: State-Indigenous Fiduciary Relationships and Australian Exceptionalism' (2016) 38(3) *Sydney Law Review* 339. Though a fiduciary duty has not been recognised, the history and law nonetheless demonstrate a special relationship between Indigenous peoples and the state in Australia.

[312] Will Kymlicka, *Multicultural Citizenship* (Clarendon Press 1995) 11, 13, 26. See also Tully (n 307 above).

[313] Pearson, 'A Rightful Place' (n 15 above) 40–43.

[314] See also Patrick Macklem, *Indigenous Difference and the Constitution of Canada* (University of Toronto Press 2001); Macklem, 'Distributing Sovereignty' (n 306 above).

[315] Frantz Fanon, *The Wretched of the Earth* (Grove Press 1963).

[316] See also Charles Taylor, 'Multiculturalism and the Politics of Recognition' in Amy Gutman (ed), *Multiculturalism* (Princeton University Press 1994) 65.

[317] Macklem argues that '[p]rinciples of distributive justice are required to explain why it is important to deviate from the ideal of equal citizenship and to promote respect for prior sovereignty through indigenous-specific distributions of political rights and responsibilities … a claim of prior sovereignty possesses persuasive power because it involves an implicit, but powerful, appeal to principles of distributive justice and equality … sovereignty is a good that has been distributed to a number of different recipients in North America by a series of mutual acts of recognition … Indian government can be viewed as a particular instance of this larger web of distributional activity.': Macklem, 'Distributing Sovereignty' (n 306 above) 1345.

constitutional culture. Indigenous constitutional recognition can be understood as reform to support equality in practice, taking into account historical and contemporary political and practical realities. This is not antithetical to liberal democratic values; rather it is complementary to such values, particularly as they operate in Australian circumstances.

Waldron cautions against recognising Indigenous peoples merely on the basis that 'they were here first' and warns against radical separatist notions of Indigenous recognition on account of the political instability and unrest such moves may cause.[318] Yet his discussion of political equality is salient to the question at hand. Indigenous constitutional recognition seeks political empowerment through formal constitutional inclusion, in contrast to the separatism, exclusion and disempowerment of the past. A First Nations constitutional voice would be a way of fostering cohesion and unity through more inclusive dialogue and deliberation, thus fortifying our political society against fragmentation and unrest. Just as federalism may be seen as a mechanism reconciling plurality with unity in aid of political stability,[319] so, too, is constitutional inclusion of the First Nations through increased dialogue and deliberation a peaceful way of processing disagreement and balancing historical difference with unity and inclusion.

The Uluru Statement's request for a voice in Indigenous affairs, in my view, accords with Waldron's conception of the fundamental purpose of democratic constitutions in this respect: in contrast to autocratic regimes which maintain the power of elites, the constitution of a democracy 'involves empowering *those who would otherwise be powerless*, the ordinary people who in most polities are the subjects not the agents of political power'.[320] The Uluru Statement pleads for a First Nations constitutional voice in their affairs to address their 'torment of powerlessness'. In calling for such reform, Indigenous advocates are reacting to their extreme minority status in the Australian constitutional system and

[318] Jeremy Waldron, 'Peoples Participating as Peoples' (n 306 above) 232–34. See also Jeremy Waldron, 'Indigeneity? First Peoples and Last Occupancy' (2003) 1(1) *New Zealand Journal of Public and International Law* 55; Waldron, 'Redressing Historic Injustice' (n 239 above); Waldron, 'Superseding Historic Injustice' (n 241 above). But note that Patrick Macklem explains that prior occupancy arguments for Indigenous recognition are more accurately a reflection of a consent-based argument: because Indigenous peoples lived on the land before the colonisers arrived, and were subject to the constitutional order imposed by the colonisers without Indigenous consent, some recognition and accommodation of Indigenous rights is arguably justified. Macklem also finds the claim of prior sovereignty to be more persuasive than arguments about prior occupancy. See Macklem, 'Distributing Sovereignty' (n 306 above) 1329, 1334.

[319] See also Will Kymlicka, *Liberalism, Community and Culture* (Clarendon Press 1989) 215; Thomas-Woolley and Keller (n 70 above).

[320] Waldron, 'Constitutionalism' (n 282 above) 24–25. For more on the dynamics of recognition and power, see Bert van den Brink and David Owen (eds), *Recognition and Power, Axel Honneth and the Tradition of Critical Social Theory* (Cambridge University Press 2007); Barbara Hobson (ed), *Recognition Struggles and Social Movements: Contested Identities, Agency and Power* (Cambridge University Press 2003).

to the reality that the *Australian Constitution* positions them as the subjects of parliamentary power – it confers upon Parliament a special power to make special laws with respect to them (as noted, the Race Power has only ever been used in relation to Indigenous people) – without specifically empowering them to reciprocally participate and engage in deliberations with respect to how such powers are exercised. A democratic constitution, and particularly a federal democratic constitution, is well placed to address the systemic disempowerment of Indigenous peoples by empowering them with a constitutional voice in political decision-making with respect to their rights and interests.

The common 'closing the gap' argument for Indigenous recognition (discussed above in section III.G) calls for legal and political systems governing Indigenous affairs to be improved in an enduring way, at the structural and constitutional level, in order to improve policy outcomes.[321] A similar practical argument is the need to preserve the culture that is unique and original to the place;[322] but this is perhaps another way of expressing the idea that the wrongs of the past – including those wrongs that unjustly suppressed Indigenous languages and cultures – should not be repeated and that enduring measures should be set in place to prevent the repetition of past wrongs. An all-encompassing way of framing the argument for Indigenous constitutional recognition within a liberal democracy is the need for rectification of past wrongs and the implementation of structural reforms for the prevention of future wrongs.[323] As Pearson argues, '[o]ur people have lived through the discrimination of the past. We have a legitimate anxiety that the past not be repeated, and that measures be put in place to *ensure things are done in a better way*.'[324]

Pearson's comments resonate with John Rawls' conception of justice as fairness. Rawls posits that justice can require an institutional guarantee of reciprocity – an assurance that the same rules will apply to all and that notions of justice will be extended fairly to all citizens. In thinking through this problem, Rawls encourages hypothetical consideration of the terms that might have been initially agreed between rational individuals who are free and equal, suggesting that 'certain principles of justice are justified because they would be agreed to in an initial situation of equality'.[325] This argument can be extended to encompass groups, particularly in a federal context, and provides a basis for understanding the justice and fairness of Australia's federal constitutional arrangements. Prior to 1901, the colonies negotiated as free and equal parties and agreed to their inclusion in the compact on equal terms, with equal representation in the future Senate. Given past discriminatory denial of Indigenous

[321] Kingsbury (n 305 above) 131.
[322] ibid 124.
[323] ibid 111, 124.
[324] Pearson, 'A Rightful Place' (n 15 above) 65.
[325] See Rawls, *A Theory of Justice* (n 2 above) 21; Rawls, *Justice as Fairness: A Restatement* (n 2 above) 15–18; Rawls, *Political Liberalism* (n 2 above).

rights, it is understandable that Indigenous peoples now seek a similar constitutional assurance of increased reciprocity in their relationship with the state. Had the parties dealt with each other as free and equal actors prior to 1901, terms for Indigenous representation and participation similar to (or perhaps stronger than) those now being advocated might already be in place.

In Australia, Indigenous calls for a *guarantee* of fairer future treatment support the need for Indigenous recognition to occur within the *Constitution*: the *Constitution* is where enduring rules, promises and guarantees are made.[326] Only the *Constitution* curtails parliamentary power. The *Constitution* is the only authority that can guarantee fairer treatment.[327] Another way to explain it, particularly apt in the Australian constitutional context, is by reference to the relational nature of the *Constitution*. Kirsty Gover, like Rawls, emphasises the hypothetical initial situation, or original state, to inform her understanding of the purpose of Indigenous recognition:

> The exchange between tribes and States in these settings is largely reparative, in the broad sense of the term: recognition is designed to repair a relationship … in State–tribal relations, recognition aims to reconstruct intergovernmental and community relationships of the kind that would have been in place, had all the parties conducted themselves justly and in good faith from first contact.[328]

The idea of repairing or improving a relationship is a helpful way of thinking about Indigenous constitutional recognition. This is a project that seeks to reform Australia's constitutional arrangements so that they better resemble the arrangements that might have been in place had discriminatory attitudes of *terra nullius* not prevailed, and had Indigenous peoples been recognised and treated as equals, sovereigns and the owners of the land when the British arrived. If the parties had conducted themselves justly and in good faith from the moment of first contact, it is likely that Indigenous peoples would have been included more fairly in the power-sharing negotiations preceding federation, and Australians may not now be discussing the need for Indigenous constitutional recognition.

Counterfactual hypotheticals can be inherently fraught, however.[329] Structural reforms in the present cannot undo what was done in the past. Nor is it possible to guess what First Nations representatives might have negotiated pre-1901 had they been given a fair chance. The important question for

[326] See Shireen Morris, 'A Practical, Constitutional Promise to Do Things With Aborigines, Not to Them', *The Australian* (29 April 2016) <https://www.theaustralian.com.au/business/legal-affairs/a-practical-constitutional-promise-to-do-things-with-aborigines-not-to-them/news-story/99c8e3707908db2830c1303dd68cc780> accessed 18 October 2019.

[327] Morris (n 300 above).

[328] Kirsty Gover, *Tribal Constitutionalism* (Oxford University Press 2010) 17.

[329] Waldron, 'Redressing Historic Injustice' (n 239 above); Waldron, 'Superseding Historic Injustice' (n 241 above) 8.

contemporary advocates and decision-makers to consider is how parties might deal with each other justly and in good faith *today*, in order to positively reform and recalibrate this constitutional relationship such that it produces better outcomes for Indigenous Australians, and the country as a whole. As noted, the successful reform must involve fairly balancing the concerns of all members of society.[330] For better and worse, we are all in this together. The descendants of non-Indigenous settlers are not leaving. The question is: what constitutional reform would make this relationship fairer, given the wrongs of the past and the persisting inequalities and injustices of the present? A First Nations constitutional voice in their affairs appears a fair and constitutionally congruent answer to this question.

C. The Tension between Recognition and Equality

According to Rawls, a liberal democracy means a system of governance in which citizens are free and equal, have an equal say through their equal vote, and have free and equal participation in the democratic system.[331] We in Australia tend to think of ourselves as a liberal democracy, despite the fact that our *Constitution* contains provisions suggesting inequality on the basis of 'race'[332] – an inequality that has had direct and painful implications for Indigenous peoples. As Gleeson observes, the *Constitution* did not and does not treat Indigenous people equally: '[t]he race power, by its very existence, calls into question the assumption of equality.'[333] An obvious solution to this problem might be to correct that inequality by establishing a paradigm of racial non-discrimination, as recommended by the Expert Panel in 2012 (discussed further in Chapter three). There are, however, significant complications to that seemingly simple solution. A racial non-discrimination guarantee, or a variation thereof, would likely not win the political consensus to proceed to a successful referendum due to objections to increased judicial review. Further, as discussion of international examples will show in Chapter four of this volume, judicially adjudicated rights guarantees may not always yield the empowerment Indigenous advocates seek. Court adjudication comes with its own risks.

Theoretically too there are limitations to the individualistic non-discrimination paradigm as the sole means for understanding collective Indigenous rights and interests. Habermas asks whether 'a theory of rights that is so individualistically constructed [can] deal adequately with struggles for recognition in which it is the articulation and assertion of collective identities that seems to be at

[330] For as Waldron reminds us: '*here we all are*'. Waldron, 'Redressing Historic Injustice' (n 239 above) 159.

[331] Rawls, *Political Liberalism* (n 2 above) 4.

[332] See *Constitution* ss 25, 51(xxvi). This issue will be discussed further in Chapter 3 of this volume. See also Morris, 'Undemocratic, Uncertain and Politically Unviable?' (n 91 above).

[333] Gleeson, 'Recognition in Keeping with the Constitution' (n 193 above) 15.

stake?'[334] A simple equality framework may be limited in this respect. Kingsbury observes that

> Non-discrimination provisions are generally not readily adapted to deal comprehensively with indigenous group rights, being premised on the protection of individuals and communities from adverse discrimination on the basis of characteristics such as race or ethnicity, with equality of all individuals as the ultimate goal. The idea of 'extra' rights for a group of individuals sits uneasily in this equality framework.[335]

Kingsbury quotes Menno Boldt's observation with respect to Canadian law, that '[a] "racism" paradigm [for analysing injustice to indigenous peoples] robs Indians of the most significant elements of Indian identity – their history, nationhood, cultures, and languages – and thereby undermines their historical and moral claims to self-determination.'[336] There is a sense in which a simple equality or non-discrimination paradigm may not easily align with the existential concerns that drive struggles for Indigenous recognition: the Indigenous desire to survive as distinct and collective peoples rather than to be individualistically assimilated into the colonising state. A tension thus appears between the practical need for protection against racial discrimination (arising as an obvious response to the fact that Indigenous peoples have for so many decades been subject to oppressive and discriminatory laws imposed by colonising governments) and the need for a framework that enables Indigenous self-determination – the freedom of Indigenous peoples, as distinct and surviving collectives, to pursue their own social, economic and cultural development.[337]

The right to self-determination is inherently related, and should not be seen as contradictory, to the right to equality.[338] The fact that the doctrine of *terra nullius* denied equal Indigenous property rights, equal humanity and equality under the law, and thus their right to exist and prosper as Indigenous peoples, demonstrates the extent to which the two principles are inter-related and can be simultaneously denied. Equality and Indigenous self-determination can evidently also be simultaneously promoted and respected.[339] As will be explored in Chapter four, in comparable settler democracies, distinct Indigenous

[334] Jurgen Habermas, 'Struggles for Recognition in the Democratic Constitutional State' in Amy Gutman (ed), *Multiculturalism* (Princeton UP 1994) 107. See also Jurgen Habermas, *The Inclusion of the Other: Studies in Political Theory* (MIT Press 1998) ch 8.

[335] Kingsbury (n 305 above) 105.

[336] Menno Boldt, *Surviving as Indians* (University of Toronto Press 1993) xv.

[337] See art 1 of both the International Covenant on Civil and Political Rights and the International Covenant on Economic, Social and Cultural Rights, and art 3 of the UN Declaration on the Rights of Indigenous Peoples. See also Noel Pearson, 'Reconciliation: To Be or Not To Be: Separate Aboriginal Nationhood or Aboriginal Self-Determination and Self-Government within the Australian Nation?' (1993) 3(61) *Aboriginal Law Bulletin* 15; Charles Perkins, 'Self-Determination and Managing the Future' in Christine Fletcher (ed), *Aboriginal Self-Determination in Australia* (Aboriginal Studies Press 1994). See also Cillian McBride, *Recognition* (Key Concepts 2013).

[338] Anaya (n 110 above) 98.

[339] The UN Declaration on the Rights of Indigenous Peoples (DRIP) in its preamble affirms 'that indigenous peoples are equal to all other peoples, while recognizing the right of all peoples to be

rights co-exist and are related to the rights of all people to be treated equally before the law. Equality principles, after all, allow for 'special measures' in the circumstances.[340] A 'special measures' analysis, however, does not adequately explain Indigenous rights: special measures are temporary, whereas Indigenous rights – particularly rights to land, culture and self-determination – are usually understood as inherent and operating in perpetuity.[341] Whichever paradigm works better as an explanation of Indigenous rights within liberal democratic arrangements, it is clear that Indigenous rights can co-exist with principles of equality and non-discrimination. Arguably, Indigenous peoples should be constitutionally guaranteed both things: equality and self-determination, for Indigenous peoples are both equal individual citizens *and* a distinct constitutional constituency. This is why the liberal equality objection to Indigenous recognition is unpersuasive, especially in a federal context like Australia. Under the federal constitutional compact, a citizen can be Australian, Victorian and of Indian heritage all at the same time (like the author). Notably, if I was Tasmanian, this would entitle me to a more powerful proportional voice in the Senate. So, too, can a citizen be Australian, Victorian and Indigenous at the same time – the difference being that a citizen's Indigeneity may give rise to certain legal rights (like native title) not available to the Indian Victorian Australian. Individual citizenship in a federation is multi-layered.[342] It enables co-existing layers of identity, affiliation and loyalty – united by a common national union under the *Commonwealth Constitution*.

Objectors to Indigenous recognition, however, tend to take a more simplistic view. They argue that a liberal democracy should treat all citizens equally and should not accommodate any recognition of Indigenous difference. Liberal arguments are often used to deny Indigenous claims for recognition.[343] However, liberal individualism too ideologically applied and untempered by pragmatic acknowledgement of the effects of history, colonisation and the power dynamics arising therefrom, risks becoming assimilationist. Charles Taylor explains:

> There is a form of the politics of equal respect, as enshrined in a liberalism of rights, that is inhospitable to difference, because a) it insists on uniform application of the

different, to consider themselves different, and to be respected as such'. The articles also recognise both Indigenous rights to equality and non-discrimination, and rights to self-determination and distinct cultural and other rights.

[340] See Convention for the Elimination of All Forms of Racial Discrimination (CERD), opened for signature 21 December 1965, 660 UNTS 195 (entered into force 4 January 1969) art 1(4): '[s]pecial measures taken for the sole purpose of securing adequate advancement of certain racial or ethnic groups or individuals requiring such protection as may be necessary in order to ensure such groups or individuals equal enjoyment or exercise of human rights and fundamental freedoms shall not be deemed racial discrimination'.

[341] In Australia, courts have tended to use a CERD 'special measures' paradigm to explain legal recognition of Indigenous rights, but this is probably because the only readily available domestic framework operates under the RDA, which explicitly incorporates 'special measures' in s 8.

[342] Chen (n 70 above) 852–53; see also Reilley (n 305 above) 412–13.

[343] See eg Bolt (n 277 above); Sheridan (n 277 above). For arguments critiquing multiculturalism, see Barry (n 277 above).

> rules defining these rights, without exception, and b) it is suspicious of collective goals … I call it inhospitable to difference because it can't accommodate what the members of distinct societies really aspire to, which is survival … I think this form of liberalism is guilty as charged by the proponents of a politics of difference.[344]

Taylor understands 'survival' as a collective goal related to the 'existential problem' that Pearson and other Indigenous leaders describe. Discussing the existential anxiety for the cultural survival of his people, as expressed by Yolngu leader Galarrwuy Yunupingu,[345] Pearson writes: '[i]t is an existential prayer. A prayer on behalf of a people fearing non-existence. Fear that the old trajectory of colonisation and its continuation in the new nation will lead to the disappearance of Yolngu from history.'[346] Pearson characterises constitutional recognition as reform that might enable Indigenous peoples to survive as distinct peoples, rather than to be crushed out of existence by the continued weight of the colonising state.

Hard-line liberal arguments against Indigenous recognition usually try to make everything about the individual and, in doing so, risk obliterating the human importance of the communal. Ideologically wielded, the argument is incongruent with Australia's constitutional reality which recognises political collectives. There are more nuanced approaches, however, that respect the ultimate wisdom of the parliamentary majority while also acknowledging the cultural, political and social importance of groups. Waldron, though a critic of judicially adjudicated rights on the basis that every individual should have an equal share of political decision-making power, nonetheless does not subscribe to the 'bludgeoning rhetoric' utilised by some hard-line liberals to deny any value in groups. For Waldron, the inherent dignity of groups cannot be ruled out 'as a matter of liberal dogma'. Rather, he cautiously accepts that groups may have 'a human importance in terms of culture, identity, destiny that goes beyond what is severally or cumulatively good for the human individuals that it comprises, an importance that cannot be characterized except in communal terms'. While acknowledgement of the dignity of groups within a democracy comes with risks – for example the elevation of certain groups above others, creating unjust division, unrest and inequality – for Waldron that in itself is 'not a reason for eschewing it, when it is appropriate. It is a reason for being careful with our characterization'.[347]

So when might recognition of group status be appropriate within a federal democracy and what would constitute a careful constitutional characterisation

[344] Taylor (n 316 above) 60–61.

[345] Galarrwuy Yunupingu, 'Truth, Tradition and Tomorrow' *The Monthly* (2008) <https://www.themonthly.com.au/issue/2008/december/1268179150/galarrwuy-yunupingu/tradition-truth-tomorrow> accessed 18 October 2019.

[346] Pearson, 'A Rightful Place' (n 15 above) 2.

[347] Jeremy Waldron, 'The Dignity of Groups', Public Law and Legal Theory Research Paper Series, Working Paper No 08-53, New York University School of Law, November 2008 <https://ssrn.com/abstract=1287174> accessed 18 October 2019, 21, 29.

of this status? I argue that, appropriately formulated, constitutional recognition of Indigenous peoples, accommodating and allowing for Indigenous survival as distinct peoples and enabling their voices to be heard in their distinct affairs, would be a modest, careful and appropriate characterisation in a federal liberal democracy like Australia. Taylor explains that some models of liberalism are 'willing to weigh the value of certain forms of uniform treatment against the importance of cultural survival, and opt sometimes in favour of the latter'.[348] Australia could be one such nation that makes space within its constitutional arrangements for Indigenous peoples to exist and prosper both as distinct peoples and as Australians – just as it made space for the former colonies to retain their distinct political identities as States in the federation. Australia's federalism recognises co-existing collectives more than it recognises individual rights. The *Constitution* already guarantees that minority voices are heard: even the smallest former colonies have equal representation in the Senate. Given its nature as a sovereignty-sharing agreement, itself a historical treaty between political communities, Australia's *Constitution* lends itself to recognition of the Indigenous political community and the Indigenous voice in Indigenous affairs.

Taylor's observation that 'liberalism can't and shouldn't claim complete cultural neutrality'[349] is important in making the argument. It is sometimes claimed that Australia's liberal democracy is neutral and favours no culture, and that therefore Indigenous recognition should not be pursued, because there is nothing structurally inequitable about the current arrangements – it is thus the Indigenous individual's or community's responsibility to protect their own culture, protect their own rights and ensure their own survival, rather than any responsibility of the state or state structures. This 'survival of the fittest'-style argument ignores power imbalances and relies on a conception of constitutional neutrality which does not ring true. As Ivison argues, 'given the history of relations between indigenous peoples and the state, it is not only pragmatically wrongheaded but morally misplaced to ask indigenous peoples to imagine the state as "neutral" in any such way.'[350] And as Taylor points out, liberalism 'is also a fighting creed'.[351]

The Australian Constitution is not culturally neutral. It is embedded with British heritage and in a foundational sense, guarantees that British culture and institutions will perpetually remain on Australian soil, so long as the *Constitution* remains in force. The *Constitution* is written in English, makes references to the Queen and sets up democratic and legal structures imported from Britain, and

[348] C Taylor (n 316 above) 61.
[349] ibid 62.
[350] Ivison, *Postcolonial Liberalism* (n 6 above) 16–17, 31. For discussion of postcolonial critiques of liberalism see 39–48.
[351] C Taylor (n 316 above) 62.

even constitutionally recognises the existence of God in the preamble. It also explicitly excluded and discriminated against Indigenous people. The *Constitution*'s establishment did not treat all cultures and peoples neutrally and its operation has not treated all cultures and peoples neutrally. The founding of Australia's *Constitution* was predicated on the fiction of Indigenous inferiority, which justified unequal treatment and non-recognition. The fact that the colonisers did not extend their application of liberal principles equally to Indigenous people dispels any myth of neutrality. Indigenous constitutional recognition, as a remedy to past illiberal non-recognition, can go some way towards rectifying this injustice.

D. Is this About 'Race'?

In discussions about Indigenous constitutional recognition, the question inevitably arises: who are we recognising? How do we define an Indigenous person? A standard three-part definition of an Indigenous Australian person has been operating in Australia since the 1980s in common law and in legislation. It requires Aboriginal and/or Torres Strait Islander descent, self-identification as an Aboriginal and/or Torres Strait Islander person, and acceptance by the community as an Aboriginal and/or Torres Strait Islander person.[352] Properly understood, Indigeneity is not about 'race', though out-dated references to race persist in some legislative definitions. The argument for Indigenous recognition on the basis that Indigenous peoples are a distinct constitutional constituency is not the same as an argument for recognition on the basis that Indigenous people are a separate 'race'.

It is sometimes argued that Indigenous recognition would have the effect of re-inserting racial distinctions back into the *Constitution*, when the intent should be to remove any racial discrimination. Two points must be made in response to this incorrect assumption. Firstly, 'race' is increasingly considered an out-dated pseudo-scientific concept, because the incorrect beliefs on which the notion was based have now been discredited. Race is better understood as a social and political construct historically used to justify division and discrimination.[353]

[352] See eg *Aboriginal Land Rights Act 1983* (NSW) s 4 'definitions'. Note, however, that identification in terms of race persists in some legislation: see eg *Native Title Act 1993* (Cth) s 253; *Aboriginal and Torres Strait Islander Commission Act* (Cth) s 4.

[353] For an in-depth discussion, see Paul C Taylor, *Race: A Philosophical Introduction* (2nd edn, Wiley 2013); Lee D Baker, *From Savage to Negro: Anthropology and the Construction of Race 1896–1954* (University of California Press 1998); Ian F Hanley Lopez, 'The Social Construction of Race: Some Observations on Illusion, Fabrication and Choice' (1994) 29(1) *Harvard Civil Rights–Civil Liberties Law Review* 1; Audrey Smedley and Brian D Smedley, 'Race as Biology is Fiction, Racism as a Social Problem is Real: Anthropological and Historical Perspectives on the Social Construction of Race' (2005) 60(1) *American Psychologist* 16.

As Ta-Nehisi Coates explains, the concept of 'race' as a biological fact has been integral to the perpetuation and justification of racism:

> Racism – the need to ascribe bone-deep features to people, then humiliate, reduce, and destroy them – inevitably follows from this inalterable condition. In this way, racism is rendered the innocent daughter of Mother Nature …
>
> But race is the child of racism, not the father. And the process of naming 'the people' has never been a matter of genealogy or physiognomy so much as one of hierarchy.[354]
>
> There is no longer any scientific basis for dividing and hierarchically ranking ethnic groups. There are no superior or inferior races. It is now widely understood that there is only one race – the human race.[355]

Secondly, Indigeneity is not the same as race, though the idea of Indigeneity and ethnicity or 'race' can be related. Pearson explains that '[i]ndigeneity … is not about race. In many northern European countries the indigenous people are white. Indigeneity is about historical connection and political status, and the rights and interests arising therefrom.'[356] Indigeneity, in the ambit of constitutional law, is most accurately described as a historical, political and legal status related to descent and inheritance; but it is not the same thing as being a member of a definitive, scientifically-defined race. For example, if the dispossessed peoples of Australia had by chance been white-skinned, like the Sámi peoples in Scandinavia, they should still today be entitled to their native title rights to remedy past dispossession, and they might still seek constitutional recognition of their distinct rights and interests so that those rights and interests are not violated or undermined. If Indigenous peoples had been white, they should still properly be characterised as a distinct constitutional constituency now requiring a just form of constitutional recognition to help enable their survival as distinct peoples and to prevent the repeat of past injustices. The distinction is subtle but important. If Indigenous recognition is on the basis of race, then such claims can more easily be criticised as arbitrary discrimination – race itself being an arbitrary and illusory category based on unjust discrimination. A better view is that recognition is required because Indigenous peoples are a distinct constitutional constituency, appropriately entitled to some distinct rights and interests arising from their historical, political and legal status as the descendants of the original occupants and owners of the land – regardless of supposed race.

[354] Ta-Nehisi Coates, *Between the World and Me* (Text Publishing 2015) 7.

[355] See Pritchard (n 76 above) 50–51. Given that the race clauses in the *Constitution* allowed for and promoted unjust discrimination on the basis of race, it may now be appropriate that such constitutional clauses be removed or appropriately amended. The Uluru Statement did not ask for such reforms, however. As a matter of practicality, the Race Power supports laws with respect to Indigenous affairs. If it were to be removed, it would need to be appropriately replaced.

[356] Pearson, 'Indigenous people need a lot more than just symbolism' (n 92 above). See also Shireen Morris, 'False Equality' in Shireen Morris (ed), *A Rightful Place: A Roadmap to Recognition* (Black Inc 2017).

As McHugh notes, reflecting on the relationship between the Māori and the Crown in New Zealand,

> the Treaty of Waitangi was not a treaty between a race and a monarch. It was a treaty between a group of tribal political formations represented through their customary leaders with another formation, an imperial one represented by and through its young Queen.[357]

Indigenous constitutional recognition seeks to reform a constitutional relationship between political communities, or constitutional constituencies. It is not about race.

Former Chief Justice, Murray Gleeson, takes a more pragmatic approach to the problem of race and its relationship with Indigenous recognition:

> The history of the twentieth century demonstrated the evil of racism, and race itself is a concept based on insecure conceptual foundations. It does not follow, however, that the term is unmentionable, or that any governmental action predicated upon race must be wrong. It has a firm footing in the Constitution …
>
> In whatever country is under consideration, being Indigenous could be regarded as a matter of history, or geography, or ethnicity. This may be unlikely to matter to the Indigenous people themselves. If, as our leaders often say, we have among us a group of people who have a special place in our history, and we are satisfied they deserve a certain form of recognition on that account, it would be driving ideology to an extreme to decline them that recognition because they form what could be regarded, and is regarded by the Constitution itself, as a racial group.[358]

The *Constitution* since 1901 has recognised the category of race and has treated Indigenous people differently on the basis of race, often unjustly. Empowering the voices of Indigenous peoples in their affairs would guard against unjust discrimination.

E. Recognition versus Sovereignty

Glen Coulthard, in the Canadian context, challenges 'the increasingly commonplace assumption that the colonial relationship between Indigenous peoples and the … state can be reconciled via a liberal "politics of recognition"'. He argues that the

> recognition-based approach to reconciling Indigenous peoples' assertions of nationhood with settler-state sovereignty via the accommodation of Indigenous identity-related claims … is still *colonial* insofar as it remains structurally committed

[357] PG McHugh, 'Treaty Principles: Constitutional Relations Inside a Conservative Jurisprudence' (2008) 39(1) *Victoria University of Wellington Law Review* 39, 50.

[358] Gleeson, 'Recognition in Keeping with the Constitution' (n 193 above) 16.

to the dispossession of Indigenous peoples of our lands and self-determining authority.[359]

It is an analysis that aligns with critiques in the Australian context that suggest Indigenous people should seek 'sovereignty' rather than mere recognition.[360] The argument views constitutional recognition as a subordinate acceptance of, rather than resistance to, continued colonial rule. It equates recognition with continued oppression and 'sovereignty' with independence, freedom and self-determination.[361]

The word 'sovereignty' has many different meanings and various uses in the debate about Indigenous constitutional recognition. Complex notions of Indigenous sovereignty can be discussed theoretically, but they must also be considered practically and strategically. Further, separatist, external understandings should be distinguished from internal, inclusive notions.[362] If separatist, international notions of sovereignty are desired, what is the political plan for achieving this? Legally, Australian courts have confirmed that the sovereignty of the Australian state cannot be challenged in domestic courts.[363] Court challenges, whether domestic or international, do not provide an avenue for making the state disappear: the Australian state is a political reality. As the story of colonisation and the frontier wars demonstrate, sovereignty practically speaking is not a matter of moral or legal right, but a military force that is asserted, often brutally. In a deeply imbalanced power relationship, it is the Australian state that wields more power. A three per cent highly disadvantaged minority will find it difficult to assert the force required to overthrow the state or reclaim their territory through force.

[359] Glen Sean Coulthard, *Red Skin, White Masks Book: Rejecting the Colonial Politics of Recognition* (University of Minnesota Press 2014) 151; Glen Coulthard, 'Subjects of Empire: Indigenous Peoples and the "Politics of Recognition" in Canada' (2007) 6(4) *Contemporary Political Theory* 437. See also Lino, *Constitutional Recognition* (n 71 above) 90–95. For other discussions sceptical of recognition see Frantz Fanon, *Black Skin, White Masks* (Pluto Press 1986); Elizabeth A Povinelli, 'The Cunning of Recognition: Real Being and Aboriginal Recognition in Settler Australia' (1998) 11(1) *Australian Feminist Law Journal* 3; Elizabeth Povinelli, *The Cunning of Recognition: Indigenous Alterities and the Making of Australian Multiculturalism* (Duke University Press 2002).

[360] See response to this view in Megan Davis, 'Constitutional Recognition Does Not Foreclose on Aboriginal Sovereignty' (2012) 8(1) *Indigenous Law Bulletin* 12.

[361] See Dylan Lino, 'Indigenous Recognition' in Rosalind Dixson (ed), *Australian Constitutional Values* (Hart Publishing 2018) 247–48. See also Andrew Schaap, 'Political Reconciliation through a Struggle for Recognition?' (2004) 13(4) *Social & Legal Studies* 524.

[362] Macklem distinguishes between these two types of sovereignty, noting that sovereignty 'means different things to different people. Its meaning is not entirely shared across particular groups, societies, or cultures, nor does sovereignty's meaning somehow inhere in the word. Instead, its meaning or value is a function of interpretive acts by those who possess it and those who seek it. Sovereignty is a contested site of interpretation, and thus remains open to transformation and application to diverse forms of human association.': Patrick Macklem, 'Distributing Sovereignty' (n 306 above) 1346–47. For discussion of how Indigenous claims of sovereignty interact with the sovereignty of nation states under international law see Patrick Macklem, 'Indigenous Recognition in International Law: Theoretical Observations' (2008) 30(1) *Michigan Journal of International Law* 177, 182–85.

[363] *Mabo* (n 25 above) 31–32; *New South Wales* (n 51 above) 388; *Coe* (n 52 above).

Aboriginal lawyer Michael Mansell urges that pragmatism rather than strict idealism may be required in the pursuit of substantive, structural reform. Though reforms for Indigenous self-determination must utilise and deal with state laws and structures, this need not equate to moral acceptance of colonial domination. As Mansell observes, 'A people who have no choice but to deal with the occupier are not necessarily agreeing to the legitimacy of the occupier's rule.' Thus, if Indigenous people are successful in achieving the structural reforms they desire, thereby making Australia a 'better country', Mansell suggests 'it may not matter whether the outcome is labelled "Australian" or "Aboriginal" sovereignty.'[364] The substantive result seems more important than adhering to purist language. Mansell's argument suggests an inclusive understanding of Indigenous sovereignty as the only workable way forward.

This accords with the practical reality. For all the ills of history, Indigenous and Non-Indigenous Australians are now living in this country together, with lives and futures irrevocably entwined. Thus, hard-line separatism may no longer be a feasible option. More importantly, however, as the history of Indigenous advocacy demonstrates, separatism is not generally sought by proponents of Indigenous constitutional recognition and structural reform. To the contrary, the predominant goal appears to be fairer inclusion and structural empowerment within Australia. Representative bodies, reserved parliamentary seats, treaties and rights guarantees are all mechanisms for inclusive Indigenous empowerment within the Australian state. Properly understood, constitutional recognition is inclusive, rather than separatist, in its understanding of Indigenous sovereignty.

While some Indigenous activists use the language of sovereignty to oppose constitutional recognition on grounds that it is too weak and subordinate to the state, at the other end of the spectrum non-Indigenous opponents have used fear-mongering about sovereignty claims to argue that Indigenous advocates for constitutional reform in fact seek to divide and fragment the Australian state in pursuit of their own separate state or nation.[365] The latter arguments misinterpret the Indigenous politics: most Indigenous activists who harbour aspirations for separate-state sovereignty in the international sense tend not to support

[364] Mansell (n 97 above) 18. Lino also suggests that because dissolving the state is 'politically unfeasible' and dissolving the Indigenous-state relationship would create new injustices, creating a fairer constitutional relationship 'is a pragmatic response in circumstances where there is no realistic alternative'. See Lino (n 361 above) 248.

[365] See eg the argument that constitutional recognition would force 'me to ask to be seen by you in a colonial system that I don't want to legitimise' and preferring a treaty, because 'Treaties are legal mechanisms between two parties that recognise one another's sovereignty'.: Nayuka Gorrie, 'Fuck Your Constitutional Recognition, I Want a Treaty', *Vice* (online, 17 March 2016) <https://www.vice.com/en_au/article/qb5zdp/fuck-your-recognition>. Contrast this with Windschuttle's argument that constitutional recognition is a backdoor way of achieving Indigenous sovereignty in Keith Windschuttle's book *The Break-Up of Australia: The Real Agenda Behind Aboriginal Recognition* (Quadrant 2016).

constitutional recognition for precisely this reason – constitutional recognition is inclusive and, to genuine separatists, it is problematically integrationist.[366]

A non-separatist, non-military, inclusive notion of surviving Indigenous sovereignty was articulated by International Court of Justice judge, Fouad Ammoun, in the *Western Sahara case* (1975). Ammoun described Indigenous peoples' sovereignty as

> a spiritual notion: the ancestral tie between the land, or 'mother nature', and the man who was born therefrom, remains attached thereto, and must one day return thither to be united with his ancestors. This link is the basis of the ownership of the soil, or better, of sovereignty.[367]

This understanding of sovereignty can co-exist peacefully and inclusively with the sovereignty of Australian governments. Internal, domestic Indigenous (as opposed to external, international) sovereignty can be expressed through notions of increased Indigenous responsibility and empowerment within domestic arrangements. The proposal for an Indigenous constitutional voice would enable greater Indigenous input into political decisions concerning Indigenous people. Offering non-binding advice, such a body would create a platform for increased Indigenous agency in Indigenous affairs. This kind of inclusive Indigenous participation is practised in many countries, as will be further discussed in Chapter four. New Zealand has a Māori Council and reserved Māori parliamentary seats. Scandinavia has Sámi Parliaments, which are Indigenous advisory bodies to government. Canada has the Assembly of First Nations and a Crown duty to consult with Aboriginal peoples. Through such mechanisms, the non-separatist sense of surviving Indigenous sovereignty can work productively with governments, and mutually respectful Indigenous-state relationships can be created. Recognition of this kind is the middle ground alternative to assimilation and annihilation of Indigenous peoples on one hand, and separatism and fragmentation of the state on the other. This is the 'radical centre' to which constitutional recognition aspires.

James 'Youngblood' Henderson, reflecting positively on how constitutional recognition and protection of Aboriginal and treaty rights under section 35 of the Canadian Constitution has enabled productive incorporation of Aboriginal sovereignty into Canadian jurisprudence, describes Aboriginal sovereignty as

[366] See for example, the delegates who dissented at the Uluru constitutional convention. Laudiana Blanco, '"We Won't Sell Out Our Mob": Delegates Walk Out of Constitutional Recognition Forum in Protest', *NITV News* (online, 25 May 2017): <https://www.sbs.com.au/nitv/nitv-news/article/2017/05/25/breaking-delegates-walk-out-constitutional-recognition-forum-protest>. See also arguments in Shireen Morris, 'Separatism through indigenous recognition an irrational fear', *The Australian*, 28 October 2016. <https://www.theaustralian.com.au/commentary/opinion/separatism-through-indigenous-recognition-an-irrational-fear/news-story/b042fef00118e5a6b727bdaf9ee731b2>.

[367] *Western Sahara (Advisory Opinion)* [1975] ICJ Rep 12, 85–86 (Vice-President Ammoun). See also *Mabo* (n 25 above) 41.

engaging notions of knowledge, understanding and relationships, rather than dominance and force:

> Aboriginal sovereignty has always operated by its own force derived from the knowledge and languages of Aboriginal peoples. In Aboriginal thought, sovereignty is not about absolute power, but the subtle art of generating and sustaining relationships. It is a distinct vision about the way humans lived together and behaved in a kinship and an ecosystem, a distinct tradition of philosophies and humanities. It is a distinct philosophy of justice and legal traditions based on spiritual and ecological understandings and linguistic conventions that are interconnected. It operates as an implicit, inherent, dramatic, epistemic, unwritten, and living concept.[368]

On Henderson's analysis, constitutional recognition of Aboriginal and treaty rights in Canada has enabled Aboriginal sovereignty to be animated through a 'resourceful constitutional analysis' in judicial interpretation of section 35.[369] It has given Aboriginal sovereignty new life and relevance.

In Australia, as the Uluru Statement suggests, constitutional recognition could mean a carving out of Indigenous authority and a sharing of power, not through judicial adjudication as in Canada – the Referendum Council makes clear that a First Nations constitutional voice should be non-justiciable[370] – but through an increased Indigenous voice in political processes with respect to Indigenous affairs. If constitutional recognition creates structural space for Indigenous peoples to be represented and recognised as distinct peoples with the state, this could be a recognition of surviving and co-existing Indigenous sovereignty or nationhood in the inclusive, peaceful sense. Reformed constitutional arrangements could allow this surviving and co-existing Indigenous sovereignty to shine through and express itself more effectively. As the Uluru Statement puts it, paraphrasing the *Western Sahara case*:

> Our Aboriginal and Torres Strait Islander tribes were the first sovereign Nations of the Australian continent and its adjacent islands, and possessed it under our own laws and customs …
>
> *This sovereignty is a spiritual notion: the ancestral tie between the land, or 'mother nature', and the Aboriginal and Torres Strait Islander peoples who were born therefrom, remain attached thereto, and must one day return thither to be united with our ancestors. This link is the basis of the ownership of the soil, or better, of sovereignty.* It has never been ceded or extinguished, and co-exists with the sovereignty of the Crown …
>
> With substantive constitutional change and structural reform, we believe this ancient sovereignty can shine through as a fuller expression of Australia's nationhood.

[368] James (Sa'ke'j) Youngblood Henderson, 'Constitutional Vision and Judicial Commitment: Aboriginal and Treaty Rights in Canada' (2010) 14(2) *Australian Indigenous Law Review* 24, 30.
[369] Ibid, 31.
[370] *Final Report of the Referendum Council* (n 147 above) 38.

Recognising and including Indigenous peoples within the constitutional compact through ensuring them a voice in their affairs, could be a practical recognition of surviving and co-existing Indigenous sovereignty in a form compatible with the sovereignty of the Australian state. As Macklem explains, the value of using the language of 'sovereignty' in such arguments is that:

> [I]t represents a legal or constitutional space in which a community can express its collective identity. Viewed in this light, sovereignty attaches to collectivities, not individuals. Invoking equality of individuals to assess the justice of distributions of sovereignty conflicts with both the nature of sovereignty's recipients and the value of sovereignty itself. The principles used to judge the distribution of sovereignty ought to reflect the collective dimension of the good being distributed. The distribution of sovereignty ought to be judged by reference to equality of peoples, not equality of individuals.[371]

Indigenous surviving sovereignty in Australia could be expressed through constitutional reform enabling increased Indigenous self-determination, agency and empowerment, without compromising Australian state sovereignty. As the Referendum Council makes clear, a First Nations constitutional voice would entail no veto.[372] Indigenous surviving sovereignty expressed through such a constitutional voice would uphold parliamentary supremacy and Australian sovereignty. This would peacefully reconcile the sovereignty of the Australian state with the surviving sovereignty of the First Nations.

F. Indigenous Self-determination within Domestic Democratic Processes

James Anaya explains the right to self-determination as deriving from a 'philosophical affirmation of the human drive to translate aspiration into reality, coupled with postulates of inherent human equality'.[373] As noted, self-determination is the right to freely pursue personal and community development: especially political, economic, social and cultural development and determination. In the context of Indigenous peoples, self-determination tends to refer to the right to self-govern,[374] exercise autonomy and political agency and make free choices about their futures as peoples within states.[375]

[371] Patrick Macklem, 'Distributing Sovereignty' (n 306 above) 1353. See also Paul Chartrand, 'Reconciling Indigenous Peoples' Sovereignty and State Sovereignty', Research Discussion Paper 26 (Australian Institute of Aboriginal and Torres Strait Islander Studies).

[372] *Final Report of the Referendum Council* (n 147 above) 36.

[373] Anaya (n 110 above) 98. See art 1 of both the International Covenant on Civil and Political Rights and the International Covenant on Economic, Social and Cultural Rights.

[374] Anaya notes that 'self-government is the overarching political dimension of ongoing self-determination': Anaya (n 110 above) 150.

[375] Declaration on the Rights of Indigenous Peoples (DRIP), arts 3–4. See also Australian Human Rights Commission, *Right to Self-Determination* <https://www.humanrights.gov.au/right-self-determination> accessed 18 October 2019.

Self-determination seeks to carve out space within the state's institutional and political structures, for Indigenous peoples to exist and to exercise authority over their lives and directions as peoples.[376] It provides a respectful and inclusive approach, in direct opposition to colonial and past policies often based on paternalism and compulsion, which limited Indigenous free choice through unilateral exercise of government force and power. While the worst oppression is in the past, some argue that the discriminatory and paternalistic treatment of Indigenous people continues today. As the 2012 Expert Panel report explained, drawing on its consultation with Indigenous communities:

> [A]t many consultations, it was suggested that current policies have limited capacity of Aboriginal and Torres Strait Islander people to exercise self-determination. Issues raised in this context included the Northern Territory Emergency Response, non-recognition of governance structure and of customary law, and administrative practices in the funding and delivery of programs to … communities. Many participants saw constitutional recognition as a way to return some self-governance to individuals and communities.[377]

Pearson concludes that 'Indigenous self-determination is a domestic democratic question', requiring nations to accommodate Indigenous peoples within national frameworks and to articulate mechanisms for self-determination within democratic and institutional arrangements.[378] Thus Indigenous self-determination should not frighten governments fearing secession and separatism.[379] Rather, self-determination – in the context of constitutional recognition at least – seeks recognition, accommodation and expression of Indigenous self-determination principles within existing constitutional and institutional arrangements. Indigenous academic Megan Davis agrees:

> [I]t is internal domestic political arrangements that accommodate indigenous peoples' voice, that give full expression to the right to self-determination … self-determination is no symbolic, wishy washy idea. It is about giving people control over their lives. It is not viewed as separatist but as enhancing democracy.[380]

In comparable liberal democracies, the Indigenous right to self-determination is increasingly operationalised. It is managed by structuring the relationship between Indigenous peoples and the colonising state to ensure that processes and procedures are fairer, less oppressive and more inclusive than in the past.[381]

[376] Pearson, 'A Rightful Place' (n 15 above) 6–7.
[377] Expert Panel Report (n 41 above) 93–94.
[378] Pearson, 'A Rightful Place' (n 15 above) 41–46.
[379] Anaya (n 110 above) 102–3, 105–6.
[380] Megan Davis, 'A Rightful Place: Correspondence. Response to Noel Pearson's *Quarterly Essay*' (n 254 above).
[381] See Chapter 4 of this volume for discussion of international examples. Anaya (n 110 above) 63; Pearson, 'A Rightful Place' (n 15 above) 41–46. See also Dylan Lino, 'The Politics of Inclusion: The Right of Self-Determination, Statutory Bills of Rights, and Indigenous Peoples' (2010) 34(3) *Melbourne University Law Review* 829, 868.

This inclusive, domestic conception of self-determination is compatible with democracy and national unity,[382] and can include guarantees and processes for fairer engagement, participation and negotiation between Indigenous peoples and government.[383] The Indigenous right to self-determination is therefore often associated with the right of Indigenous peoples to be specifically consulted and to participate in the making of laws affecting their rights and interests.[384]

The importance of consultation and consent where legislative action affects Indigenous rights is also incorporated into racial non-discrimination principles at international law. Special measures or positive measures to ensure disadvantaged groups – including Indigenous groups – equal enjoyment of their human rights, particularly in a context where there has been past or historical discrimination,[385] are supposed to be implemented with the informed consent of the beneficiaries.[386] The High Court has noted that proper consultation and the 'wishes of the beneficiaries' may be an important factor in ascertaining whether a particular law or measure is a valid special measure.[387] French CJ in *R v Maloney* explains that:

> [I]t should be accepted, as a matter of common sense, that prior consultation with an affected community and its substantial acceptance of a proposed special measure is likely to be essential to the practical implementation of that measure. That is particularly so where … the measure … involves the imposition on the affected community of a restriction on some aspect of the freedoms otherwise enjoyed by its members.[388]

Despite noting the practical importance of consultation in the effective implementation and acceptance of special measures, however, the High Court in *Maloney* found that consultation is not a decisive legal requirement of a valid special measure under Australian law. Nonetheless, there is a clear logical and practical link between non-discrimination and consultation: processes for genuine consultation and negotiation can prevent discriminatory action by

[382] 'Internal self-determination' as described by Russell A Miller, 'Collective Discursive Democracy as the Indigenous Right to Self-Determination' (2006–07) 31(2) *American Indian Law Review* 341, 346; Anaya (n 110 above) 105. See also Pearson, 'Reconciliation: To be or not to be' (n 337 above); Charles Perkins, 'Self-Determination and Managing the Future' in Christine Fletcher (ed), *Aboriginal Self-Determination in Australia* (Aboriginal Studies Press 1994).

[383] Anaya (n 110 above) 153–56.

[384] Articles 18 and 19 of DRIP.

[385] CERD, art 1(4).

[386] CERD, General Recommendation No 23, 'Indigenous Peoples', 18 August 1997 para 4(d); Australian Human Rights and Equal Opportunities Commission, *Social Justice Report 2007*, Recommendations 7, 14.

[387] 'The wishes of the beneficiaries for the measure are of great importance (perhaps essential) in determining whether a measure is taken for the purpose of securing their advancement. The dignity of the beneficiaries is impaired and they are not advanced by having an unwanted material benefit foisted on them.': *Gerhardy v Brown* (n 270 above) 135 (Brennan J).

[388] *R v Maloney* (2014) 252 CLR 168, 186.

government and are a common expression of the Indigenous self-determination principle internationally.[389]

Miller thus proposes a practical 'interpretation of indigenous peoples' self-determination that insists upon the reality of and managing the discourse between … collective entities' – Indigenous peoples and the state.[390] This requires an expression of Indigenous self-determination through national institutions.[391] Lino similarly argues that the self-determination principle is best expressed by establishing rules and procedures for fair negotiation, engagement and consultation between the state and Indigenous peoples.[392] Rather than 'juridification' of the ambiguous right to self-determination in a Bill of rights, leaving courts the authority to determine the content of the right, Lino contends that the 'law may be better put to use indirectly in structuring negotiation systems and balancing negotiating power between parties … elaborating the terms of the Indigenous-state relationship or establishing procedures for negotiation between Indigenous peoples and the state'.[393] These arguments are particularly apt in Australia, where parliamentary supremacy prevails. As Anaya explains, Indigenous self-determination within postcolonial states seeks to enable 'effective participation in the larger political order', thus 'allowing indigenous peoples to achieve meaningful self-determination through political institutions and consultative arrangements … that permit them to be genuinely associated with all decisions that affect them on an ongoing basis'.[394]

While this book explores constitutional mechanisms for Indigenous consultation, representation and participation, it will not explore constitutional mechanisms for facilitating the Indigenous right to 'free prior and informed consent' under Article 19 of DRIP. Indigenous 'free prior and informed consent' at the constitutional level may be practically unworkable and politically unviable. Miller describes it as engaging in a 'level of discourse' that may go so far as granting Indigenous people 'a veto in the covered fields'.[395] A constitutionalised veto would likely be opposed on the grounds that it undermines parliamentary supremacy.[396] Given that my aim here is to consider constitutional reform options that speak to Indigenous concerns and also respond to concerns about the compromising of parliamentary supremacy through constitutional rights

[389] Anaya (n 110 above) 153–56.
[390] Miller (n 382 above) 358.
[391] Anaya (n 110 above) 99.
[392] Lino, 'The Politics of Inclusion' (n 381 above) 867–68.
[393] ibid 867–68.
[394] Anaya (n 110 above) 153–56.
[395] Miller (n 382 above) 369.
[396] Jeffrey Goldsworthy also explains that the transfer of decision-making authority to another body would be a breach of parliamentary sovereignty: 'by forbidding Parliament to enact law without the approval of an external body-namely, the electorate-it plainly limits its substantive authority': Jeffrey Goldsworthy, 'Abdicating Parliamentary Sovereignty' (2006) 17(2) *Kings College Law Journal* 255, 276.

clauses, options for a constitutionalised consent requirement are omitted in favour of 'softer', practical and politically more feasible options to give Indigenous people an authoritative, but not binding, say in political processes with respect to Indigenous rights and interests. As Miller argues:

> The discursive commitment provided by 'consultation and cooperation' is weaker than 'free, prior and informed consent,' particularly because it lacks a consensual element … This may be justified to some extent in order to promote efficiency with respect to practical decision-making.[397]

For some, mere consultation regarding laws and policies with respect to Indigenous affairs is too weak, and no substitute for stronger notions of consent and veto. Notions of consent may be more workable where Indigenous rights are territorially confined. However, in discussions of constitutional reform which encompass the whole country, a three per cent Indigenous minority veto over majoritarian decisions appears impracticable, even in relation to decisions concerning specific Indigenous rights. Laws with respect to Indigenous rights (the law regarding Native Title, for example) must still weigh up competing Indigenous and non-Indigenous interests. It is difficult to make the argument that, where there are competing claims and concerns, the three per cent minority should have a veto over the interests of the 97 per cent majority. Further, it is unlikely that Parliament or the people would agree to such a constitutional reform. For these reasons, I do not argue for a First Nations veto power here.[398]

G. Symbolism versus Practical Reform

Within this nuanced conversation, the difficulty in distinguishing between recognition measures which enhance fairness in the relationship between Indigenous peoples and the state, and those that perpetuate unfairness, is readily apparent. As a starting point, fairness in a symbolic sense should be distinguished from fairness in practice. Sometimes, however, symbolism and practicality can collide and coincide – they can be difficult to distinguish. For example, constitutional Bills of rights (often seen, particularly in the Australian debate, as offering practical, substantive constitutional protections) can sometimes be pursued for their symbolic value more than their operational results. Indeed, many countries have a Bill of rights, but many of them do not in practice respect the human rights of

[397] Miller (n 382 above) 371.

[398] This book also does not consider arguments for separate Indigenous governments, a seventh Aboriginal State, or separate Indigenous Parliaments with law-making capacity. See Mansell (n 97 above) Chapters 9 and 10.

their citizens.[399] Observing a potential danger in pursuing litigation alone as a strategy for rights protection, Rosenberg observes that

> [s]ymbolic victories may be mistaken for substantive ones, covering a reality that is distasteful. Rather than working to change that reality, reformers may be misled (or content?) to celebrate the illusion of change. There is a danger that symbolic gains cover for actual failings.[400]

The 'illusion of change' is perhaps the greatest strategic risk in the pursuit of Indigenous constitutional recognition. It is unclear, for example, whether insertion of a racial non-discrimination clause would yield equality of outcomes and equality in practice, or whether it would be more of a symbolic statement with occasional practical effect. Conversely, some would argue that a symbolic preamble, intended to have only symbolic effect, could eventually yield practical (even if unintended) reform, perhaps through its use in judicial interpretation of the *Constitution*.[401] Others argue that symbolic statements can engender important attitudinal and cultural changes which can eventually prompt practical reform.[402] As the New Zealand example demonstrates through the Treaty of Waitangi (discussed in more detail in Chapter four) sometimes a form of recognition of itself lacking in legally enforceable power can nonetheless, over time, prompt significant practical change through the moral and political authority that it comes to wield and the political, cultural and structural reform it encourages.[403] Symbolism can be given practical substance when principles are translated into legislative action. The danger, however, is in settling for symbolism that does not and perhaps never will prompt practical change. In my view, this is why a purely symbolic constitutional change must be rejected. A purely symbolic statement may create the illusion of change, rather than actual change, such that Australian politicians and people may incorrectly feel that the problem has been solved – the Indigenous constitutional recognition box has been ticked – when in actual fact the relationship remains as practically and operationally unfair as it was before the symbolic statement was inserted.[404]

[399] Ratnapala (n 233 above) 609.

[400] Gerald N Rosenberg, 'Constitutional Cants' in Charles Stampford and Tom Round (eds), *Beyond the Republic* (Federation Press 2001) 227. On symbolism in the Indigenous constitutional recognition debate, see also Megan Davis, 'Australia's Reconciliation Process in its International Context: Recognition and the Health and Wellbeing of Australia's Aboriginal and Torres Strait Islander Peoples' (2014–2015) 18(2) *Australian Indigenous Law Review* 56, 62.

[401] Leeser (n 275 above).

[402] Frank Brennan, *No Small Change* (University of Queensland Press 2015). For more on the complex interplay between symbolism and substantive reform, see Lino, *Constitutional Recognition* (n 71 above) 101–5.

[403] It is interesting to note that, as Kingsbury explains, when the New Zealand Bill of rights was being formulated, 'many Māori were unwilling to have the Treaty placed in a formal hierarchy of written law in a way that might compromise its mana, or special authority': Kingsbury (n 305 above) 103.

[404] For discussion of symbolism generally in the Indigenous recognition debate, see Davis, 'Political Timetables' (n 135 above) 62, 81, 88.

Strategically speaking, creating the illusion of change may be worse than doing nothing. The 2007 Apology to Australia's Indigenous Peoples for the Stolen Generations, for example, was not accompanied by any practical measures or financial compensation.[405] Pearson argued that Indigenous people accepting the Apology without compensation was a strategic mistake. His fear was that '[b]lack fellas will get the words; the white fellas will keep the money. And by Thursday the stolen generations and their apology will be over as a political issue.'[406] This anxiety was well-founded. The Apology turned out to be purely symbolic and, more than a decade later, conversations about compensation are only sporadically beginning.[407] The lesson remains salient for current Indigenous struggles to achieve constitutional recognition that is more than symbolic words and includes empowering reforms to propel positive, enduring, practical change.

This book argues that Indigenous constitutional recognition should involve practical and substantive constitutional reform rather than symbolism alone. It must involve some kind of constitutional guarantee of fairer future treatment for Indigenous peoples. Australia's *Constitution*, as discussed, is a practical and pragmatic rulebook full of intergenerational promises or guarantees. It is mostly devoid of aspirational statements and symbolic content.[408] Fitting with the nature of this rulebook, constitutional recognition of Indigenous peoples should involve an appropriate constitutional guarantee – an adjusted, enduring rule or promise. Further, the type of constitutional reform adopted should be in keeping with the nature of Australia's *Constitution*. Australia's *Constitution* contains rules, procedures and principles.[409] Its rules, procedures and principles bring to life the relationships between the Commonwealth and the States, between the courts and the Parliament, and between citizens and governments under the *Constitution*. Equally, the lack of fair rules, procedures and principles with respect to Indigenous affairs is the omission that has for so long enlivened calls for Indigenous constitutional recognition. Constitutional recognition

[405] Michelle Grattan and Tony Wright, 'Rudd Rules Out Compensation', *The Age* (2 February 2008) <https://www.theage.com.au/national/rudd-rules-out-compensation-20080202-ge6oe1.html> accessed 18 October 2019.

[406] Noel Pearson, 'Contradictions Cloud the Apology to the Stolen Generations', *The Australian* (12 February 2008) <https://www.theaustralian.com.au/news/inquirer/when-words-arent-enough/news-story/e43231637f093d2d84f5d5c23c11fbd2> accessed 18 October 2019.

[407] James Robertson, 'Stolen Generations Compensation Scheme to Open', *Sydney Morning Herald* (30 June 2017) <https://www.smh.com.au/national/nsw/stolen-generations-compensation-scheme-to-open-20170630-gx20y1.html> accessed 18 October 2019; Adam Gartrell, 'Labor Promises Stolen Generations Compensation Fund', *Sydney Morning Herald* (12 February 2018) <https://www.smh.com.au/politics/federal/labor-promises-stolen-generations-compensation-fund-20180211-p4yzya.html> accessed 18 October 2019. See also Lawry (n 170 above).

[408] Goldsworthy, 'Constitutional Cultures' (n 220 above) 687–88.

[409] Jack Balkin distinguishes four types of textual devices that are employed within constitutions: rules, standards, principles and silences: see Jack Balkin, *Living Originalism* (Harvard University Press 2011). See also Brendan Lim, 'Review Essay: An Australian Reads "Living Originalism"' (2012) 34(4) *Sydney Law Review* 809, 812.

seeks to address the relationship between Indigenous peoples and the state, to make it fairer than in the past. This cannot be achieved through symbolism alone: it requires a practical change to some constitutional rules, procedures or principles.

Most importantly, a First Nations constitutional voice is what Indigenous Australians have asked for. A symbolic constitutional insertion was rejected by the Uluru Statement. There would be no point pursuing a form of Indigenous recognition that Indigenous people do not want. A minimalist, purely symbolic statement should therefore be off the table.[410]

H. Participation: The Indigenous Right of Rights in the Australian Constitutional Context?

Waldron contends that participation is the 'right of rights'. By that he means political participation is a right 'whose exercise seems peculiarly appropriate in situations where reasonable right-bearers disagree about what rights they have'.[411] Why do I keep returning to Waldron? In many ways it is because of his opposition to judicially adjudicated rights guarantees. Waldron's arguments echo the objections to judicial review that propelled political resistance to a racial non-discrimination clause as proposed by the Expert Panel in 2012 (these objections are analysed in the next chapter). Such objections gave rise to the author's exploration of a non-justiciable, political process-centred alternative: a constitutionally guaranteed Indigenous representative body, to ensure Indigenous peoples fairer participation in political decision-making with respect to their rights. The debate about Indigenous constitutional recognition needs to come to grips with a Waldronian view of rights and constitutional law, adapted to the Australian federal context where the voices of the historic political communities are guaranteed and strong attachment to parliamentary supremacy is a defining characteristic.

The importance of political participation in thinking about Indigenous constitutional recognition arises because of the inevitability of disagreement in matters of justice. This centrality of disagreement is also embraced in Ivison's work on postcolonial liberalism. As Ivison points out, 'living with disagreement … requires a belief in the effectiveness and general trustworthiness of the main political institutions'. Ivison explains,

> [t]he tension between substance and procedures is central to postcolonial liberalism, as is disagreement over justice. The legitimacy of any set of democratic procedures

[410] See also Megan Davis, 'Australia's Reconciliation Process in its International Context' (n 400 above) 62; Davis, 'Political Timetables' (n 135 above) 80–81, 88; for further discussion see Dylan Lino, 'Written Constitutions and the Politics of Recognition: Symbolism and Substance', paper presented at the *World Congress of Constitutional Law*, University of Oslo, 16–20 June, 2014.

[411] See Waldron, 'Participation' (n 247 above) 308. See also arguments made in Jeremy Waldron, *The Dignity of Legislation* (Cambridge University Press 1999).

> is dependent on substantive claims about justice, not only in terms of the actual results of the processes, but of the norms and values promoted by the procedures themselves.'[412]

Procedural fairness in political decision-making is therefore of crucial importance in decision-making about Indigenous affairs, because Indigenous peoples have good reason to mistrust colonising political institutions.

Fair procedural participation is also integral to Waldron's thinking. In relying on Parliament as the best adjudicator and defender of rights about which citizens habitually disagree, Waldron assumes that a functioning, robust legislature is a 'large deliberative body' that can deal with complex issues of justice and policy, and that law-making procedures are 'elaborate and responsible', incorporating 'various safeguards, such as bicameralism, robust committee scrutiny, and multiple levels of consideration, debate, and voting', which connect 'both formally (through public hearings and consultation procedures) and informally with wider debates in the society'.[413] Australia's Parliament, in comparison to many other countries, generally has a decent rights record and largely fulfils these criteria:[414] it is federal, bicameral and furnished with committees that fulfil scrutiny functions, through which it sometimes undertakes consultation with the public. There are in-built checks and balances. It does not, however, have a good historical record respecting Indigenous rights, resulting in Indigenous mistrust and repeated calls for constitutional reform. Reflecting this reality, the parliamentary committee set up to scrutinise laws for human rights compliance has observed that the proper consultation required for human rights compliance with respect to Indigenous affairs generally does not effectively occur.[415] A First Nations constitutional voice would address this by way of constitutional amendment as well as legislative reform, in a way that is constitutionally congruent.

As shown, Australia's *Constitution* largely positions political participation as the right of rights: it mostly uses institutional, democratic and power-sharing mechanisms to protect rights. In erring towards political mechanisms for rights protection, the *Constitution* recognises distinct political collectives. As Saunders describes:

> Federalism involves multiple overlapping political communities, each with a degree of constitutional autonomy. They are necessarily in a hierarchical relationship for some purposes. Most obviously, given the inevitability of conflict in the exercise of power, the laws of the central legislature generally are entitled to prevail. This is because the

[412] Ivison, *Postcolonial Liberalism* (n 6 above) 23, see also 92–94.

[413] Waldron, 'The Core of the Case Against Judicial Review' (n 223 above) 1361.

[414] See The Mandarin, 'Australia Stays in Top 10 in Global Democracy Index', *The Mandarin* (1 February 2018) <https://www.themandarin.com.au/88003-australia-stays-top-10-global-democracy-index/> accessed 18 October 2019.

[415] Shireen Morris, 'Parliamentary Scrutiny and Insights for a First Nations Voice to Parliament' (n 144 above). See *Human Rights (Parliamentary Scrutiny) Act 2011* (Cth).

> centre represents the wider national community. This may also justify its superiority in other respects, including the exercise of external sovereignty. Otherwise, however, the polities are not subordinate to each other.[416]

In Australia, political participation thus occurs collectively as well as individually. Recognising and including Indigenous peoples as a distinct yet co-existing constitutional constituency would build upon this understanding of Australia's *Constitution*. The *Constitution* could explicitly recognise Indigenous peoples as a distinct constitutional constituency, or historic political community, entitled to a degree of formal and guaranteed representation and participation in the political decisions made about their distinct affairs. This constitutional constituency would not be geographically confined – unlike the States – because Indigenous people live all over the country. Yet formal recognition and inclusion of the Indigenous constitutional constituency would acknowledge the existence of this co-existing and overlapping historic political community and create an additional avenue for their political participation in their affairs. Applying Saunders' logic, the political authority of this constituency within constitutional arrangements would necessarily yield to Commonwealth and State constituencies where there is disagreement, because in a democracy the 'wider national community' should prevail where there is a conflict. This approach cannot, therefore, contemplate giving the Indigenous constituency a veto. Nonetheless, reform could carve out constitutional space for Indigenous peoples to engage in continuing constructive dialogue with the state. Indigenous constitutional recognition could formally empower Indigenous peoples to participate in the dialogues set up by the *Constitution*, so that, as Schaap describes, 'citizens divided by the memories of past wrongs' might more effectively and continually 'debate and contest the terms of their political association'.[417]

The *Australian Constitution* is built on the notion that the co-existing constitutional constituencies can peacefully disagree, co-operate and collaborate.[418] The structures set in place by the *Constitution* mediate and process disagreement and create a culture of mutual respect in its resolution. These processes have generally proven conducive to peace and stability in Australia. Indigenous constitutional recognition could involve a mechanism by which Indigenous peoples are better able to respectfully express their own disagreement (or agreement, as the case may be) in matters relating to their rights and their affairs,

[416] Cheryl Saunders, 'Protecting Rights in a Federalism' (2004) 25(2) *Adelaide Law Review* 177, 182. Hawkes similarly notes that 'federalism can accommodate multiple identities and loyalties within a state, as well as different "levels" of government, some with shared sovereignty. In Australia, for example, both the Commonwealth and state governments are sovereign within their respective spheres of jurisdiction.': David C Hawkes, *Indigenous Peoples: Self-Government and Intergovernmental Relations* (UNESCO 2001) 154.

[417] Schaap (n 361 above) 538.

[418] Jeremy Waldron calls disagreement the 'circumstance of politics': see Jeremy Waldron, *The Dignity of Legislation* (n 411 above) 152–55.

to better engage in continual productive dialogue with the state. Such an idea would align with Ivison's conception of post-colonial liberalism, which accommodates a 'complex co-existence' between Indigenous peoples and the state through mechanisms for ongoing dialogue:

> [P]ostcolonial liberalism aims for a state of affairs in which the legitimacy of the norms, practices and institutions upon which people's well-being depends inheres in a form of social and political conversation – or embodied argument – about what is legitimate and illegitimate, an argument that is ultimately 'without any guarantor and without any end' …
>
> And this in turn also depends on citizens being capable of making demands for equitable treatment on these institutions and on each other; demands and forms of contestation which might bring to light forms of injustice or domination hitherto unnoticed or unrecognised.[419]

The *Constitution* could be amended to recognise, represent and give voice to the Indigenous constitutional constituency, so that this group can more fulsomely participate in the political decisions made by the majority in respect of their unique three per cent rights and interests. Such a form of recognition would be in keeping with the dialogical, layered and power-sharing arrangements of federal Australia's *Constitution*, and the culture of comity, mutual respect and reciprocity it establishes. It would acknowledge that the relationship between Indigenous peoples and the state is one which will perpetually evolve and grow through political dialogue. The *Constitution* could set in place a structure which enables this political dialogue to take place in fairer, more respectful, more civil and inclusive ways – without guaranteeing any outcomes of the dialogue. Such a dialogue would help bring to light defects or injustices in Indigenous policy, so weaknesses can be collaboratively improved. Constitutional recognition of this kind would not only help mediate and process disagreement between Indigenous peoples and the state, but also amongst the Indigenous polity itself, through the establishment of legislated representative structures to mediate intra-Indigenous disagreement. This political answer to Indigenous-state disagreement would also respond to the concerns of those who object to judicial adjudication of rights and favour political participation as the best means of resolving disagreements about rights.

Waldron's theory of political participation rests on the idea that individuals should have an equal share of political power and an equal say in the laws that affect them.[420] As noted, however, this conception does not neatly accord with Australia's federal constitutional system, which does not adopt strict individual equality in political representation. I have explained that Australia's Federation

[419] Ivison, *Postcolonial Liberalism* (n 6 above) 22–23.

[420] Waldron, 'A Right-Based Critique of Constitutional Rights' (n 223 above) 18; Jeremy Waldron, *Law and Disagreement* (Oxford Scholarship Online 1999); Waldron, 'The Core of the Case against Judicial Review' (n 223 above).

recognises distinct constitutional constituencies of varied populations and accordingly gives voice to these historic political communities. It accepts minimally populated States like Tasmania being guaranteed equal representation in the Senate, as a justifiable deviation from the strictly 'equal decisiveness' of individual votes. Ensuring Indigenous peoples an empowered say in political decisions made about them thus accords with a Waldronian view of disagreement, and the appropriate solutions for mediating disagreement, adapted to Australian circumstances. So long as the reform does not entail a veto of majoritarian decisions (as would be the case under constitutional protections of rights whereby laws may be vetoed by the High Court, to which Waldron objects), specific Indigenous participation in relevant decisions would not interfere with parliamentary supremacy – because the ultimate decision-makers are still the majority-elected representatives.

If political participation is particularly important where reasonable people have the capacity to disagree about their rights, this is especially crucial where competing interests are historically fraught – as in Indigenous affairs. Indigenous affairs involve collective claims over historical injustice and collective arguments over resources and land. If Indigenous peoples are recognised and accommodated as collective political actors (a status which can co-exist with their status as individual Australian citizens, just as the status of Tasmanians co-exists with their status as Australians) within the political decision-making procedures set up by the *Constitution*, they will be better placed to peacefully and respectfully disagree and pursue their self-determination within the state. The argument that Indigenous peoples themselves disagree and can be divided on issues is not a sustainable objection to this kind of solution, for Tasmanians also disagree with each other.

The idea that the purpose of a constitution is to manage conflicts between individuals and parties who can reasonably disagree[421] is connected to Waldron's exposition of the principle of proximity. The idea is:

> [T]hat people have a natural duty to enter into political society with those with whom they find themselves in a condition of unavoidable coexistence …
>
> Even if the explanation of our being side by side now is the existence of injustice in the past, still we have a duty to bring our present relationship under the auspices of right and legality, and that means we must form and sustain a political society among us – all of us whether we like one another, or the circumstances under which we came into one another's company, or not.[422]

This is an argument for constitutional inclusion in the face of deep and enduring conflict and disagreement. It presents a strong basis for Indigenous constitutional inclusion through perpetual, mutually respectful political dialogue.

[421] Waldron, 'Constitutionalism' (n 282 above).
[422] Drawing on Kant: Waldron, 'Redressing Historic Injustice' (n 239 above) 137–38.

In 1901 the colonies formed a unified political society, but they left Indigenous peoples out and gave them no voice in the constitutional compact. Regardless of past injustice, it is now time the First Nations were formally and specifically included in the political conversation about their rights and reconciliation. A First Nations constitutional voice would help the parties peacefully disagree and work out their differences more fairly, while leaving parliamentary supremacy intact.

Such reform would also assist with the moral legitimacy of Australia's constitutional law with respect to Indigenous people.[423] As Habermas argues, 'citizens are autonomous only if the addressees of the law can also see themselves as its authors'.[424] The addressees of the law need to feel that they participated in the making of the laws. This is especially relevant to Indigenous peoples, who historically did not consent to the imposition of the colonising law and were not party to the constitutional compact.[425] The *Constitution* specifically empowers the majority to make laws about the Indigenous minority, but it does not ensure the Indigenous minority meaningful input into those decisions. It does not require reciprocity, consultation or dialogue with Indigenous peoples. Waldron argues, in defence of political processes as the best means for resolving disputes about rights, that 'those who are to be required to comply with a decision are surely entitled to *some* sort of voice in that decision'.[426] Quoting Mill:

> If he is compelled to pay, if he may be compelled to fight, if he is required implicitly to obey, he should be legally entitled to be told what for; to have his consent asked, and his opinion counted at its worth ...[427]

It is sometimes contended that the appropriate remedy to this problem is to encourage Indigenous people to get involved in politics and get themselves elected. That is a practical challenge for a three per cent highly disadvantaged minority,[428] but more fundamentally, it is not a structural or institutional accommodation or recognition of the Indigenous constitutional constituency – it is simply telling Indigenous people to participate in the way all other

[423] Ivison argues the challenge of Indigenous constitutional recognition 'is better grasped as one of political legitimacy. The question then becomes: does the Australian state exercise legitimate power over the indigenous peoples?': Ivison, 'Pluralising Political Legitimacy' (n 53 above) 119. See also Ivison, *Postcolonial Liberalism* (n 6 above) 23.

[424] Jurgen Habermas, 'Struggles for Recognition in the Democratic Constitutional State' in Amy Gutman (ed), *Multiculturalism* (Princeton University Press 1994) 121–22.

[425] Kingsbury (n 305 above) 123; Macklem, 'Distributing Sovereignty' (n 306 above) 1329. See also Ivison, *Postcolonial Liberalism* (n 6 above) 16–18.

[426] Waldron, 'A Right-Based Critique of Constitutional Rights' (n 223 above) 38.

[427] John Stuart Mill, *Considerations on Representative Government* (Prometheus Books 1991) 173.

[428] Though currently five members of the Commonwealth Parliament (Patrick Dodson, Linda Burney, Malarndirri McCarthy, Ken Wyatt and Jacqui Lambie) are Indigenous which is approximately proportionate. See Hannah Gobbett, 'Indigenous Parliamentarians, Federal and State: A Quick Guide' (11 July 2017): <https://www.aph.gov.au/About_Parliament/Parliamentary_Departments/Parliamentary_Library/pubs/rp/rp1718/Quick_Guides/IndigenousParliamentarians> accessed 18 October 2019.

Australians participate. This does not properly grapple with Indigenous calls for an empowered, constitutional voice in their affairs. More to the point, it does not adequately grapple with the power dynamics and history of exclusion and discrimination driving Indigenous calls for a voice in their affairs. Besides which, the objection is dishonest about the extent to which Indigenous MPs can represent Indigenous peoples. Any elected Indigenous politician must represent his or her whole electorate as well as his or her political party – they cannot represent Indigenous interests alone. While a person's ethnic identity or cultural affiliation will obviously play a role in beliefs and decisions, the duty of any Australian politician, whether of Indigenous, Anglo-Celtic or Indian ethnicity, is to act as an elected representative of all of his or her constituents, not a particular ethnic group. Indigenous MPs will benefit from hearing the advice of a First Nations voice as much as non-Indigenous MPs. Notably, the current Minister for Indigenous Australians is Indigenous – Ken Wyatt. However, he is presently at odds with Indigenous opinion in his opposition to a constitutionally enshrined Indigenous voice, probably because of directives within his Party.[429] Indigenous politicians cannot be presumed to represent majority Indigenous views, for they are not elected only by Indigenous people. They must strive to represent their Parties, their electorates and ultimately all Australians. The same majoritarian forces that sway non-Indigenous politicians and make it difficult to for them to give adequate political weight to minority Indigenous views are still relevant to Indigenous political decision-makers. There is therefore a strong case for specific Indigenous participation and dialogue in laws and policies with respect to Indigenous affairs, in addition to ordinary political processes – whether or not there are Indigenous politicians.

In a liberal democracy striving for fairer treatment of Indigenous peoples, there should be no parliamentary or government interference in Indigenous rights and interests without the input, representation and participation of those people.[430] Practically, such a requirement makes sense. If Indigenous peoples were guaranteed participation in the political decisions regarding Indigenous affairs, it would improve the quality of those decisions. As Waldron argues:

> Participation by all is valuable because of the importance of assembling diverse perspectives and experiences when public decisions are being taken; and it is valuable also because the sheer experience of arguing in circumstances of human plurality

[429] Lorena Allam, 'Ken Wyatt under Fire for Ruling Out Indigenous Voice Referendum Question', *The Guardian* (19 August 2019) <https://www.theguardian.com/australia-news/2019/aug/19/ken-wyatt-under-fire-for-ruling-out-indigenous-voice-referendum-question> accessed 18 October 2019.

[430] Notably, the case for constitutionally mandated dialogue between Indigenous peoples and the state is far stronger in relation to Indigenous peoples than for other minority groups, because they are a distinct constitutional constituency subject to specific rights and interests arising from their historical dispossession and subject to special laws and policies that apply distinctly to them. No other group of Australians has specific rights and interests arising from their historical dispossession.

> helps us develop more interesting and probably more valid opinions than we could manufacture on our own.[431]

Even where no agreement can be reached through such dialogue and participation, the process of arguing about competing interests, information and ideas is worthwhile, because plurality and disagreement are valuable in themselves. The sharing of information, ideas and experience, and the having of the debate are important. Parliament's wisdom regarding Indigenous affairs would be greatly increased if it had the benefit of Indigenous views in making its laws and policies. This kind of specific participation enhances the reasonableness and fairness of public decision-making, because reciprocity 'regulates public reason'.[432] Indigenous participation in Indigenous affairs law- and policy-making would enhance the reasonableness and thus the fairness of political decisions with respect to Indigenous affairs, thus improving outcomes.

Ensuring that Indigenous views are heard in the making of political decisions that affect them speaks to the spirit of well-established moral and political principles of natural justice and procedural fairness.[433] Increased procedural fairness in the political governance of Indigenous affairs would increase the civility and respectfulness of the relationship between Indigenous peoples and the state. Chief Justice Allsop describes civility in the law as a: 'manner of human expression and social intercourse that provides the environment for the exchange and debate of conflicting ideas. It is an environment of manners and peaceful willingness to see views and ideas of others.'[434] In order to see and hear the views of others one must first recognise those others. Fairness will be enhanced if the state develops better ways of seeing and hearing Indigenous peoples' views and ideas. Civility will be enhanced if the state develops respectful procedures for the airing of divergent views on Indigenous affairs. Litigation under a new constitutional rights clause is one way for the state to hear dissenting Indigenous views and objections to political decisions, but it is not the only way. Political and procedural mechanisms – mechanisms for increased Indigenous representation and political participation – could enable peaceful dialogue and exchange, increasing the fairness of political processes and decisions with respect to Indigenous peoples.

Waldron, contrary to my argument in this book, seems to suggest that participatory rights should not be constitutionally entrenched, arguing instead for total flexibility in decision-making procedures: '[P]articipation and process is as complex and disputable as anything else in politics … People disagree about

[431] Waldron, 'A Right-Based Critique of Constitutional Rights' (n 223 above) 37.

[432] See discussion of reciprocity and deliberative democracy in Ivison, *Postcolonial Liberalism* (n 6 above) 18–23.

[433] See Chief Justice Robert French, 'Procedural Fairness: Indispensable to Justice?', Sir Anthony Mason Lecture, Melbourne Law School, 7 October 2010.

[434] Chief Justice Allsop, 'Civility, Reason, Fairness and Justice, and the Law', speech delivered at the Great Synagogue Sydney, 12 February 2014.

how participatory rights should be understood and about how they should be balanced against other values.'[435] Waldron posits that because we disagree about the best procedures to mediate disagreement, 'there have to be authoritative procedures for settling disputes about what should be our authoritative procedures'.[436] This does not negate my suggestion that Australia's *Constitution* could recognise Indigenous peoples by making space within constitutional arrangements for Indigenous people to be heard, represented and to participate in the political decisions made about their affairs. Australia's entrenched *Constitution* sets in place the basic rules and procedures by which disagreement is mediated. The entrenched nature of the *Australian Constitution* is not changing any time soon. Under section 128, however, the *Constitution* provides a mechanism by which the Australian people can democratically participate in any changes to the political decision-making procedures set up by the *Constitution* – via popular referendum.

If the Australian people voted at a referendum to alter the *Constitution* to guarantee that Indigenous peoples can always participate in the political decisions made about their rights and interests, this would be in keeping with a Waldron-style view of political participation as the 'right of rights'. Such an amendment would overcome objections to judicial review, while also realising long-standing Indigenous advocacy for increased self-determination, consultation and authority in their affairs. While the high-level requirement that Indigenous peoples be heard in their affairs would be constitutionally entrenched through a non-justiciable constitutional guarantee, the details of the First Nations voice would be set out in legislation, to allow changes over time, as needed, with the advice of the First Nations voice. It would be open to the Australian people to further modify this disagreement-mediating procedure via a referendum in the future. Parliament and the Australian people would remain ultimate decision-makers with respect to these matters.

I. Towards a Wiser Parliament and a More Reconciled Australia

A First Nations constitutional voice should be viewed as a way not only of producing better outcomes in Indigenous affairs, but also of progressing reconciliation in a philosophically deeper sense. By formally including the Indigenous constitutional constituency within Australia's political institutions and public decision-making with respect to Indigenous affairs, the nation can take a fundamental step towards healing, inclusion and national unity. The principle of proximity suggests that geographical closeness generates endemic conflict that

[435] Waldron, 'A Right-Based Critique of Constitutional Rights' (n 223 above) 39.
[436] ibid.

requires regulation and mediation under a nation's constitution.[437] Thus, 'states should be formed amongst people who occupy the same territory, whether they have any affinity with one another or not, because they are the ones who are most likely to be in conflict with one another'.[438] In the Australian colonial story, ever since first contact, the geographical proximity of historical adversaries has created disputes over rights and resources. In the relationship between Indigenous peoples and the state, the parties are coming at these disputes with vastly different cultural and historical perspectives. Morally, we have a duty to deal with such conflicts through non-violent and fair means. We did not achieve this in the past, but we can achieve it today. Indeed, it is the very role of the *Constitution* to establish procedures whereby such historic disputes and differences can be fairly settled. As noted, Australia's *Constitution* is in essence a treaty – a unity pact. It is time for the nation to move from exclusion of Indigenous peoples from this unity pact, to formal inclusion.

A First Nations voice in their affairs would belatedly include Indigenous peoples in the perpetual dialogues set up by the *Constitution*. This could bring us closer together, building shared understanding and empathy through conversation and consultation – reconciliation in action. Political dialogue, as well mediating and managing conflict, can also give rise to collaboration, partnership and shared patriotism.[439] Though it would not make 'ancient animosities disappear', inclusive dialogue over time can foster trust and solidarity.[440] Waldron expresses a salient warning, however, apt for our purposes:

> [The] ideal of constitutional patriotism and the solidarity that goes with it is not far-fetched. But this is unlikely to happen if one part of the society (even the majority) regards the territory, the soil, and the constitution as theirs in a sense that excludes at some level others who live side-by-side with them in the same locality.[441]

There is a real sense in which the *Australian Constitution* is not yet adequately owned by Indigenous Australians. It is not yet theirs.[442] Therefore, is it not yet all of ours. It has already been established that the *Constitution* is not

[437] Jeremy Waldron, 'The Principle of Proximity' (2011) Public Law and Legal Theory Research Paper Series, Working Paper No 11-08, New York University School of Law, 10: <https://ssrn.com/abstract=1742413> accessed 18 October 2019.

[438] ibid 7–8.

[439] For exploration of the idea of 'constitutional patriotism', see Jürgen Habermas, *The Inclusion of the Other: Studies in Political Theory* (Ciaran P Cronin and Pablo De Greiff eds, MIT Press, 1998).

[440] Waldron, 'The Principle of Proximity' (n 437 above) 18, 23.

[441] ibid 18. See also Jürgen Habermas, *Between Facts and Norms: Contribution to a Discourse Theory of Law and Democracy* (William Rehg tr, MIT Press 1996) 491–515, 566–67; Frank I Michelman, 'Morality, Identity and Constitutional Patriotism' (1999) 76 *Denver University Law Review* 1009; David Abraham, 'Constitutional Patriotism, Citizenship, and Belonging' (2008) 6 *International Journal of Constitutional Law (ICON)* 137.

[442] On constitutional recognition and belonging, see Ambelin Kwaymullina, 'Recognition, Referendums and Relationships' (n 86 above) 34–35.

neutral; it did not and does not treat Indigenous peoples neutrally. They were specifically excluded from the original power-sharing deal and this has not yet been rectified. How can we expect all Australians to truly share a sense of national unity, patriotism and cohesion, when one group remains excluded from the constitutional compact that created the Australian nation – the peoples that were here long before any other?

Despite past bloodshed and conflict, the broken promises and unresolved ruptures of history, Indigenous and non-Indigenous Australians still live on this continent, side by side, in close proximity. Yet the relationship still lacks trust, understanding and empathy. We are not yet reconciled. Properly understood, the Uluru Statement is a request to talk more constructively, to consult, to engage in dialogue. An ongoing political dialogue of the kind requested could build trust and consolidate cohesion.[443] Such a reform would belatedly include Indigenous peoples in the constitutional compact from which they were excluded in 1901. More than that, it could bring Australians closer together, such that we might better hear and thus learn from each other, understand one another, create better policies and produce better outcomes together.[444] The constitutionally mandated hearing of Indigenous voices could make for a wiser Parliament and fairer laws and policies with respect to Indigenous affairs. It could help create a more united and more reconciled nation.

[443] Waldron, 'The Principle of Proximity' (n 437 above) 25. See also Ivison, *Postcolonial Liberalism* (n 6 above) 92–94.

[444] See Ivison, *Postcolonial Liberalism* (n 6 above) 110–11.

3

Understanding Objections to a Racial Non-Discrimination Guarantee

I. INTRODUCTION

LET US REWIND back to 2012. When the Expert Panel delivered its recommendations for Indigenous constitutional recognition in Australia, the main substantive constitutional reform proposed was a judicially adjudicated non-discrimination guarantee.[1] It was in response to political objections to a racial non-discrimination guarantee that Indigenous leaders and constitutional experts sought out an alternative approach that might address such concerns and build the consensus that the Expert Panel's proposal did not engender.[2] The idea was to develop a non-litigious alternative that would take on board constitutionally conservative objections,[3] while also delivering the substantive and empowering constitutional reform sought by Indigenous people. Before ascertaining alternative solutions, however, the first step was to try to properly understand the objections being raised. Why was the Expert Panel's proposal enlivening opposition unconducive to referendum success? What were the concerns being expressed and the underlying values driving these concerns?

[1] Expert Panel on Constitutional Recognition of Indigenous Australians, *Recognising Aboriginal and Torres Strait Islander Peoples in the Constitution: Report of the Expert Panel* (January 2012) xxviii (Expert Panel Report) <https://antar.org.au/sites/default/files/expert_panel_report_.pdf>. The Indigenous policy organisation, Cape York Institute (CYI), where the author worked on Indigenous constitutional recognition policy under the leadership of the Indigenous leader Noel Pearson in 2011, had been a strong proponent of a racial non-discrimination guarantee in the Constitution. See Cape York Institute submission to the Expert Panel, 2011: <https://www.capeyorkpartnership.org.au/wp-content/uploads/2018/09/Constitutional-Reform-Proposal-2011.pdf> accessed 18 November 2019.

[2] This search involved collaboration with some of the opponents of a racial non-discrimination guarantee. See Shireen Morris, *Radical Heart: Three Stories Make Us One* (Melbourne University Press 2018) Chp 5.

[3] Note that this chapter is a significant re-working of an earlier article elucidating these objections. See Shireen Morris, 'Undemocratic, Uncertain and Politically Unviable? An Analysis of and Response to Objections to a Proposed Racial Non-Discrimination Clause as Part of Constitutional Reforms for Indigenous Recognition' (2014) 40(2) *Monash Law Review* 488. See Greg Craven's description of Australia's 'constitutional conservatives' whose 'central loyalty' is 'to the Constitution itself.' Greg Craven, 'The Con-Cons' Constitutional Conundrum', *The Australian* (19 February 2014) <https://www.theaustralian.com.au/opinion/columnists/the-concons-constitutional-conundrum/news-story/5a5661eb5d932b67542ec9f32a507af3>.

And what did these concerns mean for constitutional reform strategy? If a racial non-discrimination clause attracted the classic anti Bill of rights-type opposition that has proven persuasive in Australia, what kind of proposal might turn such opposition into support?[4] Without properly appreciating and comprehending objections in relation to a racial non-discrimination guarantee, the lateral thinking that gave rise to the alternative concept of an Indigenous body mandated by the *Constitution* (a new conception of what was in reality a very old idea that had long been pushed by Indigenous advocates) could not have occurred.[5] This chapter reflects my own grappling with objections to a racial non-discrimination guarantee in the wake of the Expert Panel's report. It identifies, analyses and responds to common arguments against the proposed amendment, in order to form a principled basis for exploring other more viable constitutional reform alternatives which accommodate those objections as well as Indigenous aspirations for substantive reform.

The next section examines why the Expert Panel proposed the racial non-discrimination reforms it did. The third section explains the main objections to the racial non-discrimination proposal. I characterise these objections under three broad themes: the 'undemocratic' (or majoritarian) objection, the related 'legal uncertainty' objection, and the 'political unviability' objection. The fourth section provides counter-arguments – for these were not objections I readily accepted. My consideration acknowledges, however, the constitutional reform history examined in Chapter two above, which lends weight to the argument that a racial non-discrimination guarantee in the *Constitution* may be politically unviable. The fifth section then asks whether the commonly proposed judicially adjudicated alternative – a qualified Indigenous power – might be an appropriate way of dealing with the objections, but determines that it is not: a qualified power would fall foul of the same objections. The chapter concludes that judicially adjudicated approaches – whether in a broad

[4] Notably, key constitutional conservatives who opposed a racial non-discrimination clause on the grounds that it over-empowered the judiciary, now support the alternative idea of a First Nations constitutional voice. See eg Greg Craven, 'Noel Pearson's Indigenous Recognition Plan Profound and Practical', *The Australian* (25 May 2015) <https://www.theaustralian.com.au/opinion/columnists/greg-craven/noel-pearsons-indigenous-recognition-plan-profound-and-practical/news-story/472ff0238ad4f48cd423fdd9f74a9363>; Julian Leeser, 'Uphold and Recognise' in Damien Freeman and Shireen Morris (eds), *The Forgotten People: Liberal and Conservative Approaches to Recognising Indigenous Peoples* (Melbourne University Press 2016); and see generally Damien Freeman, 'Introduction' in Damien Freeman and Shireen Morris (eds), *The Forgotten People: Liberal and Conservative Approaches to Recognising Indigenous Peoples* (Melbourne University Press 2016).

[5] See Cape York Institute, 'Submission to the Joint Select Committee Constitutional Recognition of Aboriginal and Torres Strait Islander Peoples: October 2014': <https://www.aph.gov.au/DocumentStore.ashx?id=e7940d6b-918d-4295-bea9-8089279a5c95&subId=301030> accessed 18 November 2011. See also Cape York Institute, 'Supplementary Submission to the Joint Select Committee: Establishing an Indigenous Body in the Constitution January 2015' <https://capeyorkpartnership.org.au/wp-content/uploads/2018/09/Supplementary-Submission-to-Joint-Select-Committee-January-2015.pdf> accessed 18 November 2019.

standalone guarantee or incorporated into an Indigenous power – are by definition incapable of addressing the core concern. This analysis forms the basis of my investigation of alternative, non-litigious, political and procedural constitutional reform solutions.

II. THE EXPERT PANEL'S RACIAL NON-DISCRIMINATION RECOMMENDATION

As part of its proposed reforms for Indigenous constitutional recognition, the Expert Panel recommended a new section 116A to read:

> Section 116A Prohibition of Racial Discrimination
>
> (1) The Commonwealth, a State or a Territory shall not discriminate on the grounds of race, colour or ethnic or national origin.
>
> (2) Subsection (1) does not preclude the making of laws or measures for the purpose of overcoming disadvantage, ameliorating the effects of past discrimination, or protecting the cultures, languages or heritage of any group.[6]

The Expert Panel also proposed other reforms, including removal of references to 'race' in the *Constitution*,[7] insertion of a replacement Indigenous head of power incorporating preambular recognition statements,[8] and a clause recognising Indigenous languages as original Australian languages and English as a national language.[9] The main substantive reform, however, was a guarantee against racial non-discrimination: this was the key clause intended to positively recalibrate the relationship between Indigenous peoples and the state, to ensure it is fairer than in the past.

The driving force behind the Expert Panel's recommendation was the need for a constitutional solution to the problem of racial discrimination against Indigenous people – an issue central to the question of Indigenous constitutional recognition. The allowance and promotion of racial discrimination in and under the *Constitution* is inextricably related to the history of Indigenous peoples in Australia, and to Indigenous relationships with Australian governments under the *Constitution*, which have been characterised by discrimination and exclusion.[10] As noted, Indigenous people were excluded from both the

[6] Expert Panel Report (n 1 above) xxviii.

[7] *Constitution* ss 51(xxvi), 25.

[8] A proposed new s 51A.

[9] A proposed new s 127A.

[10] Expert Panel Report (n 1 above) 167. See also Joint Select Committee on Constitutional Recognition of Aboriginal and Torres Strait Islander Peoples, 'Interim Report' (2014) 19 [2.56] <https://www.aph.gov.au/Parliamentary_Business/Committees/Joint/2015_Constitutional_Recognition_of_Aboriginal_and_Torres_Strait_Islander_Peoples/Interim_Report/index> accessed 18 November 2019 (Joint Select Committee Interim Report): '[t]he committee is mindful of the Expert Panel's view "that recognition of Aboriginal and Torres Strait Islander peoples will be incomplete without a constitutional prohibition of laws that discriminate on the basis of race".'

drafting and terms of the *Constitution* that came into force in 1901.[11] Evidence of this discrimination remains in the Constitution's text and operation. While the 1967 referendum removed the explicit exclusions of Indigenous people, it did not remove all racially discriminatory elements: section 51(xxvi), the Race Power, and section 25 remain.

Historical evidence indicates that the Race Power 'was deliberately inserted into the Constitution to allow the Commonwealth to discriminate against sections of the community on account of their race'.[12] It was initially intended by the drafters to enable the Commonwealth to pass discriminatory laws against the 'alien races',[13] particularly to exclude the 'inferior' and 'coloured'[14] peoples such as 'Asiatic or African alien[s]' from the goldfields,[15] and to more easily control 'undesirable immigrants'[16] such as Chinese, Indian, Afghan and Japanese settlers and workers.[17] The racism apparent in the colonial attitudes of the time was not confined to Indigenous people.[18] But while the Race Power provides the Commonwealth with the authority to make laws relating to 'the people of any race for whom it is deemed necessary to make special laws', in practice, the power has only ever been used in relation to Indigenous people.[19] The power

[11] See Chapter 2 above. Section 127 excluded Indigenous people from being counted as part of the population. They were also excluded from the operation of s 51(xxvi), the Race Power, because Indigenous survival was doubted or because they were considered a matter that should be the responsibility of the States. Justin Malbon, 'The Race Power under the Australian Constitution: Altered Meanings' (1999) 21(1) *Sydney Law Review* 80, 91; Geoffrey Sawer, 'The Australian Constitution and the Australian Aborigine' (1966) 2(1) *Federal Law Review* 17, 18; Bain Attwood and Andrew Markus, *The 1967 Referendum: Race, Power and the Australian Constitution* (2nd edn, Aboriginal Studies Press 2007) 1; Michael Kirby, 'Constitutional Law and Indigenous Australians: Challenge for a Parched Continent' (2012) 15 *Southern Cross University Law Review* 3, 4.

[12] George Williams, 'The Races Power and the 1967 Referendum' (2007) 11(Special Edition) *Australian Indigenous Law Review* 8, 8. Goldsworthy similarly suggests the founders omitted rights protections in their constitutional design in part because 'they did not want to be prevented from discriminating against people of other races'. Jeffrey Goldsworthy, 'Against a Constitutional Bill of Rights in Australia' in Matthew Groves, Janina Boughey and Dan Meagher (eds), *The Legal Protection of Rights in Australia* (Hart Publishing 2019) 394. Michael Kirby argues that the race power 'reflects nineteenth century concepts of racial superiority and paternalistic interventions for "the natives"' and 'is a relic of colonial thinking': Kirby, 'Constitutional Law and Indigenous Australians' (n 11 above) 16; Attwood and Markus (n 11 above) 1–2. See also Expert Panel Report (n 1 above) 13–42.

[13] Attwood and Markus (n 11 above) 2.

[14] See *Official Record of the Debates of the Australasian Federal Convention*, Third Session, Melbourne, 20 January–17 March 1898, 227–43.

[15] ibid 240–41 (Sir John Forrest).

[16] ibid 241.

[17] Constitutional Commission, 'Final Report of the Constitutional Commission: Summary, Australian Government Publishing Service' (1988) 54 (Constitutional Commission Report). See also Law Council of Australia, 'Constitutional Recognition of Indigenous Australians: Discussion Paper' (19 March 2011) 20: <http://lca.lawcouncil.asn.au/lawcouncil/images/LCA-PDF/discussion%20papers/ConstitutionalRecognitionofIndigenousAustralians.pdf> accessed 18 November 2019.

[18] Malbon (n 11 above) 93.

[19] Prior to the 1967 referendum, the power was not used.

contains no requirement that these laws be beneficial or non-discriminatory.[20] Similarly, section 25 is a 'provision as to races disqualified from voting'. While historically intended as a disincentive to discourage the States from disqualifying particular races from voting,[21] the provision nonetheless contemplates barring Australian citizens from democratic participation on account of race. In practice it did not prevent governments denying the vote to Indigenous peoples and other groups.[22]

While the explicit constitutional exclusions of Indigenous people have, since 1967, been eliminated, the continued existence of section 25 and the Race Power in the *Constitution* remain problematic. Absent a prohibition on racial discrimination, such provisions empower and allow racially discriminatory laws. This situation is arguably incompatible with Australia's international obligations to eliminate racial discrimination under the International Convention on the Elimination of All Forms of Racial Discrimination (CERD),[23] to which Australia is a party.[24] The UN Committee on the Elimination of Racial Discrimination has expressed concern at Australia's retention of sections 25 and 51(xxvi) and urged adoption of 'entrenched protection[s] against racial discrimination'.[25]

In considering how best to rectify the discriminatory non-recognition of Indigenous peoples, the Expert Panel therefore had to contend with the problem that the *Constitution* falls short of international standards regarding racial non-discrimination and of Australia's commitment to those standards.[26] Similarly, it had to deal with the problem posed by the race clauses in the context of Australia's democratic system, by reference to liberal democratic values and public expectations with respect to individual equality before the law. The Expert Panel's polling indicated that the majority of Australians (around 80–90 per cent), across political persuasions, supported the idea of a racial non-discrimination

[20] The Race Power can probably be used for beneficial or adverse use against particular races. *Kartinyeri v Commonwealth* (1998) 195 CLR 337, 378–81 [82]–[89] (Gummow and Hayne JJ); cf: at 367–68 [44]–[45] (Gaudron J), 410–11 [152] (Kirby J). Williams explains that the Court was 'split on whether the races power can still be used to discriminate against Indigenous or other peoples. This fundamental question remains unresolved': George Williams, 'Thawing the Frozen Continent' [2008] (19) *Griffith Review* 11, 27; see also Robert French, 'The Race Power: A Constitutional Chimera' in HP Lee and George Winterton (eds), *Australian Constitutional Landmarks* (Cambridge University Press 2003) 180, 206.

[21] Anne Twomey, 'An Obituary for s 25 of the Constitution' (2012) 23(2) *Public Law Review* 125, 125–29.

[22] ibid, 134–35. The history of the franchise will be further explored in Chapter 5 of this volume.

[23] International Convention on the Elimination of All Forms of Racial Discrimination, opened for signature 7 March 1966, 660 UNTS 195 (entered into force 4 January 1969).

[24] The 1988 Constitutional Commission Report stated: '[i]t is inappropriate to retain section 51(xxvi) because the purposes for which, historically, it was inserted no longer apply in this country. Australia has joined the many nations which have rejected race as a legitimate criterion on which legislation can be based.': Constitutional Commission Report (n 17 above) 54.

[25] *Report of the Committee on the Elimination of Racial Discrimination*, UN GAOR, 76th–77th sess, Supp No 18, UN Doc A/65/18 (27 August 2010) 18.

[26] Expert Panel Report (n 1 above) 160–64.

clause in the *Constitution*.[27] Many submissions advocated the value of individual equality and highlighted the problematic nature of the race provisions for a democracy like Australia.[28] Similarly, the importance of a protection against racial discrimination was powerfully propounded by Indigenous leaders,[29] arising from the fact that the democratic exclusion and differential treatment on the basis of race, allowed under and promoted in the *Constitution*, has been largely directed at Indigenous Australians. The Expert Panel therefore concluded that Indigenous recognition is intimately connected to removal of and protection from racial discrimination. Expert Panel member Noel Pearson argued:

> The racial discrimination allowed by our Constitution is inextricably linked to the Indigenous history we want recognised. So extreme was the discrimination against Indigenous people, it initially even denied that we existed. This is what Indigenous recognition is all about – overturning the fallacies of non-existence and racial inequality.[30]

Pearson persuasively characterises the non-recognition of Indigenous peoples – whether in the *Constitution* or in the English or Australian law under the doctrine of *terra nullius*, which justified the non-recognition of Indigenous polities, property rights and human rights – as a product of past racially discriminatory attitudes and beliefs.[31] In turn, Indigenous exclusion from and non-recognition in the *Constitution* sanctioned future Indigenous marginalisation.[32] The *Constitution* did not require Australians to be treated equally before the law with respect to race, and Indigenous Australians especially have suffered as a result. The Expert Panel therefore recommended removal of sections 25 and 51(xxvi), appropriate replacement of the Race Power, and adoption of a new racial non-discrimination clause to restrain governments from enacting racially discriminatory laws and policies.

27 ibid 91, 157; Patricia Karvelas, 'Most Want Race Discrimination Removed from the Constitution', *The Australian* (Sydney, 11 November 2011) 9.

28 Expert Panel Report (n 1 above) 157.

29 See Marcia Langton, 'Indigenous Exceptionalism and the Constitutional "Race Power"', speech delivered at the *Melbourne Writers' Festival*, Melbourne, 26 August 2012; Marcia Langton, 'Get Rid of Race to Stop Racism', *The Australian* (31 August 2012) 12; Patrick Dodson, 'Too Tolerant of Ugly Racism', *The Age* (31 January 2012) 13; Dan Harrison, 'Dodson Shows Support for Constitutional Ban on Racial Discrimination', *Sydney Morning Herald* (12 July 2012) 6; Patricia Karvelas, 'Pearson Puts Case for Race Clauses to Be Cut', *The Australian* (10 December 2011) 7; Noel Pearson, 'A Letter to the Australian People', Submission No 3619 to the Expert Panel on the Constitutional Recognition of Indigenous Australians; Larissa Behrendt, *Achieving Social Justice: Indigenous Rights and Australia's Future* (Federation Press 2003).

30 Noel Pearson, 'The Reward for Public Life Is Public Progress: An Appreciation of the Public Life of The Hon EG Whitlam AC QC Prime Minister 1972–1975', speech delivered at the 2013 Whitlam Oration, Whitlam Institute, University of Western Sydney, 13 November 2013.

31 ibid. See also Shireen Morris, 'Indigenous Constitutional Recognition, Non-Discrimination and Equality Before the Law: Why Reform is Necessary' (2011) 7(26) *Indigenous Law Bulletin* 7, 7.

32 Megan Davis and Dylan Lino, 'Constitutional Reform and Indigenous Peoples' (2010) 7(19) *Indigenous Law Bulletin* 3, 3.

The Expert Panel correctly identified that simple removal of the Race Power was not a sufficient solution. If removed, the Race Power would need to be replaced by a new power to ensure that the Commonwealth can continue to enact necessary laws with respect to Indigenous affairs that are currently supported by the Race Power, such as native title and Indigenous heritage protection laws.[33] Simple removal of the race clauses would not prevent the Commonwealth from using its other powers in a racially discriminatory way.[34] Any of Parliament's powers can be wielded discriminatorily and unjustly – this is the problem. To address these issues, the Expert Panel recommended a broad racial non-discrimination guarantee to restrain all the Commonwealth's powers and prevent racial discrimination.[35]

Why was a *constitutional* guarantee recommended? As was explained in the last chapter, a constitutional protection provides a more enduring and stable guarantee than legislative protection. The *Racial Discrimination Act 1975* (Cth) (RDA) has been suspended or displaced at least three times in its history – each time in relation to Indigenous people.[36] As ordinary legislation, it can be repealed or amended, or impliedly repealed or amended, by later inconsistent Acts. A constitutional guarantee against racial discrimination would provide stronger and more stable protection.

III. OBJECTIONS TO A RACIAL NON-DISCRIMINATION CLAUSE

When the Expert Panel's report was published, there were various objections to the racial non-discrimination guarantee. The proposal was described by some as a 'one clause bill of rights'[37] that would give the High Court a 'blank cheque to decide that something is a problem'.[38] First, there were concerns that such

[33] Expert Panel Report (n 1 above) 138; Sarah Pritchard, 'The "Race" Power in Section 51(xxvi) of the Constitution' (2011) 15(2) *Australian Indigenous Law Review* 44, 52.

[34] For example, s 122 also supported the Northern Territory Intervention.

[35] Expert Panel Report (n 1 above) 157–73.

[36] See eg *Hindmarsh Island Bridge Act 1997* (Cth) displaced the application of the *Racial Discrimination Act 1975* (Cth) (RDA); *Native Title Amendment Act 1998* (Cth); *Northern Territory Emergency Response Act 2007* (Cth) s 132. See also Dylan Lino, 'Thinking Outside the Constitution on Indigenous Constitutional Recognition: Entrenching the Racial Discrimination Act' (2017) 91 *Australian Law Journal* 381, 382.

[37] Dan Harrison, 'Dodson Shows Support for Constitutional Ban on Racial Discrimination' *Sydney Morning Herald* (12 July 2012) <https://www.smh.com.au/politics/federal/dodson-shows-support-for-constitutional-ban-on-racial-discrimination-20120711-21wff.html> accessed 18 November 2019; Greg Craven, 'Keep the Constitutional Change Simple', *Australian Financial Review* (Sydney, 6 February 2012) 55; Greg Craven, 'The Con-Cons' Constitutional Conundrum', *The Australian* (Sydney, 19 February 2014) 12.

[38] Patricia Karvelas, 'Historic Vote Facing Hurdles: "The Right Time" For Indigenous Recognition in the *Constitution*, Says Gillard', *The Australian* (20 January 2012) 1. See also James Allan, 'Constitutional Fiddling Brings Inherent Danger', *The Australian* (9 December 2011) 14. Craven, 'Keep the Constitutional Change Simple' (n 37 above).

a clause would be undemocratic, because it would be interpreted and adjudicated by the unelected judiciary.[39] Second, there were related concerns about the legal uncertainty of such a provision; some argued the clause was ambiguously worded and would likely lead to unintended consequences through judicial interpretation.[40] Third, there were concerns that the proposal was politically unviable and would fail at referendum.[41]

A. The 'Undemocratic' and 'Legal Uncertainty' Objections

The first two objections are closely related and entwined with a long-established opposition in Australia to constitutional rights and bills of rights.[42] The debates surrounding the recognition of Indigenous peoples and the removal of racial discrimination from the *Constitution* have therefore highlighted the ongoing tension between a litigious approach to the protection of rights and a majoritarian approach which is intent on upholding parliamentary supremacy. The former approach is usually not averse to entrenched rights guarantees and their interpretation by the judiciary; this is not seen as a contradiction to democracy but as a necessary check on unrestrained majoritarianism. The majoritarian view, however, objects to judicial adjudication of what are often contentious moral and policy questions, on the basis that these types of decisions should be left to elected representatives. It sees political procedures and democratic participation as the best mechanism for rights protection.[43]

As acknowledged in Chapter two, the Australian attachment to parliamentary supremacy and suspicion of judicially adjudicated rights guarantees is longstanding. However, for the purposes of analytical discussion and reflecting my own wrestling with these arguments, this chapter questions whether

[39] See eg Allan (n 38 above); Greg Sheridan, 'Constitutional Change will Divide Not Unite the Nation', *The Australian* (20 September 2014) <https://www.theaustralian.com.au/commentary/opinion/constitutional-change-will-divide-not-unite-the-nation/news-story/ed3fdd9de4d4b4fe0527993544f2f185> accessed 18 November 2019.

[40] See eg Anne Twomey, 'A Revised Proposal for Indigenous Recognition' (2014) 36 *Sydney Law Review* 381; Anne Twomey, 'Indigenous Constitutional Recognition Explained: The Issues, Risks and Options' (Constitutional Reform Unit, University of Sydney Law School, 26 January 2012) 7–9.

[41] Stuart Rintoul, 'Race Power Opens Pandora's Box', *The Australian* (Sydney, 22 December 2011) 9, quoting Warren Mundine and George Brandis; Patricia Karvelas, 'Laws "May Take Race Relations Backwards"', *The Australian* (Sydney, 17 December 2011) 1, quoting Nigel Scullion.

[42] See full discussion in the preceding chapter. For arguments see Goldsworthy, 'Against a Constitutional Bill of Rights in Australia' (n 12 above); Julian Leeser and Ryan Haddrick, *Don't Leave Us with the Bill: The Case against an Australian Bill of Rights* (The Menzies Research Centre, 2009).

[43] See Jeremy Waldron, 'A Right-Based Critique of Constitutional Rights' (1993) 13(1) *Oxford Journal of Legal Studies* 18; Jeremy Waldron, 'Participation: The Right of Rights' (1998) 98 *Proceedings of the Aristotelian Society* 307; Jeremy Waldron, 'The Core of the Case against Judicial Review' (2006) 115(6) *Yale Law Journal* 1346.

the common objections to a racial non-discrimination clause are sufficient and sustainable, given that Australia's *Constitution* contains explicitly discriminatory provisions and has presided over discriminatory laws and policies particularly in relation to Indigenous Australians. These factors must be taken into account when assessing whether Australia's democratic institutions and political processes, as presently established by the *Constitution*, provide sufficient mechanisms for the protection of Indigenous rights. In my view they do not. The history of discrimination against Indigenous people affirms that they do not. This is the problem for which constitutional experts must try to find the most just, legally certain and constitutionally congruent solution. One option is a judicially adjudicated racial non-discrimination guarantee, the objections to which are explored below. But there are other solutions which arguably better fit Australia's constitutional history, culture and design, which are the focus of later chapters.

(i) Australia's Constitution *is Not a Vehicle for Rights or Values*

The undemocratic and uncertainty objections to the proposed racial non-discrimination clause are founded in a common view of Australia's *Constitution* as a structural rule book,[44] rather than a rights- or values-laden document. As Professor Jeffrey Goldsworthy has described:

> The whole idea of the Constitution as an object of quasi-religious veneration, inspiration, and redemption is alien to Australians, although an increasing number would like to amend the Constitution so that it could play a more 'educative' role in spreading a 'human rights culture'. ... I concede that formally declaring the nation's commitment to abstract moral principles might serve to educate and inspire, as Abraham Lincoln suggested. But Australians seem to get by without constitutional prompting. For them, basic values and commitments are up for grabs along with everything else in politics.[45]

Further, the undemocratic objections to the proposed racial non-discrimination clause arise from a broad belief that the *Constitution* is *sensibly* structural rather than rights- or values-laden. This view sees the *Constitution* as successful because it is a basic charter of government, rather than an aspirational or moral document. The view opposes entrenchment of rights guarantees into the *Constitution* on the basis that matters of morality and values should be argued

[44] See discussion in Chapter 2 above. Sir Anthony Mason, 'The Australian Constitution in Retrospect and Prospect' in Robert French, Geoffrey Lindell and Cheryl Saunders (eds), *Reflections on the Australian Constitution* (Federation Press 2003) 8.

[45] Jeffrey Goldsworthy, 'Constitutional Cultures, Democracy, and Unwritten Principles' [2012] *University of Illinois Law Review* 683, 687–88 (citations omitted). See also Elisa Arcioni and Adrienne Stone, 'The Small Brown Bird: Values and Aspirations in the Australian Constitution' (2016) 14(1) *ICON* 60.

out by elected representatives, not declared in a *Constitution* where they must be interpreted, probably unpredictably, by unelected judges.[46]

Goldsworthy explains that unlike the United States Constitution, the *Australian Constitution* serves as a basic law, not a 'higher law'. It perhaps cannot even be considered a 'people's law', because many Australians do not even know we have a *Constitution*.[47] The *Constitution* sets up the structures in which moral debates and matters of justice can be argued out in the political realm, but it enumerates few morals or values itself. So, unlike in the USA, most Australians do not appeal to the *Constitution* when arguing matters of justice. The *Constitution* is considered a dull, 'prosaic document expressed in lawyer's language'.[48] This is how those who object to entrenchment of rights guarantees or values would prefer it stay.

The undemocratic and uncertainty objections are founded in the belief that the absence of rights guarantees and declarations of values in the *Constitution* is one of its greatest democratic strengths, and the belief that the *Constitution* is overwhelmingly successful: it works well as it is and should not be fundamentally changed. For those who oppose its fundamental alteration, the *Constitution* can represent the founders' collective wisdom; it is a treasured link with history and the past.[49] It also represents Australia's continuous and successful democracy. As Professor James Allan describes,

> Australia is one of the oldest democracies. Yes, our young nation has been a democracy, a successful democracy, longer than all but a half-dozen or so other countries. And that is in part because the Constitution we have is the best written Constitution.[50]

A continuous, stable constitution presiding over a continuous, stable democracy is regarded with pride. The influence of this mindset partly explains resistance to the entrenchment of notions such as 'equality' or 'non-discrimination' into the *Constitution*, for it may be unclear what such ideals mean in practice when interpreted by the judiciary. Because constitutional stability, continuity

[46] See Greg Craven, *Conversations with the Constitution: Not Just a Piece of Paper* (University of New South Wales Press 2004) 38–42.

[47] Goldsworthy, 'Constitutional Cultures, Democracy, and Unwritten Principles' (n 45 above) 685.

[48] ibid, quoting Sir Anthony Mason (n 44 above) 7–8. See also Craven (n 46 above) 9–10. Note also Justice Keane's description of Australia's 'small brown bird' of a Constitution. See the Hon Patrick Keane, 'In Celebration of the Constitution', speech delivered at the National Archives Commission, Queensland, 12 June 2008.

[49] See discussion of 'old constitutionalism': Craven (n 46 above) 38–42. For this kind of constitutional conservatism as it manifests in the USA, see also Bruce P Frohnen, 'Law's Culture: Conservatism and the American Constitutional Order' (2004) 27 *Harvard Journal of Law & Public Policy* 459, 463; Orrin Hatch, 'A Constitutional Conservatism for Our Time' (2015) 19 *Texas Review of Law & Policy* 199, 201–2.

[50] James Allan, 'The Document We Have Sure Ain't Broken, So Why Change It?', *The Australian* (30 January 2014) <https://www.theaustralian.com.au/opinion/the-document-we-have-sure-aint-broken-so-why-change-it/news-story/904e05f72e61653bf39e68fa17bde0d8> accessed 18 November 2011.

and legal certainty are deeply valued, constitutional imperfection seems more readily tolerated in order to avoid unpredictable future consequences. Such imperfections, in this line of thinking, are best addressed gradually by parliaments through evolutionary democratic processes, not by inserting ambiguous words into the *Constitution* which then must be interpreted by unelected judges. This attitude is inherently conservative and cautious about attempts at transformative change, especially constitutional change. It prefers slow, incremental reform to idealistically-driven radical change and is sceptical about 'seeking immediate and complete vindication of a single abstract principle.'[51] This attitude helps explain resistance to the insertion of a broad racial non-discrimination guarantee into the Australian *Constitution*.

(ii) A 'Thin' View of Democracy

In my grappling with objections to a racial non-discrimination guarantee, I eventually understood that not every opponent of the Expert Panel's proposal simply did not care about discrimination against Indigenous people, or worse, wanted Parliament to discriminate. In general, the parliamentary supremacy objection to the proposed racial discrimination prohibition is not based on the presupposition that Parliament should pass discriminatory laws, but that it should not be left to the courts to decide which laws and policies constitute unacceptable discrimination. The concern, I came to realise, was more structural than moral: while there may be agreement on the moral problem of a constitution that has presided over unjust discrimination against Indigenous peoples, there was disagreement over the appropriate structural solution. The question of concern to the objectors was: 'Who should ultimately decide – Parliament or the High Court?'

Majoritarian objections to the proposed racial non-discrimination clause and entrenched rights in general stem from a 'thin' view of democracy, under which majoritarian decision-making is all-important and ideas about the existence of any objective democratic values or rights are less important. Allan critiques what he calls a more progressive and 'morally pregnant' understanding of the term 'democracy', which imbues the term with a deeper meaning or quality than simply describing a majoritarian decision-making procedure. He argues that progressives incorrectly describe the outcomes of decisions as either democratic or undemocratic. According to Allan, it is only a decision-making process that can be democratic or undemocratic – hence the assertion that judicial decision-making is undemocratic, because judges are not elected. For Allan, therefore, written constitutions that must be

[51] Writing the US context, Hatch calls this aspect of conservatism 'prudence'. See Hatch (n 49 above) 203–4. See also Ernest Young, 'Rediscovering Conservatism: Burkean Political Theory and Constitutional Interpretation' (1994) 72 *North Carolina Law Review* 619, 622.

interpreted and applied by judges, or entrenched Bills of rights also subject to judicial review, are undemocratic because the decision-makers are unelected judges.[52]

Waldron, a chief proponent of the majority-rule view of democracy and an opponent of judicially adjudicated rights protections, writes of the democratic process that: 'according equal weight or equal potential decisiveness to individual votes is a way of respecting persons. In this sense, majority-decision is a respectful procedure – not just an admirable technical device for securing action-in-concert in the circumstances of politics'.[53] Waldron suggests we should trust and respect our fellow citizens, as autonomous and responsible rights-bearers, to make sensible decisions about rights and have appropriate concern for others in such decisions.[54] Thus, decision-making with respect to moral matters over which reasonable people disagree should be left to popularly-elected representatives rather than the judiciary, because this is the only way for individuals to have a fair and equal say in matters affecting them. As Goldsworthy puts it, 'ordinary people have a right to participate on equal terms in the political decision-making that affects their lives'.[55] This is why parliamentary supremacy in contentious moral and policy matters, which human rights questions inevitably are, is important.

The concern to ensure democratic decisiveness in human rights matters is connected to the fact that rights guarantees are usually broadly worded. The ambiguity of such clauses increases the inevitability of reasonable disagreement. Allan thus argues that because Bills of rights deal in 'moral abstractions … at a level of indeterminacy that finesses disagreement',[56] asking judges to decide the extent and practical application of such morality-laden rights gives courts increased discretion and thus power, which is to the detriment of democracy. Allan's conclusion is that 'bills of rights hand power to judges at the expense of the elected legislature. They diminish democracy'.[57] Australia, according to Allan, is 'remarkably democratic', mainly because of its absence of a Bill of rights.[58] It is on the basis of this kind of reasoning that the proposal to entrench

[52] James Allan, 'Intimations of the Decline of Democracy' (2010) 54(5) *Quadrant* 20, 20. See also James Allan, 'Oh That I Were Made Judge in the Land' (2002) 30(3) *Federal Law Review* 561, 573–76; James Allan, 'Why Australia Does Not Have, and Does Not Need, a National Bill of Rights' (2012) 24 *Giornale di Storia Constituzionale/Journal of Constitutional History* 35, 42.

[53] Jeremy Waldron, *Law and Disagreement* (Oxford University Press 1999) 114–15.

[54] Waldron, 'A Right-Based Critique of Constitutional Rights' (n 43 above) 27–28.

[55] Jeffrey Goldsworthy, *Parliamentary Sovereignty: Contemporary Debates* (Cambridge University Press 2010) 9–10.

[56] Allan, 'Intimations of the Decline of Democracy' (n 52 above) 22.

[57] ibid. See also James Allan, 'The Victorian *Charter of Human Rights and Responsibilities*: Exegesis and Criticism' (2006) 30(3) *Melbourne University Law Review* 906, in which Allan criticises the Victorian Charter of Human Rights and Responsibilities for handing too much interpretative power to the judiciary.

[58] Allan, 'Why Australia Does Not Have, and Does Not Need, a National Bill of Rights' (n 52 above) 36.

a racial non-discrimination clause in the *Constitution* has been regarded by objectors as one that would erode and disrupt Australia's remarkably successful democracy by transferring more power to the High Court.

(iii) A Belief that Entrenched Rights Clauses Do Not Necessarily Protect Rights

Scepticism regarding Bills of rights in Australia began with the inception of the *Constitution*. When the *Constitution* was being developed, the prevailing argument, particularly potent in the British and Australian legal traditions, was that the English rule of law system provided better protection for individual rights than any declared general rights that can be written down in a constitution.[59] The suspicion of entrenched rights carried significant weight in Australia. Goldsworthy explains that the founders 'deemed it both unnecessary and unwise to impose substantive fetters on their parliaments' powers. One of their reasons was that judicial interpretations of abstract rights could have unpredictable and undesirable consequences.'[60]

Despite the lack of constitutional rights guarantees, Goldsworthy argues that Australia's human rights record, while 'far from perfect', is 'at least as meritorious as that of the United States', where a constitutional Bill of rights has been in operation.[61] Professor Suri Ratnapala similarly notes that 'over 130 countries have a bill of rights in one form or another but only a minority of them can truly claim a reasonable record of respect for human rights'.[62] Supporting this assertion, a widely held view in Australia propounded by influential early writers such as Quick and Garran was that entrenched rights were not necessarily effective in protecting individual freedoms – the common law and democratic process was a far more effective method of rights protection.

[59] AV Dicey, *Introduction to the Study of the Law of the Constitution* (8th edn, Macmillan 1915) 196–99. See also Haig Patapan, 'The Dead Hand of the Founders? Original Intent and the Constitutional Protection of Rights and Freedoms in Australia' (1997) 25(2) *Federal Law Review* 211, 219–20. As Greg Craven explains: '[t]he Founders, rightly or wrongly, believed wholeheartedly in that mythical beast the "British Constitutional Genius", operating via a concept of parliamentary and responsible government, as the very best means by which to protect (and indeed to define) human rights. Consequently, such rights were to be protected by the elected Parliaments and not by the courts.': Greg Craven, 'The High Court of Australia: A Study in the Abuse of Power' (1999) 22(1) *University of New South Wales Law Journal* 216, 222.

[60] Goldsworthy, 'Constitutional Cultures, Democracy, and Unwritten Principles' (n 45 above) 687. See also Jeffrey Goldsworthy, 'The Constitutional Protection of Rights in Australia' in Gregory Craven (ed), *Australian Federation: Towards the Second Century* (Melbourne University Press 1992) 151, 151–57; Goldsworthy, 'Against a Constitutional Bill of Rights in Australia' (n 12 above) 394.

[61] Goldsworthy, 'Constitutional Cultures, Democracy, and Unwritten Principles' (n 45 above) 687.

[62] Suri Ratnapala, 'Bills of Rights in Functioning Parliamentary Democracies: Kantian, Consequentialist and Institutionalist Scepticisms' (2010) 34(2) *Melbourne University Law Review* 592, 609. See also discussion of the uncertain operation of the s 35 protection of Aboriginal rights in the Canadian Constitution, in Chapter 4 of this volume.

This belief held that democracy, by giving as equal as possible a share of power to citizens and enabling citizens to influence the laws affecting them, is adequate to protect individual rights.[63]

Not only do critics hold concerns about domestic Bills of rights, however: there is also scepticism towards 'universal' or international human rights declarations and their practical utility in the domestic context. Australian High Court judges have been criticised when they have turned to international law as an aid to constitutional interpretation.[64]

(iv) Uncertain Words

A common related objection is that there is uncertainty in the meaning of the words proposed by the Expert Panel's racial non-discrimination clause and that this may lead to unintended consequences and unwise risks.[65] Uncertainty in wording, it is argued, is likely to lead to unpredictable exercise of judicial power, by conferring on the judiciary too much discretion in interpreting the clause and thus deciding its practical operation. The objection is underpinned by a concern to maintain parliamentary supremacy and an opposition to judicial review of parliamentary action concerning largely moral and political questions. As Allan explained, he opposed the proposed racial non-discrimination clause:

> Because no one has the slightest idea … how it will be interpreted. … Anything beyond the minimalist repeal option is basically an anti-democratic proposal. It is a proposal that carries with it the potential for much greater judicial power in terms of invalidating and striking down parliament's statutes, meaning the majority of voters' statutes. … No one should sensibly be asked to buy something whose contents are in reality unknown and unknowable.[66]

As discussed below, Allan's view is perhaps rhetorically overstated: there is a significant body of racial non-discrimination case law in Australia, interpreting the RDA, that may help rationally predict how a racial non-discrimination clause in the *Constitution* would likely be applied and interpreted by the courts. Similarly, we can look to judicial interpretation of existing constitutional restraints on parliamentary power, such as section 116, to predict how courts may interpret this new kind of restraint. Nonetheless, Allan's

[63] Waldron, *Law and Disagreement* (n 53 above) 114–15; Patapan (n 59 above) 219–20. Notably, this has not just been a view held by the right of politics. Historically, the Australian Labor Party has also expressed preferences for parliamentary supremacy over the judicial adjudication of rights. See Whitlam's comments in Goldsworthy, 'Against a Constitutional Bill of Rights in Australia' (n 12 above) 396–97; see also former Labor Premier of NSW, Bob Carr's advocacy, explained in Brian Galligan and Emma Larking, 'Rights Protection: The Bill of Rights Debate and Rights Projection in Australia's States and Territories' (2007) 28 *Adelaide Law Review* 177, 191.

[64] See Hilary Charlesworth and others, 'Deep Anxieties: Australia and the International Legal Order' (2003) 25(4) *Sydney Law Review* 423, 424.

[65] See eg Twomey, 'A Revised Proposal for Indigenous Recognition' (n 40 above) 405–8.

[66] Allan (n 38 above).

point about the risk of unintended consequences in relation to the proposed clause warrants discussion. His view is not only that uncertainty would be created by inserting a racial non-discrimination guarantee into the *Constitution*, but that problematic uncertainty would be created by inserting anything new, because the words would be subject to judicial interpretation, and laws enacted by elected representatives may be struck down at judicial discretion. Allan also, therefore, opposes symbolic recognition of Indigenous peoples in the *Constitution*.[67]

(v) The Perceived Untrustworthiness of the High Court

Journalist and commentator for *The Australian*, Greg Sheridan, has argued:

> [I]t is virtually impossible to stop activist judges reading things into any part of the Constitution. Any grandiloquent word in any constitution becomes in time a licence for judges to make law. That is profoundly anti-democratic.[68]

Anxiety about potential judicial activism and the perceived undemocratic nature of judicial decision-making exacerbates concerns about constitutional reform. Constitutional experts like Nicholas Aroney, James Allan[69] and Jeffrey Goldsworthy[70] have criticised the High Court for the method some judges have taken in constitutional interpretation in recent decades, thus increasing legal uncertainty concerns. In particular, critics tend to disagree with the 'living tree' approach to constitutional interpretation, which sees the *Constitution* as a document whose meaning evolves in accordance with the developing values of society. The objectors usually prefer an originalist or 'locked-in' approach, because this reduces uncertainty.[71]

The major criticism of the 'living tree' approach to constitutional interpretation relates closely to a majoritarian understanding of democracy, in which the democratic legitimacy of decision-makers depends on whether or not they are elected. Allan and Aroney argue that the originalist approach to constitutional

[67] ibid. Notably, however, there is far more risk of interpretational ambiguity in inserting symbolic words into the *Constitution* than there is in inserting carefully drafted, technical, machinery amendments that are in keeping with essential constitutional character – this possibility will be explored in the amendment proposed in Chapter 6 of this volume.

[68] Sheridan (n 39 above).

[69] James Allan and Nicholas Aroney, 'An Uncommon Court: How the High Court of Australia Has Undermined Australian Federalism' (2008) 30(2) *Sydney Law Review* 245.

[70] Jeffrey Goldsworthy, 'Constitutional Implications Revisited' (2011) 30(1) *University of Queensland Law Journal* 9; Jeffrey Goldsworthy, 'The High Court, Implied Rights and Constitutional Change' (1995) 39(3) *Quadrant* 46.

[71] The implications of originalism versus versions of living originalism will be explored further in Chapter 5 of this volume, through the discussion of the changing judicial interpretation of the phrase 'directly chosen by the people' in ss 7 and 24 of the *Constitution*. See Allan and Aroney (n 69 above) 247–49. See also the discussion of the importance of the intentions of the original drafters of the *Constitution* in Craven (n 59 above) 220–22.

interpretation constrains judges and does not give them power elevated above ordinary citizens. The 'living tree' approach, however, gives judges an exclusive power and privilege: they can interpret and impose their personal understanding of changing societal values on the *Constitution*, in a way that ordinary citizens cannot. This, they argue, is undemocratic.[72] Even when judges purport to use a literalist approach to interpreting the text, Allan and Aroney contend that this often:

> collapses into the second ['living tree'] view of constitutions and constitutionalism sketched above, one where 99.99 percent of the population is locked-in but where judges sitting at the zenith of the court hierarchy are left free to upgrade or change or alter it as they think best or right. Insisting on 'the authoritativeness of the text and nothing but the text' when it comes to constitutionalised rights guarantees is akin to handing the judges a blank cheque.[73]

The implied rights cases[74] were criticised on a similar basis for involving judicial arguments which read in rights that some argue are not present in the constitutional text.[75] Goldsworthy explained his reaction to this perceived usurpation of the people's democratic power:

> [i]t seemed obvious to me that the Court had changed the system of government established by our *Constitution* in a substantial way, without asking me or my fellow Australians whether we approved of the change, as required by s 128.[76]

More recently, and as will be discussed in depth in Chapter five below, cases such as *Roach*[77] and *Rowe*[78] have been criticised as demonstrating a 'fast-and-loose' approach by majority judges to the task of constitutional interpretation,[79] or for finding 'spurious constitutional implications' that would not necessarily have been found had better interpretative methods been employed.[80] The concern is that some High Court judges are tending to be unduly activist and are usurping the democratic power of the people as represented by Parliament.[81] Allan, in this vein, argues that if the aim is to have a legal system which keeps up to date with

[72] Allan and Aroney (n 69 above) 249–50.

[73] ibid, 254 (citations omitted).

[74] *Australian Capital Television Pty Ltd v Commonwealth* (1992) 177 CLR 106 (*Australian Capital Television*); *Nationwide News Pty Ltd v Wills* (1992) 177 CLR 1 (*Nationwide News*).

[75] See Craven (n 59 above) 224.

[76] Goldsworthy, 'Constitutional Implications Revisited' (n 70 above) 9. See also Jeffrey Goldsworthy, 'The High Court, Implied Rights and Constitutional Change' (n 70 above) 46.

[77] *Roach v Electoral Commissioner* (2007) 233 CLR 162.

[78] *Rowe v Electoral Commissioner* (2010) 243 CLR 1.

[79] James Allan, 'The Three "Rs" of Recent Australian Judicial Activism: *Roach*, *Rowe* and (No) Riginalism' (2012) 36(2) *Melbourne University Law Review* 743, 747.

[80] Nicholas Aroney, 'Towards the "Best Explanation" of the Constitution: Text, Structure, History and Principle in *Roach v Electoral Commissioner*' (2011) 30(1) *University of Queensland Law Journal* 145, 147.

[81] Dyson Heydon, 'Judicial Activism and the Death of the Rule of Law' (2004) 10 *Otago Law Review* 493.

evolving social values, then it is better not to have a written *Constitution* at all.[82] To minimise the potential for judicial activism, however, Allan and others prefer originalism as an approach to judicial constitutional interpretation. Though Goldsworthy has questioned the dichotomy between the 'living tree' approach and originalism,[83] he nonetheless notes that Australia's *Constitution* is not one with a strong moral or rights content. The *Constitution* provides the framework within which moral debates can go on in the political sphere, but it does not generally inform their content. Therefore, Goldsworthy believes that departure from originalism in judicial decision-making, in the Australian context at least, is undemocratic.[84]

The persuasiveness of such observations depends on the nature of the constitutional clauses being interpreted and the constitutional context that informs them. Some constitutional clauses or issues leave more scope for judges to fill in gaps in meaning than others. This understanding of the existence of varying degrees of conferred interpretative scope is informed by Balkin's 'living originalism' approach, which notes that constitutions can impose rules, standards and principles, or might even remain silent on certain issues, and this creates a spectrum of valid approaches to interpretation, ranging from narrow judicial discretion to very wide discretion. The nature of the constitutional clause, or the way the *Constitution* deals with the particular issue, will affect the appropriate approach to judicial interpretation of the clause or issue.[85] The important point here, however, is that some critics believe the High Court has become wayward in its approach to constitutional interpretation. Accordingly, the risks seen as being associated with entrenching a racial non-discrimination clause in the *Constitution* are perhaps being given increased weight.

A broadly framed racial non-discrimination guarantee, as proposed by the Expert Panel, would provide the High Court with wide interpretational discretion which may increase indeterminacy. The practical meaning of the guarantee in a given set of circumstances would need to be elucidated by the judiciary. That is why objectors argue that the proposed amendment would be like handing unelected judges a 'blank cheque' to do with what they want. A racial non-discrimination clause would give judges discretion to interpret the prohibition, using (some fear) potentially wayward or activist interpretational approaches, and empowering the High Court to overrule majoritarian decisions in breach of the clause on the basis of those approaches. Objectors worry this may encourage judicial activism and undermine parliamentary supremacy and the preferred 'thin' view of democracy.

[82] James Allan and Michael Kirby, 'A Public Conversation on Constitutionalism and the Judiciary between Professor James Allan and the Hon Michael Kirby AC CMG' (2009) 33(3) *Melbourne University Law Review* 1032, 1038–39.

[83] Goldsworthy, 'Constitutional Cultures, Democracy, and Unwritten Principles' (n 45 above) 684.

[84] ibid, 685, 690.

[85] See Jack Balkin, *Living Originalism* (Harvard University Press 2011); Brendan Lim, 'Review Essay: An Australian Reads 'Living Originalism' (2012) 34(4) *Sydney Law Review* 809.

B. The 'Political Unviability' Objection

The most common non-constitutional objections to a racial non-discrimination clause were the pragmatic, political unviability objections. These objections were actually political predictions or assessments as to the likely success of the proposal, rather than substantive objections to the proposed reform.[86] Such objections often do not take issue with the normative or legal justifications for the reform; they simply claim: 'This will fail'. Predictions of failure are then presented as justification for why the proposal should not be pursued. Such political unviability objections turn the objectors into political prophets with their fingers on the pulse of Australian public opinion, but usually fail to acknowledge that the advocates themselves, as political leaders, commentators or academics with strong voices in the media, are playing a role in leading, shaping and influencing that public opinion. Political unviability predictions, repeated enough times in the public domain, can become self-fulfilling prophecies.

Some initial political viability assessments of the Expert Panel's proposed racial non-discrimination guarantee changed over time. For example, former Minister for Indigenous Affairs, Nigel Scullion, initially criticised the proposed racial non-discrimination provision on the basis that 'clauses about discrimination will lead to a much wider debate about multiculturalism' that would 'ambush the process', but later seemed to shift his view to argue that Australia should amend the *Constitution* to show that racial discrimination is unacceptable.[87] Federal Attorney-General George Brandis also appeared to modify his views to some extent.[88] Minister Ken Wyatt, however, went from recommending a racial non-discrimination clause in his Joint Select Committee's Final Report, to publicly disavowing its political viability.[89]

Political viability is an important consideration in any discussion of constitutional reform. While this consideration should not be irresponsibly wielded as a subjective veto over constitutional reform proposals, questions of viability should nonetheless be carefully considered by reform advocates in light of all available evidence. My own assessment of political viability, taking

[86] See eg the predictions about the failure of a proposed racial non-discrimination clause and the failure of an Indigenous advisory body at referendum, in Frank Brennan, *No Small Change: The Road to Recognition for Indigenous Australia* (University of Queensland Press 2015) 275, 277–79.

[87] See Patricia Karvelas, 'Laws "May Take Race Relations Backwards"', *The Australian* (Sydney, 17 December 2011) 1, quoting Nigel Scullion. See also Commonwealth, *Parliamentary Debates*, Senate, 26 February 2013, 877–79 (Nigel Scullion).

[88] Compare George Brandis' comments quoted in Rintoul (n 41 above), to his comments in Commonwealth of Australia, Official Committee Hansard, 'Constitutional Recognition of Aboriginal and Torres Strait Islander Peoples: Roundtable Discussion', Sydney, 30 April 2013, 19, 22.

[89] See Natasha Robinson, 'Ken Wyatt: Time to Get a Move on with Constitutional Recognition', *The Australian* (10 July 2015) <https://www.theaustralian.com.au/nation/time-to-get-a-move-on-with-recognition-ken-wyatt/news-story/5af9387ecc0c3859374e9f2bd10a4963> accessed 18 November 2019.

into account the objections and counter-arguments regarding a racial non-discrimination guarantee, will be considered further below.

IV. RESPONDING TO THE OBJECTIONS

A. Responding to the 'Undemocratic' Objection

(i) The Judicial Activism Concern is Probably Over-stated

A key concern of objectors to the Expert Panel's approach is that a racial non-discrimination guarantee in the *Constitution* would encourage undemocratic judicial activism. In deciding what is discriminatory or not, it is argued, judges would need to apply social values to their decisions. Such assessment of values – essentially the answering of moral and political questions – is better left to elected politicians who are more in touch with the people, not to judges, who as Goldsworthy describes, are essentially unelected 'aristocrats'.[90] Judicial activism in this context is the criticism that a court has inappropriately exceeded its adjudicatory function in breach of the doctrines of parliamentary supremacy and the separation of powers – 'betraying its own constitutional role'[91] – and that this is undemocratic.[92]

Firstly, the concern about the undemocratic nature of judicial decision-making is perhaps exaggerated. A judge's power is not unlimited. Though they are not elected, an Australian judge's authority is bestowed via democratic processes: judges are appointed by elected governments. Further, Kirby argues that judicial decision-making does not usurp the power of the people, because it is the people who choose which laws they want to dispute and bring them to court – judges do not choose which issues they resolve.[93]

Secondly, the concern about the wayward activism of the High Court is perhaps overstated and there may be an element of political bias inherent in the

[90] See Jeffrey Goldsworthy, *Parliamentary Sovereignty: Contemporary Debates* (Cambridge University Press 2010) 10–12.

[91] Craven (n 59 above) 218.

[92] See also Heydon (n 81 above) 495: 'judicial activism' is explained as 'using judicial power for a purpose other than that for which it was granted, namely doing justice according to law in the particular case. It means serving some function other than what is necessary for the decision of the particular dispute between the parties. Often the illegitimate function is the furthering of some political, moral or social programme: the law is seen not as the touchstone by which the case in hand is to be decided, but as a possible starting point or catalyst for developing a new system to solve a range of other cases. Even more commonly the function is a discursive and indecisive meander through various fields of learning for its own sake.' But see also the balanced discussion on the rise of judicial power in Australia in Nicholas Aroney and Benjamin B Saunders, 'On Judicial Rascals and Self-Appointed Monarchs: The Rise of Judicial Power in Australia' (2017) 36 *University of Queensland Law Journal* 221.

[93] Allan and Kirby (n 82 above) 1047.

claim. As many commentators have pointed out, judges in Australia are usually criticised for being activist when their decision, usually one upholding the rights of a minority, displeases political conservatives.[94] Professor George Williams has argued:

> The label is normally only applied when someone disagrees with a High Court decision that is viewed as liberal or progressive, perhaps because it protects the rights of someone like an asylum seeker or prisoner. By contrast, decisions that uphold strong, even draconian, government action against the same people tend to attract little comment.[95]

Others have argued that the term 'judicial activism' is not particularly useful as an analytical tool in discussing different approaches to judicial interpretation.[96]

In my view, the argument as to how a racial non-discrimination guarantee in the *Constitution* would *increase* inappropriate judicial activism has not been successfully articulated. Ratnapala argues that given Australia's institutional and political stability, the risks associated with entrenching some 'narrowly-focused' rights in the *Constitution* would be relatively few.[97] Similarly, in addressing the 'unelected judges' criticism of implied rights, French CJ urges that we:

> reflect upon what it is that courts already do in applying the common law which has been developed by the unelected judges of England and Australia. … [M]any of the things we think of as basic rights and freedoms come from the common law and how the common law is used to interpret Acts of Parliament and regulations made under them so as to minimise intrusion into those rights and freedoms.[98]

In other words, part of a judge's legitimate common law role is to decide matters of rights. The common law principle of legality operates to protect rights and freedoms 'in a way that is entirely consistent with the principle of parliamentary supremacy.'[99] In Australia, this important principle of statutory interpretation

[94] For this trend as it manifests in the USA, see Ernest A Young, 'Judicial Activism and Conservative Politics' (2002) 73(4) *University of Colorado Law Review* 1139.

[95] George Williams, 'When the Umpire Takes a Stand', *Sydney Morning Herald* (12 November 2011) 22. However, it should be noted that Williams' examples may not be considered symmetrical: striking down a law is usually considered more activist and interventionist than upholding a law. See also Justice Michael Kirby, 'Judicial Activism: Power without Responsibility? No, Appropriate Activism Conforming to Duty' (2006) 30(2) *Melbourne University Law Review* 576, who suggests that 'judicial activism' has become code language for denouncing important judicial decisions with which conservative critics disagree.

[96] Michael Coper, 'Concern About Judicial Method' (2006) 30(2) *Melbourne University Law Review* 554.

[97] Ratnapala (n 62 above) 616–17.

[98] Chief Justice Robert French, 'The Common Law and the Protection of Human Rights', speech delivered at the Anglo Australasian Lawyers Society, Sydney, 4 September 2009, 1–2. French explained that the term 'unelected judges' 'has been used to suggest that a kind of democratic deficit would result if judges were to be required to make decisions involving the weighing up of important but competing societal values – the kind of judgments not unusual in human rights jurisprudence.'

[99] Chief Justice Robert French, 'Human Rights Protection in Australia and the United Kingdom: Contrasts and Comparisons', speech delivered at the Anglo-Australasian Lawyers Society and

began with *Potter v Minahan* in 1908, and developed such that common law rights and freedoms could not be impinged upon by legislation, except by 'plain words' or necessary implication.[100] Later, the language shifted from 'common law' rights, to a presumption that 'individual rights and fundamental freedoms' of a more universal nature must not be abrogated unless there is a clear and unambiguous legislative intention to do so.[101] Courts have also elucidated an implied freedom of political communication, imputed from the structure of the *Constitution* and the representative democracy it establishes.[102]

Constitutional implications work both ways, however. Courts have also implied non-explicit powers in favour of the Commonwealth, such as the implied 'nationhood power'[103] and by interpreting the scope of the section 51 powers broadly.[104] This is part of courts adjudicating on the relationships between structures and institutions under the *Constitution*. Professor Adrienne Stone argues that democracy-based objections to judicial interpretation of constitutionalised rights should apply equally to judicial interpretation of structural elements of the *Constitution* and the scope of Commonwealth power, which also allow judges to decide 'matters of moral or political significance in the face of reasonable disagreement'. Therefore, 'those who object to constitutional rights should also object to structural judicial review'.[105] Indeed, in construing section 51 powers, the High Court had to decide on the scope of the section 51(xxvi) Race Power, which remains the subject of moral disagreement, and the Court found that the Parliament probably did possess the power

Constitutional and Administrative Law Bar Association, London, 5 July 2012, 23. See also discussion in Dean Meagher, 'A Common Law Bill of Rights' in Matthew Groves, Janina Boughey and Dan Meagher (eds), *The Legal Protection of Rights in Australia* (Hart Publishing 2019).

100 *Potter v Minahan* (1908) 7 CLR 277, 304 (O'Connor J); *Re Cuno; Mansfield v Mansfield* (1889) 43 Ch D 12, 17; *Melbourne Corporation v Barry* (1922) 31 CLR 174, 206. See also French (n 98 above) 8–9 [13]–[15].

101 See *Bropho v Western Australia* (1990) 171 CLR 1; *Coco v The Queen* (1994) 179 CLR 427; French (n 98 above) 9 [16].

102 *Australian Capital Television* (n 74 above); *Nationwide News* (n 74 above); *Lange v Australian Broadcasting Corporation* (1997) 189 CLR 520, 559–62; *Coleman v Power* (2004) 220 CLR 1.

103 *Australian Communist Party v Commonwealth* (1951) 83 CLR 1; *R v Sharkey* (1949) 79 CLR 121.

104 See eg the broad scope given to the external affairs power in *Koowarta v Bjelke-Petersen* (1982) 153 CLR 168 (*Koowarta*); *Commonwealth v Tasmania* (1983) 158 CLR 1 (*Tasmanian Dam Case*).

105 Adrienne Stone, 'Democratic Objections to Structural Judicial Review and the Judicial Role in Constitutional Law' (2010) 60(1) *University of Toronto Law Journal* 109, 110. Note that Goldsworthy and Aroney have criticised Stone's argument on the basis that the undemocratic objection can only apply to judicial review of rights. They draw on Waldron, who proceeds from the starting point that judicial review of constitutional rights is wrong because it is individuals themselves, as moral beings (as represented by Parliament), who are the best protectors of their own rights. Because human beings have rights, they should be trusted to protect them through self-government. Aroney therefore argues that democracy should be preferred for resolving political disputes to do with individual rights, but not necessarily other types of disputes. See Jeffrey Goldsworthy, 'Structural Judicial Review and the Objection from Democracy' (2010) 60(1) *University of Toronto Law Journal* 137; Nicholas Aroney, 'Reasonable Disagreement, Democracy and the Judicial Safeguards of Federalism' (2008) 27(1) *University of Queensland Law Journal* 129; Waldron, *Law and Disagreement* (n 53 above) 223.

to racially discriminate.[106] Judges already decide contentious moral matters in interpreting Australia's *Constitution*. Kirby in this vein refutes Allan's argument about the inappropriateness of judicial reference to values:

> The contradiction lies in his statement that we all know judges make law. Yet, on the other hand, he adheres to a 'fairy tale' view that there can be no moral input by the judge at the point of the decision. Well now, how then do the judges make the law? They make it by reference to values.[107]

In some respects, therefore, the argument about whether judges should be interpreting moral matters is misplaced in the Australian constitutional context – they already do. Judges already play a role in developing the common law and interpreting contentious moral issues under Australia's written *Constitution*. Supposedly 'activist' judges are already interpreting constitutional clauses to do with race. The judicial activism objection to a new prohibition on racial discrimination in the Constitution may therefore be overstated.

(ii) Australia' s Parliamentary Sovereignty is Already Limited by the Constitution *as Interpreted by the Courts*

In Australia, Parliament is not sovereign. Rather, the status of the Commonwealth Parliament is better described as parliamentary supremacy. This is because the Australian Parliament, unlike in the UK or in New Zealand, is limited in its law-making powers by the existence of our written and entrenched *Constitution*,[108] which binds Parliament to the rule of law as set out, or implied, by our *Constitution*. Since its inception, the *Constitution* has been interpreted by judges. Judges have engaged in structural interpretation, figuring out the nature of the Australian system of federal government and how the democracy works. In fulfilling this role, part of a judge's job is to draw implications from the constitutional text. The idea of the separation of powers is itself one such constitutional implication, drawn from section 71.[109]

As noted, courts have also had to interpret the Commonwealth's section 51 powers. Over time courts have interpreted the scope of such powers broadly, thus maximising and arguably expanding the Commonwealth Parliament's legislative authority.[110] But while Stone has argued that those who object to judicial

[106] *Kartinyeri* (n 20 above).

[107] Allan and Kirby (n 82 above) 1039–40 (citations omitted).

[108] Julie Taylor, 'Human Rights Protection in Australia and Parliamentary Supremacy' (2004) 32(1) *Federal Law Review* 61, 60.

[109] Patrick Emerton, 'Political Freedoms and Entitlements in the *Australian Constitution*: An Example of Referential Intentions Yielding Unintended Legal Consequences' (2010) 38(2) *Federal Law Review* 169, 172, citing Jeffrey Goldsworthy, 'Implications in Language, Law and the Constitution' in Geoffrey Lindell (ed), *Future Directions in Australian Constitutional Law* (Federation Press 1994) 150, 164–65.

[110] *Jumbunna Coal Mine NL v Victorian Coal Miners' Association* (1908) 6 CLR 309, 368 (O'Connor J); *Koowarta* (n 104 above); *Tasmanian Dam Case* (n 104 above). Stone (n 105 above) 118–19.

review of constitutional rights should also object to judicial review of other elements of the Constitution,[111] those objectors often have a special problem with new rights guarantees being inserted into the *Constitution* because they are usually broad and ambiguously worded restraints on parliamentary power, leaving largely moral matters to be determined by an unelected judiciary. Yet the structural, federal and empowering elements of the *Constitution* also provide written restraints on parliamentary power, and these too can involve ambiguous words enlivening moral matters – so what is the difference?

On one hand, those objecting to the racial non-discrimination prohibition are correct. The Expert Panel's proposed section 116A would restrict Parliament's law-making power: it would limit parliamentary supremacy with respect to the enactment of race-based or racially discriminatory laws. Yet why this would be a detrimental reform has not been adequately argued by objectors. After all, the *Constitution* already limits parliamentary supremacy with respect to certain matters – not least by enumerating and sharing powers in the federal scheme. The judiciary already interprets the existing race provisions, laden with controversial questions of politics and morality as they are, and judicial activism in constitutional interpretation is already a concern for commentators even though Australia has no Bill of rights. It is therefore unclear how insertion of a racial non-discrimination protection would make the situation worse – or at least, this has not been properly explained by opponents. A racial non-discrimination guarantee would change the text of the *Constitution*, reforming the situation from one in which racial discrimination is explicitly allowed, to one in which racial discrimination is generally not allowed, subject to a special measures exception. Fairness, as discussed in the preceding chapter, on its basic definition requires that people are treated equally or in a way that is reasonable in the circumstances. A racial non-discrimination clause would arguably enhance the fairness of the *Constitution* by reducing the potential for arbitrary race-based laws and helping to ensure equal treatment of citizens. It would do this by imposing a judicially adjudicated restraint, subject to exceptions, on Parliament's power to enact race-based laws. This could be a justifiable departure from the current situation, in which judges already determine the scope of Parliament's power to enact racially discriminatory laws.

Indeed, a racial non-discrimination clause would change the content of those rules in a way that is not entirely new. Analogous constitutional restraints already exist. The drafters of the *Constitution* thought it prudent to incorporate various judicially adjudicated restraints on parliamentary power, including restraints to prevent discrimination against the States.[112] Principles of non-discrimination

[111] Stone (n 105 above) 110.

[112] For example, s 116 of the *Constitution* protects freedom of religion, s 117 prevents discrimination against States' residents, and there are a variety of express limitations on Commonwealth powers: the 'just terms' qualification in s 51(xxxi), the State non-discrimination requirements in s 51(ii), as well as State consent or concurrence requirements in s 51(xxxiii), (xxxiv) and (xxxviii).

were thus implemented by the Founders in the context of federal relationships. However, the racially discriminatory attitudes of the era meant that the drafters did not include such restraints with respect to race – they instead included clauses *enabling* racial discrimination. If the Australian people were to vote at a referendum to rectify this by embedding a judicially adjudicated restraint on racially discriminatory laws and policies, this may not be the radical change critics assert. Rather, it would add to the array of judicially adjudicated limitations on parliamentary power which are already a part of Australian constitutional arrangements.

The salient question is whether the High Court should be empowered to hold Parliament accountable to a racial non-discrimination principle written into the *Constitution*. There is an argument that a political system held judicially accountable to an explicitly stated non-discrimination principle would be more democratic than the current *Constitution* which allows discrimination, because equality and non-discrimination are fundamental to a fair democracy.

(iii) The Undemocratic Objection is Somewhat Circular

There is something circular about the reasoning which favours the 'thin' view of democracy and therefore opposes entrenching a racial non-discrimination clause on majoritarian grounds. Allan, for example, on one hand argues that so-called progressives are wrong to ascribe a 'morally pregnant' democratic or undemocratic quality to the outcome of democratic decisions.[113] He says all that matters is whether the decision was made via a democratic procedure. Yet on the other hand, Allan contends that the outcome of a referendum to entrench a racial non-discrimination clause would be undemocratic, even though a referendum is clearly a democratic procedure – arguably a democratic procedure superior to the parliamentary process in terms of allowing individuals a direct say (and certainly a more democratic process than that undertaken by the original drafters of the *Constitution*, given that Indigenous people and women were not given a fair say or vote).[114] Allan contends that if the Australian people

[113] Allan, 'Intimations of the Decline of Democracy' (n 52 above) 20.

[114] Craven (n 59 above) 220–21, 226, characterises the referendum process as *more* democratic than the democratic process undertaken by the founders of the *Constitution*, which excluded Indigenous people and women: 'the Founders comprised a group of mercifully deceased, white, male Anglo-Saxons, whose racist, sexist and dietarily unacceptable assumptions should have no controlling force over the Constitution. However, the conclusive answer to such essays in anachronistic constitutional correctness lies in the democratic origins of the Constitution and the processes by which it was adopted. Put simply, from 1897, the delegates to the Conventions (except for those from Western Australia) were popularly elected. They framed their Constitution pursuant to mandates from the peoples of their respective colonies, under intense public scrutiny and surrounded by community debate. That document, which was in every sense the embodiment of their collective intentions, was in turn voted upon in a series of popular referenda and ratified. This is a formidable, indeed an unbeatable, democratic pedigree for the Australian Constitution … Of course, there is one process that clearly will produce a superior democratic will to those which originally underlay the formulation and adoption of the Constitution, and that is an amendment of the Constitution under s 128.'

were to exercise their democratic will under section 128 to insert a judicially adjudicated racial non-discrimination clause, which constrains majoritarian decision-making found to be in breach, then this outcome would be undemocratic. But Allan does not adequately address the fact that, if the proposal succeeds at referendum, then the Australian people *want* a judicially adjudicated restraint on racial discrimination. If all that matters is the democratic decision-making procedure, he should be content with whatever constitutional reforms the Australian people in their majority wisdom decide to implement.

My objection could of course be taken to the point of absurdity. For example, a successful referendum that abolishes the voting rights of all citizens and establishes a dictatorship can be legitimately criticised as an undemocratic reform, notwithstanding the democratic nature of the decision-making procedure endorsing the reform. As Waldron has argued, 'if the people voted to experiment with dictatorship, democratic principles might give us a reason to allow them to do so. But it would not follow that dictatorship is democratic'.[115] Drawing on this analysis, Stone observes that 'a democratic procedure for adopting some institution of government does not in itself make that institution democratic'.[116] In one sense, this correct observation weakens my argument that a racial non-discrimination clause inserted into the *Constitution* via a popular referendum would not be undemocratic, because the people voted for it. But in another sense, it illustrates my point that the *Constitution* is not as fair and democratic as it could be. For Allan, a judicially adjudicated constraint on majoritarianism, like that presented by a racial non-discrimination guarantee, must be undemocratic because unelected judges are the adjudicators. But the irony of democracy – that an unconstrained majority might vote to subject itself to a dictator – demonstrates that certain limitations on majoritarian decision-making, such as constraints that prevent the majority from eroding certain basic and fundamental aspects of democratic decision-making, are not necessarily undemocratic. This is arguably why the fundamental elements of the democratic process are enshrined in the *Constitution*, as our basic charter of government, and protected from ordinary legislative amendment. It may therefore be misguided for objectors to contend that a racial non-discrimination clause in the *Constitution* would be undemocratic simply because it is judicially enforced and capable of blocking some majoritarian decisions.[117] The relevant question is whether equality before the law with respect to race is a democratic essential that should be enshrined in the *Constitution*. Given the racial discrimination currently present in Australia's *Constitution*, and given the history of racially discriminatory laws and policies directed at Indigenous peoples (including laws and policies that prevented Indigenous people from participating fairly

[115] Waldron, *Law and Disagreement* (n 53 above) 255.

[116] Adrienne Stone, 'Disagreement and an Australian Bill of Rights' (2002) 26(2) *Melbourne University Law Review* 478, 485.

[117] For further explorations of the paradoxes of democracy, see Jeffrey Goldsworthy, 'Abdicating and Limiting Parliament's Sovereignty' (2006) 17(2) *King's Law Journal* 255.

and equally in democratic decision-making processes under the *Constitution*), the suggestion that such a constitutional principle is essential cannot simply be dismissed.

The fact that the proposed racial non-discrimination clause is described by objectors as undemocratic demonstrates an acceptance that elements of the *Constitution* can be undemocratic, even if they have been inserted by the people via referendum – a highly democratic procedure. In my view, the decisions by the drafters to insert sections 25, 51(xxvi) and (the now removed) section 127 were examples of a reasonably democratic process (albeit one that excluded Indigenous people) embedding undemocratic provisions into the *Constitution*. The proposed racial non-discrimination clause, if inserted by the people via a referendum, would be less susceptible to this criticism. Certainly, it would be a clause that, like most clauses in the existing *Constitution*, would be interpreted by the unelected judiciary. But it would be a democratic improvement on the current situation, which promotes and empowers differential treatment of Australian citizens on the basis of race through clauses which are also interpreted by the unelected judiciary.

(iv) The Race Clauses in the Constitution *are Themselves Undemocratic*

If Australia is, or is supposed to be a liberal democracy, and a liberal democracy means a system of governance in which citizens are free and equal, have an equal say through their equal vote and free and equal participation in the democratic system,[118] then the *Constitution* as it currently stands poses serious problems with respect to its treatment of citizens on the grounds of race – and particularly Indigenous people. If we agree that Australia's basic and practical *Constitution* provides the structures within which political arguments about morality and justice take place,[119] it must then be asked whether the *Constitution* sets up a structure whereby Australian citizens are free and equal, enjoy a fair and equal cooperation and participation in the democratic process[120] and whereby each person is shown equal respect through their equal vote,[121] with respect to race. Does the *Constitution* set up a fair, democratic process? The view that prefers the democratic process alone to protect rights presupposes first, that every section of the population is fairly guaranteed a vote, and second, that every section of the population will have a fair say in matters affecting them – they will not be unfairly hindered from participating in the democratic process. Accepting the view that the democratic process alone is sufficient to ensure that Australians are not racially discriminated against by governments presumes the neutrality and fairness of the democratic decision-making process or structure itself.

[118] John Rawls, *Political Liberalism* (Columbia University Press 2005).
[119] Goldsworthy, 'Constitutional Cultures, Democracy, and Unwritten Principles' (n 45 above) 685.
[120] Rawls (n 118 above) 4.
[121] Waldron, *Law and Disagreement* (n 53 above) 114–15.

Waldron seems to concede that majority rule cannot be regarded as impartial where there are disparate views about the democratic decision-making procedure itself.[122] Similarly, Eisgruber points out that 'in circumstances of deep and durable disagreement, it is a mistake to suppose that unrestricted majority rule, or any other procedure for resolving the disagreement, can count as neutral'.[123] The point about neutrality and fairness in the democratic decision-making process itself is important when considering the strength of Waldron's argument with respect to Australia's *Constitution*, and particularly with respect to Indigenous rights. The democratic structure set up by the *Constitution* cannot be understood as treating citizens as free and equal, when Indigenous peoples were excluded both as equal citizens from, and as negotiating parties to, the constitutional compact of 1901. Nor can the *Constitution* be said to treat citizens as free and equal when racially discriminatory clauses persist in the text, reflecting a democratic framework that may at any time, given the political will, itself be racially discriminatory. The fact of Indigenous past exclusion from democratic processes (discussed more in Chapter five below) in some jurisdictions underscores this point. Arguably, it is only correct to say that democratic procedures alone are adequate to protect rights in Australia if there exists a free and equal citizenship in Australia, and all citizens always participate fairly in that democratic procedure.

It should be noted here that the *Constitution* itself does not refer to 'citizens' or 'citizenship'. Some High Court judges have, however, established a notion of 'constitutional citizenship',[124] implied from terms such as 'the people', 'the electors', and as the opposite of 'aliens'.[125] However, omission of the term 'citizen' was a deliberate choice by the constitutional drafters.[126] There is therefore dispute about whether constitutional citizenship exists under the *Australian Constitution*,[127] as the idea of citizenship 'connotes a rights-bearing status' whereas words like 'people' and 'electors' do not.[128] For our present purposes, given that Australia is recognised as a liberal democracy, and given that the notion of Australian citizenship is a term widely used and given an everyday meaning in

[122] ibid, 299–300.

[123] Christopher L Eisgruber, 'Democracy and Disagreement: A Comment on Jeremy Waldron's *Law and Disagreement*' (2002) 6(1) *New York University Journal of Legislation and Public Policy* 35, 38.

[124] *Singh v Commonwealth* (2004) 222 CLR 322, 378–79 [134]–[135] (McHugh J) (*Singh*); cf *Koroitamana v Commonwealth* (2006) 227 CLR 31, 37 [9] (Gleeson CJ and Heydon J), 42 [31], 46 [48] (Gummow, Hayne and Crennan JJ), 49 [61] (Kirby J).

[125] In *Hwang v Commonwealth* (2005) 222 ALR 83, McHugh J described the notion of 'constitutional citizenship' as being the opposite of the constitutional term 'alien': at 89 [18]. See also Christopher Tran, 'New Perspectives on Australian Constitutional Citizenship and Constitutional Identity' (2012) 33(1) *Adelaide Law Review* 199, 201.

[126] Kim Rubenstein, *Australian Citizenship Law in Context* (Lawbook Co 2002) 29–30; Tran (n 125 above) 201.

[127] See Greg Taylor, 'Citizenship Rights and the Australian Constitution' (2001) 12(2) *Public Law Review* 205, 209–10.

[128] Tran (n 125 above) 203.

the Australian national and political discourse, I use the term 'citizenship' on the understanding that some form of common citizenship, national membership or Australian peoplehood is implied by the *Constitution*. The pertinent question is whether the individuals within this citizenship or Australian peoplehood are free and equal with respect to race, under the *Constitution*.

It is clear that, with respect to race, the *Constitution* does not establish a free and equal citizenship. Nor does it establish a structure for fair participation in democracy by all Australian citizens. The fact that Indigenous people and other non-white minorities have at various times, in some jurisdictions, been denied the right to vote demonstrates that political procedures under the *Constitution* are not sufficient protection against unjust discrimination – such procedures themselves have been discriminatory and could be again.

(v) A Liberal Democracy Requires Free and Equal Citizenship with Respect to Race

Given that Australia's *Constitution* is a structural document which sets up our political and democratic processes,[129] democratic decision-making in Australia will only be fair and democratic if the *Constitution* is fair and democratic. The *Constitution* is not fair and democratic with respect to race. The existence of the Race Power and the historical evidence informing its intended purpose do not support the existence of a free and equal citizenship with respect to race.

During the Constitutional Conventions, there was debate about whether, once admitted to the country, the 'coloured or inferior' races should be given equal citizenship. Sir Samuel Griffith was concerned about being 'flooded' by 'eastern people',[130] perhaps indicating that the power was meant to apply to immigrants. But these comments were part of an argument about whether discriminating against Australian citizens on the basis of race was acceptable. The existence of various other powers to deal with immigration and foreign affairs, including section 51(xix) the 'naturalization and aliens' power, section 51(xxvii) the 'immigration and emigration' power, section 51(xxviii) the 'influx of criminals' power and section 51(xxix) the 'external affairs' power, support a contention that the Race Power was initially intended to discriminate both against foreign outsiders and those people who had become Australian citizens, but who were of non-white ethnic backgrounds.

Convention delegate James Howe argued that 'we should as far as possible make Australia home for Australians and the British race alone' and emphasised the importance of Parliament retaining power to control 'coloured persons' in

[129] Goldsworthy, 'Constitutional Cultures, Democracy, and Unwritten Principles' (n 45 above) 685.
[130] *Official Record of the Debates of the National Australasian Convention*, Sydney, 8 April 1891, 703 (Sir Samuel Griffith).

various ways.[131] John Reid's comments at the time support this notion, but for more benevolent reasons. As the Expert Panel explained:

> John Reid … agreed with Forrest that it was 'certainly a very serious question whether the internal management of these coloured persons, once they have arrived in a state, should be taken away from the state'. He was prepared, however, to give that power to the Commonwealth because 'it might be desirable that there should be uniform laws in regard to those persons, who are more or less unfortunate persons when they arrive here'.[132]

As noted, the 1967 referendum removed the exclusion of Indigenous people from the ambit of the Race Power, but it did not confirm that the power could only be used for beneficial rather than discriminatory purposes.[133] Leaving to one side the policy argument that benevolent government action might more appropriately address demonstrable individual and community disadvantage and need rather than race,[134] Reid's benevolent intentions must be read alongside the other malevolent purposes: the Race Power was inserted to control, exclude and subordinate those who were not white.

The existence of section 51(xxvi) provides evidence against the existence of a free and equal citizenship under Australia's *Constitution*. The counter-argument is that, because the Race Power applies in theory to everyone equally, now that the exclusion of Indigenous peoples has been removed, the power is not discriminatory, as it could be used for or against any so-called 'race'. In reality, however, the Race Power has only ever been used with respect to Indigenous people.[135] While the power may in theory be used to target any section of the population on the basis of race, it is still a power to target Australians on purely racial

[131] *Official Record of the Debates of the Australasian Federal Convention*, Melbourne, 28 January 1898, 251 (James Howe).

[132] Expert Panel Report (n 1) 6 (citations omitted), quoting *Official Record of the Debates of the Australasian Federal Convention*, Melbourne, 27 January 1898, 241 (John Reid).

[133] Though judgments were split, in *Kartinyeri* (n 20 above) 378–81 [82]–[89] two Justices, Gummow and Hayne JJ, held that this power could be used to pass laws for the benefit of any race, or laws to the detriment of any race'. Similarly in *Koowarta* (n 104 above) 186 (citations omitted), Gibbs CJ held: '[i]t would be a mistake to suppose that s 51(xxvi) was included in the *Constitution* only for the purpose of enabling the Parliament to make laws for the special protection of people of particular races. Quick and Garran, in their *Annotated Constitution of the Australian Commonwealth*, correctly observed that by "sub-sec xxvi the Federal Parliament will have power to pass special and discriminating laws relating to 'the people of any race'". Such laws might validly discriminate against, as well as in favour of, the people of a particular race.'

[134] Noel Pearson, 'Next Step Is for the Nation to Leave Race Behind', *The Australian* (25 May 2013) 19; Shireen Morris, '2013 Reconciliation Week Blog: Why We Need Constitutional Reform: Recognition and Equality Before the Law' on *Castan Centre for Human Rights Law: The Official Blog* (29 May 2013) <http://castancentre.com/2013/05/29/why-we-need-constitutional-reform-recognition-and-equality-before-the-law/> accessed 18 November 2019.

[135] See eg *World Heritage Properties Conservation Act 1983* (Cth), *Aboriginal and Torres Strait Islander Heritage Protection Act 1984* (Cth), *Native Title Act 1993* (Cth), and *Corporations (Aboriginal and Torres Strait Islander) Act 2006* (Cth) which all relate specifically to Indigenous peoples and rights. See Expert Panel Report (n 1) 33; Pritchard (n 33 above) 52.

grounds. It means that Parliament is theoretically empowered to prevent Asian Australians from buying houses in Melbourne, or to prevent African Australians from earning equal wages.

The existence of section 25, which contemplates barring races from voting, also supports this contention. The High Court has pointed to section 25 to show that there is no equality before the law with respect to voting or citizenship under the *Constitution*.[136] Twomey, however, challenges the assumption that section 25 is racially discriminatory, pointing to its anti-racist intent and its derivation from the US 14th Amendment,[137] a view supported by Kirby J, who saw the clause as a disincentive or deterrent to racial disqualification from voting.[138] Twomey nonetheless notes that section 25 'did not apply to discourage discrimination against Australian Aboriginal people with respect to voting rights in the States for as long as s 127 existed'[139] and 'the consequences of s 25 were easily avoided'.[140] While it is correct that section 25 was inserted to discourage the States from barring races from voting, it is nonetheless a provision that acknowledges that excluding races from voting is allowed within the democratic system created by the *Constitution*,[141] an assertion supported by the existence of the Race Power, which allows differential treatment of citizens on racial grounds.

The right to vote is a crucial right of citizenship and demonstrates the 'equal respect'[142] given to citizens' views in the democratic process. The fact that the *Constitution* contemplates taking this basic right of citizenship away, and indeed the fact that this basic participatory right *has been* historically denied to Indigenous people and others on the basis of race, demonstrates the way in which such clauses undermine notions of equal Australian citizenship, as well as the notion of guaranteed political participation that is free from racial discrimination. But simple removal of the race clauses does not solve the problem. Taking out these provisions would not create a guarantee of equal treatment. Apart from the Race Power, other powers can be used to discriminate (the Northern Territory Intervention,[143] which many argued was discriminatory, was also supported by the Territories Power, section 122) and removing section 25 would simply delete a dead-letter disincentive – it does not prevent discrimination.

[136] *Singh* (n 124 above) 368 [107] (McHugh J); *Attorney-General (Cth) ex rel McKinlay v Commonwealth* (1975) 135 CLR 1, 20–21 (Barwick CJ), 44 (Gibbs J), 62 (Mason J). See also Twomey, 'An Obituary for s 25 of the Constitution' (n 21 above) 136–37.

[137] Twomey, 'An Obituary for s 25 of the Constitution' (n 21 above) 126–29.

[138] *Mulholland v Australian Electoral Commission* (2004) 220 CLR 181, 254–55 [213].

[139] Twomey, 'An Obituary for s 25 of the Constitution' (n 21 above) 135.

[140] ibid 135–36 (citations omitted).

[141] See Chapter 5 of this volume for a more in-depth discussion.

[142] Waldron, *Law and Disagreement* (n 53 above) 115.

[143] *Northern Territory National Emergency Response Act 2007* (Cth); *Social Security and Other Legislation Amendment (Welfare Payment Reform) Act 2007* (Cth); *Families, Community Services and Indigenous Affairs and Other Legislation Amendment (Northern Territory National Emergency Response and Other Measures) Act 2007* (Cth); *Appropriation (Northern Territory National Emergency Response) Act (No 1) 2007–2008* (Cth); *Appropriation (Northern Territory National Emergency Response) Act (No 2) 2007–2008* (Cth).

B. Responding to the 'Uncertainty' Objection

A narrowly and carefully drafted racial non-discrimination clause in the *Constitution* may involve less legal uncertainty than some imagine. There is a vast body of case law under the RDA which can be drawn upon to predict how such a clause would likely be interpreted by Australian courts – depending of course on how much the words of the constitutional clause differ from the relevant RDA clauses, and taking into account the reality that constitutional context and implications are different to legislative context and implications.

Drawing upon the *Maloney* decision, which considered the validity under the RDA of Alcohol Management Plans (AMPs) on Palm Island, it may be surmised that AMPs in alcohol-affected Indigenous communities would be held to be valid special measures under racial non-discrimination law principles, and consent or consultation with Indigenous people will not be considered a strict legal requirement of a special measure unless specifically articulated in the text, though it may be a factor considered in the analysis.[144] Native Title and land rights laws would most likely be held to be valid special measures, as *Gerhardy v Brown* demonstrated.[145] Measures to address Indigenous social and economic disadvantage, like the education support provided under ABSTUDY, have also been held to be valid special measures under the RDA.[146] However, laws mandating lower wages for Indigenous people may likely be in breach of a racial non-discrimination clause and may not be considered valid special measures, as was demonstrated in the *Palm Island Wages Case*.[147]

To further enhance predictability in the operation of a constitutional racial non-discrimination clause, it may help if the clause was drafted in a way that closely mimics the RDA. It may also help to make its operation narrower, by framing the provision as a restraint on lawmaking, more in line with the 'equality before the law' approach taken by s 10 of the RDA. The Expert Panel's proposed provision says that '[t]he Commonwealth, a State or a Territory shall not discriminate on the grounds of race, colour or ethnic or national origin'.[148] This is broad enough to potentially encompass administrative as well as legislative action.[149] A more predictable approach may be to draft a clause which states that 'no law shall discriminate on grounds of race' or to talk about 'equality before the law with respect to race', together with an articulation of the allowable special measures exceptions in a way that is consistent with the formulation given in Article 1(4) of CERD, as currently incorporated under section 8 of the RDA.

[144] *R v Maloney* (2014) 252 CLR 168.
[145] *Gerhardy v Brown* (1985) 159 CLR 70. Though as discussed in the previous chapter, Indigenous land rights are probably more appropriately understood as distinct Indigenous rights, rather than as special measures under a non-discrimination paradigm.
[146] *Bruch v Commonwealth* [2002] FMCA 29.
[147] *Bligh v Queensland* [1996] HREOCA 28 (*Palm Island Wages Case*).
[148] Expert Panel Report (n 1 above) xviii.
[149] See Twomey, 'Indigenous Constitutional Recognition Explained' (n 40 above) 8.

Sensible approaches to drafting may help with certainty. However it must be accepted that, even if the operation of the clause may be less uncertain than some imagine, legal uncertainty cannot be eliminated from a judicially adjudicated restraint on parliamentary power. Whether such a constitutional guarantee would in practice give rise to positive change for Indigenous people is also an important question which would depend on the litigation, the approach of the courts to interpretation of the provision and its application to the facts. As will be shown in Chapter four below in discussion of the Canadian situation, constitutional rights guarantees may not always lead to Indigenous rights being decisively protected against state power. Similarly in Australia, the judicial tendency may be to defer to Parliament when answering the contentious question of whether a law or policy constitutes a valid special measure, as has often been the case under the RDA.[150] In contentious human rights issues, courts may be reluctant to robustly intervene and therefore may opt for deference to legislative and policy discretion. It cannot be assumed that litigation under a new rights guarantee will result in favourable outcomes for Indigenous litigants. The unavoidable reality is that High Court adjudication of a new constitutional rights guarantee will entail some uncertainty and changeability over time. Outcomes may be difficult to predict and can be influenced by trends in judicial interpretation and social and political circumstances, as well as the facts of each case. Judicial overreach (as usually argued by Bill of rights critics) is not the only risk arising from such guarantees. Given the judicial tendency towards deference in the adjudication of constitutional rights guarantees,[151] the possibility of judicial underreach should be seriously considered by reform advocates.

The core question remains whether the High Court should be empowered to strike down laws that the Court determines to be in breach of racial non-discrimination principles. This 'who should decide?' concern lies at the crux of objections.

C. Responding to the Political Unviability Objection

As distinct from the structural and legal objections discussed above, the political unviability criticisms oppose proposals for reform on the basis that they will 'fail at a referendum'. Such objections are difficult to respond to because

[150] See eg *R v Maloney* (2014) 252 CLR 168; see also deference to 'reasonably made political assessments' in *Gerhardy v Brown* (1985) 159 CLR 70, 143. Discussion in Geoffrey Lindell, 'The Justiciability of Political Questions: recent developments' in HP Lee and George Winterton (eds), *Australian Constitutional Perspectives* (Law Book Co 1991) 203–7.

[151] For the High Court's narrow interpretation of existing constitutional rights, see Aroney and Saunders (n 92 above) 229–30. This will be further discussed in Chapter 4 by reference to judicial approaches to s 35 of the Canadian Constitution.

they focus on political predictions rather than substantive legal or political arguments in favour of or against the racial non-discrimination proposal. Often, the people predicting a virulent 'no' case, divisive sentiment and subsequent referendum failure can be the same people making and leading that 'no' case and divisive sentiment. The political unviability objections may also ignore polling which demonstrates the public popularity of the racial non-discrimination idea.[152]

While, admittedly, the Expert Panel's polls were conducted absent a 'no' campaign, the instinctive popularity of the racial non-discrimination ideal arises from a widespread belief in the importance of individualised, even-handed and 'colour-blind' justice, the shared sense of the importance of an equal and 'fair go' for each person, and the arbitrariness and unfairness of treating Australian citizens differently on the basis of an outdated classification like 'race'. The underpinning value driving these sentiments is the ideal of equality before the law, as well as the importance of national unity and social cohesion. Treating everyone equally, rising above racial divisions and creating a more unified and cohesive nation and society are ideas that, if argued in a positive way, could potentially capture the Australian imagination in a way that renders the proposal politically viable.

Notably, national unity and national loyalty as political angles featured strongly in the conservative push for Indigenous constitutional recognition. Former Prime Minister Tony Abbott, at the time Leader of the Opposition, began his Second Reading Speech to the *Aboriginal and Torres Strait Islander Peoples Recognition Bill 2013*,[153] declaring: 'Australia is a blessed country. Our climate, our land, our people, our institutions rightly make us the envy of the earth, except for one thing – we have never fully made peace with the First Australians.'[154] Australia's failure to make peace with Indigenous Australians, Abbott argued, was one of our only national blemishes. Abbott thus linked the constitutional recognition of Indigenous peoples to a potential achievement of national unity: a way to stop being an 'incomplete' and 'torn people', and to become 'one nation'. In an uncharacteristic critique of the forefathers' collective wisdom, Abbott called upon the nation 'to atone for the omissions and for the hardness of heart of our forebears to enable us all to embrace the future as a united people'.[155] The reasons offered for Indigenous constitutional recognition were based in national pride and national unity, arguments that align with the idea of national loyalty as a basis on which to foster reconciliation between religions, classes and backgrounds, with common citizenship operating as a uniting

[152] Expert Panel Report (n 1 above) 90–92, 157.

[153] This was an Act which set out parliamentary commitment to Indigenous constitutional recognition.

[154] Commonwealth, *Parliamentary Debates*, House of Representatives, 13 February 2013, 1123 (Tony Abbott).

[155] ibid.

and equalising influence grounded in consensus, rather than force.[156] These kinds of arguments could have formed the basis for a campaign to sell a racial non-discrimination guarantee, as part of the Indigenous recognition package, to the Australian community. Abbott, however, opposed the reform which he called a 'one-line bill of rights', preferring instead a merely symbolic statement of Indigenous recognition.[157]

National loyalty and unity often entails reverence for the *Constitution* as a symbol of national pride and history. The sentiment can thus also entail resistance to proposals for substantive constitutional change. When considering political viability, the likelihood of opposition must also be considered. Calls for constitutional reform, particularly to protect Indigenous rights, can be seen as a moral critique of Australia's British constitutional history and heritage. Similarly, national loyalty and pride can entail denial of a significant problem requiring resolution – essentially a denial that there was a discriminatory history with real, lived ramifications for Indigenous people.[158] Amplification of the significance of the race clauses or Indigenous non-recognition as a 'blemish on our nationhood'[159] or a 'stain on our soul'[160] can be seen as a threat to national pride and a criticism of national history, exacerbating resistance to the racial non-discrimination proposals – and indeed any substantive reform proposals in the cause of Indigenous constitutional recognition. Because there may be underlying denial that the allowance of race-based differential treatment in the *Constitution* had any real adverse effects, there is therefore denial that the *Constitution* needs substantive reform. This denial is a political problem that cannot be avoided, no matter what form of Indigenous recognition is adopted. It is an incorrect belief that must be confronted through mutually respectful conversation and debate.

In relation to the political viability of a racial non-discrimination guarantee, as frustrating as self-fulfilling prophecies of referendum doom can be, it is also

[156] Roger Scruton, *A Political Philosophy: Arguments for Conservatism* (Continuum 2006) 18.

[157] Paul Kelly, 'Bill of Rights Would Kill Referendum, Says Tony Abbott', *The Australian* (6 September 2014) <https://www.theaustralian.com.au/nation/bill-of-rights-would-kill-referendum-says-tony-abbott/news-story/172020c7d41e7aeec78fce7e81f495c3> accessed 18 November 2019.

[158] See Sheridan (n 39 above). On one hand Sheridan admits: '[t]here is no doubt that throughout Australian history Aborigines suffered terrible injustice. Australian history, like that of all nations, contains plenty of good and plenty of bad. John Howard is right to hail the grandeur of the Australian achievement in nation building. Noel Pearson is right to draw our attention once more to the capricious cruelty and killings that occurred often in colonial times. I am not someone who denies historical injustice done to Aborigines.' Yet, Sheridan also argues that in removing 'the anachronistic clause that allows Canberra to make laws that help Aborigines … we are remedying a problem that does not exist. The commonwealth parliament does not make laws designed to hurt Aborigines, just as it doesn't make laws designed to hurt Parsis or Irish Australians or the disabled or scientists.'

[159] Expert Panel Report (n 1 above) xii.

[160] Commonwealth, Parliamentary Debates, House of Representatives, 13 February 2013, 1123 (Tony Abbott), citing Paul Keating, 'Redfern Speech', speech at Redfern Park, Redfern, Sydney, 10 December 1992.

important to acknowledge the lessons of Australian constitutional history. As explained in Chapter two, Australia's attachment to parliamentary supremacy is deep and enduring, as is the longstanding resistance to a constitutional, or even a legislated, federal Bill of rights. Wentworth's attempt to insert a racial non-discrimination guarantee prior to 1967 did not gain traction because of concerns about empowering the judiciary to strike down Parliament's laws. Every past attempt at inserting a new rights guarantee into the *Constitution* has failed or fizzled out. In 2012, the political pushback against the so-called 'one clause bill of rights' was virulent. It must also be remembered that Parliament must initiate any constitutional reform. Public popularity, as indicated in the Expert Panel's poll in relation to a racial non-discrimination clause, is thus not the only indicator of political viability. Parliament as initiator is also the gatekeeper of constitutional reform, and the reality is that Parliament is unlikely to support proposals that restrain or diminish its own power. Alternative solutions that preserve parliamentary supremacy must therefore be explored.

V. IS A QUALIFIED POWER THE ANSWER?

After the Expert Panel's recommendations attracted opposition, a commonly proposed alternative to a broad racial non-discrimination guarantee was a qualified Indigenous legislative power. As noted, it is generally accepted that if the 'race' clauses are removed from the *Constitution*, section 51(xxvi), the Race Power, would need to be replaced to ensure that the Commonwealth retains its power to enact necessary laws for Indigenous affairs.[161] Given this necessity, and faced with political objections to a broad racial non-discrimination guarantee, some suggested incorporating a more limited non-discrimination qualification into the replacement power instead. The common proposal of a qualified Indigenous power, in practice a racial non-discrimination clause that applies to Indigenous people only,[162] would provide constitutional protection that is narrower in scope than the Expert Panel's racial non-discrimination clause proposal.[163] It would not explicitly restrain other Commonwealth powers

[161] Joint Select Committee on Constitutional Recognition of Aboriginal and Torres Strait Islander Peoples, Parliament of Australia, 'Progress Report' (October 2014) 4–5 (Joint Select Committee Progress Report); Joint Select Committee Interim Report (n 10 above) 9–10; Expert Panel Report (n 1 above) 137–38; Pritchard (n 33 above) 52.

[162] Rosalind Dixon and George Williams, 'Drafting a Replacement to the Races Power in the Australian Constitution' (2014) 25(2) *Public Law Review* 83; Twomey, 'A Revised Proposal for Indigenous Recognition' (n 40 above); Joint Select Committee Interim Report (n 10 above) 19; Joint Select Committee Progress Report (n 161 above) 4–9; Joint Select Committee, 'Final Report' (2015) Recommendation 5 (Joint Select Committee Final Report).

[163] Dixon and Williams (n 162 above) 88; Twomey, 'A Revised Proposal for Indigenous Recognition' (n 40 above) 409.

that may be used to legislate for Indigenous people, though as will be explained below, it would probably do so through judicial interpretation.[164]

As explained below, though various forms of qualification to a new Indigenous power were suggested in the wake of political reactions to the Expert Panel's recommendations, none of these revised proposals successfully addresses the core objections to judicial review discussed above: all are susceptible to the same criticisms as a broader racial non-discrimination guarantee.

A. Options for Judicially Adjudicated Qualifications to an Indigenous Power

(i) 'Advancement' or 'Benefit'

The Expert Panel's proposed replacement power was a new section 51A, which would read:

> Recognising that the continent and its islands now known as Australia were first occupied by Aboriginal and Torres Strait Islander peoples;
>
> Acknowledging the continuing relationship of Aboriginal and Torres Strait Islander peoples with their traditional lands and waters;
>
> Respecting the continuing cultures, languages and heritage of Aboriginal and Torres Strait Islander peoples;
>
> Acknowledging the need to secure the advancement of Aboriginal and Torres Strait Islander peoples;
>
> the Parliament shall, subject to this Constitution, have power to make laws for the peace, order and good government of the Commonwealth with respect to Aboriginal and Torres Strait Islander peoples.[165]

The incorporation of Indigenous recognition statements into the head of power, rather placing them at the front of the *Constitution* in a general preamble, was to prevent the statements from influencing interpretation of the whole *Constitution*, thereby minimising unintended consequences arising from uncertain poetic language.[166] Twomey argues this is a clever way to effectively constrain the interpretation of the recognition statements so that they would most likely only affect the interpretation of the section 51A power,[167] rather than the entire *Constitution*. The word 'advancement' in this proposal does not substantively limit the scope of the power itself; it provides preambular context to inform judicial interpretation of the power's operation and could therefore

[164] Dixon and Williams (n 162 above) 87–88; Twomey, 'A Revised Proposal for Indigenous Recognition' (n 40 above) 409.

[165] Expert Panel Report (n 1 above) 144–57.

[166] ibid 116–19, 128–31; Joint Select Committee Interim Report (n 10 above) 22–27.

[167] Twomey, 'A Revised Proposal for Indigenous Recognition' (n 40 above) 406–8. Others prefer the idea of a general preamble. See Craven, 'Keep the Constitutional Change Simple' (n 37 above).

be described as a soft qualification – in contrast to a power to make laws with respect only to 'the advancement of Indigenous peoples', in which the limitation is built-in rather than preambular, creating a substantive qualification. Nonetheless, the Expert Panel included the word 'advancement' in the preamble to the power to 'ensure that the purpose of the power is apparent' and to inform the scope that should be given to the substantive power for the purposes of interpretation,[168] thus indirectly limiting the power's potential for discriminatory use against Indigenous people.[169]

'Advancement' appears to reference special measures, defined, in Article 1(4) of the International Convention on the Elimination of all forms of Racial Discrimination, as measures for the advancement of disadvantaged groups to ensure the equal enjoyment of fundamental rights and freedoms.[170] Several submissions to the Expert Panel supported using 'advancement',[171] however this word has also been subject to criticism.[172] Twomey argues that because the qualification is in the preamble to the power, it may not operate to prevent adverse use of the power, because the High Court would likely find that there is no ambiguity in the conferral of power to legislate for Indigenous people, and so it would not have to resort to the preamble to resolve any ambiguity.[173] Others object that 'advancement' is condescending: it defines Indigenous people in terms of disadvantage,[174] using 'deficit language' to highlight socio-economic hardship which it is hoped will be one day overcome (and should therefore not be conceptually enshrined in the *Constitution*).[175] Similarly it might imply that Indigenous people are 'backward' and need to be advanced.[176] Indeed, much historical discrimination has occurred under government policies enacted in the name of Indigenous 'advancement', demonstrating the subjectivity of adjudicating on these kinds of questions.[177] Others raised concerns that qualifying the

[168] Expert Panel Report (n 1 above) 150.

[169] ibid 151.

[170] CERD art 1(4) states: '[s]pecial measures taken for the sole purpose of securing adequate advancement of certain racial or ethnic groups or individuals requiring such protection as may be necessary in order to ensure such groups or individuals equal enjoyment or exercise of human rights and fundamental freedoms shall not be deemed racial discrimination …'. See also Twomey, 'A Revised Proposal for Indigenous Recognition' (n 40 above) 394–95; Dixon and Williams (n 162 above) 86.

[171] See submissions referred to in Expert Panel Report (n 1 above) 148–50.

[172] Twomey, 'A Revised Proposal for Indigenous Recognition' (n 40 above) 394–95; Dixon and Williams (n 162 above) 86.

[173] Twomey, 'A Revised Proposal for Indigenous Recognition' (n 40 above) 395; Anne Twomey, 'The Race Power: Its Replacement and Interpretation' (2012) 40(3) *Federal Law Review* 413, 425–28.

[174] Note Peter Dawson's comments in Commonwealth of Australia, Official Committee Hansard (n 88 above) 15.

[175] See Indigenous Youth Engagement Council, 'Recognise This: Indigenous Youth Report on Constitutional Recognition' (National Centre of Indigenous Excellence 2013) 32.

[176] Twomey, 'A Revised Proposal for Indigenous Recognition' (n 40 above) 395.

[177] Jon Altman, 'Will Constitutional Recognition Advance Australia Fair?' *New Matilda* (10 February 2012).

new head of power with a word like 'benefit' or 'advancement' would do little to quell concerns about past racial discrimination against Indigenous people, or to guarantee against, or at least render challengeable, similar discriminatory government action in the future. Without a broad racial non-discrimination clause, governments could use other heads of power to enact racially discriminatory laws.[178]

The foremost legal problem with 'advancement' is its uncertain legal meaning.[179] The Expert Panel hoped that racial non-discrimination and special measures jurisprudence might be enlivened by reference to 'advancement'.[180] However, it is not clear that this would be the case through the use of 'advancement' alone.[181] 'Advancement' is not considered a term of 'received legal meaning'[182] because the lack of domestic precedent makes it difficult to predict the interpretation courts might adopt.[183] It would be up to the judiciary to determine what 'advancement' means in given circumstances and, without a racial non-discrimination clause in the *Constitution* (as was also proposed by the Expert Panel), it is not totally clear that racial non-discrimination and special measures principles would apply. As a result of this legal ambiguity and the possible condescension of the term, the subsequent Joint Select Committee report did not recommend using the word in its revised version of section 51A.[184]

The word 'benefit' was also proposed by many submissions[185] and is vulnerable to the same criticisms.[186] Like 'advancement', the notion of 'benefit' is highly subjective: were past protectionist policies for the benefit and advancement of Indigenous peoples? The state would have argued they were, whereas the Indigenous challengers might have argued they were unjust and harmful. Such questions leave courts to decide contentions matters of morality and policy. Even though the scope of this uncertainty would apply only to one head of power and to Indigenous people only, a qualified Indigenous power of this kind would likely attract the same objections as the Expert Panel's racial non-discrimination guarantee: it is still empowering the judiciary to invalidate Parliament's laws on the basis of ambiguous words like 'benefit' or 'advancement'. It is still creating legal uncertainty and undermining parliamentary supremacy over contentious policy matters.

[178] Sean Brennan, 'Submission on Content of a Referendum Package', Submission to the Expert Panel (2011) 7.

[179] Twomey, 'A Revised Proposal for Indigenous Recognition' (n 40 above) 395; Dixon and Williams (n 162 above) 87.

[180] Twomey, 'A Revised Proposal for Indigenous Recognition' (n 40 above) 395.

[181] Though note that the Expert Panel proposed the qualified power as well as a racial non-discrimination clause.

[182] See eg Commonwealth of Australia, Official Committee Hansard (n 88 above) 19, 22.

[183] Sean Brennan, 'Constitutional Reform and Its Relationship to Land Justice' (2011) 5(2) *Land, Rights, Laws: Issues of Native Title* 1, 6.

[184] Joint Select Committee Final Report (n 162) Recommendation 5.

[185] Expert Panel Report (n 1) 148–50.

[186] Pritchard (n 33 above) 53.

(ii) 'But Not So as to Discriminate Adversely against Them'

Another option proposed was to create an Indigenous power to make laws with respect to Indigenous people 'but not so as to discriminate adversely against them'.[187] Variations of this option were recommended by the Joint Select Committee as an alternative to 'advancement' but also as an alternative to the Expert Panel's proposed racial non-discrimination clause.[188] The qualification is framed as an 'express limitation'. This formulation explicitly uses the word 'discriminate' and so would be more legally certain than 'benefit' or 'advancement', because there is Australian discrimination law that can be drawn upon.[189] Similarly, it might be preferable for those who are concerned about the condescension of words like 'benefit or 'advancement'. 'But not so as to discriminate adversely' may convey that equality and non-discrimination principles should apply.

High Court precedent indicates that 'express qualifications' incorporated within a Commonwealth power are usually interpreted to restrict other Commonwealth powers as well, where those powers are used to legislate for the same subject matter.[190] Therefore, the Court would likely interpret an express qualification to the new Indigenous power in a similarly broad way, to constrain the Commonwealth's other legislative powers where exercised in relation to Indigenous matters.[191] This is an important argument, because other powers are used to support laws with respect to Indigenous people, sometimes in a way that is considered discriminatory.[192]

Ultimately, whether or not an express qualification to the Indigenous power would be construed broadly is subject to judicial interpretation. It is not certain, because the limitation on other powers would not be explicitly stated, but implied. Interestingly, however, the Joint Select Committee in its 2015 Final Report recommended two versions of a qualified power with a limitation that

[187] Dixon and Williams (n 162 above) 87; Twomey, 'A Revised Proposal for Indigenous Recognition' (n 40 above) 408.

[188] Joint Select Committee Final Report (n 162 above) Recommendation 5; Joint Select Committee Interim Report (n 10 above) 15; Twomey, 'A Revised Proposal for Indigenous Recognition' (n 40 above) 408–9.

[189] However, it may be difficult to predict whether RDA case law would be drawn upon in interpreting the *Constitution*, particularly if the wording differs from the Act.

[190] *Bourke v State Bank of New South Wales* (1990) 170 CLR 276, 285; *New South Wales v Commonwealth* (2006) 229 CLR 1, 127 (*Workchoices Case*); *Attorney-General (Victoria) v Andrews* (2007) 230 CLR 369, 406; *Wurridjal v Commonwealth* (2009) 237 CLR 309, 484–86; *Nintendo Co Ltd v Centronics Systems Pty Limited* (1994) 181 CLR 134, 160.

[191] *Bourke* (n 190 above) with respect to the s 51(xiii) power; Dixon and Williams (n 162 above) 87–88. As Dixon and Williams note, there is also contention about what an 'express qualification' is: see the *Workchoices Case* (n 190 above).

[192] The Northern Territory Intervention was also reliant on s 122. *Wurridjal* (n 190 above) 387, 435. See also Sean Brennan 'Wurridjal v Commonwealth: the Northern Territory Intervention and Just Terms for the Acquisition of Property' (2009) 33(3) *Melbourne University Law Review* 934; Brooke Greenwood, 'The Commonwealth Government's Northern Territory Emergency Response Act: Some Constitutional Issues' (2009) V *Cross Sections* 21, 22.

also *expressly* qualifies all other Commonwealth powers, so they too cannot be used adversely against Indigenous people – essentially creating a racial non-discrimination guarantee that applies to Indigenous people only.[193] Under this formulation, the uncertainty about whether other powers are limited is removed, because the limitation is explicitly stated, but uncertainty as to practical impacts and operation remains.

If the limitation on other Commonwealth powers is not explicitly stated, it may nonetheless be reasonable to predict that the High Court would interpret the limitation in a broad way,[194] so that it impliedly limits other Commonwealth powers when exercised in respect of Indigenous matters. Yet the High Court may also consider that if the drafters of the amendment had intended to constrain all the Commonwealth's powers such that they could not be used in a discriminatory way against Indigenous people, then an explicit clause constraining the Commonwealth in this broad way would have been put to the Australian people at a referendum. The High Court may consider it informative that the broad racial non-discrimination protection was dropped from the referendum proposal, perhaps supporting a contention that the qualified Indigenous power is intended to be interpreted narrowly.[195] The only certain way to prevent Parliament from using its broad powers in a racially discriminatory way against Indigenous people would be to adopt a broad racial non-discrimination clause, as proposed by the Expert Panel, or a clause protecting Indigenous people only from discrimination, expressly constraining all powers. A qualified Indigenous power is a weaker option. Some Indigenous leaders therefore considered it a poor trade for the broad protection offered by the Expert Panel's section 116A.[196]

Like 'benefit' or 'advancement', the meaning of the term 'discriminate adversely' in the context of a constitutional head of power would be uncertain in its operation.[197] While the 'but not so as to discriminate adversely' qualification carries fewer uncertainties and would be likely to enliven racial non-discrimination principles, this kind of qualified power does not appropriately address the objections to a racial non-discrimination clause. Indeed, a qualified power in this formulation would arguably be more uncertain than the Expert Panel's section 116A proposal, for four reasons. First, the Expert Panel's section 116A(1) specifically prohibits discrimination on the grounds of 'race,

[193] Joint Select Committee Final Report (n 162 above) Recommendation 5.

[194] Twomey agrees that qualified the Indigenous power would in effect qualify the other Commonwealth powers, giving the qualification a broad scope: Twomey, 'A Revised Proposal for Indigenous Recognition' (n 40 above) 409.

[195] This intention can also be made clear in the Second Reading Speech, but this would not be treated as primary evidence.

[196] Noel Pearson, 'Debate the Substance, Not the Inconvenience', *The Australian* (18 April 2014) <https://www.theaustralian.com.au/nation/noel-pearson-debate-the-substance-not-the-inconvenience/news-story/791467632e14960c8268753d4deb22af> accessed 18 November 2019.

[197] Joint Select Committee Interim Report (n 10 above) 20.

colour or ethnic or national origin', clearly using the terminology of the RDA and CERD.[198] Second, the Panel's proposed section 116A(2) provides a clear special measures sub-clause, which obviates the kinds of measures that are not racial discrimination: those that are 'for the purpose of overcoming disadvantage, ameliorating the effects of past discrimination, or protecting the cultures, languages or heritage of any group'. Third, section 116A would be a stand-alone clause not complicated by being attached to an Indigenous-specific head of power. Thus, the judiciary would not have to read in any broader operation of the limitation on Commonwealth power – it would be textually explicit. Fourth, the Expert Panel's proposed section 116A does not contain the word 'adversely'. There is no mention of 'adverse' discrimination in CERD's definition of racial discrimination. Usually in racial discrimination law, 'discrimination' already means adverse discrimination, or discrimination which impairs the equal enjoyment of fundamental human rights.[199] Allowable positive discrimination is encapsulated by the law of 'special measures': measures to promote the equal enjoyment and exercise of human rights.[200]

Any 'but not so as to discriminate adversely' qualification would still refer ambiguous words and contentious moral and political matters for judicial adjudication, raising the possibility that Parliament's laws will be struck down by the High Court. The words of qualification would contain equivalent if not greater ambiguity than the Panel's proposed section 116A, leaving wide scope for judicial discretion. Given that the purpose of considering alternatives to the Expert Panel's proposed racial non-discrimination clause in the first place is presumably to address the objections hindering political progress, these same objections must also be considered with respect to proposals for a qualified Indigenous power. Under a qualified power, it would still be up to courts to ultimately decide what

[198] Article 1(1) of CERD provides: '[i]n this Convention, the term "racial discrimination" shall mean any distinction, exclusion, restriction or preference based on race, colour, descent, or national or ethnic origin'. Section 9(1) of the RDA provides: '[i]t is unlawful for a person to do any act involving a distinction, exclusion, restriction or preference based on race, colour, descent or national or ethnic origin'. Section 10(1) provides: '[i]f, by reason of, or of a provision of, a law of the Commonwealth or of a State or Territory, persons of a particular race, colour or national or ethnic origin do not enjoy a right that is enjoyed by persons of another race, colour or national or ethnic origin, or enjoy a right to a more limited extent than persons of another race, colour or national or ethnic origin, then, notwithstanding anything in that law, persons of the first-mentioned race, colour or national or ethnic origin shall, by force of this section, enjoy that right to the same extent as persons of that other race, colour or national or ethnic origin.'

[199] RDA s 9(1); CERD Article 1(1).

[200] At international law, CERD provides the following definition of 'special measures' in art 1(4), also referred to in s 8 of the RDA: '[s]pecial measures taken for the sole purpose of securing adequate advancement of certain racial or ethnic groups or individuals requiring such protection as may be necessary in order to ensure such groups or individuals equal enjoyment or exercise of human rights and fundamental freedoms shall not be deemed racial discrimination, provided, however, that such measures do not, as a consequence, lead to the maintenance of separate rights for different racial groups and that they shall not be continued after the objectives for which they were taken have been achieved.'

constitutes 'adverse discrimination' in the circumstances. While the uncertainty concerns should be less than in relation to a racial non-discrimination clause – because the judicially adjudicated limitation is confined to the Indigenous power, thus ostensibly only affecting a narrow array of laws[201] – this assurance is undermined by the argument that the limitation will be interpreted broadly to qualify Commonwealth powers generally.[202] The same criticism obviously also applies to drafting formulations explicitly constraining all Commonwealth powers.

The proposed 'but not so as to discriminate adversely' qualification does not take on board the legal uncertainty and parliamentary supremacy objections raised in relation to a racial non-discrimination clause – a fact Committee Chairman Wyatt evidently realised a few weeks too late. After recommending three versions of a racial discrimination restraint in his Committee's 2015 Final Report (two of which applied to Indigenous people only and were incorporated into the Indigenous power), Wyatt stated that a racial non-discrimination clause would be unlikely to win the necessary political consensus for a successful referendum.[203]

VI. CONCLUSION

This chapter has examined objections to a racial non-discrimination guarantee in the *Constitution* in order to properly understand the arguments and apply arising insights to alternative constitutional reform solutions. It has also questioned whether such objections are sufficient and sustainable in the Australian context, where unelected judges already interpret Australia's written federal *Constitution* and already interpret provisions with respect to race. The democratic procedures set up by the *Constitution* are not free from unjust discrimination, and such procedures alone have not proven sufficient to protect Australians – especially Indigenous people – from the unjust discrimination of the past. This is the problem for which constitutional experts should try to find the most certain, just and constitutionally congruent solution. A racial non-discrimination clause would represent one kind of constitutional promise – a judicially adjudicated constitutional promise – that past wrongs will not be repeated or will at least be challengeable if repeated.[204] On principle, this is a justifiable solution. On balance, however, it does not seem a politically viable solution. Nor is it the most

[201] See Expert Panel Report (n 1) 33. Pritchard (n 33 above) 52; Joint Select Committee Progress Report (n 161 above) 4–5; Joint Select Committee Interim Report (n 10 above) 9–10.

[202] Dixon and Williams (n 162 above) 87–88.

[203] See Robinson (n 89 above).

[204] For discussion of constitutional recognition as requiring a promise, see Chapter 2 of this volume. See also Shireen Morris, 'What Promise will the Nation Make?' in Damien Freeman and Shireen Morris, *The Forgotten People: Liberal and Conservative Approaches to Recognising Indigenous Peoples* (Melbourne University Press 2016).

constitutionally congruent or legally certain solution for Australia's 'Bill of rights'-free *Constitution*. And the problem of legal certainty should not just be a concern for Bill of rights opponents; it should also be considered by Indigenous rights reformers. As will be discussed in the next chapter in relation to Canada's approach to Indigenous constitutional recognition, judicially-adjudicated rights guarantees do not always lead to Indigenous rights being robustly defended against state power. Legal uncertainty can run both ways.

More importantly, a racial non-discrimination guarantee is not what Indigenous Australians, after careful consideration and deliberation, have now asked for in the Uluru Statement. The Uluru Statement was a decisive shift away from the Expert Panel's approach, to a political and participatory First Nations constitutional voice. This shift was wise. Australia's *Constitution* mostly protects rights through political, institutional and power-sharing mechanisms, and history demonstrates that judicially adjudicated restraints on parliamentary power are unlikely to succeed at a referendum. The lateral shift towards political and participatory mechanisms for Indigenous empowerment appears a sensible way to build the consensus necessary for success. It is also more aligned with the long history of Indigenous advocacy for greater self-determination that was discussed in the preceding chapter, and may ultimately be more empowering for Indigenous people in practice.

4

International Inspiration

IN 2014, IN light of objections to a racial non-discrimination guarantee and in search of alternative ideas, I was lucky enough to be able to organise a research trip to New Zealand as part of my work at Cape York Institute. Together with a delegation of Indigenous leaders and another constitutional expert, we met with Māori leaders, lawyers and politicians as well as other scholars and experts. The trip was enlightening. It opened my eyes to the possibilities for political, procedural and institutional forms of constitutional recognition that empower Indigenous voices within constitutional arrangements, as alternatives to judicially adjudicated approaches.

This chapter builds on my New Zealand experience and seeks inspiration from the international context. Drawing first on principles of the UN *Declaration on the Rights of Indigenous Peoples* (DRIP),[1] it then examines how Indigenous peoples are constitutionally recognised in comparable democracies with minority Indigenous populations – New Zealand, Canada, and briefly, the Scandinavian countries of Norway, Sweden, and Finland. Here I focus particularly on constitutional and institutional mechanisms that enable Indigenous peoples to be heard in their affairs.

I. UN DECLARATION ON THE RIGHTS OF INDIGENOUS PEOPLES

Australia endorsed DRIP in 2009, but its key principles are yet to be domestically implemented in a meaningful way.[2] Of greatest relevance here are DRIP's principles relating to Indigenous self-determination, consultation and participation in decisions affecting their rights. Article 3 provides that: 'Indigenous peoples have the right to self-determination. By virtue of that right they freely determine their political status and freely pursue their economic, social and

[1] *United Nations Declaration on the Rights of Indigenous Peoples*, GA Res 61/295, UN Doc S/RES/61/295 (2 October 2007, adopted 13 September 2007) (DRIP).

[2] For more on the status of Indigenous peoples in international law, see Patrick Macklem, 'Indigenous Recognition in International Law: Theoretical Observations' (2008) 30(1) *Michigan Journal of International Law* 177.

cultural development.'[3] Article 4 further requires that 'Indigenous peoples, in exercising their right to self-determination, have the right to autonomy or self-government in matters relating to their internal and local affairs, as well as ways and means for financing their autonomous functions.'[4] The Uluru Statement's call for empowerment through a constitutionally guaranteed First Nations voice is a request for greater self-determination through formal inclusion and fairer participation in public decision-making with respect to their rights and interests. It is a request for self-determination in the inclusive, domestic sense. As Wilson and Selle explain, self-determination can be understood as the amalgamation of the separate yet connected ideas of autonomy and integration:

> In the case of Indigenous peoples, autonomy refers to their ability to exercise some degree of control over decisions that affect their daily lives. Integration, on the other hand, refers to their ability to influence decisions made by non-Indigenous governments, which, in many areas, still have the authority to make decisions that affect Indigenous communities.[5]

In enabling Indigenous self-determination within dominant states, DRIP emphasises the importance of institutions that enable Indigenous political agency and varying degrees of autonomy in their affairs.[6] Article 5 provides that:

> Indigenous peoples have the right to maintain and strengthen their distinct political, legal, economic, social and cultural institutions, while retaining their right to participate fully, if they so choose, in the political, economic, social and cultural life of the State.

DRIP thus makes provision for Indigenous peoples to represent their interests through dedicated institutions within the state, as well as participating as equal citizens in ordinary democratic processes. Articles 18 and 19 focus on the importance of Indigenous participation and consultation in political decisions affecting Indigenous rights. Article 18 provides that: 'Indigenous peoples have the right to participate in decision-making in matters which would affect their rights, through representatives chosen by themselves in accordance with their own procedures, as well as to maintain and develop their own indigenous decision-making institutions.' Similarly, Article 19 requires that:

> States shall consult and cooperate in good faith with the indigenous peoples concerned through their own representative institutions in order to obtain their free, prior and informed consent before adopting and implementing legislative or administrative measures that may affect them.

[3] The right of all peoples to self-determination is also recognised in art 1 of the *International Covenant on Civil and Political Rights* and the *International Covenant on Economic, Social and Cultural Rights*.

[4] See discussion of self-determination in Chapter 2 of this volume.

[5] Gary N Wilson and Per Selle, 'Indigenous Self-Determination in Northern Canada and Norway' (IRPP STUDY No 69, February 2019) 11.

[6] S James Anaya, *Indigenous Peoples in International Law* (2nd edn, Oxford University Press 2004) 150; Wilson and Selle (n 5 above) 9.

These consultation obligations echo the requirements outlined in the International Labour Organization (ILO) *Convention No 169 on Indigenous and Tribal Peoples in Independent Countries*.[7]

Like all international human rights instruments, DRIP is not legally enforceable until implemented through Australian legislation.[8] Though Australia has endorsed its principles, the High Court found in *R v Maloney*[9] that consultation is not a legal requirement of a special measure under the *Racial Discrimination Act 1975* (Cth), as this is not expressly articulated in the domestic law.[10] Australia is not living up to its agreed human rights standards in relation to DRIP: governments often enact laws and policies with respect to Indigenous peoples without their genuine participation or consultation, let alone their consent. As the Parliamentary Joint Committee on Human Rights (PJCHR) – the parliamentary committee tasked with scrutinising bills for international human rights compliance[11] – has emphasised, although DRIP's requirement of consultation is not legally binding in Australia,[12] genuine Indigenous participation and engagement is nonetheless crucial to safeguarding Indigenous rights.[13] Assessing the controversial *Stronger Futures* legislation[14] in 2013, the PJCHR noted

> the critical importance of ensuring the full involvement of affected communities, in this case primarily Indigenous communities, in the policymaking and policy

[7] See, particularly, arts 6 and 7 of International Labour Organization, *Convention No 169 on Indigenous and Tribal Peoples in Independent Countries*, opened for signature 27 June 1989, 28 ILM 1382 (1989) (entered into force 5 September 1991). For the ILO's relevance to Scandinavian countries (discussed below), see Barbara Ann Hocking, 'Evaluating Self-Determination of Indigenous People through Political Processes and Territorial Rights: The Status of the Nordic Saami from an Australian Perspective' (2000) 11 *Finnish Yearbook of International Law* 289, 302–4.

[8] *Dietrich v The Queen* (1992) 177 CLR 292 (Mason CJ and McHugh J); *Kioa v West* (1985) 159 CLR 550, 570 (Gibbs CJ).

[9] *R v Maloney* (2014) 252 CLR 168.

[10] ibid 185–86. See also Patrick Wall, Case Note: 'The High Court of Australia's Approach to the Interpretation of International Law and its Use of International Legal Materials in *Maloney v The Queen* [2013] HCA 28' (2014) 15(1) *Melbourne Journal of International Law* 228.

[11] See Shireen Morris, 'Parliamentary Scrutiny and Insights for a First Nations Voice to Parliament' in Laura Grenfell and Julie Debeljak (eds), *Law Making and Human Rights* (Thomson Reuters 2020).

[12] DRIP is also not included in the human rights instruments listed in s 3 of the *Human Rights (Parliamentary Scrutiny) Act 2011* (Cth). But as a 2013 PJCHR report stated: 'While the Declaration is not currently listed as one of the international instruments against which the committee is to scrutinise bills and legislation for human rights compatibility, many international lawyers and others accept that in many respects the Declaration spells out the details of relevant obligations under the human rights treaties listed in the committee's terms of reference. It is also considered to represent customary international law binding on Australia in many, though not all, respects. The government has accepted the relevance of the Declaration to the work of the committee': Parliamentary Joint Committee on Human Rights, *Stronger Futures in the Northern Territory Act 2012 and related legislation* (11th Report of 2013, 26 June 2013) 14–15, [1.57]–[1.58].

[13] ibid 34 [1.122]. This was also emphasised by Brennan J in *Gerhardy v Brown* (1985) 159 CLR 70, 135: 'The wishes of the beneficiaries for the measure are of great importance (perhaps essential) in determining whether a measure is taken for the purpose of securing their advancement.'

[14] Comprising various statutes: *Stronger Futures in the Northern Territory Act 2012* (Cth); *Stronger Futures in the Northern Territory (Consequential and Transitional Provisions) Act 2012* (Cth); *Social Security Legislation Amendment Act 2012* (Cth).

> implementation process. The right to self-determination guaranteed by article 1 of each of the International Covenants on Human Rights, as well as the UN Declaration of the Rights of Indigenous Peoples, require[s] meaningful consultation with, and in many cases the free, prior and informed consent of, Indigenous peoples during the formulation and implementation of laws and policies that affect them. This means ensuring the involvement of affected communities in decisions as to whether to adopt particular measures, in their implementation, and in their monitoring and evaluation. To do otherwise risks producing the disempowerment and feelings of exclusion and marginalisation … which are fundamentally at odds with the principles of respect for the dignity and autonomy of persons recognised in the human rights treaties and the UN Declaration on the Rights of Indigenous Peoples. The committee recognises the significant steps that the government has taken in this regard, but considers that more needs to be done.[15]

Nations around the world implement mechanisms for Indigenous representation, consultation and participation in different ways, depending on history, politics and circumstances, with varying degrees of success.[16] Domestic interpretations of Indigenous self-determination differ internationally, depending on the dynamics and characteristics of the Indigenous peoples and the nations involved.[17] The following sections explore how comparable democracies with minority Indigenous populations – namely, New Zealand, Canada, and the Scandinavian countries of Norway, Sweden and Finland – incorporate into their constitutional and institutional arrangements mechanisms to recognise and empower Indigenous peoples through active Indigenous participation in political decision-making with respect to their affairs.

II. NEW ZEALAND

In 2013, in the context of political ambivalence towards the Expert Panel's recommendations for constitutional recognition, former Australian Prime Minister Tony Abbott (then Leader of the Opposition) invoked New Zealand as a positive role model for Indigenous recognition and reconciliation. 'We only have to look across the Tasman to see how it all could have been done so much better', Abbott said. 'Thanks to the Treaty of Waitangi in New Zealand two peoples became one nation.'[18] In pointing to the Treaty as a beacon of reconciliatory

[15] PJCHR, *Stronger Futures* (n 12 above) 75 [1.275].

[16] For an analysis of how minority and Indigenous representation may strengthen representational links, encourage positive attitudes toward government and foster political participation (with a focus on the USA and New Zealand), see Susan A Banducci, Todd Donovan and Jeffrey A Karp, 'Minority Representation, Empowerment, and Participation' (2004) 66(2) *The Journal of Politics* 534.

[17] Wilson and Selle (n 5 above) 8.

[18] Commonwealth, *Parliamentary Debates*, House of Representatives, 13 February 2013, 1123 (Tony Abbott).

achievement, Abbott rhetorically urged national unity and cohesion over division. But while his observation about the unifying purpose of the Treaty in New Zealand may be broadly correct,[19] Abbott's vision of 'two peoples' peacefully becoming 'one nation' was romanticised.[20] As with most colonial relationships, the relationship between Māori and the Crown in New Zealand is turbulent. It is a relationship marked by highs and lows, promises and betrayals, wars and reconciliations; just like the relationship between Indigenous peoples and the Crown (and settlers) in Australia. Nonetheless, there is much Australia can learn from New Zealand about moving beyond a discriminatory past and setting in place practical measures for a fairer relationship. In this fundamental challenge, New Zealand has achieved better progress than Australia.[21] As Labor Opposition Leader, Anthony Albanese, tweeted on Waitangi Day 2020:

> We can learn a lot from our mates across the ditch about reconciliation with First Nations people.
>
> New Zealand has led the way. It's time for Australia to follow.
>
> It's time to support the Uluru Statement from the Heart.

A. Constitutional Context

New Zealand's constitution is a collection of statutes and conventions, some legally enforceable, and others carrying moral and political weight – like the Treaty of Waitangi.[22] The *Constitution Act 1986* is New Zealand's main formal statement of constitutional arrangements and can be amended via ordinary legislative procedures.[23] In contrast to Australia, New Zealand's constitutional

[19] '[I]ts purpose was to establish a relationship between two peoples in one nation': Constitutional Advisory Panel, *New Zealand's Constitution: A Report on a Conversation* (November 2013) 35.

[20] Abbott's rhetoric has also been criticised as assimilationist. Kirsty Gover characterises Abbott's view as framing reconciliation 'as a process that should erase differentiation between Indigenous and settler Australians', citing Abbott's speech at the *RECOGNISE* Inaugural Gala Dinner on 11 December 2014, where he said: 'I am a supporter of constitutional recognition because I want our country to transcend the "them and us" mindset to embrace "all of us" in [a] spirit of generous inclusion … Not "them" and "us" anymore – just us.' See Kirsty Gover, 'From the Heart: The Indigenous Challenge to Australian Public Law' in Jason NE Varuhas and Shona Wilson Stark (eds), *The Frontiers of Public Law* (Hart Publishing 2020) 210.

[21] Note that this section on New Zealand is a significant reworking of an earlier article, Shireen Morris, 'Lessons from New Zealand: Towards a Better Working Relationship between Indigenous Peoples and the State' (2014/2015) 18(2) *Australian Indigenous Law Review* 67.

[22] Kenneth Keith, 'On the Constitution of New Zealand: An Introduction to the Foundations of the Current Form of Government' (Department of the Prime Minister and Cabinet, 1990, updated 2008 and 2017) <https://dpmc.govt.nz/our-business-units/cabinet-office/supporting-work-cabinet/cabinet-manual/introduction> accessed 8 December 2019.

[23] See Noel Cox, *Technology and Legal Systems* (Ashgate 2006) 4. One exception is s 17 of the *Constitution Act 1986* (NZ). The *Electoral Act 1993* (NZ) also contains some semi-entrenched provisions: see Anthony H Angelo, *Constitutional Law in New Zealand* (Wolters Kluwer 2011) 17–18.

arrangements are not entrenched.[24] There is no hierarchy under which constitutional laws are given special status, and no 'supreme law' under which ordinary legislation can be struck down by the courts.[25] This flexible constitutional structure has arguably enabled 'adaption to changing circumstances', allowing 'the values of government' to 'stay in line with changing social values',[26] predominantly through political processes rather than the courts. To proponents of the political process as the best mechanism for rights adjudication, this makes New Zealand a particularly democratic nation.[27] A strong form of parliamentary sovereignty prevails in New Zealand,[28] in contrast to Australia's parliamentary supremacy, in which the Parliament's power is curtailed by an entrenched Constitution, as interpreted by the courts.[29]

The Treaty of Waitangi and the New Zealand *Bill of Rights Act 1990* (NZBORA) are important parts of New Zealand's constitutional framework. They are considered 'foundational documents' which have established important constitutional principles, including the principle 'that the Government must govern according to the law'.[30] Despite this, the unentrenched status of these documents means their principles can never trump parliamentary will,[31] which means Māori rights are susceptible to political infringement. Māori advocates chose not to include Treaty principles in the NZBORA, fearing this would lead to their rights being narrowed and weakened.[32] But the legal vulnerability of

[24] Interestingly, however, in New Zealand, a referendum can be requested via a successful petition under the *Citizens Initiated Referenda Act 1993* (NZ) or on government initiative. These referenda can be either binding, which means government must act on the result, or indicative (non-binding). In New Zealand, referenda have been held in relation to compulsory military training, parliamentary terms, and electoral reform: see 'What is a Referendum?', *Elections: New Zealand Electoral Commission* <http://www.elections.org.nz/voting-system/referenda> accessed 8 December 2019.

[25] Nick Mereu, 'A Written Constitution for New Zealand?' (2009) 2(1) *New Zealand Law Students Journal* 217, 219.

[26] Constitutional Advisory Panel, *New Zealand's Constitution* (n 19 above) 24. For example, as will be explained below, New Zealand's electoral arrangements changed in 1993 with the introduction of proportional representation. See Andrew Geddis and Caroline Morris, 'All is Changed, Changed Utterly: The Causes and Consequences of New Zealand's Adoption of MMP' (2004) 32(3) *Federal Law Review* 451.

[27] It is an arrangement which, in James Allan's view, may be preferable to Australia's more static and 'locked in' constitutional architecture: James Allan and Michael Kirby, 'A Public Conversation on Constitutionalism and the Judiciary between Professor James Allan and the Hon Michael Kirby AC CMG' (2009) 33(3) *Melbourne University Law Review* 1032, 1038. For opposing arguments, see Jeanette Jameson, 'Indigenous People: An American Perspective on the Case for Entrenchment of Māori Rights in New Zealand Law' (1993) 2(3) *Pacific Rim Law & Policy Journal* 345.

[28] For a leading Australian exposition on the principles of parliamentary sovereignty, see Jeffrey Goldsworthy, *Parliamentary Sovereignty: Contemporary Debates* (Cambridge University Press 2010).

[29] See Chapter 2 of this volume for discussion on Australia's constitutional arrangements and parliamentary supremacy. See also Julie Taylor, 'Human Rights Protection in Australia and Parliamentary Supremacy' (2004) 32(1) *Federal Law Review* 57, 58–60.

[30] Constitutional Advisory Panel, *New Zealand's Constitution* (n 19 above) 23.

[31] ibid 25, 30.

[32] Kirsty Gover, 'The Treaty and Human Rights in New Zealand Law: Can We Add the Declaration and Stir?' in Andrew Erueti (ed), *International Indigenous Rights in Aotearoa New Zealand* (Victoria University Press 2018) 49–50; KJ Keith, 'The New Zealand Bill of Rights Act 1990: An Account

Māori rights has prompted some to call for 'constitutional transformation' to entrench stronger protections.[33]

New Zealand's flexible constitutional arrangements must be taken into account when applying insights to Australia's more difficult-to-amend Constitution. On one hand, such flexibility means Māori rights may be less securely protected. On the other hand, it has facilitated institutional reform over time to incorporate new mechanisms for Māori recognition and empowerment.[34] The difference in constitutional rigidity, together with the greater numerical power of Māori in New Zealand[35] and the lack of a founding treaty in Australia, may help explain why Indigenous constitutional recognition in Australia has proved more difficult.

B. The Treaty of Waitangi

The signing of the Treaty of Waitangi can be viewed as a moment of historical accord which laid the groundwork for 'harmonious race relations' between Māori and Pākehā people.[36] The Treaty has been described as 'the promise of two peoples to take the best possible care of each other'.[37] Despite this aspiration, New Zealand's history 'since the signing of the Treaty has been marked by repeated failures to honour these founding promises'.[38] Nonetheless, the Treaty

of its Preparation' (2013) 11 *New Zealand Journal of Public and International Law* 1, 12. McHugh argues that: 'Māori lost an important opportunity when their representatives rejected inclusion of a Treaty principles clause in the Bill of Rights Act 1990 (BORA). This would have given those principles a clear application throughout the public sector': PG McHugh, 'Treaty Principles: Constitutional Relations Inside a Conservative Jurisprudence' (2008) 39(1) *Victoria University of Wellington Law Review* 39, 67.

[33] Margaret Mutu, 'Behind the Smoke and Mirrors of the Treaty of Waitangi Claims Settlement Process in New Zealand: No Prospect for Justice and Reconciliation for Māori without Constitutional Transformation' (2018) 14(2) *Journal of Global Ethics* 208. Notably, the former UN Special Rapporteur on Indigenous peoples also called for the 'principles enshrined in the Treaty of Waitangi and related, internationally protected human rights to be provided security within the domestic legal system of New Zealand so that these rights are not vulnerable to political discretion': UNHRC, 'Report of the Special Rapporteur on the Rights of Indigenous Peoples, James Anaya: The Situation of Maori People in New Zealand' (31 May 2011) UN Doc A/HRC/18/35/Add.4, 1–2.

[34] It has facilitated 'dynamic' recognition. See Benjamen Franklen Gussen, 'A Comparative Analysis of Constitutional Recognition of Aboriginal Peoples' (2017) 40(3) *Melbourne University Law Review* 867, 889–90.

[35] Māori are 15% of New Zealand's population: 'New Zealand Population 2019' (*World Population Review*, 28 August 2019) <http://worldpopulationreview.com/countries/new-zealand-population/> accessed 8 December 2019.

[36] David V Williams, 'Te Tiriti o Waitangi: Unique Relationship between Crown and Tangata Whenua?' in IHJ Kawharu (ed), *Waitangi: Māori and Pakeha Perspectives of the Treaty of Waitangi* (Oxford University Press 1989) 64.

[37] Bishop Manu Bennett, quoted in Human Rights Commission, *Human Rights in New Zealand/ Ngā Tika Tangata O Aotearoa* (HRC 2010) 39, as cited in Human Rights Commission, *Human Rights and the Treaty of Waitangi: Te Mana i Waitangi* (HRC 2003).

[38] *Human Rights in New Zealand* (n 37 above) 39.

established a special relationship between Māori and the Crown, reflecting 'an understanding of the fundamental elements of the relationship and about how *iwi* and *hapū* would work with the Crown in developing the country's future'.[39] It was an acknowledgement of shared founding authority and an agreement to work in partnership. This understanding proved crucial to the development of institutional structures recognising the special relationship.

In legal terms, the Treaty can be described as mostly ineffective, as laws can be and are passed which contravene the Treaty.[40] Like other international treaties, the Treaty of Waitangi is only enforceable to the extent that it is expressly incorporated into legislation.[41] It has never been incorporated in its entirety and so does not provide an independent source of Māori rights. As noted, judicialisation of the Treaty has at various times been resisted by Māori. Palmer notes that some Māori felt incorporating the Treaty into legislation could 'diminish its status', transforming it from 'a powerful normative symbol with moral legitimacy into a mere legal instrument' that can be amended:

> If the Treaty is outside the law its moral and normative power can continue untouched, as a reference point for political agitation. Inside the law, it becomes an instrument of the legal system and a plaything for lawyers and judges.[42]

Over time, however, the Treaty has become symbolically, politically and morally powerful. As Palmer explains:

> It symbolized and still symbolizes a mutual agreement between two peoples that gave the Crown legitimacy to exercise a governance role in New Zealand and accorded some level of protection to Māori. Despite the uncertainty and argument over its terms the Treaty remains a potent symbol of nation-building.[43]

The Treaty's preamble acknowledges the British monarchy, the native prior occupants and immigrants, and is said to establish a bicultural foundation for New Zealand.[44] The preamble establishes the Treaty's purpose as protecting Māori rights and property, recognising British sovereign authority, and establishing law and order and conditions for justice, for both the native population and the Crown's subjects. Article 1 declares that the native chiefs cede their sovereignty and authority absolutely, and without reservation, to the British Crown (however, this interpretation is disputed, as the Māori text employs a concept

[39] Constitutional Advisory Panel, *New Zealand's Constitution* (n 19 above) 29. See also Aditya Vasudevan, 'Restoring Rangatiratanga: Theoretical Arguments for Constitutional Transformation Ko Nga Take Ture Māori' (2017) 23 *Auckland University Law Review* 91.

[40] Constitutional Advisory Panel, *New Zealand's Constitution* (n 19 above) 13.

[41] *Hoani Te Heuheu Tukino v Aotea Dist Māori Land Bd* [1941] AC 308 (PC).

[42] Matthew SR Palmer, 'Constitutional Realism about Constitutional Protection: Indigenous Rights under a Judicialized and a Politicized Constitution' (2006) 29 (1) *Dalhousie Law Journal* 1, 31.

[43] ibid 29.

[44] ET Durie, 'Justice, Biculturalism and the Politics of Law' in Margaret Wilson and Anna Yeatman (eds), *Justice and Identity: Antipodean Practices* (Allen & Unwin 1995) 33.

that differs from the English concept of 'sovereignty').[45] Article 2 guarantees Māori tribes 'full exclusive and undisturbed' possession of their properties as long as they wish to retain those properties; but says that the tribes yield to the Crown the exclusive and pre-emptive right of alienation at agreed prices.[46] Article 3 says that 'in consideration therefore', the Crown grants the Māori 'royal protection' and imparts 'all the rights and privileges of British subjects'. It guarantees Māori equal citizenship and equality before the law, but may also establish a duty of protection whereby the Crown is supposed to act in the best interests of Māori people.[47]

The Treaty in and of itself did not prevent discrimination against Māori.[48] Racially discriminatory views that saw Māori as inferior led the courts to declare the Treaty legally invalid on the basis that Māori were politically incapable of entering into a valid agreement with the Crown.[49] The 1877 *Wi Parata* case found the 'Māori tribes were incapable of performing the duties, and therefore of assuming the rights, of a civilised community'. Because Māori were considered 'primitive barbarians', the Supreme Court held that government could 'acquit itself, as best it may, of its obligation to respect native proprietary rights', and thus could be 'the sole arbiter of its own justice'.[50] Though the Privy Council overturned the discriminatory reasoning in 1901,[51] New Zealand courts ignored its decision and continued to disregard the Treaty.[52] In 1941, the Privy Council fell into line with New Zealand courts and declared that the Treaty was not enforceable unless incorporated into legislation.[53] New Zealand's history,

[45] In 1989, anthropologist Hugh Kawharu developed an English translation of the Māori version of the Treaty to more accurately reflect the understanding of the signing chiefs. Kawharu translated 'kāwanatanga' as 'government'. Translated meanings continue to be debated: 'Te Tiriti O Waitangi/The Treaty of Waitangi', *New Zealand History* <https://nzhistory.govt.nz/files/documents/treaty-kawharu-footnotes.pdf> accessed 8 December 2019. See also Constitutional Advisory Panel, *New Zealand's Constitution* (n 19 above) 29.

[46] Article 2 has also been interpreted to give Māori the right to live as Māori, or the right to self-determination: see *Human Rights in New Zealand* (n 37 above) 39.

[47] *New Zealand Māori Council v Attorney-General* [1987] 1 NZLR 641, 705.

[48] Carwyn Jones, 'Strengthening Partnership between States and Indigenous Peoples: Treaties, Agreements and Other Constructive Arrangements' (Office of the United Nations High Commissioner for Human Rights, Geneva, 16–17 July 2012) 2. See also Jacinta Ruru, 'Asserting the Doctrine of Discovery in Aotearoa New Zealand: 1840–1960s' in Robert J Miller and others (eds), *Discovering Indigenous Lands: The Doctrine of Discovery in the English Colonies* (Oxford University Press 2010).

[49] This is an outcome reminiscent of Batman's attempted treaty with the Kulin people in Australia, discussed in Chapter 2 of this volume, which was declared legally invalid by colonial authorities. Jacinta Ruru, 'Finding Support for a Changed Property Discourse in Aotearoa New Zealand in the United Declaration of the Rights of Indigenous Peoples' (2011) 15(4) *Lewis & Clark Law Review* 951, 964.

[50] *Wi Parata v Bishop of Wellington* (1877) 3 NZ Jur (NS) 72 (SC) 78, 77, 78.

[51] *Nireaha Tamaki v Baker* [1901] AC 561 (PC) 577.

[52] Ruru, 'Finding Support' (n 49 above) 965.

[53] *Hoani* (n 41 above). This principle is followed today.

like Australia's, includes violence and discrimination[54] in the dispossession of Indigenous people, despite the Treaty.[55]

C. Movement Towards Practical Recognition of Māori

Yet as attitudes and politics changed, the Treaty came to be seen as the foundation for a positive re-calibration of the relationship between Māori and the Crown.[56] The Treaty is now said to establish biculturalism,[57] a principle of partnership between Māori and the state and a duty to negotiate reasonably and in good faith.[58] These principles have become ingrained,[59] and now incorporate a duty to consult that has developed moral and political force, though in general, these principles are not legally actionable unless spelt out in legislation.[60] References to 'principles of the Treaty' are now incorporated into many significant pieces of legislation.[61]

Reinforcing the predominantly political approach to Māori recognition, New Zealand courts have exercised deference to Parliament in applying the Treaty. As McHugh explains:

> To the extent there has grown a jurisprudence of Treaty principles it has been an inherently conservative one. Far from pushing the boundaries of that jurisprudence the courts have been cautious and more concerned with ensuring due process.

[54] Noel Cox, 'The Treaty of Waitangi and the Relationship between the Crown and the Māori in New Zealand' (2003) 28(1) *Brooklyn Journal of International Law* 123, 140.

[55] Ruru, 'Finding Support' (n 49 above) 960–62.

[56] Augie Fleras and Paul Spoonley, *Recalling Aotearoa: Indigenous Politics and Ethnic Relations in New Zealand* (Oxford University Press 1999) 115–27; see also *Human Rights in New Zealand* (n 37 above) 131–47. Note that, in New Zealand, the use of 'the Crown' to denote the New Zealand state has proved strategically useful in enabling discussions about history and reparations that do not ascribe guilt and culpability to contemporary individuals. See Janet McLean, 'Crown, Empire and Redressing the Historical Wrongs of Colonisation in New Zealand' [2015] (2) *New Zealand Law Review* 187.

[57] Fleras and Spoonley (n 56 above) 115–27; see also *Human Rights in New Zealand* (n 37 above) 39.

[58] *New Zealand Māori Council* (n 47 above); *Te Runanga o Wharekauri Rekohu Inc v Attorney-General* [1993] 2 NZLR 301, 304, 306. See *Human Rights in New Zealand* (n 37 above) 39. See also, DRIP (n 1 above) which states in its preamble: 'Treaties are the basis for a strengthened partnership between Indigenous people and the state.'

[59] Philip Joseph, 'The Māori Seats in Parliament: Te Oranga O Te Iwi Māori – A Study of Māori Economic and Social Progress' (New Zealand Business Roundtable, May 2008).

[60] See also, McHugh (n 32 above); Jack Oliver-Hood, 'Ko Nga Take Ture Māori: Our Significantly Indigenous Administrative Law – The Treaty of Waitangi and Judicial Review' (2013) 19 *Auckland University Law Review* 53; MH Durie, 'The Treaty of Waitangi Perspectives for Social Policy' in IHJ Kawharu (ed), *Waitangi: Māori and Pakeha Perspectives of the Treaty of Waitangi* (Oxford University Press 1989) 280.

[61] See Mark Barnett and Kim Connolly-Stone, 'The Treaty of Waitangi and Social Policy' (December 1998) 11 *Social Policy Journal of New Zealand* <http://www.msd.govt.nz/about-msd-and-our-work/publications-resources/journals-and-magazines/social-policy-journal/spj11/treaty-of-waitangi-and-social-policy.html> accessed 8 December 2019.

> The profile of the jurisprudence has been facilitative, geared mostly around getting the relevant parties in constructive dialogue within the terms of the statutory regime.[62]

The Treaty established an ongoing political dialogue between treaty partners. Practical measures have since been implemented to facilitate this dialogue and ensure that Māori voices are heard through national institutional arrangements. These include the New Zealand Māori Council, the recommendatory functions of the Waitangi Tribunal, which have helped propel direct Treaty negotiations as well as practical forms of Māori cultural recognition, and reserved Māori parliamentary seats.

(i) The New Zealand Māori Council

The Māori Council structure arose out of Māori political advocacy in the 1800s and derived from the Kotahitanga (Māori King) movement and the Māori parliaments. The structure was not recognised by the Crown until 1962, when the Māori Council's general functions and purpose were articulated in legislation.[63] The Māori Council is a consultative and advisory body, empowered to make representations to government regarding Māori affairs.[64] Its role includes considering and promoting Māori social and economic advancement and harmonious inter-ethnic relations, and collaborating with state departments and other organisations on Māori affairs initiatives such as employment, education, health and cultural revitalisation.

Māori over 20 years of age are entitled (but not compelled) to vote in Māori Committee elections, and any person, whether or not they are Māori, may stand for election if they are ordinarily resident in the area or have 'marae affiliations' to the area.[65] The representative structure is spearheaded by a smaller group of elected representatives, formed from a collective of Māori committees within each Māori district. Māori Council districts[66] are distinct from the Māori electorates which operate for the purposes of the Māori roll in the election of Māori reserved parliamentary seats.[67] Committee areas within districts are the declared tribal committee areas under the *Māori Social and Economic Advancement Act 1945*.[68] The Māori Council thus provides an

[62] McHugh (n 32 above) 66. As will be seen, there are similarities with the Canadian approach in this respect.

[63] *Māori Community Development Act 1962* (NZ) s 18; see 'Our History', *Te Kaunihere Māori o Aotearoa: New Zealand Māori Council*: <https://web.archive.org/web/20171012094826/https://maoricouncil.com/2013/02/02/our-history/> archived 12 October 2017.

[64] *Māori Community Development Act 1962* (NZ), s 18.

[65] *Māori Community Development Act 1962* (NZ), s 19.

[66] Declared at any time by resolution of the New Zealand Māori Council: *Māori Community Development Act 1962*, s 14.

[67] There are currently 16 Māori Council districts across New Zealand.

[68] *Māori Community Development Act 1962* (NZ), s 8.

elected, representative structure to connect local Māori leaders with national leadership.[69]

The Māori Council has represented Māori in claims against the Crown[70] and has been an important vehicle for national advocacy. It has helped give Māori a recognised voice in their affairs and assisted in consolidating Māori co-operation and consensus between tribes: important elements for effective national advocacy. A review of the Act was undertaken in 2010.[71] In 2013, then Minister for Māori Affairs, Dr Pita Sharples, criticised the Act for being outdated in its incorporation of arguably discriminatory elements, like empowering Māori wardens to evict Māori people from bars.[72] In 2014, the Waitangi Tribunal responded to a Māori Council claim that the government review did not comply with Treaty principles.[73] The Tribunal's finding explained that, while its role and efficacy has changed over time and the Act may need updating, the Māori Council is the result of a negotiated compact between Māori and the Crown to provide an institutional structure for Māori autonomy, self-government and self-determination. The recommendation demonstrates the extent to which the Treaty established an ongoing relationship between Māori and the Crown, together with an expectation of Māori empowerment in this relationship. The Māori Council is one resulting facet of this expectation.

Given that Māori are best placed to lead, consult with Māori and advise government on Māori policy, it appears sensible that New Zealand has formally recognised a national structure to enable Māori to exercise influence, empowerment and a voice in their affairs. The flexibility of the Act establishing the Māori Council is also instructive. If Australia is to adopt its own Indigenous representative, consultative and advisory body, it is important to ensure that its structure and functions can evolve over time as necessary, while also ensuring that its political authority and permanency can be maintained in changing circumstances.

[69] It may be that part of the success of the Māori Council is that it provides a counter-balance to tribal authorities – it is one of various ways for Māori to be heard. See Kirsty Gover and Natalie Baird, 'Identifying the Māori Treaty Partner' (2002) 52(1) *The University of Toronto Law Journal* 39, 43–45.

[70] See, for example, *New Zealand Māori Council v Attorney-General* (n 47 above) ('the Lands case').

[71] Māori Affairs Committee, *Inquiry into the Operation of the Māori Community Development Act 1962 and related issues* (49th Parliament, House of Representatives, December 2010).

[72] Adam Bennett, 'Fears for Future of Māori Council', *New Zealand Herald* (27 September 2013). However, see comments by the current Executive Director, Matthew Tukaki, in 2019: 'When [the 1962 Act] was first written – it was largely written and guided by some very wise people including Sir Turi Carroll, who was one of the first chairs of the Māori Council – it was because we had a problem with alcohol back then. Today, while it might not be flattering, one could very much argue that drugs such as P and Ice [methamphetamine] have become a problem in place of alcohol, as it was defined back then. So I say, acts of parliament and legislation are not meant to be pretty but they're meant to be able to be interpreted for whatever the challenge of the day might be.' Leonie Hayden, 'The firebrand: meet the new man at the helm of the Māori Council', *The Spinoff* (1 December 2019) <https://thespinoff.co.nz/atea/01-12-2019/the-firebrand-meet-the-new-man-at-the-helm-of-the-maori-council/> accessed 10 February 2020.

[73] Waitangi Tribunal, *Report on the Māori Community Development Act Claim* (2014) xvi.

Notably, the Referendum Council, responding to the Uluru Statement, proposed precisely this – a First Nations voice that would be constitutionally guaranteed, but legislatively articulated,[74] enabling both stability and flexibility.

Unlike Māori, Indigenous Australians have no founding treaty or established partnership principles to which they can appeal. There is therefore a strong argument that, for Indigenous Australians, a First Nations voice must be embedded into the constitutional compact so that it is enduring and authoritative. As discussed in Chapter two above, the Australian Constitution is itself like a treaty. Indigenous peoples should be included in this compact, so their voice in their affairs can be constitutionally guaranteed.

(ii) The Waitangi Tribunal and Cultural Recognition

Since 1975, Māori have been recognised and represented through the processes of the Waitangi Tribunal. The Tribunal hears and recommends resolutions for addressing breaches of the Treaty of Waitangi, which can then inform direct negotiations.[75] Through these processes, grievances can be aired, stories told and histories documented. Settlements involve financial and cultural redress and recognition, as well as official Crown apologies for past Treaty breaches.[76] The Treaty settlement process establishes a truth and reconciliation mechanism for New Zealand and provides an active and ongoing process for Māori recognition and agreement-making. The Tribunal's recommendations are generally non-binding but carry political and moral force.[77]

Negotiations occur between Māori and the Crown, but do not involve the general public – although Waitangi Tribunal reports are published and publicly available. This contained conversation, in addition to use of 'the Crown' as a distancing device,[78] may have usefully 'relieved the public of "guilt by association"', such that 'New Zealanders today are not held accountable for the sins of their colonial past'.[79] Though public attitudes towards Waitangi Tribunal mechanisms have varied over time, governments on either side have remained committed to the process,[80] demonstrating the long-term political impact of

[74] *Final Report of the Referendum Council* (30 June 2017) Recommendation 1, 36.

[75] *Treaty of Waitangi Act 1975* (NZ). Jones, 'Strengthening Partnership' (n 48 above).

[76] FM Brookfield, *Waitangi and Indigenous Rights: Revolution, Law and Legitimation* (Auckland University Press 1999) 158. See also Fleras and Spoonley (n 56 above) 132.

[77] However, in 1988, the Waitangi Tribunal was conferred power to make binding recommendations in specific limited circumstances. It has only once used this power: Janine Hayward, 'Treaty of Waitangi Settlements: Successful Symbolic Reparation' in Joannah Luetjens, Michael Mintrom and Paul 't Hart (eds), *Successful Public Policy* (Australian National University Press 2019) 404; Richard P Boast, 'The Waitangi Tribunal: "Conscience of the Nation" or Just Another Court?' (1993) 16(1) *UNSW Law Journal* 223, 227–28.

[78] See McLean (n 56 above).

[79] Hayward (n 77 above) 400.

[80] ibid. Note, however, Tiopira McDowell who argues that, 'while the Crown publicly offered a series of moral, legal, social and political principles to explain its motivations and objectives in

the Treaty. For Hayward, the settlements process creates an enduring 'political conversation sustained over several decades between the treaty partners'. In this relationship, both parties have 'evolved and been shaped by the necessary political manoeuvring, negotiation, tension and compromise'.[81] This demonstrates what can be achieved through engaged political dialogue, given the right political conditions: the non-justiciability of the settlements process has not limited its impact. As McHugh explains, 'non-justiciability does not mean an absence of public law consequence. Rather, it means the courts will not be the sole or primary agent of that consequence in the claims-settlement arena'.[82] The settlements occur in the political arena, propelled by a sense of partnership and good faith. This sense of partnership and long-term commitment to shared dialogue is notably absent in the Australian Indigenous-state dynamic, despite rhetoric to the contrary.[83] This is why constitutional reform is needed in the Australian context – to reset the relationship and create a dynamic of partnership and dialogue that is underpinned by a constitutional promise.

Key Treaty settlements demonstrate the way in which this process can address financial as well as cultural losses. The Waikato-Tainui settlement, enacted into legislation in 1995, addressed decades of historical warfare and failed attempts at fair negotiation.[84] The settlement deed included compensation of land and cash valued at NZ$170 million.[85] Queen Elizabeth II signed the *Waikato Raupatu Claims Settlement Act 1995* incorporating it into New Zealand law, and personally delivered the apology[86] acknowledging past injustices and Treaty breaches. The apology included expressions of 'profound regret … for the loss of lives' and 'the devastation of property and social life', the wrongful confiscations of land and resources, and the 'crippling impact on the welfare, economy and development of Waikato'. It acknowledged the

> sense of grief, the justice of which under the Treaty of Waitangi has remained unrecognised, has given rise to Waikato's two principles 'i riro whenua atu, me hoki

settling treaty claims, the Crown's primary motivation was to divert Māori away from their legal rights, to contain the Crown's fiscal liabilities, to maintain the acceptability of treaty claims settlements to the non- Māori public': see Tiopira McDowell, 'Diverting the Sword of Damocles: Why Did the Crown Choose to Settle Māori Historical Treaty Claims?' (2018) 64(4) *Australian Journal of Politics and History* 592.

[81] Hayward (n 77 above) 401.

[82] McHugh (n 32 above) 67.

[83] ibid 57. Although this may now be changing with the government's commitment to a co-design process between Indigenous people and government, to settle the details of a First Nations voice. See Joint Select Committee on Constitutional Recognition relating to Aboriginal and Torres Strait Islander Peoples, *Final Report* (November 2018) Recommendations.

[84] *Waikato Raupatu Claims Settlement Act 1995* (NZ); 'The Treaty in Practice: The Waikato-Tainui Claim' (*New Zealand History*, 7 July 2014) <http://www.nzhistory.net.nz/politics/treaty/the-treaty-in-practice/waikato-tainui> accessed 8 December 2019.

[85] 'The Treaty in Practice' (n 84 above).

[86] Richard S Hill, *Ngā Whakataunga Tiriti: Treaty of Waitangi Settlement Process – Different Paths to Settlement* (*Te Ara: The Encyclopedia of New Zealand*, 13 July 2102) <http://www.TeAra.govt.nz/en/video/33050/royal-apology-to-tainui-1995> accessed 8 December 2019.

whenua mai' (as land was taken, land should be returned) and 'ko to moni hei utu mo te hara' (the money is the acknowledgment by the Crown of their crime).

The apology agreed 'to provide redress' by returning 'as much land as is possible that the Crown has in its possession to Waikato'.[87] It was thus an apology accompanied by practical redress, in contrast to the National Apology in Australia which, as noted in Chapter two above, was symbolic only, not accompanied by compensation and narrowly limited to wrongs with respect to the Stolen Generation.

The *Te Reo Māori* claim argued that Māori language was a cultural 'treasure'; a right protected under Article 2 of the Treaty.[88] In 1987, the Tribunal made several recommendations for appropriate redress, which included recognising te reo Māori as an official language of New Zealand. This and many other recommendations were subsequently taken up by the government.[89] Māori was recognised as an official language in legislation,[90] and the fact that Māori language rights are protected under the Treaty is recognised in the preamble to the *Māori Language Act 1987* (NZ).[91] The Māori Language Commission was established under the Act[92] to promote New Zealand as a bicultural nation.[93]

The cultural component of the Waitangi Tribunal settlements has helped to propel recognition of Māori culture and heritage in a tangible way. The New Zealand National Geographic Board[94] undertakes dual-language place naming, with Māori place names sometimes flowing from Treaty settlements, then included in the relevant settlement legislation.[95] The process of dual naming 'recognises the equal and special significance of both the original Māori and non-Māori names',[96] and New Zealand itself now carries its Māori name: Aotearoa. Māori culture is increasingly seen as New Zealand's culture. Witness the way in which variations of the traditional Māori Haka are performed by New Zealand sports teams, including national teams like the All Blacks, as an expression not only of Māori culture and heritage, but also of New Zealand

[87] *Waikato Raupatu Claims Settlement Act 1995*, s 6. The Māori version is recorded in s 5.

[88] Article 2 has also been interpreted to give Māori the right to live as Māori, or the right to self-determination: see *Human Rights in New Zealand* (n 37 above) 39.

[89] ibid 47–48; Jones, 'Strengthening Partnership' (n 48 above).

[90] *Māori Language Act 1987*, s 3.

[91] The Preamble states: 'Whereas in the Treaty of Waitangi the Crown confirmed and guaranteed to the Māori people, among other things, all their taonga: And whereas the Māori language is one such taonga.'

[92] *Māori Language Act 1987*, s 6.

[93] *Human Rights in New Zealand* (n 37 above) 47–48; Jones, 'Strengthening Partnership' (n 48 above).

[94] Set up under the *New Zealand Geographic Board (Ngā Pou Taunaha o Aotearoa) Act 2008*.

[95] 'Treaty of Waitangi: Claims Settlement Names' (Land Information New Zealand: Toitū Te Whenua, last updated 9 March 2018) <http://www.linz.govt.nz/regulatory/place-names/propose-place-name/treaty-waitangi-claims-settlement-names> accessed 8 December 2019.

[96] ibid.

culture and heritage. By contrast, a few seconds of an Aboriginal war dance performed by Australian footballer, Adam Goodes, on the field during a special 'Indigenous Round' of Aussie Rules football in 2015, prompted widespread contention in Australia. By some it was taken not as a celebration, but as an affront. The consternation demonstrated that Australia has not yet come to terms with the Indigenous parts of its national heritage and history.

New Zealand's settlements process has helped create a sense of respect for Māori culture and worldviews. The landmark Te Awa Tupua (Whanganui River Claims Settlement) of 2017[97] recognises that 'Te Awa Tupua is an indivisible and living whole, comprising the Whanganui River from the mountains to the sea, incorporating all its physical and metaphysical elements'[98] and also recognises the river as a legal person.[99] The settlement provides for joint management and collaborative development of a policy plan for managing the river, and includes financial and cultural redress as well as a Crown apology for past wrongs.[100] Interestingly, the settlement articulates the 'intrinsic values' that represent the essence of Te Awa Tupua, including recognition of the river as a 'source of spiritual and physical sustenance'.[101] The settlement demonstrates the extent to which agreement-making can involve a sharing of cultural understanding and the development of shared values through negotiation.[102]

The settlements mechanisms in New Zealand encourage an understanding of Māori recognition as a practical work in progress. Settlements allow recognition to incrementally continue and political dialogue to occur in an ongoing way. The Crown has committed to reaching a final settlement with each Māori tribe, with each settlement intended to be a final resolution of all historical grievances so that Māori and the Crown can build a constructive partnership for the future.[103] This process, started in 1975, is now reaching its conclusion.[104] According to Hayward, the settlements process has had far-reaching positive impacts: it has 'laid bare New Zealand's colonial history, established new relationships between the Crown and iwi (tribes) and reestablished an economic and cultural base for future local and regional Māori development'.[105]

[97] *Te Awa Tupua (Whanganui River Claims Settlement) Act 2017* (NZ).

[98] ibid, s 12.

[99] ibid, s 14.

[100] ibid, ss 69, 70.

[101] ibid, s 13.

[102] But some argue that it does not go far enough: see Toni Collins and Shea Esterling, 'Fluid Personality: Indigenous Rights and the *Te Awa Tupua (Whanhanui River Claims Settlement) Act 2017* in Aotearoa New Zealand' (2019) 20(1) *Melbourne University Law Review* 1.

[103] Damien Freeman, 'Addressing Aboriginal Disadvantage: That's What I Call a Defining Moment', *The Australian* (6 September 2014).

[104] The aim is for historic settlements to be concluded by 2020. See Hayward (n 77 above) 399; Constitutional Advisory Panel, *New Zealand's Constitution* (n 19 above) 33.

[105] Hayward (n 77 above) 400. For an opposing view as to the justice and effectiveness of the Waitangi Tribunal settlements, see Mutu (n 33 above).

Along with the other practical forms of Māori recognition, the settlements process may be seen as measures which have 'supplemented the deficient legitimacy of the legal order … that began in 1840', such that the 'Māori expectations based on the Treaty and also in some measure on the historical record of dealings between coloniser and colonised, have been partly fulfilled'.[106] New Zealand has used contemporary agreement-making and settlements to reform and reframe the relationship between Māori and the Crown, making it fairer than in the past. In considering mechanisms for Indigenous recognition in Australia, there is much that can be learnt from New Zealand's Waitangi Tribunal negotiations and settlements. The Uluru Statement's call for a Makarrata Commission demonstrates an aspiration to move Australia towards an agreement-making and truth-telling process. The design of this process could learn from the Waitangi Tribunal and the settlements process undertaken in New Zealand.

(iii) Māori Reserved Seats in Parliament

Reserved Māori seats in Parliament are an important part of the practical recognition of Māori in New Zealand, and have arguably become part of political expectations arising from the Treaty.[107] New Zealand has had reserved Māori seats since 1867.[108] The reserved seats sit in the House of Representatives and are chosen through a Māori electoral roll not attached exclusively to particular Māori territory. Rather, every Māori person, wherever they reside, may choose whether to vote on the Māori roll or the general roll.[109] The Māori electoral population,[110] as ascertained by the number of Māori people who have registered on the Māori roll, is divided into Māori electoral districts.[111] The Māori districts cover the entire country and territorially co-exist with the general roll.

One view is that the Māori seats were initially implemented as a tool for political control and minimisation of Māori power, as Māori in the 1860s were in the majority.[112] Lloyd explains that at 'a time when Māori greatly outnumbered non-Māori, dedicated seats allowed the political power of Māori to be constrained, limiting their vote to the Māori electoral roll and the four Māori seats alone'.[113] Others argue that the seats were implemented to address the

[106] Brookfield (n 76 above) 158.
[107] Constitutional Advisory Panel, *New Zealand's Constitution* (n 19 above) 39.
[108] See Catherine Iorns Magallanes, 'Indigenous Political Representation: Identified Parliamentary Seats as a Form of Indigenous Self-Determination' in BA Hocking (ed), *Unfinished Constitutional Business?* (Aboriginal Studies Press 2005) 106; Brian Lloyd, 'Dedicated Indigenous Representation in the Australian Parliament' (Research Paper No 23, Parliamentary Library, Politics and Public Administrations Section, 2009).
[109] *Electoral Act 1993* (NZ), s 76.
[110] A Māori person for electoral purposes is today defined as a person of 'the Māori race of New Zealand' and the descendants of such a person: ibid, s 3(1).
[111] ibid, s 45.
[112] Magallanes (n 108 above) 106–7.
[113] Lloyd (n 108 above) 5.

problem that the Māori were disenfranchised because of the property rules that were a condition of voting rights. Only males over 21 with an individual property title were allowed to vote.[114] Māori practised communal ownership,[115] and though they could undertake processes to gain individual title, this was slow and many were mistrustful of aggressive Crown tactics to individualise Māori title as a way of eroding Māori governance and authority.[116] Accordingly, many Māori men who should otherwise have been allowed to vote were not democratically represented.[117]

The allocation of reserved seats was initially a temporary measure, purportedly to ensure that the Māori were represented while governments undertook the process of giving Māori males individual property titles.[118] However, the number of seats given was not at all proportionate to the number of Māori men in the population, so the seats were probably 'discriminatory tokenism',[119] rather than a genuine attempt at proportional representation.[120] Some argue the move involved 'no high intentions or moral principles',[121] but was a 'way of rewarding Māori loyalists and placating Māori rebels'.[122] Others say that there was some element of responding to international pressure, especially since the Crown was generating tax revenue from the Māori people.[123] Whatever the many reasons, the existence of the reserved seats was further extended.[124]

Universal suffrage in New Zealand was achieved in 1893 but was split into two race-based voting rolls. From 1893 to 1975, 'full-blood' Māori had to be on the Māori voting roll, 'half-bloods' (or 'half-castes') could choose which roll to be on, and any person with less than half Māori lineage had to be on the European roll.[125] In 1975, Māori were given the choice of which roll they wanted to be on, and the European roll was renamed the 'general roll'.[126] The reserved Māori seats remained, perhaps out of 'indifference and neglect',[127] but also perhaps as an affirmative way to address historical wrongs through promoting

[114] Joseph (n 59 above).

[115] Sarah McClelland 'Māori Electoral Representation: Challenge to Orthodoxy' (1997) 17(3) *New Zealand Universities Law Review* 272, 275; New Zealand Parliamentary Library, 'The Origins of the Māori Seats' (Parliamentary Library Research Paper, May 2009) 3.

[116] 'The Origins of the Māori Seats' (n 115 above) 6.

[117] ibid, 3; Andrew Geddis, 'A Dual Track Democracy? The Symbolic Role of the Māori Seats in New Zealand's Electoral System' (2006) 5(4) *Election Law Journal* 347, 352.

[118] 'The Origins of the Māori Seats' (n 115 above) 3.

[119] Joseph (n 59 above) 14.

[120] Alan Ward, *A Show of Justice: Racial 'Amalgamation' in Nineteenth Century New Zealand* (Auckland University Press 1973) 209.

[121] Tina Dahlberg, 'Māori Representation in Parliament and Tino Rangatiratanga' (1996) 2(1) *He Pukenga Korero* 62, 63.

[122] 'The Origins of the Māori Seats' (n 115 above) 8.

[123] ibid; Claudia Orange, *The Treaty of Waitangi* (Allen & Unwin 1987) 184.

[124] Geddis (n 117 above) 352.

[125] ibid 353.

[126] Jeremy Sparrow, *The Truth About the Māori Seats* (LLB (Honours) thesis, University of Otago 2010) 5.

[127] Joseph (n 59 above) 5.

a stronger Māori political voice. As Lloyd explains, the uncertain status of the reserved seats remained until the 1980s, 'after which there was a transition to Multiple Member Proportional voting (MMP) in national elections', which 'has played a significant part in increasing Māori parliamentary representation',[128] such that 'New Zealand achieved parity between the proportion of Māori in its population and the proportion of Māori representatives in parliament following the 2002 national elections'.[129] Similarly, there are now more Māori sitting in general seats.[130] Notably however, since 1967, though MPs in the reserved seats must be elected by voters on the Māori roll, there is no legal requirement that representatives sitting in the Māori seats must be Māori. In 1967, 'the 100-year-old disqualification preventing Europeans from standing as candidates in Māori seats was removed' and Māori were reciprocally able to stand in the non-Māori seats. Nonetheless, there has not yet been a non-Māori elected to a Māori reserved seat.[131]

The gradual consolidation of Māori reserved seats through the MMP reforms is described by Jack Nagel as evidence of how 'historical and political processes can improve on conscious design, producing social inventions that no institutional planner could have devised'.[132] The flexibility of New Zealand's constitutional arrangements have proved crucial in allowing this to occur. According to Nagel, the MMP reforms were the result of political 'consultation, deliberation, and decision by consensus'. They involved politicians changing their minds and coming to grasp the value of specific of Māori representation – an example of politically-driven, pragmatic reform producing worthwhile constitutional innovation.[133]

As noted, the Māori reserved seats have come to be associated with Treaty of Waitangi principles,[134] and may now symbolise the position of Māori as a 'Treaty partner' in the governance of the nation.[135] However, there have been criticisms of the reserved seats on the basis that they contravene equality before the law principles.[136] The 1993 Royal Commission on the Electoral System recommended that the reserved seats be abolished;[137] however, these recommendations were not adopted. Some argue that the Māori seats undermine

[128] Lloyd (n 108 above) 5–6.

[129] ibid 4.

[130] BV Harris, 'The Treaty of Waitangi and the Constitutional Future of New Zealand' [2005] (2) *New Zealand Law Review* 189, 199.

[131] 'The Origins of the Māori Seats' (n 115 above) 19. This approach reflects the approach taken in the Māori Council representation.

[132] Jack H Nagel, 'Constitutional Reform and Social Difference in New Zealand' (1996) 4(2) *Cardozo Journal of International and Comparative Law* 373, 374.

[133] ibid 390, 393.

[134] Geddis (n 117 above) 358.

[135] Lloyd (n 108 above) 7.

[136] Constitutional Advisory Panel, *New Zealand's Constitution* (n 19 above) 39.

[137] New Zealand Royal Commission on the Electoral System, *Towards a Better Democracy* (1986) 86.

fair proportional representation of all New Zealanders: they are 'discriminatory privilege',[138] or reverse discrimination.[139] The Treaty principles argument too has been refuted, because the Treaty does not *expressly* establish reserved seats:[140] 'the concepts of partnership and the Crown's duty of active protection define the Treaty relationship but neither concept mandates separate Māori representation'.[141] Others argue that the reserved seats institutionalise 'Māori separatism'.[142] The debate about reserved seats in New Zealand is paralleled by the Australian debate about the compatibility of Indigenous recognition with the principle of equality before the law in a liberal democracy.[143]

As discussed in Chapter two above, equality before the law is not cut and dried, especially in a liberal democracy with surviving, formerly excluded and oppressed Indigenous peoples. Liberalism allows for positive measures to ensure equality of opportunities and fair and equal participation, given the historical and contemporary circumstances. This is reflected in the allowance of 'special measures' at international law, as a positive expression of the racial non-discrimination principle, and allows for affirmative measures to promote equal opportunities and ensure that all groups have equal enjoyment of their human rights, particularly given the past denial of rights.[144] In New Zealand, however, the reserved seats are better justified as a manifestation of an original sovereignty-sharing, or power-sharing, agreement which recognises Māori as a distinct constitutional constituency under the Treaty. While Treaty promises were historically breached by the more powerful Crown, reserved seats are a way of equalising the historically imbalanced power relationship. The reserved seats can be justified as a way of ensuring a political structure for fairer ongoing debate about the meaning of the terms of the Treaty – especially important given the longstanding disputes about linguistic and substantive interpretation. The reserved seats enable political debate, dialogue and disagreement between Treaty partners to occur in a fairer way. It is a political form of Indigenous constitutional recognition.

New Zealand has no entrenched Constitution, no entrenched Bill of rights, and the Treaty is not legally binding unless legislated, which is subject to political will. In this environment of strong parliamentary sovereignty, reserved Māori seats can be understood as a political and procedural mechanism for

[138] Joseph (n 59 above) 14–15.

[139] Sparrow, *The Truth About the Māori Seats* (n 126 above) 13; Joseph (n 59 above) 11–12. See also Rawiri Taonui, 'New Zealand Elections: Māori Seats Once Again Focus of Debate' (*The Conversation*, 8 September 2017) <https://theconversation.com/new-zealand-elections-maori-seats-once-again-focus-of-debate-83293> accessed 8 December 2019.

[140] Joseph (n 59 above) 86.

[141] ibid 17.

[142] ibid 17–21.

[143] See arguments discussed in Chapter 2 of this volume.

[144] *International Convention on the Elimination of Racial Discrimination*, opened for signature 21 December 1965, 660 UNTS 195 (entered into force 4 January 1969) art 1(4).

protecting Māori interests and ensuring Māori a voice in political debates, thus allowing the meaning of Treaty principles to be more fairly contested within democratic processes, rather than decisively determined by the courts. If New Zealand had an entrenched 'supreme law' Constitution which protected Māori rights through rights guarantees, it would be up to the judiciary to interpret the clauses and strike down breaching laws in order to protect Māori minority rights. With reserved Māori seats, however, Māori representatives have a formal platform through which to influence Parliament's laws at their inception and pro-actively negotiate the accommodation of Māori rights on an ongoing basis in the political arena. Reserved Māori seats may thus be a more democratic and pre-emptive solution to the legal vulnerability of Māori rights than legal entrenchment of the Treaty, or a constitutionalised Bill of rights. It is a procedural and political form of recognition that involves Māori as active partners and political participants in the governance of the nation, rather than as occasional litigants.

D. Insights for Australia

There are four key lessons Australia can take from New Zealand. First, the New Zealand example demonstrates that judicially adjudicated constitutional rights guarantees are not the only way to protect and recognise Indigenous rights and interests; Indigenous rights can also be recognised and protected through representative, political and procedural mechanisms. Indigenous recognition can be achieved through mechanisms for Indigenous peoples to be heard, to be represented, and to participate as a distinct constitutional constituency in political processes regarding their affairs, as the Uluru Statement requests. In Australia, Indigenous recognition could entail a constitutional guarantee that Indigenous peoples will always have a voice in the political decisions made about them. There are various ways that this could occur. The possibility of Indigenous seats will be explored but ultimately not recommended in Chapter five below. A constitutionally mandated Indigenous representative and advisory body was recommended by the Referendum Council. We could imagine this as an Indigenous Australian adaptation of the Māori Council, but with constitutional status. This idea will be further explored and advocated in Chapter six below.

Second, New Zealand's settlement processes demonstrate the importance of agreement-making for Indigenous empowerment, and work alongside mechanisms to politically empower Indigenous voices. Like New Zealand, Australia should explore ways of enhancing its agreement-making with Indigenous peoples. The Uluru Statement calls for a Makarrata Commission, set up in legislation, to supervise agreement-making and truth-telling between Indigenous peoples and the state. This could build on existing structures. Australia already has settlement mechanisms for agreements between Indigenous peoples and government under the Native Title Tribunal structure,[145] and under State land rights regimes. The Au$1.3 billion Noongar settlement in Western Australia, to be paid in annual instalments of Au$50 million over 12 years into a Noongar Future Fund, and including the handing over of 320,000 hectares of land to the Noongar,[146] may be comparable to a treaty settlement.[147] Noel Pearson argues that native title and land rights regimes, along with other initiatives for reform and recognition in Indigenous affairs, could form 'very good foundations … for First Nations to make agreements with government on the full range of issues that affect their people and their future'. Pearson argues that the streams of innovation currently being pursued in Indigenous affairs[148] could lead into what may one day be understood as regional First Nations treaties.[149] Warren Mundine, former Chair of the Indigenous Advisory Council, similarly contends that 'a formal agreement or declaration between Australia and its first peoples' is needed 'between Australia and each Aboriginal and Torres Strait Islander tribal group, nation to nation', and that drawn-out Native Title cases should be fairly settled:[150]

> In the next term of Federal parliament, Australians will be asked to pass a referendum that formally recognises Indigenous people in the Australian Constitution. Wouldn't it be fitting if we also implement a system of governance that recognises the Indigenous nations and gives members of those nations the ability to govern matters concerning their traditional lands, assets, culture, language and heritage.[151]

Countless Indigenous advocates have called for governance structures and agreement-making to encourage Indigenous self-determination and leadership in their affairs.[152] The Australian government could work towards a settlement process with the First Nations, similar to that undertaken in New Zealand, as part of a package of reforms for Indigenous recognition.[153] The settlements that occur in Australia through the native title regime could be expanded to include

[145] Under the *Native Title Act 1993* (Cth).

[146] Kathryn Diss, 'Claimants Ink $1.3 Billion Western Australia Noongar Native Title Deal', *ABC News* (30 March 2015) <https://www.abc.net.au/news/2015-03-30/south-west-noongar-native-title-deal-inked/6357746> accessed 10 December 2019.

[147] Harry Hobbs and George Williams, 'The Noongar Settlement: Australia's First Treaty' (2018) 40(1) *Sydney Law Review* 1.

[148] Particularly the proposed Empowered Communities structural reforms which seek to rebalance the power relationship between Indigenous peoples and government in communities that opt-in: see Wunan Foundation, *Empowered Peoples Design Report* (2015).

[149] Michael McKenna, 'Noel Pearson's Regional Treaty Push', *The Australian* (19 June 2015); Noel Pearson, 'In Pursuit of a Regional, Reciprocal Responsibility Settlement for Cape York' (*National Native Title Conference*, Port Douglas, 18 June 2015).

[150] Patricia Karvelas, 'Warren Mundine: Treaty Needed with Each First Nation', *The Australian* (11 December 2014).

[151] Warren Mundine, 'Shooting an Elephant: Four Giant Steps' (Garma Festival Corporate Dinner, 10 August 2013) 5.

[152] See history of Indigenous advocacy for constitutional recognition in Chapter 2 of this volume.

[153] See also Damien Freeman and Nolan Hunter, 'When Two Rivers Become One' in Shireen Morris (ed), *A Rightful Place: A Roadmap to Recognition* (Black Inc 2017).

cultural redress and recognition, and an accounting of history and formal apologies, in addition to land and financial compensation. If this process were pursued wholeheartedly, it could significantly improve our sense of national self-esteem in Indigenous affairs.

Third, like New Zealand, Australia could implement legislative reforms to recognise Indigenous cultures and languages. If constitutional entrenchment of a clause recognising Indigenous languages (as was recommended by the Expert Panel in 2012)[154] is unachievable, perhaps this recognition can occur in legislation. An *Australian Languages Act* could map the Indigenous Australian language groups and recognise them as official Australian languages. Dual place naming mechanisms could be set up under the Act, connecting with any settlement mechanisms, as happens in New Zealand. An Australian Languages Commission could be established to document, promote, teach and revitalise Australian Languages.[155] Referring to Indigenous Australian languages and cultures as *Australian* languages and cultures through such initiatives could help all Australians feel ownership and connection with Australian languages, cultures and heritage as the original heritage of the land – thus shifting the common perception that English is Australia's unofficial national language, or that Western culture is, or should be, the predominant 'Australian' culture (although, of course, the Act could make appropriate and equal recognition of the importance of English as well). New Zealand has succeeded in making Māori heritage a celebrated part of New Zealand's national identity. Australia can do the same through practical cultural recognition through legislation and policy. This could be part of the Indigenous recognition package.

The fourth broad lesson from New Zealand is that Indigenous recognition should be enduring, operational and practical – not static and symbolic. Recognition in Australia can and should mean much more than a symbolic preamble or 'plaque' inserted into the Constitution, or a revised Race Power containing some preambular symbolic statements.[156] The New Zealand example encourages us to think practically and creatively in our search for appropriate, politically viable solutions that address the working, operational relationship between Indigenous peoples and the state. There can be a multiplicity of measures put in place to make this relationship fairer. These can include measures for an Indigenous representative and consultative body, specific Indigenous representation in political processes, articulation of agreed principles to guide the relationship, settlement and agreement processes to redress past wrongs and promote

[154] Expert Panel on Constitutional Recognition of Indigenous Australians ('Expert Panel'), *Recognising Aboriginal and Torres Strait Islander Peoples in the Constitution: Report of the Expert Panel* (January 2012); see recommendation for a new s 127A.

[155] See arguments made in Noel Pearson, 'Indigenous Tongues Deserve Recognition as Official Languages', *The Australian* (20 February 2016); Noel Pearson, 'Mind Our Language', *The Monthly* (April 2016).

[156] See Shireen Morris and Noel Pearson, 'Indigenous Constitutional Recognition: Paths to Failure and Possible Paths to Success' (2017) 91(5) *Australian Law Journal* 35.

reconciliation, and practical measures for cultural and language recognition. But given that Australia has an entrenched Constitution, advocates for Indigenous constitutional recognition have had to consider which is the most important reform – and the most politically sellable reform – that warrants constitutional enshrinement through a referendum. The Uluru Statement provides the appropriate answer to this question: a First Nations constitutional voice.

The New Zealand example demonstrates the value of an enduring commitment to political dialogue between Indigenous peoples and the state. Australia has no founding treaty to which Indigenous advocates can appeal in creating such a dialogue. As McHugh describes, the 'Australian Government has resolutely refused to enter into a similar history of political relations that Canada and New Zealand have experienced throughout their national existence.'[157] In Australia, constitutional reform is needed to reset the relationship, and create a new partnership based on dialogue. A First Nations constitutional voice would be a non-justiciable, political-constitutional commitment – but still a constitutional commitment – to ongoing political dialogue between Indigenous peoples and the state.[158] Like the commitments in the Treaty of Waitangi, such a constitutional promise would carry political and moral force.

III. CANADA

A. Constitutional Context

Canada shares with Australia and New Zealand a British constitutional inheritance bequeathed through colonisation. In some ways, Canada shares more similarities with Australia than New Zealand. Canada and Australia are both larger, federalised nations, whereas New Zealand is a smaller, unitary state.[159] Like Australia, Canada's Constitution is entrenched.[160] In Canada and Australia, Indigenous people are a small minority: Aboriginal people form approximately 4.9 per cent of the Canadian population[161] – a much smaller proportion

[157] McHugh (n 32 above) 57.

[158] For more on non-justiciable constitutional commitments, or 'constitutional directives', in comparative perspective, see Tarunabh Khaitan, 'Constitutional Directives: Morally-Committed Political Constitutionalism' (2019) 82(4) *Modern Law Review* 603.

[159] New Zealand abolished its provincial system in 1877 and its upper house in 1950, via ordinary legislative change: Palmer, 'Constitutional Realism' (n 42 above) 10.

[160] However constitutional change does not require a referendum. See Part V of the *Constitution Act 1982*.

[161] In Canada, 'Aboriginal peoples' as defined in s 35(2) of the Canadian Constitution refers to First Nations, Métis, and Inuit peoples. Like Australia, there are many First Nations groups across Canada. See 'Aboriginal Peoples in Canada: Key Results from the 2016 Census', *Statistics Canada* (last modified 2 July 2019) <https://www150.statcan.gc.ca/n1/daily-quotidien/171025/dq171025a-eng.htm> accessed 10 December 2019. Although some sources say the Aboriginal population is 4%: 'Canada Population 2019', *World Population Review* (11 October 2019) <http://worldpopulationreview.com/countries/canada-population/> accessed 10 December 2019.

than New Zealand's 15 per cent Māori population, but more than Australia's three per cent Indigenous minority. These differences in democratic proportion inform the power dynamics of the respective relationships.

As in New Zealand and Australia, the colonisation of Canada involved discrimination, denial of Aboriginal existence and sovereignty[162] and denial of Aboriginal rights,[163] which led to contemporary Aboriginal disadvantage.[164] This also led to ongoing Aboriginal advocacy for recognition, empowerment and constitutional reform. The anniversaries of their colonial founding enliven Indigenous protest in both countries: the Canadian Aboriginal tepee protest on Parliament Hill in Ottawa mirrors the Aboriginal Tent Embassy protest outside Australia's Parliament House in Canberra.[165] In Canada, however, efforts have been made to constitutionally ameliorate past injustice through Indigenous constitutional recognition: section 35 of the 1982 Constitution[166] recognises and affirms Aboriginal and treaty rights.

There appear three main mechanisms that work to give Canadian Aboriginal peoples a voice in their affairs. The first is the duty to consult Aboriginal

[162] In Canada, like in Australia and New Zealand, discriminatory attitudes were applied by the colonisers to justify denial of rights and expropriation of land. See John Borrows, 'The Durability of *Terra Nullius*: *Tsilhqot'in Nation v British Columbia*' (2015) 48(3) *University of British Colombia Law Review* 701; Michael Asch, 'From *Terra Nullius* to Affirmation: Reconciling Aboriginal Rights with the Canadian Constitution' (2002) 17(2) *Canadian Journal of Law & Society / La Revue Canadienne Droit et Société* 23; Howard Adams, *Tortured People: The Politics of Colonisation* (Theytus Books 1999); Alan Cairns, *Citizens Plus: Aboriginal Peoples and the Canadian State* (University of British Columbia Press 2000) 17–40.

[163] Just as the Treaty of Waitangi was invalidated by colonial courts (although this was later overruled), a similar history is evident in Canada. For example, *R v Syliboy*, a 1928 Nova Scotia case, held that a 1752 treaty was invalid because: '[T]he Indians were never regarded as an independent power. A civilized nation first discovering a country of uncivilized people or savages held such country as its own until such time as by treaty it was transferred to some other civilized nation. The savages' rights of sovereignty even of ownership were never recognized. Nova Scotia had passed to Great Britain not by gift or purchase from or even by conquest of the Indians but by treaty with France, which had acquired it by priority of discovery and ancient possession; and the Indians passed with it': [1929] 1 DLR 307, 313–14; 50 CCC 389. This was overruled in 1985, in *Simon v The Queen* [1985] 2 SCR 387, 24 DLR (4th) 390. See Cheryl Knockwood, 'The Mi'kmaq-Canadian Treaty Relationship: A 277 Year Journey of Rediscovery' in Ardith Walkem and Halie Bruce (eds), *Box of Treasures or Empty Box? Twenty Years of Section 35* (Theytus Books Ltd 2003) 43–44, 48–52.

[164] See Calla Wahlquist, '"It's the Same Story": How Australia and Canada are Twinning on Bad Outcomes for Indigenous People', *The Guardian* (25 February 2016): <https://www.theguardian.com/world/2016/feb/25/indigenous-australians-and-canadians-destroyed-by-same-colonialism> accessed 10 December 2019; Joan Kendall, 'Circles of Disadvantage: Aboriginal Poverty and Underdevelopment in Canada' (2001) 31(1)–(2) *American Review of Canadian Studies* 43.

[165] See Susan Neylan, 'Canada's Dark Side: Indigenous Peoples and Canada's 150th Celebration' (2018) 11(9) *Origins* <https://origins.osu.edu/article/canada-s-dark-side-indigenous-peoples-and-canada-s-150th-celebration> accessed 10 December 2019; Tim Leslie, 'The History of the Aboriginal Tent Embassy', *ABC News* (27 January 2012) <https://www.abc.net.au/news/2012-01-27/the-history-of-the-aboriginal-tent-embassy/3796630> accessed 10 December 2019. See also Shireen Morris, 'Don't Change the Date, Change its Meaning', *Meanjin* (24 January 2018) <https://meanjin.com.au/blog/dont-change-the-date-change-the-date/> accessed 10 December 2019.

[166] *Constitution Act 1982*, being Schedule B to the *Canada Act 1982* (UK) c 11 (*Constitution Act 1982* or the Constitution).

peoples in government decisions affecting their rights, which arises from the idea of the honour of the Crown[167] and is required by section 35 of the Constitution.[168] The second is the Assembly of First Nations (AFN) – a national Aboriginal representative organisation which advocates to government on behalf of Aboriginal peoples and monitors government policy in relation to Aboriginal affairs.[169] The AFN can perhaps be viewed as a Canadian equivalent to the Māori Council in New Zealand.[170] The third is treaty- and agreement-making: both Canada and New Zealand forged historical treaties between Indigenous peoples and the Crown (in New Zealand there was one treaty, in Canada there were multiple treaties).[171] Both countries continue contemporary agreement-making – New Zealand through historic and contemporary Treaty settlements and Canada through contemporary land agreements.[172] The Canadian Truth and Reconciliation Commission into Indian residential schools also completed its work in 2015.[173] The Commission's historical truth-telling processes appear similar to discussions about historical wrongs undertaken in Waitangi Tribunal processes.[174] In both countries, historical treaty/treaties have formed the basis of ongoing relationships

[167] David M Arnot, 'The Honour of the Crown' (1996) 60 *Saskatchewan Law Review* 339; Brian Slattery, 'Aboriginal Rights and the Honour of the Crown' (2005) 29 *Supreme Court Law Review* 433.

[168] *Haida Nation v British Columbia (Minister of Forests)*, 2004 SCC 73 (CanLII), [2004] 3 SCR 511 [20]. The duty to consult is the focus of this section.

[169] 'The AFN National Executive is made up of the National Chief, 10 Regional Chiefs and the chairs of the Elders, Women's and Youth councils. Regional Chiefs are elected every three years by Chiefs in their regions. Chiefs, who are elected by the citizens and members of their respective communities, elect the National Chief every three years': 'About AFN', *Assembly of First Nations* <afn.ca/about-afn/> accessed 10 December 2019. There are also other important Aboriginal organisations, including the Congress of Aboriginal Peoples, Inuit Tapiriit Kanatami, Métis National Council, and the Native Women's Association of Canada.

[170] Although the Māori Council is set up in legislation.

[171] See Alice Petrie, 'Treaties and Self-determination: Case Studies from International Jurisdictions' (Research & Inquiries Unit, Parliamentary Library & Information Service, Research Note No 8, June 2018).

[172] See Peter W Hogg, 'The Constitutional Basis of Aboriginal Rights' (2010) 15(1) *Lex Electronica* 179, 194–95.

[173] See National Centre for Truth and Reconciliation, 'Honouring the Truth, Reconciling for the Future: Summary of the Final Report of the Truth and Reconciliation Commission of Canada' (Truth and Reconciliation Commission of Canada, 31 May 2015). This initiative arose out of the advocacy of the AFN and other organisations, which supported victims to take the federal government and churches to court. The litigation resulted in a settlement, called the Indian Residential Schools Settlement Agreement, which provided compensation and called for the establishment of a Truth and Reconciliation Commission. See Rosemary Nagy, 'The Truth and Reconciliation Commission of Canada: Genesis and Design' (2014) 29(2 Law and Colonisation) *Canadian Journal of Law & Society* 199. Notably, the Canadian history of Aboriginal residential schools parallels the Stolen Generations history in Australia.

[174] However, the focus on residential schools means it was narrower in scope. See Naiomi Metallic, 'The Relationship Between Canada and Indigenous Peoples: Where Are We?' in The Law Society of Upper Canada (ed), *Special Lectures 2017 – Canada at 150: The Charter and the Constitution* (Irwin Law 2017).

between Indigenous peoples and the Crown, which are renewed and renegotiated over time. In Canada, as Wilson and Selle explain,

> much of the focus of political negotiations between Indigenous communities and non-Indigenous governments has been on land claims and self-government agreements that are designed to entrench self-rule. In part, this process seeks to restore the autonomy taken away from Indigenous peoples as a result of colonization.[175]

The most important difference between Canada and New Zealand is constitutional culture. In New Zealand, political constitutionalism endures and parliamentary sovereignty prevails.[176] In Canada, the new Constitution of 1982 included a Charter of Rights and Freedoms which empowered the judiciary to strike down Parliament's laws for constitutional inconsistency,[177] subject to parliamentary override.[178] The new constitutional order replaced parliamentary supremacy with constitutional supremacy,[179] expanding the scope of judicial review.[180] By contrast, New Zealand's constitutional and political culture, like Australia's, tends to retain some suspicion of judicial review.[181] As Palmer asserts, there is an important 'constitutional parallel between the relative judicialization of Canada's constitution and the relative politicization of New Zealand's constitution'.[182] Compared to New Zealand, Canada has taken a more litigious approach to Indigenous constitutional recognition.

B. Judicially Driven Reconciliation: The Balancing of Interests Under Section 35

In 1982, the inclusion of section 35 in the Canadian Constitution represented 'the culmination of a long and difficult struggle in both the political forum and the courts for the constitutional recognition of aboriginal rights'.[183] Before this,

175 Wilson and Selle (n 5 above) 11.

176 See Geoffrey Palmer and Matthew Palmer, *Bridled Power: New Zealand's Constitution and Government* (4th edn, Oxford University Press 2004).

177 See *Constitution Act 1982*, s 52. See also Palmer, 'Constitutional Realism' (n 42 above) 11, 16–17.

178 *Canadian Charter of Rights and Freedoms*, Part I of the *Constitution Act 1982*, being Schedule B to the *Canada Act 1982* (UK) c 11 ('*Canadian Charter of Rights and Freedoms*') s 33. Notably the parliamentary override provision has very rarely been used. See Rosalind Dixon, 'The Supreme Court of Canada, Charter Dialogue, and Deference' (2009) 47(2) *Osgoode Hall Law Journal* 235, 248–49.

179 James (Sa'ke'j) Youngblood Henderson, 'Constitutional Vision and Judicial Commitment: Aboriginal and Treaty Rights in Canada' (2010) 14(2) *Australian Indigenous Law Review* 24, 26–29.

180 Peter W Hogg, *Constitutional Law of Canada* (4th edn, Carswell 1997) 803; Palmer, 'Constitutional Realism' (n 42 above) 11.

181 As Palmer explains, where the introduction of MMP voting in New Zealand arguably saw more power accumulate to the legislature, Canada's constitutional reform saw more power transfer to the judiciary: Palmer, 'Constitutional Realism' (n 42 above) 16.

182 ibid 18–19.

183 *R v Sparrow*, 1990 CanLII 104 (SCC), [1990] 1 SCR 1075, 1105.

government had power to extinguish Aboriginal rights.[184] Section 35 ostensibly changed this, providing constitutional recognition and protection to Aboriginal and treaty rights.[185] Other constitutional provisions required Aboriginal involvement in their affairs. Section 35.1 requires consultation with Aboriginal peoples on constitutional amendments directly affecting them.[186] Section 37 (before it was repealed) required that a constitutional conference with Aboriginal representatives be convened to determine the interpretation of the Aboriginal rights protected by section 35.[187] Several constitutional conferences were held but they did not conclusively determine the meaning of section 35, which was left to the courts to resolve.[188]

There is ongoing disagreement about the meaning of section 35. Through the constitutional conferences, many Aboriginal people came to view section 35 as encompassing an Aboriginal right to self-government,[189] whereas government

[184] Section 91(24) of the *Constitution Act, 1867* empowers the Canadian federal government to deal exclusively with 'Indians, and Lands reserved for the Indians'. *Delgamuukw v British Columbia*, 1997 CanLII 302 (SCC), [1997] 3 SCR 1010, 1039–40; *R v Van der Peet*, 1997 CanLII 302 (SCC), [1996] 2 SCR 507, 538. Kent McNeil, 'The Vulnerability of Indigenous Land Rights in Australia and Canada (2004) 42(2) *Osgoode Hall Law Journal* 271, 287–88. See Peter W Hogg, *Constitutional Law of Canada* (5th edn, Caswell 2007) ch 28; Margaret Stephenson, 'Indigenous Lands and Constitutional Reform in Australia: A Canadian Comparison' (2011) 15(2) *Australian Indigenous Law Review* 87, 88. See also Margaret A Stephenson, 'Canadian Provincial Legislative Powers and Aboriginal Rights Since *Delgamuukw*: Can a Province Infringe Aboriginal Rights or Title?' (2003) 8 *International Trade and Business Law Annual* 55; Kent McNeil, 'Aboriginal Title and the Division of Powers: Rethinking Federal and Provincial Jurisdiction' (1998) 61(2) *Saskatchewan Law Review* 431; Stephenson, 'Indigenous Lands' ibid 88.

[185] The section provides:

(1) The existing aboriginal and treaty rights of the aboriginal peoples of Canada are hereby recognized and affirmed.
(2) In this Act, 'aboriginal peoples of Canada' includes the Indian, Inuit and Métis peoples of Canada.
(3) For greater certainty, in subsection (1) 'treaty rights' includes rights that now exist by way of land claims agreements or may be so acquired.
(4) Notwithstanding any other provision of this Act, the aboriginal and treaty rights referred to in subsection (1) are guaranteed equally to male and female persons.

[186] Stephenson, 'Indigenous Lands' (n 184 above) 87.

[187] As Palmer explains, 'The Canadian custom of negotiations with First Nations was bolstered by the section 37 conferences and confirmed by the precedent of full inclusion of four national aboriginal organizations as a third order of government, along with 11 first ministers and two territorial leaders, in the discussions leading to the failed Charlottetown Accord in 1992': Palmer, 'Constitutional Realism' (n 42 above) 24.

[188] Stephenson, 'Indigenous Lands' (n 184 above) 87, 89; Kent McNeil and David Yarrow, 'Has the Constitutional Recognition of Aboriginal Rights Adversely Affected their Definition?' (2007) 37 *Supreme Court Law Review* 177, 178.

[189] See arguments in *R v Pamajewon*, 1996 CanLII 161 (SCC), [1996] 2 SCR 821. See also Kent McNeil, 'The Decolonisation of Canada: Moving Toward Recognition of Aboriginal Governments' (1994) 7(1) *Western Legal History* 113, 126; Stephenson, 'Indigenous Lands' (n 184 above) 89–90. See also Patrick Macklem, 'First Nations Self-Government and the Borders of the Canadian Legal Imagination' (1991) 36(2) *McGill Law Journal* 382; Mildred C Poplar, 'We were Fighting for Nationhood not Section 35' in Ardith Walkem and Halie Bruce (eds), *Box of Treasures or Empty Box? Twenty Years of Section 35* (Theytus Books Ltd 2003); Frances Abele and Michael J Prince, 'Four Pathways to Aboriginal Self-Government in Canada' (2006) 36(4) *American Review of Canadian Studies* 568.

saw this as reliant on agreements negotiated with the state.[190] In 1992, a final round of constitutional conferences resulted in the Charlottetown Accord, which advocated that a new 'Canada clause' be inserted in the *Constitution Act, 1867* to recognise Aboriginal peoples as 'the first people to govern this land', as well as their 'right to promote their languages, cultures and traditions and to ensure the integrity of their societies'.[191] The Charlottetown Accord sought to constitutionally recognise Aboriginal rights to self-government, but it was rejected when put to Canadian voters at a referendum.[192] There have been no constitutional conferences since.

Section 35 sits outside the 1982 Charter of Rights and Freedoms, and section 25 requires that Charter rights and freedoms cannot be construed to abrogate or derogate from Aboriginal rights.[193] This should make the protection of Aboriginal rights more powerful, because section 35 is not limited by the balancing mechanism provided in section 1 of the Charter.[194] However, courts have adopted balancing mechanisms akin to section 1 in interpreting section 35,[195] highlighting a judicial need for rules and structure to guide adjudication of broadly defined rights.[196] While, on the text of section 35, it appears that Aboriginal and treaty rights cannot now be extinguished via legislative action;[197] this principle has been construed as not absolute[198] and in practice courts have limited the section's protection.[199]

The two-part justification test articulated in *R v Sparrow* requires government to demonstrate that the proven rights infringement occurred in pursuit of a 'compelling and substantial' legislative objective,[200] and that the infringement accords with the special fiduciary relationship between the Crown and

[190] House of Commons Special Committee on Indian Self-government, Parliament of Canada, *Indian Self-government in Canada: Report of the Special Committee* (1983) 44; Palmer, 'Constitutional Realism' (n 42) 24.

[191] McNeil and Yarrow (n 188 above) 179.

[192] Stephenson, 'Indigenous Lands' (n 184 above) 90.

[193] Note, there is no consensus on what this provision entails. See *R v Kapp*, 2008 SCC 41 (CanLII), [2008] 2 SCR 483. See also Gussen (n 34 above) 885–86.

[194] Section 1 of the Charter provides: 'The *Canadian Charter of Rights and Freedoms* guarantees the rights and freedoms set out in it subject only to such reasonable limits prescribed by law as can be demonstrably justified in a free and democratic society.'

[195] *Sparrow* (n 183 above) 1108–9.

[196] See Palmer, 'Constitutional Realism' (n 42) 21, referring to *Sparrow* (n 183 above) 1113. See also Macklem, 'First Nations' (n 189 above) 448; John Borrows, 'Measuring a Work in Progress: Canada, Constitutionalism, Citizenship and Aboriginal Peoples' in Ardith Walkem and Halie Bruce (eds), *Box of Treasures or Empty Box? Twenty Years of Section 35* (Theytus Books Ltd 2003) 234–35.

[197] The provision is described as giving 'a measure of control over government' and providing a 'strong check on legislative power', which holds 'the Crown to a substantive promise': *Sparrow* (n 183 above) 1110.

[198] *Sparrow* (n 183 above) 1109, 1119. Stephenson, 'Indigenous Lands' (n 184 above) 94.

[199] See also Emmanuelle Richez, 'Rights-Based Judicial Review and Substantive Equality for Aboriginal Peoples: The Case of Canada' (2013–14) 17(2) *Australian Indigenous Law Review* 26, 38.

[200] *Sparrow* (n 183 above) 1110.

the Aboriginal peoples.[201] Factors of relevance in the infringement analysis include whether there has been as little infringement as possible in achieving the policy objective, whether fair compensation has been paid to the victim(s), and whether the Aboriginal groups affected have been consulted with respect to the infringing action.[202] Thus, we see the duty to consult emerge as evidence used in the justification analysis to help courts determine whether a breach of Aboriginal rights protected under section 35 can be justified. This balancing test gives government ways around the demands of section 35,[203] which requires that Aboriginal and treaty rights are constitutionally 'recognised and affirmed'. The result is that, despite constitutional protection, Aboriginal and treaty rights can be legislatively infringed if the breaching action passes the *Sparrow* test.[204] Incorporation of balancing factors in the justification analysis, such as a valid legislative objective, the payment of compensation and whether there has been consultation[205] – which have been read into section 35 and are not part of its text – are integrated into the softening process, which appears to work in favour of Crown power.[206]

This was further demonstrated in *Delgamuukw*[207] and *Gladstone*[208] where, on Kent McNeil's analysis, the Supreme Court 'prepared the way for giving precedence to private interests by providing the Crown with broad powers to infringe Aboriginal title' – despite the fact that it should enjoy 'protection against

[201] ibid 1109, 1113–14. For discussion of why a justification analysis based on a fiduciary relationship was read in by the court, although it was not present in the constitutional text, see Borrows, 'Measuring a Work in Progress' (n 196 above) 234–35. For arguments on why such fiduciary relationships are needed in Australia, see Kirsty Gover, 'The Honour of the Crowns: State-Indigenous Fiduciary Relationships and Australian Exceptionalism' (2016) 38(3) *Sydney Law Review* 339. See also Brian Slattery, 'First Nations and the Constitution: A Question of Trust' (1992) 71(2) *Canadian Bar Review* 261.

[202] *Sparrow* (n 183 above) 1119.

[203] McNeil, 'Vulnerability of Indigenous Land Rights' (n 184 above) 289.

[204] *Van der Peet* (n 184 above) 538 [28]. McNeil, 'Vulnerability of Indigenous Land Rights' (n 184 above) 288. See also *R v Badger*, 1996 CanLII 236 (SCC), [1996] 1 SCR 771, which confirmed provincial legislatures can also infringe Aboriginal treaty rights using the *Sparrow* test. See also Catherine Bell, '*R v Badger*: One Step Forward and Two Steps Back?' (1997) 8(2) *Constitutional Forum* 21.

[205] *Sparrow* (n 183 above) 1119.

[206] For Christie, the *Sparrow* test 'illustrates the extent to which a colonial mentality infects contemporary jurisprudence, and how the duty to consult emerges from an essentially colonial agenda': Gordon Christie, 'A Colonial Reading of Recent Jurisprudence: *Sparrow*, *Delgamuukw* and *Haida Nation*' (2005) 23(1) *Windsor Yearbook of Access to Justice* 17, 38. However, Macklem notes that, by incorporating a duty to consult, 'the Court in *Sparrow* laid down a framework for the constitutional protection of First Nations interests which is strongly supportive of the active involvement of native people in the formation of laws which govern their lives': Macklem, 'First Nations' (n 189 above) 449.

[207] *Delgamuukw* (n 184 above). In this case, the Supreme Court defined Aboriginal title as a *sui generis* right: [1997] 3 SCR 1010, at 1083.

[208] *R v Gladstone*, 1996 CanLII 160 (SCC), [1996] 2 SCR 723.

legislative interference that has been its due as a constitutionally entrenched Aboriginal right since 1982'.[209] Lamer CJ noted in *Delgamuukw* that:

> In the wake of *Gladstone*, the range of legislative objectives that can justify the infringement of aboriginal title is fairly broad. Most of these objectives can be traced to the *reconciliation* of the prior occupation of North America by aboriginal peoples with the assertion of Crown sovereignty, which entails the recognition that 'distinctive aboriginal societies exist, and are a part of, a broader social, political and economic community' (at para 73). In my opinion, the development of agriculture, forestry, mining, and hydroelectric power, the general economic development of the interior of British Columbia, protection of the environment or endangered species, the building of infrastructure and the settlement of foreign populations to support those aims, are the kinds of objectives that are consistent with this purpose and, in principle, can justify the infringement of aboriginal title.[210]

The Court found that infringements could be justified in certain circumstances, noting that balancing of interests was a 'necessary part of the reconciliation of aboriginal societies with the broader political community of which they are part'.[211] Yet, given that these anticipated objectives are considered in a hypothetical situation where a breach of section 35 has already been shown, the *Delgamuukw* list seems to offer the Crown very wide discretion to infringe Aboriginal rights.[212] As Borrows notes, the Supreme Court's use of the concept of reconciliation 'implies a search for a middle ground, between conflicting positions'.[213] Yet the middle ground of 'reconciliation' has allowed for legislative infringement of constitutionally protected Aboriginal rights,[214] in effect poking holes through the protective shield of the text of section 35. Echoing McLachlin J's dissent in *Van der Peet*,[215] McNeill suggests that such decisions demonstrate the courts' pragmatic balancing of political and economic interests, rather than a strict legal interpretation of section 35, to the inevitable detriment of Aboriginal interests.[216] As Tully observes, the *Delgamuukw* legislative objectives closely resemble 'the early justification of dispossession in terms of the superiority of European derived societies and their developmental imperatives'.[217]

[209] McNeil, 'Vulnerability of Indigenous Land Rights' (n 184 above) 299.

[210] *Delgamuukw* (n 184 above) [165].

[211] ibid [161], quoting *Gladstone* (n 208 above) [73].

[212] McNeil, 'Vulnerability of Indigenous Land Rights' (n 184 above) 293.

[213] Borrows, 'Measuring a Work in Progress' (n 196 above) 239–42.

[214] See also Mark D Walters, 'The Jurisprudence of Reconciliation: Aboriginal Rights in Canada' in Will Kymlicka and Bashir Bashir (eds), *The Politics of Reconciliation in Multicultural Societies* (Oxford University Press 2008) 181–82.

[215] *Van der Peet* (n 184 above) 664–68.

[216] McNeil, 'Vulnerability of Indigenous Land Rights' (n 184 above) 299–300. See also Borrows, 'Measuring a Work in Progress' (n 196 above) 243–44.

[217] James Tully, 'The Struggles of Indigenous Peoples For and Of Freedom' in Ardith Walkem and Halie Bruce (eds), *Box of Treasures or Empty Box? Twenty Years of Section 35* (Theytus Books Ltd 2003) 287.

The narrowing of Aboriginal rights under section 35 can also be seen in the Supreme Court's interpretation of the nature of rights protected. In *Sparrow*, the justices adopted a purposive approach to the interpretation of section 35 and affirmed a 'generous, liberal interpretation of the words in the constitution provision',[218] in line with honour of the Crown principles.[219] The Court also found that the protection of 'existing' Aboriginal rights meant rights that had not been extinguished before the *Constitution Act 1982* came into force.[220] Such rights were to be 'affirmed in a contemporary form rather than in their primeval simplicity and vigour'.[221] In *Van der Peet*, however, reconciliation principles were applied in a way that constrained protection of Aboriginal rights by confining them to pre-existing customs and traditions.[222] This frozen-in-time approach[223] to the characterisation of Indigenous rights is arguably paralleled in the Australian *Yorta Yorta case*, which rejected the Yorta Yorta's application to recognise surviving native title, on the basis that 'the forbears of the claimants had ceased to occupy their lands in accordance with traditional laws and customs' and because 'there was no evidence they continued to observe those laws and customs'.[224] Pearson argues that this restrictive approach in Australia was a 'discriminatory estimation of the nature of native title' which, on this narrow interpretation, amounted only to 'whatever berry-picking rights indigenous claimants must be able to prove by reference to their traditional laws and customs as they existed in 1788'.[225] In Australia, the narrow interpretation

[218] *Sparrow* (n 183 above) 1106; see also 1119.

[219] *R v Taylor and Williams*, 1981 CanLII 1657 (ON CA), (1981) 34 OR (2nd) 360, 367. See also Gover, 'The Honour of the Crowns' (n 201 above).

[220] *Sparrow* (n 183 above) 1092.

[221] ibid 1093. Stephenson, 'Indigenous Lands' (n 184 above) 92–93. See also McNeil and Yarrow (n 188) 180–81; Brian Slattery, 'Understanding Aboriginal Rights' (1987) 66 *Canadian Bar Review* 725, 782.

[222] *Van der Peet* (n 184 above) 548. Stephenson, 'Indigenous Lands' (n 184 above) 92.

[223] See John Borrows, 'Frozen Rights in Canada: Constitutional Interpretation and the Trickster' (1997) 22(1) *American Indian Law Review* 37; Alexandra Kent, 'The *Van der Peet* Test: Constitutional Recognition or Constitutional Restriction?' (2012) 3(2) *The Arbutus Review* 20; Russel Lawrence Barsh and James Youngblood Henderson, 'The Supreme Court's *Van der Peet* Trilogy: Naïve Imperialism and Ropes of Sand' (1997) 42 *McGill Law Journal* 993. Note that Dwight Newman suggests the Supreme Court adopted this reasoning to avoid economic consequences which it saw as unacceptable. See Dwight Newman, 'Consultation and Economic Reconciliation' in Patrick Macklem and Douglas Sanderson (eds), *From Recognition to Reconciliation: Essays on the Constitutional Entrenchment of Aboriginal and Treaty Rights* (University of Toronto Press 2016) 220–21. See also PG McHugh, 'A Common Law Biography of s 35' in Patrick Macklem and Douglas Sanderson (eds), *From Recognition to Reconciliation: Essays on the Constitutional Entrenchment of Aboriginal and Treaty Rights* (University of Toronto Press 2016) 152.

[224] *Yorta Yorta v Victoria* (2002) 214 ALR 422, 458 (Gleeson CJ, Gummow and Hayne JJ). See also 492–94 (Callinan J).

[225] Noel Pearson, 'Promise of Mabo Not Yet Realised', *The Australian* (29 May 2010). Although, note that in *Mabo*, it was also found that 'traditional law or custom is not … frozen as at the moment of establishment of a Colony': *Mabo v Queensland (No 2)* (1992) 175 CLR 1, 110. See also Elizabeth Povinelli, who argues that Australian native title law perpetuates colonial power dynamics to impose upon Indigenous people an impossible standard of traditional and cultural 'authenticity': Elizabeth Povinelli, *The Cunning of Recognition: Indigenous Alterities and the Making of Australian Multiculturalism* (Duke University Press 2002).

of native title rights has occurred as a result of the judicial interpretation of section 223 of the *Native Title Act 1993* (Cth),[226] and case law flowing from *Mabo*[227] – both of which were, in practical reality, compromises balancing Indigenous and non-Indigenous interests.[228] Similarly, in Canada, Lamer CJ in *Van der Peet* emphasised that, because Aboriginal rights benefit only one segment of Canadian society,[229] these rights had to be reconciled with Non-Aboriginal rights.[230] Various scholars argue this judicially-driven reconciliation of interests has led to Indigenous rights protections being accorded a narrow and weak interpretation.[231]

Rights inquiries will always involve balancing rights against other conflicting rights and taking into account countervailing matters of public interest. Canadian jurisprudence refers to this balancing as 'reconciliation'.[232] Yet whether judicial balancing is necessarily the best way of resolving disputes between historically fraught competing interests is an open question, relevant to constitutional reform in Australia. On consideration of Canada and Australia, McNeil suggests courts are generally hesitant to resolve the fundamental issues arising from colonisation and dispossession:

> [R]egardless of the strengths of legal arguments in favour of Indigenous peoples, there are limits to how far the courts in Australia and Canada are willing to go to correct the injustices caused by colonialism and dispossession. Despite what judges may say about maintaining legal principle, at the end of the day what really seems to determine the outcome in these kinds of cases is the extent to which Indigenous rights can be reconciled with the history of British settlement without disturbing the

[226] Section 223 provides: 'The expression *native title* or *native title rights and interests* means the communal, group or individual rights and interests of Aboriginal peoples or Torres Strait Islanders in relation to land or waters, where:

(a) the rights and interests are possessed under the traditional laws acknowledged, and the traditional customs observed, by the Aboriginal peoples or Torres Strait Islanders; and
(b) the Aboriginal peoples or Torres Strait Islanders, by those laws and customs, have a connection with the land or waters; and
(c) the rights and interests are recognised by the common law of Australia.'

[227] *Mabo v Queensland (No 2)* (n 225 above); Shireen Morris, 'Re-evaluating *Mabo:* The Case for Native Title Reform to Remove Discrimination and Enable Economic Opportunity' (*Land, Rights, Laws: Issues of Native Title* – Native Titles Research Unit, AIATSIS Issues Paper, Vol 5, Issue 3, 2012).

[228] According to Pearson, the Australian compromise in relation to land rights 'was that the original owners were entitled to whatever was left over': Pearson, 'Promise of Mabo' (n 225 above). See also McNeil, 'Vulnerability of Indigenous Land Rights' (n 184 above) 273–86; McHugh, 'A Common Law Biography' (n 223 above) 152.

[229] *Van der Peet* (n 184 above) 535. McNeil and Yarrow (n 188 above) 190.

[230] McNeil and Yarrow (n 188 above) 186–91.

[231] See McNeil and Yarrow (n 188 above) 191; Stephenson, 'Indigenous Lands' (n 184 above) 92. See Metallic (n 174 above) 15–16; Borrows, 'Measuring a Work in Progress' (n 196 above); Borrows, 'Frozen Rights' (n 223 above).

[232] For more on the unique use of reconciliation in Canadian jurisprudence, see Walters (n 214 above); Andrew Lokan, 'From Recognition to Reconciliation: The Functions of Aboriginal Rights Law' (1999) 23(1) *Melbourne University Law Review* 65.

> current political and economic power structure. I think this is a reality that Indigenous peoples need to take into account when deciding whether courts are the best places to obtain redress for historical wrongs and recognition of present-day rights. It may be advantageous to formulate strategic approaches that avoid surrendering too much power to the judicial branch of the Australian and Canadian state.[233]

McNeil highlights the difficulty in asking courts to resolve conflicts arising from questions of sovereignty, which are highly political in nature. Just as a court cannot invalidate the political power that gives rise to its own authority,[234] so too may courts find it difficult to robustly pronounce on Indigenous rights in a way that, as McNeil puts it, disturbs the 'current political and economic power structure'. Whether courts are necessarily the most appropriate mechanism for the prosecution and protection of Indigenous rights is therefore an important strategic question for constitutional reformers. While many gains in Aboriginal rights can be seen through judicial adjudication, sometimes judicial interpretation can also work to limit Indigenous rights in favour of government power. There is an argument, then, that Indigenous empowerment and self-determination may be best achieved in the political realm – although this entails challenges of its own, especially for minority Indigenous populations.

On the other hand, empowered by judicially adjudicated rights clauses, courts may play an important role in spurring the political realm to action it might not otherwise take. Canadian courts in practice facilitate dialogue not only between courts and legislatures, but also between First Nations and governments.[235] Rather than providing absolute protection of Aboriginal rights as the text of the provision seems to require, section 35 in practice provides a mechanism through which courts prompt the political arms of government to behave with honour in their dealings with Indigenous peoples. This can be seen in the development of the Canadian duty to consult.

C. The Duty to Consult

The most significant development in Canadian jurisprudence around section 35 has been the implication of a duty to consult with Aboriginal peoples in matters concerning their rights.[236] In *Delgamuukw*, the court's urgings of good faith

[233] McNeil, 'Vulnerability of Indigenous Land Rights' (n 184 above) 300–301.

[234] *Coe v Commonwealth (No 2)* (1993) 214 CLR 422; *Mabo* (n 225 above) 31–32; *New South Wales v The Commonwealth* (1975) 135 CLR 337, 388.

[235] Matthew SR Palmer, 'Constitutional Realism' (n 42) 26. See also James B Kelly and Michael Murphy, 'Shaping the Constitutional Dialogue on Federalism: Canada's Supreme Court as Meta-Political Actor' (2005) 35(2) *Publius* 217.

[236] See Lorne Sossin, 'The Duty to Consult and Accommodate: Procedural Justice as Aboriginal Rights' (2010) 23(1) *Canadian Journal of Administrative Law & Practice* 93; E Ria Tzimas, '*Haida Nation* and *Taku River*: A Commentary on Aboriginal Consultation and Reconciliation' (1998) 29 *Supreme Court Law Review* 461; Gordon Christie, 'Developing Case Law: The Future

political negotiations and consultation called on the political realm to take more responsibility in the process of reconciliation.[237] Lamer CJ noted that, '[u]ltimately, it is through negotiated settlements, with good faith and give and take on all sides', that 'the reconciliation of the pre-existence of aboriginal societies with the sovereignty of the Crown' will be achieved.[238] In *Haida Nation*, the Canadian Supreme Court urged that negotiated settlements, including consultation and accommodation of Aboriginal concerns, were preferable to litigious solutions.[239] A focus on good process and procedure in the relationship between Aboriginal peoples and the Crown is central to these decisions. As Palmer explains, 'the Court's primary role appears to have been to push executive government to take the interests of indigenous peoples seriously', through prods and prompts which 'often manifest as procedural requirements upon the Crown in engaging with indigenous peoples'. This reflects 'the importance of process for the health of these relationships',[240] but also judicial deference to the Legislature and the Executive in inherently political questions.[241] Yet, at times in the jurisprudence, it almost seems as if the Supreme Court is shifting responsibility back onto the political arms of government as a way of avoiding forceful enforcement of section 35.

In interpreting section 35, the Court has imported the idea of the honour of the Crown to guide its reasoning. The honour of the Crown is an ancient British concept, connected to the Crown's fiduciary duty with respect to Aboriginal peoples,[242] which has evolved to shape the Crown-Aboriginal relationship.[243] As McLachlin CJ explains in *Haida Nation*, the duty to consult arises from the idea of the honour of the Crown, which requires that Aboriginal rights be determined, recognised and respected, and requires an honourable Crown 'to participate in processes of negotiation'. This expectation of fair engagement requires consultation and, where necessary, accommodation of Aboriginal interests.[244] The duty to consult and accommodate is therefore 'grounded in

of Consultation and Accommodation' (2006) 39(1) *University of British Columbia* 139; Janna Promislow, 'Irreconcilable? The Duty to Consult and Administrative Decision Makers' (2013) 22(1) *Constitutional Forum Constitutionnel* 63; E Ria Tzimas, 'To What End the Dialogue?' (2011) 54 *Supreme Court Law Review* 493.

237 This urging of the political arms occurred in many other cases too. See Borrows, 'Measuring a Work in Progress' (n 196 above) 244–45.

238 *Delgamuukw* (n 184 above) [186].

239 *Haida Nation* (n 168 above) [14]. See also John M Evans, 'Current Constitutional Issues in Canada' (2013) 51(2) *Duquesne Law Review* 323, 345.

240 Palmer, 'Constitutional Realism' (n 42) 23; Borrows, 'Measuring a Work in Progress' (n 196 above) 238.

241 For discussion of this shift towards process in the judicial adjudication of constitutional rights guarantees in Canada, see Colleen Sheppard, 'Inclusion, Voice, and Process-Based Constitutionalism' (2013) 50(3) *Osgoode Hall Law Journal* 547.

242 Gover, 'The Honour of the Crowns' (n 201 above).

243 Slattery provides detailed theories on how the honour of the Crown arose: Slattery, 'Honour of the Crown' (n 167 above).

244 *Haida Nation* (n 168 above) [17]–[25]. See also Tzimas, 'To What End' (n 236 above).

the assertion of Crown sovereignty which pre-dated the Union'.[245] It is both required by and informs section 35 – although it does not appear explicitly in the text:[246]

> Section 35 represents a promise of rights recognition, and '[i]t is always assumed that the Crown intends to fulfil its promises'. This promise is realized and sovereignty claims reconciled through the process of honourable negotiation. It is a corollary of s 35 that the Crown act honourably in defining the rights it guarantees and in reconciling them with other rights and interests. This, in turn, implies a duty to consult and, if appropriate, accommodate.[247]

The duty to consult arises where there is proven Aboriginal title, or where the Crown contemplates that an Aboriginal right may be adversely affected by certain conduct, even if the right has been claimed but not yet proven.[248] In Hogg's view, the duty was initially intended as 'an interim protection measure, designed to safeguard aboriginal interests while rights were in dispute or a treaty was under negotiation',[249] but it has since been extended such that a Minister's decision can be quashed for failure to appropriately consult.[250]

For Aboriginal advocate Henderson, the duty to consult is an 'inspiring obligation' that forms part of a 'deepened understanding of democracy of peoples and the innovative modalities of shared sovereignty'.[251] It represents a 'promise of dialogical governance' and a 'constitutionalization of an openness to dialogue' that could significantly transform the constitutional relationship between Aboriginal peoples and the Crown.[252] If implemented fulsomely and in good faith, Henderson suggests that the duty could be a 'remedy to the long history of cunning abeyance and avoidance of a dead-beat Crown and the bureaucracies that have continuously and intractably quibbled over the constitutional responsibilities for the failures and poverty of Aboriginal peoples'. Alternatively, a more pessimistic prediction would see the duty perpetuating such 'quibbling and abeyance', by failing to shrug off colonial narratives.[253] For Gordon Christie, however, the duty to consult is part of a jurisprudence that confirms colonial power over Aboriginal nations: it continues the expropriation

[245] *Haida Nation* (n 168 above) [59].

[246] ibid [20], [25], [29], [38].

[247] ibid [20].

[248] Zena Charowsky, 'The Aboriginal Law Duty to Consult: An Introduction for Administrative Tribunals' (2011) 74(2) *Seskatchewan Law Review* 213, 214.

[249] Hogg, 'Constitutional Basis' (n 172 above) 193.

[250] See eg, *Mikisew Cree First Nation v Canada*, 2005 SCC 69 (CanLII), [2005] 3 SCR 388. If the Crown fails to consult when required, various remedies are available, including injunctive relief, damages, or an order that consultation or accommodation be carried out: *Rio Tinto Alcan Inc v Carrier Sekani Tribal Council*, 2010 SCC 43 (CanLII), [2010] 2 SCR 650 [37].

[251] James (Sa'ke'j) Youngblood Henderson, 'Dialogical Governance: A Mechanism of Constitutional Governance' (2009) 72(1) *Saskatchewan Law Review* 29, 31.

[252] ibid 33.

[253] ibid 31.

and exploitation of Aboriginal rights and lands – just more politely, in a 'kinder and gentler' way.[254]

The unwritten nature of the duty to consult has given rise to uncertainty.[255] In defining its content, the Supreme Court in *Haida Nation* took guidance from New Zealand. Quoting the New Zealand Ministry of Justice's Guide for Consultation with Māori (1997), the Court held that meaningful consultation is not just exchanging information. It should involve testing policy proposals before they are finalised, seeking Aboriginal opinions on those proposals, 'not prompting but listening with an open mind', and importantly, being open to accommodation, 'which means being prepared to alter the original proposal'.[256] Despite such guidance, the duty as outlined left room for ambiguity in its practical operation and has resulted in some confusion as to its scope and content.[257] For clarity, the government issued guidelines regarding how to fulfil the duty and a Consultation and Accommodation Unit was established.[258] Bryant, however, argues that the content of the judicially articulated duty remains obscured by unknowable 'legalese'. This legal uncertainty has effectively put government in a 'straitjacket' that slows down decision-making and paralyses policy innovation. Absurdity can arise whereby government must pre-consult on how to consult. Rather than endless consultative delays and uncertainty, Bryant proposes a more decisive Aboriginal consent requirement.[259]

In 1990, Macklem similarly argued for the duty to consult to be 'deepened and extended' to become 'a constitutional requirement of an equal partnership between governments and First Nations in the drafting of laws which affect s 35(1) rights', such that 'native consent to laws that affect their interests could become a precondition of constitutionality'.[260] Given that the Court has made clear that the duty to consult does not entail an Aboriginal right of

[254] Christie argues that the courts 'are effectively working in concert with the other arms of the state, continuing the colonial oppression of the original peoples … The duty to consult must be understood in light of this analysis': Christie, 'A Colonial Reading' (n 206 above) 42.

[255] Hogg, 'Constitutional Basis' (n 172 above) 194–95.

[256] *Haida Nation* (n 168 above) [46].

[257] Tzimas, '*Haida Nation* and *Taku River*' (n 236 above) 463–64; Charowsky (n 248 above) 214; Sheppard (n 241 above) 563–64.

[258] See Government of Canada, *Aboriginal Consultation and Accommodation: Updated Guidelines for Federal Officials to Fulfil the Duty to Consult* (2011). This has not resolved all uncertainty. For a discussion of consultation and accommodation where there is conflict as to which First Nations speak for which land, see Ian Peach, 'Who Speaks for Whom? Implementing the Crown's Duty to Consult in the Case of Divided Aboriginal Political Structures' (2016) 59(1) *Canadian Public Administration* 95. Clarity may be improving, however. See Neil Craik, 'Process and Reconciliation: Integrating the Duty to Consult with Environmental Assessment' (2016) 53(2) *Osgoode Law Journal* 632.

[259] Michael J Bryant, 'The Case for an Aboriginal Veto' in Patrick Macklem and Douglas Sanderson (eds), *From Recognition to Reconciliation: Essays on the Constitutional Entrenchment of Aboriginal and Treaty Rights* (University of Toronto Press 2016).

[260] Macklem, 'First Nations' (n 189 above) 449; see also, 455.

veto over government decisions,[261] it seems unlikely that courts would apply an Aboriginal consent requirement to legislation affecting Aboriginal rights.[262] As a matter of constitutional law, however, section 35 provides a substantive constitutional limit on Parliament's legislative power with respect to Aboriginal rights. As noted, prior to 1982, Parliament could legislate to extinguish Aboriginal rights, but section 35 changed this, albeit subject to the balancing test provided in *Sparrow* in 1990. Section 52 states that the 1982 Constitution is supreme law and that inconsistent legislation will be invalid.[263] It therefore follows that a failure to consult, as required under section 35, should invalidate relevant legislation with respect to Aboriginal rights. After all, if a Minister's decision can be quashed for failure to consult under section 35, why should relevant legislation adversely impacting Aboriginal rights not also be invalidated for failure to consult in its development?[264] If the duty to consult is required by section 35, as Canadian courts hold, then the duty should also apply to the making of legislation, because section 35 limits parliamentary power. Accordingly, if Macklem's proposed Aboriginal consent requirement cannot be read into section 35, whereas a duty to consult can be read in (as the case law demonstrates), it appears reasonable that this duty should apply to Parliament's legislative processes with respect to Aboriginal rights. Further, given sections 35 and 52, this duty to consult should be a precondition of legislative validity.

[261] *Haida Nation* (n 168 above) [48]: 'This process does not give Aboriginal groups a veto over what can be done with land pending final proof of the claim. The Aboriginal "consent" spoken of in *Delgamuukw* is appropriate only in cases of established rights, and then by no means in every case. Rather, what is required is a process of balancing interests, of give and take.' See also Evans (n 239) 346; Bryant (n 259).

[262] However, in *Tsilhqot'in* it was held that: 'Once Aboriginal title is established, s 35 of the Constitution Act, 1982 permits incursions on it only with the consent of the Aboriginal group or if they are justified by a compelling and substantial public purpose and are not inconsistent with the Crown's fiduciary duty to the Aboriginal group': *Tsilhqot'in Nation v British Columbia*, 2014 SCC 44 (CanLII), [2014] 2 SCR 257 [2], [76]. See also Val Napoleon, 'Tsilhqot'in Law of Consent' (2015) 48(3) *University of British Colombia Law Review* 873.

[263] As Hogg explains, 'the exclusion of section 35 from the Charter of Rights also had the effect of rendering the override clause of section 33 inapplicable to aboriginal or treaty rights': Hogg, 'Constitutional Basis' (n 172 above) 182. See also Kent McNeil, 'Aboriginal Governments and the Canadian Charter of Rights and Freedoms' (1996) 34(1) *Osgoode Hall Law Journal* 61, 72–73. Note, Yukon used the override provision to make clear that special representation for the Council of Yukon First Nations (then the Council of Yukon Indians) to the Land Planning Board and Committees (*Land Planning and Development Act 1982* (Yukon) ss 4 and 18) did not breach the equality before the law guarantee of s 15 of the Charter. However, this was probably unnecessary, because s 15(2) allows for special measures or 'affirmative action', and s 25 requires that Charter provisions cannot diminish Aboriginal rights. See Tsvi Kahana, 'The Notwithstanding Mechanism and Public Discussion: Lessons from the Ignored Practice of Section 33 of the Charter' (2008) 44(3) *Canadian Public Administration* 255, 258. See also Laurence Brosseau and Marc-Andre Roy, 'The Notwithstanding Clause of the Charter' (Legal and Social Affairs Division, Parliamentary Information and Research Service, Publication No 2018-17-E, 7 May 2018) 7. Thus, s 35 provides stronger constitutional protection than Charter protection.

[264] See Henderson, 'Constitutional Vision' (n 179 above) 37; Henderson, 'Dialogical Governance' (n 251 above) 53.

D. *Mikisew Cree*: Does the Duty to Consult Apply to Proposed Legislation?

In the 2018 *Mikisew Cree* case,[265] the Court was asked to determine 'whether the honour of the Crown gives rise to a justiciable duty to consult when ministers develop legislation that could adversely affect the Mikisew's treaty rights'. Up until this point, the Court had left open the question of whether the law-making process is 'Crown conduct' triggering the duty.[266] Contrary to my argument above, the majority found that the duty to consult does not apply to executive actors when they are exercising legislative power.

While the Supreme Court unanimously agreed that the Federal Court had erred by reviewing the Mikisew Cree's case because it was not within its jurisdiction,[267] the justices were split on whether the duty applied to the development of legislation. While Karakatsanis J noted 'the close relationship between the honour of the Crown and s 35' and affirmed the honour of the Crown as a 'constitutional principle',[268] the majority nonetheless found the duty to consult only applies to executive action.[269] This was because 'the development of legislation by ministers is part of the law-making process' which is 'generally protected from judicial oversight'.[270] Karakatsanis J therefore declined to apply the duty to consult to the law-making process, because this would 'require courts to improperly trespass onto the legislature's domain'.[271] Her Honour also highlighted various practical concerns with applying a duty to legislative processes, noting that,

> in the long chain of events contributing to the development of legislation, disentangling what steps the duty to consult applies to (because they are executive) and what actions are immune (because they are parliamentary) would be an enormously difficult task.[272]

[265] *Mikisew Cree* concerned two pieces of legislation impacting Canada's environmental protection regime. The Mikisew Cree First Nation was not consulted on either of these omnibus bills during their development, so they went to court and argued that the Crown had a duty to consult them in the development of the legislation, which had the potential to adversely affect their treaty rights to hunt, trap, and fish under Treaty No 8. The reviewing judge declared that the duty to consult was engaged and that the Mikisew were entitled to notice of the relevant provisions of the bills, as well as an opportunity to make submissions. But, on appeal, a majority of the Federal Court of Appeal disagreed. The Mikisew then appealed.

[266] *Mikisew Cree First Nation v Canada*, 2018 SCC 40 (CanLII), [2018] 2 SCR 765 [29].

[267] As Brown J explained: 'The Federal Court is not a court of inherent jurisdiction. It follows that Parliament must grant jurisdiction in order for the Federal Court to hear and decide a matter'. The reviewing judge therefore did not have jurisdiction because the *Federal Courts Act* does not allow for judicial review of parliamentary activities, and also because such review would breach principles of parliamentary sovereignty, the separation of powers, and parliamentary privilege: ibid [18], [99], [116]–[133].

[268] ibid [24].

[269] ibid [50].

[270] ibid [34].

[271] ibid [35].

[272] ibid [40].

Karakatsanis J noted, however, that these conclusions did not apply to processes for the adoption of subordinate legislation.[273] So, according to the majority, when ministers develop regulations, the honour of the Crown applies; when ministers develop or propose legislation, the duty does not apply.

Yet Karakatsanis J appeared uneasy about the resultant gap in the legal protection under section 35.[274] Acknowledging that 'permitting the Crown to do by one means that which it cannot do by another would undermine the endeavour of reconciliation',[275] she suggested that while the duty to consult does not apply to the law-making process, other doctrines may nonetheless be developed to 'ensure the consistent protection of section 35 rights and to give full effect to the honour of the Crown'.[276] Firstly, it was suggested that it may be inconsistent with section 35 to 'legislate in a way that effectively removes future Crown conduct which would otherwise trigger the duty to consult'.[277] Secondly, declaratory relief was proposed 'where legislation is enacted that is not consistent with the Crown's duty of honourable dealing toward Aboriginal peoples to address the gap in legal protection'.[278]

Brown J, approved by Rowe J, agreed that the honour of the Crown and the related duty to consult does not apply to law-making:

> The entire law-making process – from initial policy development to and including royal assent – is an exercise of legislative power which is immune from judicial interference. The making of policy choices is a legislative function, while the implementation and administration of those choices is an executive function. This precludes judicial imposition of a duty to consult in the course of the law-making process.[279]

Brown J held that the honour of the Crown applies to executive power but not legislative power, noting that 'the Crown does not enact legislation. Parliament does'.[280] But His Honour disagreed robustly with Karakatsanis J's openness to other forms of relief in relation to legislative action that may negatively impact Aboriginal rights.[281] While Brown J appears correct in pointing out the internal inconsistency in Karakatsanis J's position, this inconsistency arguably arises because Her Honour's conclusion, like Brown J's conclusion, is incorrect.

[273] ibid [51].
[274] ibid [43].
[275] ibid [44].
[276] ibid [45].
[277] ibid [46], citing *Ross River Dena Council v Yukon*, 2012 YKCA 14 (CanLII), 358 DLR (4th) 100.
[278] *Mikisee Cree* (2018) (n 266 above) [47].
[279] ibid [102].
[280] ibid [135].
[281] Brown J argues: '[M]y colleague's reasons invoking the honour of the Crown appear to leave open the possibility that validly enacted legislation (which has not been or could not be the subject of a s 35 infringement claim) might be declared to be "not consistent with [the honour of the Crown]" (para 47) due to some failure to uphold the honour of the Crown. But in doing so, [Karakatsanis J] runs up against those same constitutional principles of separation of powers and parliamentary privilege which furnish the entire constitutional basis for her conclusion that no duty to consult is owed in respect of legislative processes': ibid [140].

Section 35 limits parliamentary power. If section 35 includes a duty to consult, then the duty to consult should apply to the exercise of legislative powers, including legislative processes. Whether the honour of the Crown refers to the Crown construed as only the Executive, or the Crown construed in a broader sense to mean 'the state',[282] including Parliament, should be irrelevant: the honour of the Crown, after all, does not appear in the text of section 35. In *Sparrow*, it was found that section 35 provides a constitutional guarantee or promise[283] and a 'strong check on legislative power'.[284] *Haida Nation* subsequently affirmed that, while the duty to consult is grounded in the honour of the Crown,[285] it is also a 'corollary' of section 35.[286] It is part of the 'process of fair dealing' arising out of the need to reconcile the sovereignty of the Crown with the sovereignty of First Nations – a 'process flowing from rights guarantees by section 35(1) of the Constitution Act, 1982'.[287]

Properly understood, therefore, section 35 imposes a constitutional limit on the *sovereignty* of the Canadian Crown and of the Canadian Parliament.[288] As noted, section 52 provides that Canadian parliamentary sovereignty is limited by the Constitution and that legislation inconsistent with the Constitution can therefore be invalidated. Accordingly, section 35 constitutionally limits Parliament's legislative power, which is why legislation that breaches section 35 can be invalidated for constitutional inconsistency.[289] Parliamentary sovereignty – and parliamentary processes – must therefore yield to the requirements of section 35. If the duty to consult applies to Ministers discharging their administrative and executive duties, it seems odd that such duties would not also apply to the same Ministers when they are developing policies and proposing laws that may adversely impact Aboriginal rights. If section 35 requires a duty to consult, then the duty should apply to Parliament in the exercise of its powers: it should apply to parliamentary processes too.

(i) Extra-textual Uncertainty: Who is this 'Honourable Crown' and Who Does the Honour Shield?

Inherent in this question is confusion about the meaning of 'the Crown' and lack of clarity about the honour of the Crown.[290] In *Mikisew Cree*, the Supreme

[282] See P Cobbett, '"The Crown" as Representing "the State"' (1903–1904) 1(1) *Commonwealth Law Review* 23.

[283] *Sparrow* (n 183 above) 1110.

[284] ibid 1110.

[285] *Haida Nation* (n 168 above) [16].

[286] ibid [20], [38].

[287] ibid [32].

[288] *Sparrow* (n 183 above) 1109: '[W]e find that the words "recognition and affirmation" incorporate the fiduciary relationship … and so import some restraint on the exercise of sovereign power'.

[289] *Mikisew Cree* (2018) (n 266 above) [43]; *Sparrow* (n 183 above) 1110.

[290] The idea of the honour of the Crown was incorporated into the reasoning supporting the justification test set out in *Sparrow* (n 183 above) 1109.

Court's argument that 'the Crown' in 'the honour of the Crown' refers only to the Executive and not to the Legislature seems an over-simplification that ignores the ambiguity and variability of the term.[291] According to Janet McLean, using 'the Crown' to signify the executive branch became more common from the 1860s.[292] Later, the term was disparaged as a 'convenient cover for ignorance', which served to distract citizens from 'asking difficult questions' about who is exercising power and what kind of power is being exercised.[293] For Henderson, the Crown is a 'mystical concept that represents the constitutional authority for the existence of federal or provincial governments' and 'a vague legal fiction of British law'. But the *honour* of the Crown 'transforms the mystical and symbolic concept of the Crown into a protecting entity' that 'shields the rights of Aboriginal peoples from negative government action'.[294] Given that the principle was imported to aid interpretation of section 35, as a kind of 'constitutional therapy for the ill of colonization',[295] it should be construed to protect Aboriginal rights from Crown power. Henderson thus argues that the Crown's honour 'demands good faith consultation when government contemplates or establishes legislation or policy that might impact on an asserted Aboriginal or treaty right',[296] because 'all manifestations of the Crown are obligated to consult with First Nations'.[297] The Mikisew apparently assumed a similar broad operation of the duty.[298]

Here one can see the divergent expectations of what the honour of the Crown requires, demonstrating the difficulty with extra-textual principles of this kind.[299] Though the principle's ostensible purpose was to protect Aboriginal rights by obliging the Crown to behave ethically, the result in *Mikisew Cree* is ironically the inverse: the hazy concept of the Crown and the Crown's honour are used to *narrow* Crown obligations and protect it from consultative responsibilities. Rather than shielding Aboriginal rights, the concept instead shields the state from increased accountability through Aboriginal input into

[291] Anne Twomey, 'Responsible Government and the Divisibility of the Crown' (Legal Studies Research Paper No 08/137, University of Sydney Law School, November 2008) 6–8; Cheryl Saunders, 'The Concept of the Crown' (2015) 38(3) *Melbourne University Law Review* 873.

[292] Janet McLean, *Searching for the State in British Legal Thought* (Cambridge University Press 2012) 140.

[293] FW Maitland, *The Constitutional History of England* (Cambridge University Press 1908) 418. See also Saunders (n 291 above) 875.

[294] Henderson, 'Dialogical Governance' (n 251 above) 30–31.

[295] ibid 51.

[296] ibid 55, citing *Haida Nation* (n 168 above) [27].

[297] Henderson, 'Dialogical Governance' (n 251 above) 58.

[298] Robert Jago, 'Why Canada's Duty to Consult With Indigenous Peoples Isn't Negotiable', *The Walrus* (2 November 2018).

[299] McHugh notes that the honour of the Crown is 'not an exacting principle or standard', but 'a means by which the Court can characterise Crown conduct as inadequate or falling short of contemporary standards set by judges'. He suggests that the doctrine has been applied with little differentiation between 'a past where s 35 was in force and one where it was not': McHugh, 'A Common Law Biography' (n 223 above) 161.

legislative processes affecting their rights. It has protected parliamentary sovereignty, in spite of the constitutional check on parliamentary power provided by section 35.

The uncertain and often contradictory use of extra-textual principles in the interpretation of section 35 warrants closer scrutiny. In *Sparrow*, the honour of the Crown was used on the one hand ostensibly to supplement and strengthen the protection afforded by section 35. This was because, in the Supreme Court's view, while section 35 contained 'no explicit language' authorising it to 'assess the legitimacy of any government legislation that restricts aboriginal rights', the words 'recognition and affirmation' in section 35 nonetheless imported honour of the Crown principles.[300] Yet the suggestion that the Court is not authorised to review government legislation contradicts the Court's observation in the same judgment that section 35 provides a 'strong check on legislative power'.[301] It also contradicts section 52 of the Constitution, which imposes an obligation on the Court to determine the law consistently with the Constitution and to invalidate laws to the extent of inconsistency with the Constitution.[302] As McNeil points out, the Court in *Sparrow* 'seriously limited the protection accorded by section 35(1)', yet 'there is nothing in the 1982 Constitution Act itself which justifies' the limitations imputed. McNeil warns that such limitations may render the protections of section 35 'largely illusory'.[303]

A similar observation applies to the fiduciary duty, which also does not appear in the text of section 35. Considering the Court's importation of fiduciary obligations as part of the infringement and justification analysis, Borrows notes the irony of a doctrine intended 'to protect Aboriginal peoples from the arbitrary power of government' being 'turned on its head and used as a justification for infringing constitutionally protected Aboriginal rights'.[304] The imported concept of reconciliation has worked in a similarly double-edged way. Reconciliatory aspirations should restrain government power in favour of Aboriginal interests – helping re-balance this unequal power relationship – but 'reconciliation' has instead been employed in the jurisprudence 'as an objective that permits the infringement of Aboriginal rights'.[305] It would appear that

[300] *Sparrow* (n 183 above) 1109.

[301] ibid 1110.

[302] *Canada v Mossop*,1993 CanLII 164 (SCC), [1993] 1 SCR 554, 582; *Nova Scotia (Workers' Compensation Board) v Martin*, 2003 SCC 54 (CanLII), [2003] 2 SCR 504 [28].

[303] Kent McNeil, 'The Constitution Act, 1982, Sections 25 and 35' [1988] (1) *Canadian Native Law Reporter* 1, 12. See also Borrows, 'Measuring a Work in Progress' (n 196 above) 234–35.

[304] Borrows, 'Measuring a Work in Progress' (n 196 above) 235. Felix Hoehn similarly notes that: 'Although the Crown's fiduciary duty ostensibly protects the Aboriginal interest, its existence and formulation underlines the vulnerable and inferior nature of the Aboriginal title in relation to the underlying interest the Crown asserts based on its "discovery" of the land': Felix Hoehn, 'Back to the Future: Reconciliation and Indigenous Sovereignty After *Tsilhqot'in*' (2016) 67 *University of New Brunswick Law Journal* 109, 122.

[305] Borrows, 'Measuring a Work in Progress' (n 196 above) 242.

judicial resort to extra-textual principles to aid interpretation of section 35 is not working in favour of Aboriginal rights.

Arnot argues that the honour of the Crown, properly understood, should be 'the conscience of the country'.[306] He notes, however, the principle's ancient British origins as an idea originally intended to protect the monarch's good name, which (cynically viewed) was 'often deployed to cloak the misconduct of ministers and to reassure British subjects that the power of the state remained in responsible and chaste hands that would not dare to behave selfishly'.[307] During the nineteenth century, the honour of the Crown became a concept that automatically justified the behaviour and decisions of Crown ministers, such that 'the shield was neatly converted into a sword'. As Arnot notes, 'Aboriginal nations have felt the edge of that sword.'[308] This double-edged potential is evident in judicial application of the honour of the Crown to Aboriginal rights under section 35 and can be seen in *Mikisew Cree*, where the hazy concept of 'the Crown' works to diminish government accountability under section 35.[309] Whereas in New Zealand, the concept of 'the Crown' has enabled the government to pursue direct political negotiations with Māori in a way that usefully shields the public from moral culpability for past wrongs,[310] in the Canadian context, the ambiguity of the term has worked to shield Parliament in judicial decisions.

It may be that extra-textual concepts are necessarily utilised by the courts to elucidate the ambiguous meaning of section 35. But the principles imported – reconciliation, honour of the Crown, fiduciary duty and so on – are themselves ambiguous, thus recreating the original problem. In the end, courts still need to resolve the conflicts between competing rights and interests. The resulting narrowing of Aboriginal rights protection demonstrates that the uncertainty inherent in this constitutional rights guarantee does not always lead to creative judicial overreach in favour of the vulnerable group in question, as commonly suggested by Bill of rights critics; it can also result in judicial underreach, to the detriment of Aboriginal rights (even in arguable contradiction to the requirements of the constitutional text). For constitutional reform advocates, *Mikisew Cree* is a reminder of the risk involved when constitutional rights guarantees in effect prompt courts to undertake the balancing of competing political, economic and social concerns. While Aboriginal rights may be recognised and

[306] Arnot (n 167 above) 345.
[307] ibid 340.
[308] ibid 341.
[309] As Cheryl Saunders explains: 'In Canada … emphasis on the extent to which the constitution is unwritten appears to have preserved a concept of the Crown as a more vigorous constitutional principle, which nevertheless has been shaped by a variety of forces, including the relationship with Indigenous peoples': Saunders (n 291 above) 896. On the reliance on unwritten principles in the interpretation of the Canadian Constitution, see also Henderson, 'Dialogical Governance' (n 251 above) 42–43.
[310] See McLean (n 56 above).

protected in a limited way through resulting litigation, courts may also ultimately balance the scales in favour of the majority, the government and the structural status quo – even when interpreting a provision arguably intended to constitutionally reform the status quo.

Given the words of section 35, and given that the Constitution is Canada's supreme law, these outcomes are troubling. While historical principles may be used to resolve ambiguities in constitutional text, surely the meaning of such principles should ultimately adapt to the 1982 written Constitution as the new, supreme law – not the other way around. Yet in *Mikisew Cree*, we see the honour of the Crown – a concept developed before the new constitutional requirement of section 35 came into force[311] – being applied in a way that has arguably weakened the constitutional protection.[312] Indeed, by using historical principles to interpret the new constitutional requirement, the Supreme Court may be applying outdated colonial understandings of the Aboriginal-Crown relationship, thereby potentially undermining the transformative potential of the constitutional guarantee.[313] While it is true that applying the duty to consult to parliamentary processes would have gone against long-established constitutional principles – the separation of powers and parliamentary sovereignty, for example – the text of section 35, and the duty to consult case law precedents arguably required the Court to adapt such concepts to give the duty to consult and section 35 their full constitutional strength. The Court instead stayed firmly grounded in longstanding traditions – traditions arguably rooted in the top-down assertion of Crown sovereignty over Aboriginal peoples and rights.[314]

(ii) Dissent: The Duty to Consult Applies to Legislative Processes

In contrast to the majority judgments, Abella J's dissent found the duty to consult does apply to legislative processes:

> The honour of the Crown governs the relationship between the government of Canada and Indigenous peoples. This obligation of honour gives rise to a duty to consult and accommodate that applies to all contemplated government conduct with the potential to adversely impact asserted or established Aboriginal and treaty rights,

[311] Jamie D Dickson, *The Honour and Dishonour of the Crown: Making Sense of Aboriginal Law in Canada* (Purich Publishing 2015) 24–30; Slattery, 'Honour of the Crown' (n 167 above) 444–45; Arnot (n 167 above) 340–42.

[312] Indeed, Rowe J affirms this point: 'Section 35 rights are not absolute. Like other provisions of the Constitution Act, 1982, s 35 is both supported and confined by broader constitutional principles. The honour of the Crown arises from the fiduciary duty that Canada owes to Indigenous peoples following the assertion of sovereignty; it is an overarching guide to Canada's dealings with Indigenous peoples': *Mikisew Cree v Canada* (2018) (n 266 above) 153. Here, that fiduciary duty has arguably weakened constitutional rights.

[313] See also Metallic (n 174 above) 15–16; Walters (n 214 above) 175–78.

[314] See also McHugh, 'A Common Law Biography' (n 223 above) 161.

> including, in my view, legislative action … As a constitutional imperative, the honour of the Crown cannot be undermined, let alone extinguished, by the legislature's assertion of parliamentary sovereignty.[315]

The dissent argued that the Court should 'reconcile, not choose between, protecting the legislative process from judicial interference and protecting Aboriginal rights from the legislative process', and thus that the duty to consult had to be reconciled with parliamentary sovereignty.[316] Because section 35 is a constitutional guarantee, the logical result is that the duty to consult could limit parliamentary sovereignty and thus the legislative process. This was seen as 'inevitable if the guarantee under section 35 is to be taken seriously', as 'there would be little point in having a constitution if legislatures could proceed as if it did not exist when expedient'.[317]

Abella J also highlighted the utility of early consultation in the prevention of rights abuses, noting that: 'Ongoing consultation is preferable to the backward-looking approach of subsequent challenges, since it protects s. 35 rights from irreversible harm and enhances reconciliation'.[318] Similarly, in terms of practical workability, Abella J noted the 'flexibility inherent in the duty to consult doctrine' which meant the 'unique challenges raised in the legislative sphere' could be addressed in a tailored way by the 'spectrum of consultation and accommodation duties that may arise'. The dissent noted that common duties of consultation, such as the giving of notice to affected parties and the opportunity to make submissions, were 'hardly foreign to the law-making process', and could be adapted to fulfil the duty to consult in the legislative context. Further, the duty would only be triggered where the Crown, 'with knowledge of the potential existence of the Aboriginal right or title in question, contemplates enacting legislation that might adversely affect it'.[319] Thus it was not too broad to be practically unimplementable.

Nonetheless, a successful challenge for failure to consult in the legislative process would not necessarily invalidate legislation: declaratory relief would generally be the appropriate remedy. This was because: 'In the legislative context, a declaration allows courts to shape the legal framework while respecting the constitutional role of another branch of government to act within those constraints.'[320] This outlines a way of reconciling the duty to consult with parliamentary sovereignty in the Canadian context. After all, while Parliament may be shielded from judicial review of its internal procedures, it should not be shielded from its responsibilities arising under honour of the Crown principles or from the requirements of section 35. Such responsibilities may not necessarily

[315] *Mikisew Cree* (2018) (n 266 above) [55].
[316] ibid [84].
[317] ibid [85].
[318] ibid [78]. Note that the majority acknowledged this too: at [26].
[319] ibid [92].
[320] ibid [97].

be judicially enforced and adjudicated, but they can still be identified to exist and apply – and should be enforced politically. In the spirit of this approach, the dissent concludes with a nudge, urging the political arms to appropriately adjust their procedures:

> While it is not the role of the courts to dictate the procedures legislatures adopt to fulfil their consultation obligations, they may consider whether the chosen process accords with the special relationship between the Crown and Indigenous peoples of Canada.[321]

The dissenting finding that the duty to consult *does* apply to the legislative process appears correct. Section 35 is part of Canada's supreme law. It limits the legislative powers of Parliament. If a duty to consult is part of section 35, then this duty should apply to the making of legislation. The Constitution tempers parliamentary sovereignty in this respect. Just as in Australia it can be said that Parliament is not sovereign but supreme, because its powers are constrained by the Constitution; so too are the powers of Canada's Parliament constrained by its Constitution.[322]

The dissent hints at a compromise way forward that the majority could have adopted: a way of affirming that the duty to consult does apply to the development of legislation, without compromising principles like the separation of powers or parliamentary supremacy. Rather than framing the issue around a *justiciable* duty to consult in the making of laws detrimentally affecting Aboriginal rights, the Supreme Court could have investigated a *non-justiciable* duty to consult in such legislative development.[323] It was arguably open to the Court to find that the duty to consult in the making of laws with respect to Aboriginal rights is constitutionally required by section 35, but also that this is a non-justiciable requirement that will not result in invalidation of the law – because, in the words of the Australian High Court judge, Justice McTiernan: 'Parliament is master in its own household.'[324] While this conclusion would not strictly accord with sections 35 and 52, which arguably require justiciability and invalidation where there is inconsistency with the Constitution, it would be a more satisfactory conclusion than the majority result in *Mikisew Cree*.

A non-justiciable, but nonetheless constitutional, duty to consult in the development and making of laws affecting Aboriginal rights appears workable. In practice, Parliament and government will need to ensure they consult with Aboriginal peoples when making laws and policies about them. Parliament and government will need to adapt their procedures to hear Aboriginal voices in the

321 ibid [93].

322 As noted, the s 33 Charter override provision does not apply to s 35 (n 263 above).

323 Dwight Newman discusses the utility of justiciability in relation to the duty to consult in Newman (n 223) 221.

324 *Victoria v Commonwealth* (1975) 134 CLR 81, 138, 118. See Kirsty Magarey, 'Alcopops Makes the House See Double: "The Proposed Law" in Section 57 of the Constitution' (Law and Bills Digest Section, Parliamentary Library, Research Paper No 32 2008–09).

making of laws and policies that affect them. Parliament and government will need to issue the relevant notifications and call for submissions and conduct hearings or negotiations. These are not issues a court can readily resolve. These are issues of politics, policy and process that are properly left to the political arms.[325] Courts, however, can play a useful role in prompting and prodding the politics.[326]

E. Insights for Australia

Assessment of the operation of section 35 reveals a gap between the self-determination and empowerment sought by many Aboriginal advocates and the reality of what section 35 litigation has been able to deliver. In 1994, Henderson observed that section 35 helped 'define a new constitutional context of self-determination for Aboriginal peoples' by recognising property rights and treaty rights as important sources of constitutional law.[327] But he noted that:

> The affirmation of these constitutional acts did not resolve the existing structural, political problems in Canadian federalism or Canadian democracy ... no changes in the political order have occurred ... the conventional political order continues to deny Aboriginal peoples full participation in Canada's political and economic federalism. Aboriginal peoples have no voice to assert these rights in Parliament or in the legislative assemblies. They are still organized lobbyists or plaintiffs outside the formal structure of government.[328]

Henderson suggested that the recognition of Aboriginal rights in the Canadian Constitution, while a positive step forward, did not formally include Aboriginal peoples as active participants in the 'political order'.[329] Nor did it empower the Aboriginal voice within the 'formal structure of government'.[330] Likewise, the

[325] As McHugh notes, the New Zealand example demonstrates that contemporary settlements can occur productively as a product of political will, without the impetus of an entrenched s 35 style constitutional guarantee. See McHugh, 'A Common Law Biography' (n 223 above) 163.

[326] Borrows, 'Measuring a Work in Progress' (n 196 above) 238.

[327] James 'Youngblood' Henderson, 'Empowering Treaty Federalism' (1994) 58(2) *Saskatchewan Law Review* 241, 244.

[328] ibid 244.

[329] ibid 244; see also Henderson, 'Dialogical Governance' (n 251 above) 56.

[330] ibid 244; see also Papillon, who argues that 'Without formal status as federal partners, Aboriginal peoples and their governments also have no statutory voice in the shared institutions of "intrastate federalism", such as the federal Parliament, the Cabinet, or the Supreme Court, other than what their demographic weight calls for': Martin Papillon, 'Canadian Federalism and the Emerging Mosaic of Aboriginal Multilevel Governance' in Herman Bakvis and Grace Skogstad (eds), *Canadian Federalism: Performance, Effectiveness, and Legitimacy* (3rd edn, Oxford University Press 2012) 288. The comments support Lino's insight that entrenchment of a high-level right to self-determination in a Bill of rights might not give Indigenous people the political agency and day-to-day practical involvement they seek: Dylan Lino, 'The Politics of Inclusion: The Right of Self-determination, Statutory Bills of Rights, and Indigenous Peoples' (2010) 34(3) *Melbourne University Law Review* 829, 867–68.

entrenchment of a high-level recognition of Aboriginal rights in the Canadian Constitution did not of itself address the call for political participation and stronger political empowerment in their affairs. Something more, or different, was needed to genuinely ensure Indigenous participation and consultation in political decisions made about them. Henderson effectively highlights the remaining institutional and democratic deficiency, which Canadian courts have tried to gently – but not decisively – remedy through the duty to consult.

Of course, section 35 has done some good. Where the political arms have not taken enough action to recognise and protect Indigenous rights or empower Aboriginal peoples within the political order, courts, empowered by section 35, have played an important prompting role.[331] Yet while section 35 provides a valuable 'safety net' without which the Canadian government might have been able to continue to trample and ignore Aboriginal interests, the Supreme Court has also established 'loopholes' that enable government to circumvent its responsibilities.[332] There are benefits that follow from a court-enforced rights guarantee, but there are also downsides and risks. If Indigenous empowerment is the true aim,[333] courts may not ultimately be the right vehicle for remedying such deficiencies in the political order.[334] Courts may remain confined by pre-existing traditions, even when new constitutional clauses require fresh thinking. Borrows observes that section 35 'influences political and legal culture, but it also largely follows it'. He therefore urges Canadians not to rely on the Constitution or section 35 as reliable avenues for reform or nation-building, because it may be unfair to expect the judiciary to comprehensively reform the relationship between Aboriginal peoples and the state.[335]

This is an important insight: it may be expecting too much to ask courts to solve these fundamental problems. Such issues go to the wielding of political power – issues of sovereignty – and courts, whilst they strive for independence are also institutions of the dominant power. Walkem argues that Canadian

[331] As Nigel Bankes points out, drawing also on the Sámi example discussed in the next section, such leadership can emerge from any branch of government and can then manifest in a dialogue about Indigenous rights. See Nigel Bankes, 'Themes and Reflections: A Perspective from Canada' in Christina Allard and Susann Funderud Skogvang (eds), *Indigenous Rights in Scandinavia: Autonomous Sámi Law* (Routledge 2016) 16–18.

[332] Knockwood (n 163 above) 57.

[333] See Poplar (n 189 above); Lee Maracle, 'The Operation was Successful but the Patient Died' in Ardith Walkem and Halie Bruce (eds), *Box of Treasures or Empty Box? Twenty Years of Section 35* (Theytus Books Ltd 2003).

[334] As Papillon argues, 'there are inherent limits to what the courts can do in redefining the status and role of Aboriginal governments. The interpretation of Aboriginal rights by the Supreme Court, however liberal it may be, will remain constrained by the parameters of the Canadian Constitution, from which it derives its own authority. Though important in establishing a more leveled playing field and interpreting negotiated agreements, tribunals can neither create new institutions of governance nor completely replace the political process in redefining the constitutional foundations of our relationships ... Given the lack of legitimacy of existing institutions, the redefinition of the relationship between Aboriginal peoples and the Canadian federation should ideally stem from negotiations between mutually consenting parties': Papillon (n 330 above) 291.

[335] Borrows, 'Measuring a Work in Progress' (n 196 above) 247.

courts, as 'instruments of colonial society' and colonial aspirations, have tended to interpret section 35 in a way that is 'not unduly disruptive of Canadian society'.[336] For Maracle too, 'the problem is the colonial law' and 'the solution offered by s 35 is an entrenchment of colonial law'.[337] A gap therefore emerges between Aboriginal aspirations for real empowerment and what section 35 has delivered in practice. Section 35 has facilitated a 'limited recognition' of Aboriginal peoples, 'while upholding overarching state power'.[338] Canadian courts have played a role in maintaining the stability of the status quo,[339] even when interpreting a clause that calls for constitutional transformation.[340] Given that the main vehicle for rights protection under section 35 is litigation, the reach of this mechanism is also limited.[341] Arguably, if the aim is to genuinely reform the power relationship between Aboriginal peoples and the state, the political arms of government may be better placed to lead change.[342] Perhaps that is why courts have refrained from robust interpretation of section 35, preferring to prompt political negotiation. But empowering reform requires political will, leadership and a willingness by government to share power to create a fairer relationship. Herein lies the perpetual conundrum: whether it is through litigation or political negotiation, Indigenous minorities are always faced with the power of the state.[343]

The Canadian experience shows that broad constitutional rights guarantees may not always generate the political empowerment, agency and involvement in political decision-making that Indigenous advocates may seek. Judicially adjudicated constitutional guarantees of Indigenous rights, though often assumed to be more effective than political and procedural mechanisms, can in practice also work in ways that weaken Aboriginal rights protection. The risk is not only uncertain judicial overreach (as usually argued by Bill of rights critics), but also uncertain judicial underreach to the detriment of Aboriginal rights. As has been observed in the Irish context, such deference in the interpretation of constitutional rights can give rise to a paradox: 'although the judiciary adopts an attitude

[336] Ardith Walkem, 'Constructing the Constitutional Box: The Supreme Court's s 31(1) Reasoning' in Ardith Walkem and Halie Bruce (eds), *Box of Treasures or Empty Box? Twenty Years of Section 35* (Theytus Books Ltd 2003) 199–201.

[337] Maracle (n 333 above) 314.

[338] Walkem (n 336 above) 216.

[339] The Canadian court has also demonstrated a concern to maintain stability and peace in societal relations. See Borrows, 'Measuring a Work in Progress' (n 196 above) 235.

[340] Although Lee Maracle argues that s 35 was never meant to create a nation-to-nation relationship. See Maracle (n 333 above) 310–11.

[341] ibid 314.

[342] Note that Prime Minister Justin Trudeau, in 2018, proposed that a statutory framework should be implemented to shift reconciliation away from litigation. See Joanne Cave, 'From Rights Recognition to Reconciliation: Reflecting on the Government of Canada's Proposed Indigenous Rights Recognition Framework' (2019) 77(2) *University of Toronto Faculty of Law Review* 59.

[343] See Halie Bruce and Ardith Walkem, 'Bringing Our Living Constitutions Home' in Ardith Walkem and Halie Bruce (eds), *Box of Treasures or Empty Box? Twenty Years of Section 35* (Theytus Books Ltd 2003) 349.

of judicial restraint out of respect for democracy and the constitutional separation of powers', in practice this attitude may undermine democratic standards and the 'supremacy of the Constitution.'[344] Judicial review of constitutional rights clauses thus comes with the risk of judicial over-restraint. In my view, therefore, the Uluru Statement and the Referendum Council's call for a First Nations voice takes a sensible approach to Indigenous constitutional recognition, by minimising judicial intervention and seeking Indigenous empowerment via political processes. While non-justiciability comes with its own risks and challenges, it is the most constitutionally congruent approach in the Australian context and arguably the best approach for securing the kind of structural empowerment that Indigenous advocates appear to seek.

Judicial hesitance at impinging upon the parliamentary sphere, demonstrated by the majority in *Mikisew Cree*, underscores the limitations inherent in the judiciary adjudicating procedural, political duties to consult with Indigenous peoples. Judges are used to making decisions on matters of law, not policies and laws-in-the-making. Courts are traditionally hesitant to get involved in the processes of the legislature[345] and may shy away from robust, reforming adjudication of political questions. These factors may explain some of the inconsistencies arising in *Mikisew Cree*: duty to consult jurisprudence led the courts into an uncomfortable intellectual corner. The substantive weakening of section 35 increased the centrality of the duty to consult, but the duty to consult in turn led to the logical request that it also be applied to the making of laws detrimentally affecting Aboriginal rights. That the Court declined to take this logical further step highlights the limited reach of the court-created duty. Some advocates thus urge 'a new path forward' that delivers a more concrete 'place at the table' for Aboriginal people 'in the development of the colonizers' laws'.[346] Courts cannot create this: only the politicians can make room in negotiation with Aboriginal people.

For Australia, constitutional reform advocates should appreciate the risk that any new judicially adjudicated rights guarantee may be similarly read down by judges for pragmatic, political and economic reasons and to maintain stability and continuity. This would be in line with the deferential approach historically taken by Australian courts in interpreting the few existing constitutional restraints on parliamentary power: as Aroney and Saunders note, 'The rights that are contained in the Constitution have typically been given a relatively narrow construction.'[347] In light of such realities, the suggestion that a duty to

[344] Maria Cahill and Sean O Conaill, 'Judicial Restraint Can Also Undermine Constitutional Principles: An Irish Caution' (2017) 36 *University of Queensland Law Journal* 259, 259.

[345] Jago (n 298 above).

[346] Bruce McIvor and Kate Gunn, 'Change of Direction Required: Case Comment on Mikisew Cree First Nation', *First Peoples Law* (15 October 2018) <https://www.firstpeopleslaw.com/index/articles/371.php> accessed 15 December 2019.

[347] See Nicholas Aroney and Benjamin B Saunders, 'On Judicial Rascals and Self-Appointed Monarchs: The Rise of Judicial Power in Australia' (2017) 36 *University of Queensland Law*

consult in the Australian context should be justiciable,[348] because justiciability equals robustness and effectiveness, must be questioned. In my view, it would be preferable to leave Indigenous consultation processes to the political arms to articulate and develop, under the imprimatur of a non-justiciable constitutional guarantee of a First Nations voice, as the Referendum Council suggests. The duty to consult should be stated explicitly and clearly, not as a general justiciable rights-style guarantee, but as a specific and explicit requirement in the Constitution so that Parliament and government must abide by it in law- and policy-making procedures. A constitutional amendment guaranteeing a First Nations voice in Australia should be drafted to be non-justiciable, as the Referendum Council recommends, anchoring the consultation requirement in politics rather than litigation. This should be a constitutional law that is adjudicated and enforced by Parliament, not the High Court.[349] Further, the requirement to consult and hear Indigenous voices in law- and policy-making with respect to Indigenous affairs should apply explicitly to Parliament as well as the Executive, to avoid narrow *Mikisew Cree*-type outcomes.

From my Australian perspective, there may be lessons for Canada here too. Perhaps Canadians could draw inspiration from the Uluru Statement to devise a Canadian version of a First Nations voice to Parliament. For example, Canada could consider formalising and constitutionalising processes through which the AFN (or an appropriate structure or structures) might engage with Parliament and government on policy- and law-making in respect of Aboriginal rights. The duty to consult could be explicitly and procedurally spelt out in the Constitution. Such a reform would not be a big step for Canada: their Constitution already requires Aboriginal consultation in constitutional reforms impacting Aboriginal rights. Just as the removed section 37 required constitutional conferences be held with Aboriginal peoples, so too could a new provision require Parliament and the Executive to consult with Aboriginal people when making laws and policies substantially affecting Aboriginal rights and interests. The clause could require Parliament to enact legislation setting out appropriate procedures and could

Journal 221, 229–30. This judicial deference to parliamentary power can arguably be seen in the way that the Australian High Court has narrowly interpreted the s 92 guarantee that 'trade, commerce, and intercourse among the States' shall be 'absolutely free' (see *Cole v Whitfield* (1988) 165 CLR 360), as well as the religious freedom restraint in s 116 (see Luke Beck, *Religious Freedom and the Australian Constitution* (Routledge 2018) 161–63) and s 41 (see Jonathan Crowe and Peta Stephenson, 'An Express Constitutional Right to Vote? The Case for Reviving Section 41' (2014) 36 *Sydney Law Review* 205; and Anne Twomey, 'The Federal Constitutional Right to Vote in Australia' (2000) 28 *Federal Law Review* 125).

[348] Megan Davis and Rosalind Dixon, 'Constitutional Recognition through a (Justiciable) Duty to Consult? Towards Entrenched and Judicially Enforceable Norms of Indigenous Consultation' (2016) 27(4) *Public Law Review* 249.

[349] For a discussion of how non-justiciability can be achieved in constitutional drafting, see Chapter 6. See also Shireen Morris, 'The Argument for a Constitutional Procedure for Parliament to Consult with Indigenous Peoples When Making Laws for Indigenous Affairs' (2015) 26(3) *Public Law Review* 166, 179–86; Shireen Morris, 'The Torment of Our Powerlessness: Indigenous Constitutional Vulnerability and the Uluru Statement's Call for a First Nations Voice' (2018) 41(3) *UNSW Law Journal* 629, 653–65.

be drafted to be non-justiciable. Breach of the requirement need not invalidate laws, but would operate as a powerful moral, political and indeed constitutional requirement. Thus, it could emulate the Uluru Statement approach currently being debated in Australia.

IV. SÁMI PARLIAMENTS: NORWAY, SWEDEN AND FINLAND

The Scandinavian countries of Norway, Sweden, and Finland are home to minority Indigenous populations who since 'time immemorial' have struggled for recognition of their rights.[350] In these nations, Sámi self-determination has found practical expression through the Sámi Parliaments, which are representative and advisory bodies that enable Sámi input into Sámi affairs.[351] The Sámi Parliaments provide informative parallels with the concept of a First Nations constitutional voice in development in Australia.[352]

A. Constitutional Context

The Sámi population in Northern Europe is estimated to be around 80,000 across Norway, Sweden, Finland and Russia. Around 40,000 Sámi live in Norway (less than one per cent of the population),[353] approximately 20,000 live in Sweden, and Finland hosts the smallest Sámi population of about 8,000.[354] Sámi are an even more extreme minority than Indigenous peoples in Australia.[355] Unlike in

[350] Use of the phrase 'time immemorial' is common to describe Sámi rights in Scandinavian countries. See Jacinta Ruru, 'A Comparative Gaze with Aotearoa New Zealand' in Christina Allard and Susann Funderud Skogvang (eds), *Indigenous Rights in Scandinavia: Autonomous Sami Law* (Routledge 2016) 30.

[351] See John B Henriksen, 'The Continuous Process of Recognition and Implementation of the Sámi People's Right to Self-determination' (2008) 21(1) *Cambridge Review of International Affairs* 27. Wilson and Selle describe this as an example of 'shared rule'. See Wilson and Selle (n 5 above) 24–26.

[352] This section will not discuss Sámi land and husbandry rights. For an in-depth discussion, see Christina Allard, 'Some Characteristic Features of Scandinavian Laws and their Influence on Sami Matters' in Christina Allard and Susann Funderud Skogvang (eds), *Indigenous Rights in Scandinavia: Autonomous Sami Law* (Routledge 2016).

[353] 'Norway Ethnic Groups', *Study.com* <https://study.com/academy/lesson/norway-ethnic-groups.html> accessed 15 December 2019. See also Hurst Hannum, *Autonomy, Sovereignty, and Self-Determination: The Accommodation of Conflicting Rights* (University of Pennsylvania Press 1990) 247.

[354] 'Sami in Sweden', *Sweden Sverige* (updated 11 September 2019) <https://sweden.se/society/sami-in-sweden/> accessed 15 December 2019; see also 'Sámi Facts', *Cultural Survival* (December 2008) <https://www.culturalsurvival.org/publications/cultural-survival-quarterly/sami-facts> accessed 15 December 2019.

[355] Sámi population numbers are difficult to ascertain because there is no Sámi Census, but see: Minority Rights Group International, *State of the World's Minorities and Indigenous Peoples 2012: Case Study – Sami Rights to Culture and Natural Resources* (28 June 2012) <https://www.refworld.org/docid/4fedb3de37.html> accessed 15 December 2019.

Canada and New Zealand, there are no historical treaties between the Sámi and Scandinavian governments.[356]

Like Indigenous peoples elsewhere, the Sámi suffered a history of discrimination and exclusion by dominant states,[357] and arguments about Sámi inferiority were used to justify exclusion and dispossession. In Sweden, for example, hierarchical ideas about race and culture in the 1800s asserted that Sámi 'nomads were culturally inferior to farmers', thus justifying expropriation of land.[358] It was argued that Sámi possessed 'racial characteristics' that made them inferior to the 'civilized' population.[359] Equal education was denied and the children of nomadic Sámi were prevented from accessing public primary schools.[360] In 1922, the Swedish Parliament opened a Swedish Institute of Racial Biology to protect the superior nature of the 'Swedish race'.[361] Although Lappland was set aside for traditional Sámi culture,[362] discriminatory ideas promoting Sámi inferiority did not begin to dissipate until after the Second World War.[363] In Norway, explicit assimilationist policies were pursued, including policies supressing Sámi languages, and assimilation also occurred in Finland.[364] The gradual encroachment of Sámi homelands was evident across these countries.[365]

The shift from exclusion and suppression towards Sámi political empowerment and recognition of Sámi rights was gradual.[366] A 1973 government decree established approximately 10 per cent of Finland's territory as traditional Sámi homeland.[367] Sámi language began to be promoted in schools in the 1970s, and 1985 legislation allowed it to be the primary language taught in the Sámi home region.[368] Finland's 1999 *Constitution Act of Finland*[369] included a fresh emphasis on human rights and enabled judicial review.[370] Section 17 recognises and

[356] Christina Allard, 'The Rationale for the Duty to Consult Indigenous Peoples: Comparative Reflections from Nordic and Canadian Legal Contexts' (2018) 9 *Arctic Review on Law and Politics* 25, 27.

[357] Henriksen (n 351 above) 28–29.

[358] Ministry of Agriculture, Food and Consumer Affairs and the Sámi Parliament, *The Sami: An Indigenous People in Sweden* (2005) 14 <http://www.samer.se/2137> accessed 15 December 2019. On gradual incursions into Sámi land, see Hannum (n 353 above) 249–51.

[359] ibid 14.

[360] ibid 15.

[361] For more on Sámi discrimination, see Tomas Cramer, 'Superlawyers and Sami in Sweden' (1986) 55(1)–(2) *Nordic Journal of International Law* 58.

[362] Hannum (n 353 above) 251.

[363] *The Sami* (n 358 above) 15.

[364] Hannum (n 353 above) 251.

[365] Christina Allard and Susann Funderud Skogvang (eds), *Indigenous Rights in Scandinavia: Autonomous Sami Law* (Routledge 2016) 4.

[366] See generally, essays in ibid; Henriksen (n 351 above) 28–31; Hocking (n 7 above) 294–96.

[367] Pertti Pesonen and Olavi Riihinen, *Dynamic Finland: The Political System and the Welfare State* (Studia Fernica Historica 2002) 70.

[368] Hannum (n 353 above) 255.

[369] *Constitution Act of Finland* (731/1999). The Constitution contains a special amendment procedure in s 73.

[370] Allard, 'Some Characteristic Features' (n 352 above) 54.

protects Sámi language and culture rights.[371] Section 121 provides that: 'In their native region, the Sámi have linguistic and cultural self-government, as provided by an Act.'

Norway's 1814 Constitution is entrenched and enduring and includes a Bill of rights.[372] A 1959 Royal Commission on Sámi Questions asserted that all children had the right to learn their mother tongue. Numerous government-appointed Sámi advisory bodies were created to advise on Sámi affairs. In 1980, a Sámi Rights Committee and a Commission on Sámi Cultural and Educational Matters were established. Recommendations were influenced by international human rights instruments, particularly Article 27 of the International Covenant on Civil and Political Rights,[373] and called for constitutional recognition of Sámi cultural rights.[374] In 1988, Sámi cultural and language rights were recognised and protected under a constitutional amendment.[375]

In Sweden, there was a similar trend towards increased constitutional recognition of Sámi over time. The Swedish Constitution is known as the 'fundamental law' and is specially entrenched.[376] In 1989, a commission of inquiry recommended recognition of Sámi people as an Indigenous minority in the Constitution and proposed policies to promote Sámi culture, strengthen Sámi husbandry rights and establish an elected Sámi Parliament.[377] The Parliament recognised Sámi as an Indigenous people in 1977 and acknowledged Sámi as one of its national minorities in 1999.[378] Sweden subsequently implemented policies

[371] Section 17 provides: 'The Sámi, as an indigenous people, as well as the Roma and other groups, have the right to maintain and develop their own language and culture. Provisions on the right of the Sámi to use the Sámi language before the authorities are laid down by an Act. The rights of persons using sign language and of persons in need of interpretation or translation aid owing to disability shall be guaranteed by an Act.'

[372] Norway's Constitution is the second oldest written Constitution in the world and can only be amended through a special parliamentary procedure (art 112).

[373] Article 27 provides: 'In those States in which ethnic, religious or linguistic minorities exist, persons belonging to such minorities shall not be denied the right, in community with the other members of their group, to enjoy their own culture, to profess and practise their own religion, or to use their own language.'

[374] Hannum (n 353 above) 252–54.

[375] Article 108 of the Norwegian Constitution provides: 'The authorities of the state shall create conditions enabling the Sámi people to preserve and develop its language, culture and way of life.'

[376] This is said to include the *Instrument of Government*, the *Act of Succession*, the *Freedom of the Press Act*, and the *Fundamental Law on Freedom of Expression*, the central provisions of which are in the *Instrument of Government*. See Sevriges Riksdag, *The Constitution of Sweden: The Fundamental Laws and the Riksdag Act* (2016) 9 <https://www.riksdagen.se/globalassets/07.-dokument--lagar/the-constitution-of-sweden-160628.pdf> accessed 15 December 2019.

[377] Coral Dow and John Gardiner-Garden, 'Indigenous Affairs in Australia, New Zealand, Canada, United States of America, Norway and Sweden' (Parliament of Australia, Background Paper 15 1997–98, 6 April 1998).

[378] 'The Sami Parliament', *Sametinget*, 2 <https://www.sametinget.se/101727> accessed 15 December 2019.

to enable the transmission of Sámi language and culture in schools.[379] Since 2011, the Swedish Constitution has recognised Sámi as a people. Article 2 of the 1974 Instrument of Government requires that: 'The opportunities of the Sámi people and ethnic, linguistic and religious minorities to preserve and develop a cultural and social life of their own shall be promoted.' Article 17 states that the right of Sámi to practise reindeer husbandry is to be regulated in law.

In Allard's view, the protection given to Sámi culture in these respective constitutions does not in reality play a significant role, because the 'Scandinavian constitutions are traditionally weak compared to those of common law systems, and their provisions are seldom evoked before the courts'.[380] In contrast to Canada, principles of Sámi consultation and negotiation have not seemed to emerge through litigation arising out of these constitutional guarantees of Sámi rights;[381] rather, they have been supported largely through legislative and policy action.[382] However, Broderstad argues that the gradual progression of Sámi rights shows how both 'political compromise and legal decisions' further Sámi self-determination. In this process, courts have played an important role in 'problematizing former understandings, policies, and approaches', thus applying pressure on the political system to adapt its practice.[383] The enactment of the Sámi Parliaments, however, has been particularly crucial in enabling the Sámi to influence political decisions and argue for their rights.[384]

B. The Sámi Parliaments

Sámi Parliaments have been established in Finland (1973),[385] Norway (1987) and Sweden (1992). Each is set up in legislation and acts as a representative and consultative body that advises the respective governments on Sámi affairs. The Sámi Council, formed in 2000, connects the Sámi Parliaments of Norway,

[379] Swedish Discrimination Ombudsman, *Discrimination of the Sami: The Rights of the Sami from a Discrimination Perspective* (2008) 14–16 <https://www2.ohchr.org/english/issues/indigenous/ExpertMechanism/3rd/docs/contributions/SwedishEqualityOmbudsman_2.pdf> accessed 15 December 2019.

[380] Allard, 'Some Characteristic Features' (n 352 above) 50, fn 8.

[381] See also Allard, 'Rationale for the Duty' (n 356 above) 27.

[382] As Allard explains: 'As a distinct Scandinavian trait, Scandinavian governments have generally sought to address Sami rights issues through government commissions and bills. But increasingly Sami land and resource rights are also being pursued through national and international courts': Allard, 'Some Characteristic Features' (n 352 above) 51.

[383] Else Grete Broderstad, 'Implementing Indigenous Self-determination: The Case of the Sámi in Norway', *E-International Relations* (30 May 2014) <https://www.e-ir.info/2014/05/30/implementing-indigenous-self-determination-the-case-of-the-sami-in-norway/> accessed 15 December 2019. On how seminal cases led to important legislative reform in Norway, see Malgosia Fitzmaurice, 'The New Developments Regarding the Saami Peoples of the North' (2009) 16(1) *International Journal on Minority and Group Rights* 67, 95–99.

[384] Broderstad, 'Implementing Indigenous Self-determination' (n 383 above).

[385] Although the more recent Act was adopted in 1992.

Sweden, and Finland and includes the permanent participation of Sámi from Russia, enabling the Sámi to have a transnational voice in international affairs as well as domestic voices in national affairs. The Sámi Parliaments can be seen as institutional mechanisms enabling Sámi self-determination and related rights of consultation and participation in laws and policies affecting their rights.[386] As Allard notes, the focus is on dialogue and reaching mutual agreement through negotiation. In contrast to Canada's juridically-driven duty to consult, which emerged by reference to the 'honour of the Crown', Scandinavian duties to engage with Sámi peoples have generally been politically-led and influenced by reference to international law.[387]

In Norway, the *Sámi Act 1987* was enacted 'to enable the Sámi people in Norway to safeguard and develop their language, culture and way of life',[388] echoing the intent of the constitutional provision. The Act established the modes of election and operation of the Sámi Parliament. Section 2.1 defines the Sámi Parliament's business as 'any matter that in the view of the parliament particularly affects the Sámi people', and notes that 'the Sameting may on its own initiative raise and pronounce an opinion on any matter coming within the scope of its business'. Notably, its duties have increased and expanded over time. In 1993, the Sámi Parliament took responsibility for funding Sámi language promotion and also took over the Norwegian Cultural Council's work in relation to Sámi culture. By 2002, it had assumed responsibility for promoting Sámi artists, museums, festivals and other cultural activities.[389] The institution thus fulfils a representative as well as an administrative role.

Levels of engagement with the state have also increased over time. In 2005, the Norwegian government and the Sámi Parliament signed a Consultation Agreement, which accords Sámi significant input in the drafting of legislation and the development of policy affecting them.[390] Article 1 of the Agreement states that the objective of the agreed consultation procedures are to

> contribute to the implementation in practise of the State's obligations to consult indigenous peoples under international law; achieve agreement between State authorities and the Sámi Parliament whenever consideration is being given to legislative or administrative measures that may directly affect Sámi interests; facilitate

[386] See also Adrian Liviu Ivan and Ruxandra Emanuela Nut, 'Sami People and the Rights to Self-Determination' (2015) 9(2) *Society & Politics/Societate si Politica* 28; Eva Josefsen, 'The Sami and the National Parliaments: Direct and Indirect Channels of Influence' in Kathrin Wessendorf (ed), *Challenging Politics: Indigenous Peoples' Experiences with Political Parties and Elections* (International Work Group for Indigenous Affairs 2001) 64–93.

[387] Allard, 'Rationale for the Duty' (n 356 above) 26.

[388] *Sámi Act* (Act of 12 June 1987. No 56) (Norway) s 1.1.

[389] Wilson and Selle (n 5 above) 26–27.

[390] 'Procedures for Consultations between State Authorities and the Sami Parliament [Norway]', *Government.no* (updated 14 August 2018) <https://www.regjeringen.no/en/topics/indigenous-peoples-and-minorities/Sami-people/midtspalte/PROCEDURES-FOR-CONSULTATIONS-BETWEEN-STA/id450743/> accessed 15 December 2019.

> the development of a partnership perspective between State authorities and the Sámi Parliament that contributes to the strengthening of Sámi culture and society; and to develop a common understanding of the situation and developmental needs of the Sámi society.

In practice, according to Allard, the Consultation Agreement has led to Sámi having 'substantial influence on … the drafting of new legislation such as the Finnmark Act, 2005, the Reindeer Herding Act, 2007, the Planning and Building Act, 2008 and the Nature Diversity Act, 2009'.[391] As Broderstad explains, the landmark *Finnmark Act*[392] was the result of a 'unique political process' involving 'consultation between the standing committee on justice of the Norwegian parliament, the Sámi parliament, and Finnmark county council', demonstrating a 'fundamentally new approach on the part of the Norwegian parliament for dealing with the legislative process'.[393] Notably, the *Finnmark Act* also empowered the Sámi Parliament to issue guidelines regarding the use of uncultivated land, which can then be approved by the Minister,[394] thus delivering processes for further practical empowerment of Sámi in their affairs.

Consulting Sámi in the development of legislation appears to be becoming normal practice in Norway. According to Broderstad:

> Between 40 and 50 consultations on legislation and policies are carried out annually, with a majority leading to consensus. The topics are diverse, including consultations on education, health, language, national parks, cultural heritage, hunting and fishery regulations, reindeer husbandry, windmills, power stations, and mining.[395]

Under the Consultation Agreement, the consultation required is not limited to the Sámi Parliament and may include other Sámi groups. Further, the terms of the agreement can be changed, but only if the parties agree to alternative arrangements.[396] The agreement demonstrates a productive commitment to procedures for state-Sámi engagement and partnership.[397] Through such processes, the Norwegian 'Sámi Parliament has developed into a political body with a real say'.[398]

The Norwegian *Sámi Act*, as well as setting up the Sámi Parliament, also includes measures for cultural and language recognition. Section 1.5 declares

[391] Allard, 'Rationale for the Duty' (n 356 above) 29.

[392] Section 1 states the Act's purpose as facilitating 'the management of land and natural resources in the county of Finnmark in a balanced and ecologically sustainable manner for the benefit of the residents of the county and particularly as a basis for Sami culture, reindeer husbandry, use of noncultivated areas, commercial activity and social life'.

[393] Else Grete Broderstad, 'The Promises and Challenges of Indigenous Self-Determination: The Sami Case' (2011) 66(4) *International Journal* 893, 904.

[394] Fitzmaurice (n 383 above) 101.

[395] Broderstad, 'Implementing Indigenous Self-determination' (n 383 above).

[396] Allard, 'Rationale for the Duty' (n 356 above) 30.

[397] See Broderstad, 'Promises and Challenges' (n 393 above) 902. See also Wilson and Selle (n 5 above) 29.

[398] Broderstad, 'Promises and Challenges' (n 393 above) 901.

that the 'Sámi and Norwegian are languages of equal worth', and section 2.13 provides that: 'At meetings of the Sameting all persons have the right to speak Sámi or Norwegian as they wish.' Chapter 3 of the Act sets out further Sámi language rights, including establishing a Sámi Language Council. The Sámi Parliament of Norway is housed in a building architecturally designed to resemble a traditional Sámi tipi. The Act thus facilitates political empowerment as well as cultural recognition and expression.

The Sámi Parliament of Finland is also an elected advisory body whose objective is to 'look after the Sámi language and culture, as well as to take care of matters relating to their status as an indigenous people'.[399] Although an advisory body, it has power to allocate state funding for Sámi language and culture.[400] The Act states in section 1 that:

> The Sámi, as an indigenous people, have linguistic and cultural autonomy in the Sámi homeland as provided in this Act and in other legislation. For the tasks relating to cultural autonomy the Sámi shall elect from among themselves a Sámi Parliament.

The Act also sets out matters for which an 'obligation to negotiate' (which is defined as consultation: 'the opportunity to be heard and discuss matters') is enlivened.[401] Section 9 states that such negotiation is required 'in all far-reaching and important measures which may directly and in a specific way affect the status of the Sámi as an indigenous people and which concern the following matters in the Sámi homeland', and lists the relevant matters, including 'community planning; the management, use, leasing and assignment of state lands, conservation areas and wilderness areas'; and 'any other matters affecting the Sámi language and culture or the status of the Sámi as an indigenous people'. Notably, however, the duty is territorially limited to the Sámi homeland and confined to engagement with the Sámi Parliament, although Sámi activists are advocating that the scope of this duty to consult be expanded.[402] According to Josefsen, the Finnish duty to consult does not operate robustly in practice, as 'No comprehensive formal structures or joint arenas of significance have been established between the Saami Parliament and the Finnish Government to ensure that the intention in the legislation regarding Saami influence is met.'[403]

The Sámi Parliament of Sweden is also an elected body; however, its chairman is appointed by government and it is also a state agency. In this respect, the Swedish institution can be described as the weakest in terms of enabling empowered Sámi participation in Sámi affairs.[404] Sweden stands out from Norway and

[399] *Act on the Sámi Parliament* (974/1995), s 5(1).

[400] Hocking (n 7 above) 298.

[401] The legislation also clarifies that 'failure to use this opportunity [to be heard] in no way prevents the authority from proceeding in the matter', thus eliminating any possibility of a veto by abstention.

[402] Allard, 'Rationale for the Duty' (n 356 above) 31–33.

[403] Eva Josefsen, *The Saami and the National Parliaments: Channels for Political Influence* (2010) 8 <http://archive.ipu.org/splz-e/Chiapas10/saami.pdf> accessed 15 December 2019.

[404] Hocking (n 7 above) 301; Fitzmaurice (n 383 above) 83.

Finland because it lacks any legislated requirements for the state to consult with the Sámi on Sámi matters. While consultation with Sámi in Sweden tends to occur in the form of corporate engagement with respect to mining projects as part of their environmental assessment,[405] Sweden has been the most hesitant when it comes to Sámi recognition.[406] Sámi advocates in Sweden have therefore urged stronger constitutional protection of Sámi rights.[407]

Trudel et al note that, while the Sámi in Scandinavia have achieved better recognition and empowerment than Indigenous peoples in Australia, there is further to go. In Finland, for example, an important 2015 Bill affecting Sámi rights was introduced without proper Sámi consultation.[408] While the literature indicates that the Sámi Parliament of Norway, and the Norwegian Consultation Agreement, have been most effective in ensuring Sámi participation and consultation in legislation and policy affecting their rights, across Scandinavia there is more work to be done.

After many years of negotiations between Sweden, Norway and Finland, Sámi aspirations for strengthening rights to participation and self-determination were reflected in the Nordic Sámi Convention which was signed in 2017.[409] Article 14 affirms the place of the Sámi Parliaments as the main vehicle for the 'realization of the Saami people's right of self-determination'. Article 16 provides a right of negotiation, requiring that:

> In matters of major importance to the Saami, negotiations shall be held with the Saami parliaments before decisions on such matters are made by a public authority. These negotiations must take place sufficiently early to enable the Saami parliaments to have a real influence over the proceedings and the result.

Article 18 emphasises the right of Sámi to voice their concerns on Sámi matters, requiring that 'Saami parliaments shall be given the opportunity to be heard during the consideration by national assemblies of matters that particularly concern the Saami people' and stipulates that regulations should be issued setting out appropriate procedures. Article 21 broadens state duties to consult beyond just the Sámi Parliaments, to Sámi villages, reindeer herders' communities, village assemblies, and other Sami organisations as necessary. These principles emphasise the procedural importance of negotiation, engagement

[405] Allard, 'The Rationale for the Duty' (n 356 above) 34.

[406] Henriksen (n 351 above) 34.

[407] Ingwar Ahren, 'Small Nations of the North in Constitutional and International Law' (1995) 64 *Nordic Journal of International Law* 457, 461.

[408] Elisabeth Roy Trudel, Leena Heinamaki and Philipp Kastner, 'Saami Still Struggle for Recognition', *Arctic Deeply* (7 June 2016): <https://www.newsdeeply.com/arctic/community/2016/06/07/saami-still-struggle-for-recognition> accessed 15 December 2019.

[409] *Nordic Saami Convention* (English version) <https://www.sametinget.se/105173> accessed 15 December 2019. See also Fitzmaurice (n 383 above) 116; Margret Carstens, 'Sami Land Rights: The Anaya Report and the Nordic Sami Convention' (2016) 15(1) *Journal on Ethnopolitics and Minority Issues in Europe* 75; Timo Koivurova, 'The Draft for a Nordic Saami Convention' (2006/07) 6 *European Yearbook of Minority Issues* 103.

and consultation, building on the frameworks begun by the Sámi Parliaments. The Convention demonstrates that the enactment of a Sámi Parliament in each country was the beginning of an ongoing process of negotiation and engagement in Sámi-state relationships.

C. Insights for Australia

Reflecting on the success of Norwegian arrangements, Broderstad notes that 'A representative political body had to be in place before the development of procedures of political inclusion could take place.'[410] The Scandinavian examples demonstrate what may be achieved when Indigenous peoples – even extremely small minority populations – are institutionally supported and empowered to represent themselves and assert their voices in political decision-making with respect to their rights: if political conditions are right, they can participate in negotiations and consultations on legislation and policy, that may also lead to development of further agreed procedures for political inclusion and empowerment over time. The operation of the Sámi Parliaments in these countries also demonstrates that constitutional recognition of Indigenous peoples through a clause declaring and recognising Indigenous rights and culture, as observed in the Norwegian, Swedish and Finnish constitutions, needs political action and institutional reform to bring such high-level aspirations into practical and operational reality. The Sámi Parliaments are institutional mechanisms by which Sámi can assert their self-determination to varying degrees. Each has propelled, to varying degrees, processes and procedures for ongoing Indigenous-state engagement, negotiation, and consultation. The Norwegian example in particular demonstrates that consultation in the making of legislation need not hamper parliamentary supremacy; rather it can be implemented directly by government to enhance Indigenous-state relations. If political actors show initiative, legislative and policy processes can be adapted to incorporate Indigenous empowerment and dialogue.

In Australia, a First Nations voice will need a constitutional imperative to have authority and longevity, but it will also need negotiated legislation bringing the institution to life.[411] The Scandinavian Sámi Parliaments, like the Māori Council, are useful in generating ideas for how such legislation could be designed and how engagement procedures might work in practice. The Norwegian example demonstrates that an Indigenous representative body, if well-designed and implemented, may be able to negotiate further procedures to enhance its role. For example, the Uluru Statement also advocated for a Makarrata Commission

[410] Broderstad, 'Promises and Challenges' (n 393 above) 905.
[411] *Final Report of the Referendum Council* (n 74 above) Recommendation 1, 36.

to supervise agreement-making and truth-telling.[412] This could be something a First Nations voice could advocate and help develop. Importantly, Sámi Parliaments demonstrate that a First Nations voice to Parliament is not a novel idea. Similar Indigenous bodies are operating elsewhere, with varying success. These international examples can be adapted to Australian circumstances. While no model is simply transportable – the First Nations of Australia are unique, and Australian politics and constitutional culture are also unique, requiring a tailored, domestic solution – international examples are nonetheless helpful in informing and inspiring domestic approaches.

A further lesson for Australia is that the Act setting up the Indigenous body can go beyond simply setting up a representative institution: it can declare the importance and status of Indigenous languages and cultures and other matters of symbolic and practical significance. The connection between Indigenous political empowerment and cultural and language recognition is evident in both the Scandinavian and New Zealand contexts. A *First Nations Voice Act* in Australia could not only set up the First Nations body – it could recognise Indigenous Australian languages as the original languages and set up a Languages Commission to revitalise and transmit these Australian languages.

V. CONCLUSION

The international context should be a source of inspiration for the Australian debate about Indigenous constitutional recognition. These examples demonstrate that a First Nations voice to enable Indigenous peoples to have a fairer say in laws and policies made about their rights, is not a novel idea – it is a modest approach that is already happening elsewhere.[413]

The New Zealand example demonstrates what can be achieved through institutional mechanisms for Indigenous political empowerment – measures that ensure Indigenous people have a voice in their affairs. These measures can respect parliamentary supremacy and fit with a political and procedural approach to rights protection. The Canadian example shows that such a political approach to empowering Indigenous voices may be preferable to a litigious approach. Judicial adjudication of Indigenous rights comes with its own risks. The empowerment of Indigenous voices in their affairs, in my view, is therefore best achieved in the political realm, rather than through judicial adjudication of a justiciable duty to consult. The Scandinavian example shows that, given the right political conditions, such an approach can yield positive results, even for

[412] Notably, the Swedish Sámi Parliament has been advocating for a Truth and Reconciliation Commission: see Per-Olof Nutti, 'Statement about the Work for a Truth Commission on Historical Events and Abuse of the Sami People in Sweden' <https://www.sametinget.se/120809> accessed 15 December 2019.

[413] See also Gover, 'From the Heart' (n 20 above) 206.

extreme minority Indigenous populations. Like New Zealand, the Sámi Parliaments show how Indigenous institutional empowerment can be productively coupled with fulsome recognition of Indigenous languages and cultures.

The Uluru Statement calls for a First Nations voice and the Referendum Council recommends a constitutionally guaranteed Indigenous representative and advisory body. Such a body could draw inspiration from the Māori Council, the Canadian AFN and the Sámi Parliaments, adapted to Australian circumstances. The case for a constitutional guarantee requiring the Australian Parliament to establish such a body will be made in Chapter six.

5

The Legislative Possibility of Reserved Indigenous Seats in Parliament

I. INTRODUCTION

THE NEW ZEALAND example, discussed in Chapter four, demonstrates how political and procedural forms of constitutional recognition can empower Indigenous voices to be heard in their affairs, thus providing a proactive and pre-emptive protection of Indigenous rights through the political arena. The Māori parliamentary seats are an important form of Māori constitutional recognition, enabling Māori self-determination and ongoing dialogue between Treaty partners. Such political mechanisms present an informative contrast to the judicially adjudicated constitutional recognition that predominates in Canada under section 35. In Australia, ongoing resistance to new judicially adjudicated rights guarantees means that political avenues for constitutional recognition should be explored.

In the history of Indigenous advocacy for recognition and reform,[1] reserved Indigenous seats in Parliament has been a recurring theme.[2] This chapter explores the possibility of legislated reserved Indigenous seats in Australia's federal Parliament under current constitutional arrangements,[3] particularly in light of changing judicial interpretation of the phrase 'directly chosen by the people' in sections 7 and 24.

II. CONSTITUTIONAL CONSTRAINTS

As explained in the preceding chapter, New Zealand has had reserved Māori seats since 1867. The Australian constitutional context is fundamentally different,

[1] See history in Chapter 2 of this volume.

[2] For more current advocacy see Michael Mansell, *Treaty and Statehood: Aboriginal Self-Determination* (The Federation Press 2016) 35–41; Rosie Lewis, 'Reserved Seats for Aboriginal MPs, Says Jacquie Lambie', *The Australian* (14 September 2014); Misha Schubert, 'Indigenous Want Reserved Seats in Parliament: Congress', *The Age* (31 July 2011).

[3] Michael Mansell argues that constitutional reform is not necessary for the implementation of reserved Indigenous seats: Mansell (n 2 above) 35–41. It is also questionable whether constitutional reform implementing reserved seats would succeed at a referendum. See discussion in Glynn Evans and Lisa Hill, 'The Electoral and Political Implications of Reserved Seats for Indigenous Australians (2012) 47(3) *Australian Journal of Political Science* 491, 493–94.

however. Whereas New Zealand has no entrenched Constitution and its legislative flexibility to determine electoral arrangements is accordingly unconstrained, Australia's entrenched *Constitution* in part delegates to Parliament the authority to decide electoral arrangements and in part constrains Parliament's power to do so. The hazy line between legislative freedom and constitutional control of electoral arrangements is in practice drawn by the High Court, through interpretation of the relevant constitutional clauses. Whether the Commonwealth Parliament could legislate, under current constitutional arrangements, to create Indigenous reserved seats depends on the High Court's interpretation of the relevant constitutional clauses.

When Aboriginal rights activist William Cooper called for reserved seats in 1937, the Australian Solicitor-General concluded it would be a constitutional impossibility because of lack of Commonwealth authority.[4] Prime Minister Ben Chifley drew a similar conclusion in response to Indigenous advocacy in 1949.[5] As Chesterman explains, however, these conclusions were influenced by exclusions of Indigenous people in constitutional clauses which were later amended or repealed through the 1967 referendum, including section 127 which had excluded Indigenous people from being counted as part of the population for voting purposes, and section 51(xxvi) which previously excluded Indigenous people from the scope of the Race Power.[6] The Commonwealth, subject to the *Constitution*, now has a power to legislate with respect to Indigenous matters. The main constitutional clauses that may constrain the legislative implementation of reserved Indigenous seats are sections 7, 24 and possibly 29.

A. Section 7

Section 7 establishes the Australian Senate.[7] The provision allows Parliament to legislate to alter the number of Senators in the composition of the State, but the Original States must each maintain an equal number of Senators.[8] Section 7

[4] Solicitor-General George S Knowles, 'Opinion: A431/1, 1949/1591' (National Archives of Australia, Canberra, 14 January 1938); quoted in John Chesterman, 'Chosen by the People? How Federal Parliamentary Seats Might be Reserved for Indigenous Australians without Constitutional Amendment' (2006) 34(2) *Federal Law Review* 261, 270.

[5] Letter from Prime Minister Ben Chifley to Shadrach James (A432, 1949/258, National Archives of Australia, 28 March [date unclear] 1949), quoted in Chesterman (n 4 above) 270.

[6] Ibid.

[7] Section 7 provides: 'The Senate shall be composed of senators for each State, directly chosen by the people of the State, voting, until the Parliament otherwise provides, as one electorate … Until the Parliament otherwise provides there shall be six senators for each Original State. The Parliament may make laws increasing or diminishing the number of senators for each State, but so that equal representation of the several Original States shall be maintained and that no Original State shall have less than six senators'.

[8] Barwick J notes that 'the relative populations of the States have always varied considerably. Thus, there can be no question that equality of voting strength throughout Australia was intended or provided for in s 7': *Attorney-General (Cth); Ex rel McKinlay v Commonwealth* (1975) 135 CLR 1, 18.

allows the creation of additional Senators. It may therefore enable reserved Indigenous Senate seats, so long as the number of Senators in each Original State remains equal.

Section 7 also provides that each State must vote as one electorate, but only 'until Parliament otherwise provides'. This indicates that the Commonwealth can legislate to divide State electorates.[9] Parliament may, therefore, in theory be able to legislate to give each State an Indigenous electorate, overlayed upon its general electorate. Indigenous citizens in each State could choose whether to vote on the general roll for Senate elections, or on an Indigenous electoral roll for that State, as happens in New Zealand on a national scale. This would entail a national Indigenous electoral roll, divided by State electoral boundaries. However, this simple interpretation of section 7 requires a certain construction of the clause's key phrase, 'directly chosen by the people', which will be discussed further below.

B. Section 24

Section 24 establishes the Australian House of Representatives.[10] The provision requires that members are 'directly chosen by the people of the Commonwealth' and creates a nexus between the numbers in the Senate and the House of Representatives, such that the total members in the House of Representatives must be approximately double the number of Senators. As Reilley notes, there is some flexibility in this requirement.[11] The legislative implementation of four new Territory Senators, which impacted the proportionality between the Senate and the House of Representatives, was found to be constitutionally valid in 1975.[12]

[9] In September 2019, former leader of the National Party Barnaby Joyce raised the idea of increasing the regional representativeness of the Senate by dividing each State into six regions, each represented by two Senators – therefore retaining the current number of 12 Senators per State. Joyce argued that this would address the problem that many Senators are currently based in the big cities and do not truly represent regional interests. Rosie Lewis, 'Joyce Pushes Senate Plan', *The Australian* (9 September 2019).

[10] 'The House of Representatives shall be composed of members directly chosen by the people of the Commonwealth, and the number of such members shall be, as nearly as practicable, twice the number of the senators. The number of members chosen in the several States shall be in proportion to the respective numbers of their people, and shall, until the Parliament otherwise provides, be determined, whenever necessary, in the following manner: (i) a quota shall be ascertained by dividing the number of the people of the Commonwealth, as shown by the latest statistics of the Commonwealth, by twice the number of the senators; (ii) the number of members to be chosen in each State shall be determined by dividing the number of the people of the State, as shown by the latest statistics of the Commonwealth, by the quota; and if on such division there is a remainder greater than one-half of the quota, one more member shall be chosen in the State. But notwithstanding anything in this section, five members at least shall be chosen in each Original State.'

[11] Alexander Reilley, 'Dedicated Seats in the Federal Parliament for Indigenous Australians' (2001) 2(1) *Balayi: Culture, Law and Colonialism* 73, 98.

[12] *Western Australia v The Commonwealth (First Territorial Senators Case)* (1975) 134 CLR 201; *Commonwealth v Queensland* (1977) 139 CLR 585.

Section 24 also requires that members in each State are proportionate to population numbers in that State. In practice, each member represents a geographic area called an electoral division, the boundaries of which change as population varies.[13]

If the geographical nature of electoral districts is constitutionally required, this could potentially preclude the legislative establishment of reserved Indigenous seats in the House of Representatives. Reilley suggests that section 24

> might mean that dedicated seats in the House of Representatives would have to be State based. Section 7 of the Constitution places a similar constraint on electoral districts for the Senate. Since Senators are elected from the different States, electoral boundaries for the Senate do not cross State boundaries. The current constitutional arrangement requires that electoral boundaries be geographically located within State boundaries. This means that a nationwide Aboriginal electoral register could not be established without constitutional reform.[14]

C. Section 29

In 1961, a parliamentary inquiry investigated 'whether it was constitutionally possible to establish "an aboriginal electorate throughout the Commonwealth, regardless of State boundaries, on the model of the New Zealand electorates for Maoris"'.[15] The advice was that section 29 would prevent it.[16] Section 29 specifies that an electoral division must not be formed out of 'parts of different States',[17] indicating that electoral divisions for the House of Representatives must be drawn within State boundaries.

In 1961, Solicitor-General Kenneth Bailey concluded that Indigenous reserved seats in the House of Representatives through an Indigenous nationwide electorate, as in New Zealand, could not be created primarily because section 29 specifies that electoral divisions cannot cross over State boundaries. But when asked whether Indigenous electorates could be legislatively created

[13] 'About the House of Representatives', *Parliament of Australia* <http://www.aph.gov.au/About_Parliament/House_of_Representatives/About_the_House_of_Representatives> accessed 20 December 2019.

[14] Reilley (n 11 above) 99. Note that Mansell also suggests that s 24 may make implementation of reserved Indigenous seats in the House of Representatives difficult. See Mansell (n 2 above) 35–36.

[15] Chesterman (n 4 above) 275.

[16] KH Bailey, 'Opinion' (3 August 1961), cited in Chesterman, ibid 271. See also Mansell (n 2 above) 30–31.

[17] Section 29 provides: 'Until the Parliament of the Commonwealth otherwise provides, the Parliament of any State may make laws for determining the divisions in each State for which members of the House of Representatives may be chosen, and the number of members to be chosen for each division. A division shall not be formed out of parts of different States. In the absence of other provision each State shall be one electorate.'

within States, Bailey also saw section 29 as an obstacle preventing an 'ethnic division' within a State.[18] Bailey advised that:

> [T]here are sufficiently clear indications in the wording of the section itself that the 'divisions' in the States, contemplated by the section, are territorial areas rather than, for instance, ethnic groups ... [I]t follows I think that the Parliament cannot create what may perhaps best be described as an *ethnic division*.[19]

Sawer, another eminent lawyer of the time, seemed to agree that electoral divisions must be geographical.[20] However, this is not directly evident from the words of section 29. There seems nothing in section 29 that prevents additional, overlapping Indigenous electorates, so long as the Indigenous electorates do not cross over State boundaries. As Chesterman notes, section 29 prohibits electoral divisions which cross over State boundaries, but it confers broad flexibility on Parliament to determine the nature of electoral divisions within each State. The phrase 'until Parliament otherwise provides' confers legislative flexibility to change arrangements and does not explicitly rule out electoral divisions from overlapping with each other within a State.[21] Chesterman argues that a 'robust reading' of section 29 'would even possibly enable the Indigenous populations of two or three entire states to form one electorate, so long as the electorate was not created from "parts of different States"'.[22]

Any new Indigenous electorates would still need to comply with the technical nexus and proportionality requirements in section 24, which complicates the issue. Section 7 seems to allow for more legislative flexibility in the Senate than sections 24 and 29 allow in the House of Representatives. Therefore, reserved Senate seats may be more readily implementable.

III. HOW MUCH LEGISLATIVE FLEXIBILITY DOES THE *CONSTITUTION* CONFER?

Sections 7, 24 and 29 confer upon Australian Parliaments legislative flexibility to evolve national voting arrangements, while also providing constitutional constraints. Many other clauses do the same, sharing authority to determine political arrangements between the Commonwealth and the States.[23] While the

[18] KH Bailey, 'Opinion' (7 June 1961), quoted in Chesterman (n 4 above) 275.
[19] ibid.
[20] Geoffrey Sawer, 'Opinion' (28 July 1961), quoted in Chesterman (n 4 above) 276.
[21] ibid 276–77.
[22] ibid.
[23] For example, s 30 states that, 'until the Parliament otherwise provides', the qualification of electors shall be prescribed by law in each State, 'as the qualification of electors of the more numerous House of Parliament of the State'. It lets each State decide its own franchise until the Commonwealth Parliament decides to intervene. Under s 51(xxxvi), the Commonwealth has the power subject to the Constitution to enact the 'until the Parliament otherwise provides' type of laws. 'Until the Parliament otherwise provides' provisions have been described as 'transitional provisions', which are said

Constitution sets up the initial electoral framework, it delegates to Australian Parliaments responsibility for evolving that framework.[24] That this flexibility was constitutionally conferred is important, because it allowed the franchise to legislatively expand over time.

A. The Gradual Expansion of the Franchise

In the lead-up to federation, Indigenous people were generally not encouraged to participate in voting. In the late 1800s, Queensland[25] and Western Australia[26] enacted legislation specifically denying Indigenous people the right to vote, and the Northern Territory (then part of South Australia) denied the vote to certain non-white citizens and immigrants.[27] Women were also excluded until 1895, when South Australia granted women the right to vote. Other colonies followed suit in the years after.[28]

When the *Constitution* came into force, section 41 guaranteed people with the right to vote in their State elections the right to also vote in Commonwealth elections, but only while their State right continues.[29] The section acknowledges that the franchise can expand and change, but also that States might again shrink their franchise. From early in the federation, section 41 was interpreted very narrowly.[30] The Commonwealth protection only applied where State voting

to have effect until the Commonwealth Parliament legislates otherwise, at which point the legislative provisions take primacy. See Jonathan Crowe and Peta Stephenson, 'An Express Right to Vote? The Case for Reviving Section 41' (2014) 36(2) *Sydney Law Review* 205, 222.

[24] *Roach v Electoral Commissioner* (2007) 233 CLR 162, 172–73.

[25] The *Elections Act 1885* (Qld) s 6 provided that, 'no aboriginal native of Australia, India, China or of the South Sea Islands shall be entitled to be entered on the roll except in respect of a freehold qualification'.

[26] The *Constitution Act Amendment Act 1899* (WA) s 26 provided that, 'no aboriginal native of Australia, Asia, or Africa, or person of the half-blood, shall be entitled to be registered, except in respect of a freehold qualification'.

[27] The *Electoral Code 1896* (SA) s 16 provided that, 'in the Northern Territory immigrants under the *Indian Immigration Act 1882* and all persons except natural-born British subjects and Europeans or Americans naturalized as British subjects, are disqualified from voting'.

[28] Australian Electoral Commission, *History of the Indigenous Vote* (August 2006). See also Anne Twomey, 'An Obituary for s 25 of the Constitution' (2012) 23(2) *Public Law Review* 125, 133. For more on the evolution of the franchise, see Anne Twomey, 'The Federal Constitutional Right to Vote in Australia' (2000) 28(1) *Federal Law Review* 125, 143–46; Jennifer Norberry, 'The Evolution of the Commonwealth Franchise: Tales of Inclusion and Exclusion' in Graeme Orr, Brian Mercurio and George Williams (eds), *Realising Democracy: Electoral Law in Australia* (Federation Press 2003) 80.

[29] Section 41 provides: 'No adult person who has or acquires a right to vote at elections for the more numerous House of the Parliament of a State, shall, while the right continues, be prevented by any law of the Commonwealth from voting at elections for either House of Parliament of the Commonwealth.' The section means that 'no adult who has the right to vote for the lower house of his or her state legislature may be deprived of the right to elect the Commonwealth Parliament'. See Crowe and Stephenson (n 23 above) 207.

[30] John Quick and Robert Garran, *The Annotated Constitution of the Australian Commonwealth* (Legal Books, reprinted 1995 [1901]) 486–87.

rights had been acquired *before* the enactment of the *Constitution*,[31] and groups acquiring the right to vote in their State after 1901 could be denied the right to vote in Commonwealth elections. The *Commonwealth Franchise Act 1902* (Cth) section 4 provided:

> No aboriginal native of Australia Asia Africa or the Islands of the Pacific except New Zealand shall be entitled to have his name placed on an Electoral Roll unless so entitled under section forty-one of the Constitution.

In 1924, an Indian man, Mitta Bullosh, challenged his exclusion from Commonwealth voting on the basis that he was indeed allowed to vote in his State elections, under section 41. The Magistrate's Court upheld his claim and said that the provision should be interpreted as having prospective operation (namely to include all citizens who had secured the vote in their State since the passage of the 1902 Act), rather than just retrospective operation (including only those citizens enfranchised prior to that Act).[32] The Commonwealth later withdrew its appeal to the High Court and altered the *Commonwealth Franchise Act* to allow Indian people the right to vote.[33] But laws excluding Indigenous people did not change until much later,[34] and section 41 was eventually interpreted as a transitional provision that became spent after the franchise became universal.[35]

The incremental legislative steps allowing for the enfranchisement of women, non-white naturalised foreigners and Indigenous people mostly converged into equality in voting rights in 1965.[36] In 1967, the removal of section 127 further confirmed the treatment of Indigenous people as equal members of the Australian population for electoral purposes, but there were remaining discriminatory elements and powers. These included section 25, which contemplates and disincentivises barring races from voting,[37] and section 51(xxvi), the Race Power, which now includes Indigenous people within its scope and can probably be

[31] Russell McGregor, *Indifferent Inclusion: Aboriginal People and the Australian Nation* (Aboriginal Studies Press 2011) xxiv.

[32] ibid.

[33] For full discussion see Twomey, 'The Federal Constitutional Right to Vote in Australia' (n 28 above) 134.

[34] In 1949, the *Commonwealth Electoral Act 1949* (Cth) allowed Indigenous people who had completed military service, or who already had the right to vote in their State, to participate in Commonwealth elections. In 1962, the Act was amended to provide that Indigenous people could enrol to vote in federal elections, but it was not compulsory for them to enrol as it was for other Australians. At this time, Indigenous people also gained the right to vote in Western Australia and the Northern Territory. Queensland was the last State to follow suit in 1965, and then Indigenous people had the same voting rights as other Australians: ibid.

[35] *R v Pearson; Ex parte Sipka* (1983) 152 CLR 254; Crowe and Stephenson (n 23 above) 208; *Snowdon v Dondas* (1996) 188 CLR 48, 71–72; but see Twomey, 'The Federal Constitutional Right to Vote in Australia' (n 28 above) 141–42.

[36] Although, it was not compulsory for Aboriginal people to vote until 1984: Reilley (n 11 above) 74; *History of the Indigenous Vote* (n 28 above).

[37] Twomey, 'Obituary for s 25' (n 28 above).

used to enact adversely discriminatory legislation.[38] These provisions together, in my view, leave open the possibility (absent High Court intervention in the vein of *Roach* and *Rowe* discussed below) that Parliament could again use its power to enact racially discriminatory laws preventing Indigenous people, or any other ethnic group, from voting.[39]

B. What Does 'Directly Chosen by the People' Mean?

If Parliament has a great amount of legislative flexibility to determine electoral arrangements, then it may be possible for it to legislate for Indigenous reserved seats under current constitutional arrangements. Chesterman argues that 'the scope given in the *Constitution* to allow the meaning and practice of democracy to develop now … permits the creation of set Indigenous seats'.[40] But if the key constitutional phrases are interpreted in a way that restricts the kinds of reforms that Parliament can make to electoral law, then Parliament's flexibility to legislate for Indigenous reserved seats is more uncertain. It may depend on how the High Court interprets the phrase 'directly chosen by the people'. Ascertaining whether legislated reserved seats are constitutionally possible entails examining whether 'the people' excludes the possibility of an Indigenous-only electorate within each State under section 7, and whether 'directly chosen by the people' excludes the possibility, for example, of some Senate seats chosen only by Indigenous people.

The High Court approach to construction of this key phrase has changed over time.[41] Earlier decisions affirmed Parliament's broad powers with respect to electoral law and confirmed that voting rights could be taken away as well as conferred. In 1975 in *McKinlay*, the High Court acknowledged that Parliament has ultimate authority to determine the rules for who can vote and how. Barwick CJ emphasised that 'the people of the State' in section 7

> cannot mean that all the people of the States are to have a vote in the Senate elections … it would be both an unreasonable and an impractical interpretation to read it as securing the franchise to every child and teenager in the population. If, on the other hand, the word 'people' is read as referring to the electors of the State it is quite evident from other provisions of Part III that adult suffrage in each State was not intended or required by the expression 'directly chosen by the people'.[42]

[38] Section 51(xxvi) gives the Commonwealth the power to pass laws with respect to 'the people of any race for whom it is deemed necessary to make special laws': *Kartinyeri v Commonwealth* (1998) 195 CLR 337.

[39] See also Elisa Arcioni, 'Excluding Indigenous Australians from the People: A Reconsideration of Sections 25 and 127 of the Constitution' (2012) 40(3) *Federal Law Review* 287.

[40] Chesterman (n 4 above) 274.

[41] For a discussion of this development, see Sarah Murray, 'The People as a Source of Constitutional Principle: The Australian Constitution and the Contours of Representative Government' (2017) 29 *Singapore Academy of Law Journal* 882.

[42] *McKinlay* (n 8 above) 18.

Barwick CJ noted that women and Indigenous people were historically precluded from voting, demonstrating Parliament's flexible legislative power to determine voting rights under the *Constitution*.[43] Other cases similarly confirmed this broad and flexible authority.[44] Gummow and Hayne JJ observed in *Mulholland*:

> The recurrent phrase in the Constitution 'until the Parliament otherwise provides' accommodates the notion that representative government is not a static institution ... care is called for in elevating a 'direct choice' principle to a broad restraint upon legislative development of the federal system of representative government.[45]

McHugh J noted that the 'Constitution does not mandate any particular electoral system' and that the type of electoral system, the details of electoral divisions and the franchise were matters left by the *Constitution* for parliaments to determine.[46] Drawing on this attitude, Chesterman does not interpret the constitutional constraints imposed by sections 7, 24, or 29 as insurmountable barriers to the implementation of Indigenous reserved seats, stating:

> [W]henever constitutional grounds are relied upon to challenge electoral laws and practices, the High Court has almost always deferred to Parliament's power in this regard. As Gerard Carney has written, in Australia there has been a 'virtual lack of successful constitutional challenges to the electoral regime. The recognition of an implied freedom of political communication in 1992 is the one glaring exception to this trend' ...
>
> ... The scope given in the *Constitution* to allow the meaning and practice of democracy to develop now, I would submit, permits the creation of set Indigenous seats.[47]

But Chesterman published these observations in 2006 and Carney in 2003,[48] before the significant *Roach* and *Rowe* decisions, which may demonstrate an interpretational trend that reduces Parliament's flexibility to determine electoral details.

Earlier cases understood sections 7 and 24 as conferring broad legislative power upon the Parliament, because they interpreted the words 'directly chosen by the people' as what Patrick Emerton would call a 'legally constituted kind', rather than a sociologically or politically constituted kind.[49] Whereas the meaning of the 'people' for Barwick J, in *McKinlay*, refers to the legally constituted

[43] ibid.

[44] *McGinty v Western Australia* (1996) 186 CLR 140; *Langer v Commonwealth* (1996) 186 CLR 302; *Mulholland v Electoral Commission* (2004) 220 CLR 181.

[45] *Mulholland* (n 44 above) 237.

[46] ibid 207.

[47] Chesterman (n 4 above) 273–74.

[48] Gerard Carney, 'The High Court and the Constitutionalism of Electoral Law' in Graeme Orr, Bryan Mercurio and George Williams (eds), *Realising Democracy: Electoral Law in Australia* (Federation Press 2003) 170, 171.

[49] Patrick Emerton, 'Political Freedoms and Entitlements in the Australian Constitution: An Example of Referential Intentions Yielding Unintended Legal Consequences' (2010) 38(2) *Federal Law Review* 169, 191–98.

electors – the electors being a group that under the *Constitution* must be understood as defined by electoral law – *Roach* and *Rowe* and the implied rights cases interpret the phrase as a sociological or political fact to which the *Constitution* refers: a fact which can change over time. In practical terms, a legally constituted interpretation means that Parliament largely decides the meaning of the phrase through legislation – which arguably leaves more room for Indigenous reserved seats, depending of course on political will. A sociologically or politically constituted interpretation means the High Court decides the meaning of the phrase – which may render the constitutional possibility of legislated reserved seats more uncertain. The approach to construction of the phrase is explored further below.

C. Legal Kinds versus Sociological and Political Kinds

Roach and *Rowe* built on the reasoning in the implied rights cases of the 1990s, which imposed implied restrictions on Parliament's power to deny political communication as a consequence of the constitutional requirement under sections 7 and 24 that representatives must be 'directly chosen by the people'.[50] Some have argued that these decisions were not appropriately rooted in the correct meanings of the constitutional clauses or that they were driven by judicially activist attempts at achieving a desired just outcome.[51]

In Emerton's view, the decisions can be explained through consideration of the referential intentions of the drafters of the *Constitution* in the construction of the phrase 'directly chosen by the people'.[52] Given that the drafters deliberately chose a phrase with a certain amount of inherent ambiguity, Emerton argues that the court is therefore empowered 'to declare legislation or other governmental acts unconstitutional if they unduly burden political communication or otherwise interfere with direct choice'. For Emerton, this 'is simply a particular instance of the courts' general power to ensure that Australian

[50] *ACTV v Commonwealth* (1992) 177 CLR 106; *Lange v Australian Broadcasting Corporation* (1997) 189 CLR 520. See also Glenn Patmore, 'The Right to Participate: Revisiting *Roach* and *Rowe*' in Glenn Patmore and Kim Rubenstein (eds), *Law and Democracy: Contemporary Questions* (Australian National University Press 2014).

[51] See for example, Nicholas Aroney, 'Towards the "Best Explanation" of the Constitution: Text, Structure, History and Principle in *Roach v Electoral Commissioner*' (2011) 30(1) *University of Queensland Law Journal* 145; James Allan, 'The Three "R's" of Judicial Activism: *Roach*, *Rowe* and (No)'riginalism' (2012) 36(2) *Melbourne University Law Review* 743; Greg Craven, 'The High Court of Australia: A Study in the Abuse of Power' (1999) 22(1) *University of New South Wales Law Journal* 216, 222; Jeffrey Goldsworthy, 'The High Court, Implied Rights and Constitutional Change' (1995) 39(3) *Quadrant* 46; Anne Twomey, '*Rowe v Electoral Commissioner* – Evolution or Creationism?' (2012) 31(2) *University of Queensland Law Journal* 181; Jeffrey Goldsworthy, 'Original Meanings and Contemporary Understandings in Constitutional Interpretation' in HP Lee and Peter Gerangelos (eds), *Constitutional Advancement in a Frozen Continent: Essays in Honour of George Winterton* (Federation Press 2009).

[52] Emerton (n 49 above) 193.

organs of government act within power'.[53] While the *Constitution* confers on Parliament broad authority to flexibly determine the nature of the franchise, the *Constitution* also confers on courts power to adjudicate matters arising under the *Constitution* and therefore to determine what is meant by a 'direct choice by the people' thus identifying the appropriate limits on parliamentary power. Crucially, in Emerton's view, judicial inquiry into the constitutional meaning of this key phrase need not be limited to legal inquiry. It might legitimately involve sociological and political inquiry.[54] This is where divergence of opinion occurs.

Emerton points out that 'the people' can refer to a zoological kind, a philosophical kind, a social and political kind, or a legally constituted kind.[55] He acknowledges that the term may indeed appropriately be interpreted as a legal kind,[56] but argues it may also legitimately refer to a social and political kind.[57] Emerton's analysis rates the two most relevant types of 'referential chains' – one concerning legal facts and one concerning sociological and political facts – as equally acceptable approaches to interpretation of the phrase.[58] Yet if any referential chain is acceptable, then constitutional meanings may be highly changeable.[59]

Whether one prefers a confined or open number of interpretational choices in such instances is connected to whether one is predominantly in favour of 'originalism'[60] as the appropriate method of constitutional construction, or 'living originalism'[61] (also referred to as 'evolutionary originalism'[62] or the 'living tree' approach).[63] Balkin's living originalism distinguishes four types of

[53] ibid 194–95.

[54] See also Jonathan Crowe, 'The Narrative Model of Constitutional Implications: A Defence of *Roach v Electoral Commissioner* (2019) 41(1) *University of New South Wales Law Journal* 91.

[55] Emerton (n 49 above) 195–96.

[56] 'The relevant evidence is found in ss 8, 10, 30, 31 and 51(xxxvi) of the *Constitution*. These provisions establish, as the default Commonwealth franchise, that pertaining under the law of each State for the more numerous house of parliament in that State, but confer upon the Commonwealth Parliament the power, subject to the *Constitution*, to displace the operation of these State laws and to settle the franchise for Commonwealth elections … It may be … that the framers took themselves to have referred to a kind constituted by the conjoint operation of State and Commonwealth laws according to the rules set forth in these sections of the *Constitution*': ibid 196.

[57] ibid 196–97.

[58] ibid 198.

[59] See also George Winterton, 'Extra-constitutional Notions in Australian Constitutional Law' (1986) 16 *Federal Law Review* 223.

[60] For an explanation of originalism, see Jeffrey Goldsworthy, 'Originalism in Constitutional Interpretation' (1997) 25(1) *Federal Law Review* 1.

[61] Jack Balkin, *Living Originalism* (Harvard University Press 2011); Brendan Lim, 'Review Essay: An Australian Reads "Living Originalism"' (2012) 34(4) *Sydney Law Review* 809; Jeffrey Goldsworthy, 'Constitutional Cultures, Democracy, and Unwritten Principles' [2012] (3) *University of Illinois Law Review* 683.

[62] Jeremy Kirk, 'Constitutional Implications (I): Nature, Legitimacy, Classification, Examples' (2000) 24(3) *Melbourne University Law Review* 645, 660.

[63] Although there are differences in how these doctrines are explained: Bradley W Miller, 'Beguiled by Metaphors: The "Living Tree" and Originalist Constitutional Interpretation in Canada' (2009) 22(2) *Canadian Journal of Law and Jurisprudence* 331. See also Allan (n 51 above) 747.

textual devices that are employed within constitutions:[64] rules, standards, principles, and silences.[65] Where there are constitutional principles, standards, and silences, as opposed to rules, there is a wide degree of variation in acceptable interpretation. As Lim explains, 'the choice to enact a standard or principle, instead of a rule, is a choice to delegate rather than to constrain'.[66] But delegate to whom?

If the delegation is to the courts, this will give rise to uncertainty and change in the interpretation of constitutional clauses over time – driven by litigation. Lim explains that: 'Balkin not only tolerates this indeterminacy, he embraces it.'[67] Indeterminacy is to be expected under living originalism, because a judge's 'scope of legitimate choice increases as one moves away from the narrowest versions of originalism on the interpretative spectrum'.[68] Where constitutional words are ambiguous, Balkin does not insist that one interpretation must prevail over another. If the delegation is to Parliament, however, the scope for change and indeterminacy is also wide, but the change is driven politically – by legislative evolution rather than changing judicial interpretation.

Lim correctly identifies the phrase 'directly chosen by the people' as entailing significant indeterminacy. It is a standard, not a rule.[69] The key question is: to which arm of government is determination of the standard delegated? This may be central in ascertaining whether the *Constitution* allows legislative scope to implement Indigenous reserved seats and whether that legislation is likely to survive a constitutional challenge.

D. The Significance of *Roach* and *Rowe*

The *Roach* and *Rowe* decisions, contrary to earlier cases, seem to view the phrase 'directly chosen by the people' as a delegation to the judiciary, not Parliament. Yet the reasoning supporting this conclusion is unclear. In *Roach*, Gleeson CJ agreed with Barwick CJ that the *Constitution* 'reflects a high level of acceptance' of parliamentary supremacy in 'the scheme of government': 'Nowhere is this more plainly illustrated than in the extent to which the Constitution left it to parliament to prescribe the form of our system of representative democracy.'[70] Gleeson CJ observed that universal adult suffrage in Australia 'was the result of legislative action'.[71] But despite acknowledging the previous primacy of Parliament in determining electoral arrangements, Gleeson CJ reasoned that,

[64] Balkin (n 61 above).
[65] For a good summary, see Lim (n 61 above) 812.
[66] ibid 816.
[67] ibid 814.
[68] Kirk (n 62 above) 560.
[69] Lim (n 61 above) 821, 826–27.
[70] *Roach* (n 24 above) 173.
[71] ibid 4.

over time, the meanings of constitutional words can change because the historical facts informing them have changed.

To support this conclusion, Gleeson CJ cited the example of 'foreign power' under section 44(i) which, in 1901, excluded the UK, but which, after *Sue v Hill*,[72] came to include the UK because of Australia's changed relationship with the UK.[73] A word such as 'alien' now also has an altered constitutional meaning for the same reason.[74] Gleeson CJ in *Roach* found that the meaning of 'directly chosen by the people' had similarly changed due to altered historical facts. Agreeing with the minority judgments of McTiernan and Jacobs JJ in *McKinlay*,[75] Gleeson CJ held that

> universal adult suffrage was a long established fact, and that anything less could not now be described as a choice by the people … we have reached a stage in the evolution of representative government which produces that consequence … the words of ss 7 and 24, because of changed historical circumstances including legislative history, have come to be a constitutional protection of the right to vote.[76]

French CJ concurred in *Rowe*:[77]

> The content of the constitutional concept of 'chosen by the people' has evolved since 1901 and is now informed by the universal adult-citizen franchise which is prescribed by Commonwealth law. The development of the franchise was authorised by ss 8 and 30 of the Constitution, read with s 51(xxxvi). Implicit in that authority was the possibility that the constitutional concept would acquire, as it did, a more democratic content than existed at federation. That content, being constitutional in character, although it may be subject to adjustment from time to time, cannot now be diminished.[78]

French CJ referred to legislative development of voting rights as evidence of what Gleeson CJ described as the now 'irreversible evolution' of constitutional meaning. This irreversible evolution is said to be driven by legislative development, reflecting 'a persistent view by the elected representatives of the people of what the term "chosen by the people" requires'.[79] Yet this is confusing, because the facts in *Roach* and *Rowe* demonstrate that the view of elected politicians had become less persistent – because legislation was enacted to curtail or limit voting rights, which the court then invalidated on the basis that it was contrary to the irreversible evolution. A potential criticism of the High Court's reasoning, then, is that the Court took itself to be a better interpreter of the views

[72] *Sue v Hill* (1999) 199 CLR 462.
[73] *Roach* (n 24 above) 173–74.
[74] *Nolan v Minister for Immigration and Ethnic Affairs* (1988) 165 CLR 178. See also Emerton (n 49 above) 189.
[75] *McKinlay* (n 8 above) 36.
[76] *Roach* (n 24 above) 174.
[77] As part of the majority in *Rowe v Electoral Commissioner* (2010) 243 CLR 1.
[78] ibid 18.
[79] ibid.

of elected representatives than the elected representatives themselves. In effect, the High Court found that the Parliament had become bound by limits forged through the legislation enacted by earlier Parliaments – a move that does not seem supported by the constitutional text. While the apparent incongruence can perhaps be explained as the majority adopting a 'living originalist' approach to constitutional construction of the words 'directly chosen by the people' as a constitutional standard, entailing 'words of generality' which are properly 'contingent upon contemporary construction',[80] the reasoning is nonetheless difficult to comprehend.

Hayne J, supported by Heydon J in the minority in *Roach*, agreed that the phrase embodies a standard, but doubted that this entails a meaning that can fundamentally change over time.[81] They suggested that the content of the standard is political (what Emerton would refer to as 'legal') and thus to be determined by Parliament. The majority seemed to agree that the standard is political and hence evolving, yet conclude that the political standard may be determined by the courts: the relevant political standard has irreversibly evolved through legislation, thus permitting the High Court to intervene to adjudicate its limits. Emerton observes that the majority attributed to the constitutional framers 'in their use of *people*, the intention to refer to a kind constituted primarily non-legally, by facts of civic engagement'. This approach acknowledges that: 'Parliament is to enjoy a margin of appreciation in respect of these facts, but is not to be the constitutor of them.'[82] On this understanding, there can be a political and social reality with respect to 'the people' that is independent of parliamentary action. Thus, for Emerton, it is acceptable for the courts to adjudicate questions of who 'the people' are, as a political and sociological question rather than just as a legal one, even if that yields a practical result that diminishes parliamentary supremacy over electoral arrangements.[83]

The non-legally constituted interpretation of 'directly chosen by the people' adopted by the High Court increases uncertainty as to whether Parliament would be within its powers to legislate for Indigenous reserved seats. If the phrase is given a legally constituted meaning, then Parliament retains more flexible authority to legislate who gets to vote and how and what a direct choice by the people is to mean. But under a living originalist interpretation it might be argued that the Indigenous seats are not 'directly chosen by the people' because 'the people' must include all the people of the State for each Senate seat, not just Indigenous people, and thus that the reserved seats are inconsistent with the *Constitution*. It might be argued that the franchise has evolved to a point where it cannot be fundamentally changed, or that the 'facts of civic engagement' of Indigenous people within the electoral regime now prevent Parliament

[80] Lim (n 61 above) 826–27.
[81] *Roach* (n 24 above) 219.
[82] Emerton (n 49 above) 199.
[83] See also Crowe (n 54 above).

from treating Indigenous people differently within electoral law. By contrast, a strictly legally constituted interpretation would probably leave it to Parliament to define by electoral law the details of what is meant by 'directly chosen by the people' in the changing social and political circumstances.

That said, even under a sociological and political interpretation of the phrase, the High Court would likely take into account the intended inclusive nature of the Indigenous reserved seats as an action to enhance Indigenous political participation rather than deny it. The case law demonstrates that the High Court usually adopts an interpretation curtailing parliamentary power and flexibility as a way of defending rights or preventing exclusion from democratic participation, rather than to prevent active inclusion of a marginalised group.[84] Given the inclusive purpose of reserved seats, the High Court would likely be less interventionist.

E. In Favour of a Legally Constituted Interpretation of 'Directly Chosen by the People'

The approach adopted by the High Court in *Roach* and *Rowe*, although achieving inclusive policy outcomes, is arguably not the most compelling interpretation of the words 'directly chosen by the people' in the constitutional context. I argue this on four grounds. First, there are other constitutional clauses which indicate that the phrase is best interpreted by reference to legally constituted kinds, not sociological and political kinds. Second, the plenary power conferred on Parliaments to drive electoral evolution logically means the franchise must be able to retract as well as expand – it cannot be irreversible. Third, the evolving meaning of 'foreign power' and 'alien' is of limited relevance as a useful analogy for interpretation of this constitutional phrase: the changed legal meaning of 'foreign power' and 'alien' is incorrectly equated with the changed sociological and political meaning of 'directly chosen by the people'. Fourth, there are persuasive policy arguments with respect to maintaining legal certainty, equality before the law and constitutional authority that highlight the downsides of excessive indeterminacy in constitutional meaning and therefore support a legally constrained interpretational approach.

(i) Other Constitutional Clauses Indicate that the Phrase is Best Interpreted as a Legally Constituted Kind

The construction of the voting 'people' as a legally constituted kind is coherent with the *Constitution* as a whole,[85] which delegates to State and federal

[84] *Murphy v Electoral Commissioner* (2016) 261 CLR 28, 73. See also *Roach* (n 24 above); *Rowe* (n 77 above).

[85] As Hayne J argues, it 'should go without saying that the provisions of ss 7, 8, 24 and 30 must all be read in the context provided by the whole of the Constitution': *Roach* (n 24 above) 211.

Parliaments the authority to determine the details of the franchise and electoral law. Section 30 authorises the States to determine their own franchise, until the Commonwealth Parliament intervenes.[86] Section 29 allows the States to determine their own electoral divisions, until the Commonwealth legislates otherwise. Section 51(xxxvi) empowers the Commonwealth to legislate with respect to 'matters in respect of which this Constitution makes provision until the Parliament otherwise provides'. Many other clauses also delegate to Parliament power to determine the franchise.[87] Even section 128 acknowledges that 'the qualification of electors of members of the House of Representatives' may not be 'uniform throughout the Commonwealth', demonstrating that the States could have retained different voting rules.[88] All these provisions must be weighed against the restraints in sections 7 and 24.[89] Hayne J observed in *Roach*:

> Because the power to delineate the franchise was given to the parliament, the ambit of exceptions to or disqualifications from the franchise was a matter for the parliament itself, so long always as the generality of 'directly chosen by the people' was preserved.[90]

The historical context supports this interpretation. Future parliaments were left to determine the franchise because the drafters of the *Constitution* could not agree on who should be allowed to vote. There was particular disagreement about including women in the franchise.[91] The disagreement was reflected in various remaining constitutional clauses, particularly sections 25 and 41. Section 25 provides a disincentive for the States to ban particular races from voting,[92] reflecting the historical reality that States sometimes did this. The section demonstrates, in my view, that banning races from voting is a legislative action contemplated as possible within Australia's constitutional system, and weakens the argument that the franchise has now constitutionally evolved to mandate universality.[93] Twomey notes that the High Court turned a 'blind eye' to the implications of section 25 in declaring a universal franchise.[94]

[86] In *Roach*, Hayne J states that: 'The drafting history of what became s 30 shows that the parliament's power under that section was given so that the parliament itself could determine the franchise upon which it was elected. That is, the purpose of the conferral of legislative power under s 30 was to provide the parliament with the power to determine which groups should be given the franchise': (2007) 233 CLR 162, 206.

[87] These are listed in Hayne J's judgment: ibid 211.

[88] ibid 211–12.

[89] ibid 212.

[90] ibid 206.

[91] 'the debate centred upon women's suffrage, and whether the Constitution should conclude that issue by providing for adult suffrage. The outcome of the Adelaide convention was to adopt a clause which, in relevant respects, was in the form submitted to the convention. The issue of women's suffrage was left for the new Federal Parliament to decide': ibid 209.

[92] See Twomey, 'Obituary for s 25' (n 28 above) 126–28.

[93] *McKinlay* (n 8 above) 44, 62; *Singh v Commonwealth* (2004) 222 CLR 322, 368 [107] (McHugh J); *Hwang v Commonwealth* (2005) 222 ALR 83, 88–89 [16], [17] (McHugh J).

[94] See Twomey, 'Obituary for s 25' (n 28 above) 137.

Similarly, section 41 demonstrates that the universal franchise is not constitutionally required.[95] In *Pearson*, section 41 was described as a transitional provision that no longer has any effect,[96] making it a 'mere historical artefact'.[97] But Crowe and Stephenson observe the irony in the fact that, in declaring a universal franchise, '*Roach* and *Rowe* make only passing reference to the one constitutional provision that enshrines an express right to vote' – namely section 41.[98] Section 41 was perhaps ignored in the judicial reasoning because its content demonstrates that the Commonwealth right to vote only applies 'while the right continues' under State law, indicating that the Constitution contemplates that the franchise, once legislatively expanded, can be retracted. It may be that section 41 has 'vanished from the constitutional discourse'[99] because it does not fit with the High Court's theory of irreversible constitutional enfranchisement.

When all such clauses are read together in the constitutional context, it is apparent that the franchise can be legislatively contracted. In *McKinlay*, Gibbs and Mason JJ supported this view, finding that sections 25, 30, 41 and 128 demonstrate that the *Constitution* allows for disenfranchisement on the basis of sex, race and property.[100] The main clear restraint imposed by the *Constitution* is therefore arguably a political one, to be effected through democratic procedures and federal checks and balances.[101] As Aroney argues, 'the Constitution *does* contain a safeguard against electoral abuse: that safeguard is the supervisory role of the federal Parliament'.[102] This understanding is in keeping with Australia's political approach to rights protection and seems the more persuasive legal interpretation. Lim points out that under Balkin's theory of living originalism in constitutional construction, 'we may articulate and supplement the constitutional text through construction, but we may not contradict it'.[103] Even though the phrase 'directly chosen by the people' is more like a standard than a rule, it must still be interpreted and applied consistently with the rest of the *Constitution*. The *Constitution* as a whole indicates that the standard is for Parliament to determine and evolve as necessary.

(ii) Parliaments have Plenary Power to Drive Electoral Evolution – So the Franchise can Expand or Retract

The view that maintains Parliament's power to determine the franchise is consistent with Isaacs J's description of the power to make laws with respect

[95] *King v Jones* (1972) 128 CLR 221. Twomey explains the relationship between ss 25 and 41: Twomey, 'Obituary for s 25' (n 28 above) 129–30.
[96] *Pearson* (n 35 above).
[97] Crowe and Stephenson (n 23 above) 208.
[98] ibid 207.
[99] ibid.
[100] *McKinlay* (n 8 above) 44, 62.
[101] Aroney (n 51 above) 161.
[102] ibid.
[103] Lim (n 61 above) 811.

to elections as a 'plenary power'.[104] As French CJ describes, this means 'it is a power subject to the limitations imposed by the Constitution'.[105] The words 'directly chosen by the people' do impose limitations. What is less clear is what can reasonably be read into those limitations, or how it is that these words can refer to 'the people' as a legally constituted kind (determined by Parliament's electoral laws) at one time, and then a sociologically and politically constituted kind at another. The proposition that electoral law can evolve in one direction but not in another has not been adequately explained.[106]

The nature of plenary power is such that laws can be enacted and repealed. Goldsworthy notes that courts since the nineteenth century have characterised Australian Parliaments as legislatures akin to those in Britain.[107] The orthodox view is that the words 'for the peace, order and good government' in section 51 (and the words 'for the peace, welfare and good government' that appear in some State Constitutions) indicate 'the widest law-making powers appropriate to a sovereign'.[108] In a general sense, the Commonwealth Parliament is thus bound by the British doctrine of parliamentary sovereignty except where constitutional provisions displace it.[109] Australian parliamentary supremacy therefore adheres to the principle that Parliament cannot bind its successors,[110] unless there are constitutional provisions which indicate otherwise. This principle appears incompatible with evolutionary irreversibility through legislative action.[111]

The majority reasoning applied in *Roach* and *Rowe*, however, would seem to indicate that legislative reform can sometimes amount to constitutional reform in matters of electoral rights, and that the 'statutory franchise' has become a constitutional franchise. This seems to present a back-door avenue for constitutional entrenchment through legislative reform, in contradiction to section 128 of the *Constitution*, which requires a referendum for constitutional amendment.[112]

[104] *Smith v Oldham* (1912) 15 CLR 355, 363, quoted in *Rowe* (n 77 above) 14 [8].

[105] *Rowe* (n 77 above) 14.

[106] See also Twomey, '*Rowe v Electoral Commissioner*' (n 51 above) 184, 188.

[107] Jeffrey Goldsworthy, 'The Constitutional Protection of Rights in Australia' in Greg Craven (ed), *Australian Federation* (Melbourne University Press 1992) 152.

[108] *Ibralebbe v R* [1964] AC 900, 923 (PC). But see Ian D Killey, 'Peace, Order and Good Government: A Limitation on Legislative Competence' (1989) 17(1) *Melbourne University Law Review* 24, 42–43.

[109] Goldsworthy, 'Constitutional Protection of Rights' (n 107 above) 152.

[110] See also Jeffrey Goldsworthy, *Parliamentary Sovereignty: Contemporary Debates* (Cambridge University Press 2010); Gerard Carney, 'An Overview of Manner and Form in Australia' (1989) 5 *Queensland University of Technology Law Journal* 69, 70–71.

[111] Twomey agrees that irreversibility is 'contrary to the plenary nature of the legislative power conferred by the Constitution': Twomey, '*Rowe v Electoral Commissioner*' (n 51 above) 202.

[112] As Twomey observes, the decision in *Rowe* undermines, 'both the principle of parliamentary sovereignty and the role of the people in constitutional change by effectively permitting the Parliament, through the enactment of legislation, to change the meaning of the Constitution and to entrench laws without a referendum under s 128 of the Constitution'. The reasoning 'entails the attribution of power to the Parliament to change the meaning of the Constitution': Twomey, '*Rowe v Electoral Commissioner*' (n 51 above) 181, 188.

A statutory franchise, in contrast to any constitutional one, should be inherently flexible. Yet in *Roach* and *Rowe* it was concluded that inherent in the authority conferred upon Parliament to determine that franchise, was the possibility that the franchise 'would acquire, as it did, a more democratic content than existed at federation' and that: 'That content, being constitutional in character, although it may be subject to adjustment from time to time, cannot now be diminished.'[113]

Hayne J rejects this analysis in *Rowe*, noting that the evolutionary expansion of the franchise, which was driven by parliaments, does not permit the further conclusion that the *Constitution* itself has developed or that the concept of representative government has 'evolved into a constitutional norm'.[114] Heydon J similarly disagrees with the notion of evolutionary irreversibility in *Roach*, observing that the *Australian Constitution* allows Parliament to adapt and expand electoral policy, but also to retreat and retract it if 'change was found wanting in light of experience'. To deny this flexibility, his Honour suggests, would encourage governments to become 'gerontocratic and ossified, faithful to only one technique of government', a trait ironically more characteristic of 'totalitarian regimes'.[115] These minority arguments, while they may deliver less inclusive policy outcomes, nonetheless appear the more legally and constitutionally compelling. Aroney observes the 'circularity and indeed vacuity in the proposition that the standards to be applied as constitutional requirements are themselves to be determined by reference to the standards adopted by the Parliament over the course of time'.[116] There is similar circularity in the argument that a standard evolved by Parliament may be used to justify the High Court overruling Parliament's attempt to further adjust and evolve that standard.

(iii) The Evolving Meanings of 'Foreign Power' and 'Alien' are of Limited Relevance

The cited analogy between the changed meaning of 'foreign power' in the *Constitution* and the supposedly changed meaning of 'directly chosen by the people' is arguably unpersuasive.[117] The altered historical circumstances in relation to Australia's relationship with the UK are not accurately analogous to the changing historical circumstances with respect to enfranchisement in Australia. The changed meaning of 'foreign power' is a legitimate example of a legally constituted kind whose meaning changed because of altered *legal* facts. It is not

[113] *Rowe* (n 77 above) 18. For discussion on how legislation has informed the Court's understanding of 'the people' under the *Constitution*, see Elisa Arcioni, 'Democracy and the Constitution: The People Deciding the Identity of "the People"' in Glenn Patmore and Kim Rubenstein (eds), *Law and Democracy: Contemporary Questions* (ANU Press 2014) 14–18.

[114] *Rowe* (n 77 above) 70–71.

[115] *Roach* (n 24) 224.

[116] Aroney (n 51 above) 161.

[117] Hayne J picks up on this weakness in *Roach* (n 24 above) 219–20, as does James Allan in Allan (n 51 above) 766–67.

an example of a sociologically and politically constituted kind, the meaning of which changed because *sociological and political* facts changed. Gleeson CJ's use of the term 'historical facts' to make this analogy in *Roach* is problematically ambiguous.[118]

The meaning of 'foreign power' changed because legal facts changed (although sociological and political facts might have changed as well). Initially, the British colonies of Australia were subject to the legislative authority of the British Parliament. In 1931, the UK relinquished its legislative authority over Australia's Commonwealth Parliament through the *Statute of Westminster*, which provided legal recognition of the independence of the Crown's dominions.[119] In 1942, Australia ratified the free and equal status of its government.[120] Then, in 1986, the *Australia Acts* amended the *Statute of Westminster*[121] and gave the States full independence from the UK,[122] severing remaining legal links.[123] With the passing of the *Australia Acts*, the legislative power of the UK with respect to Australia was totally abdicated.[124] Australia's constitutional relationship with the UK was thereby irreversibly changed due to a specific set of uniquely altered and irreversible legal facts. The UK Parliament cannot legislate to get the relationship back to how it was, because UK laws no longer affect Australia. This alters the meaning of relevant Australian constitutional provisions, which must now be interpreted in light of the changed legal facts under the *Australia Acts* and the *Statute of Westminster*; documents of quasi-constitutional status which contribute to Australia's constitutional framework.

The irreversible nature of the *Australia Acts* reform, an action which required the concurrence of all State parliaments as well as UK legislation, is different to the purported constitutional evolution of the franchise under ordinary electoral law.[125] The *Australia Act* and the *Statute of Westminster* are quasi-constitutional because they are effectively entrenched and subject to special amendment requirements. The reforms enacted under those Acts are irreversible in a way ordinary electoral legislation is not. While the meanings of 'foreign

[118] Allan highlights the mix of 'factual determinations and the evaluative moral sentiments' utilised in this analogy: Allan (n 51 above) 767. See also Twomey, '*Rowe v Electoral Commissioner*' (n 51 above) 184–85.

[119] Anne Twomey, *The Australia Acts 1986: Australia's Statutes of Independence* (The Federation Press 2010) 21–23; Leslie Zines, *The High Court and the Constitution* (5th edn, The Federation Press 2008) 431, 439.

[120] This was achieved through the *Statute of Westminster Adoption Act 1942* (Cth), which overrode the *Colonial Laws Validity Act 1865* (UK).

[121] *Australia Act 1986* (Cth) s 12.

[122] See James McConvill, 'The United Kingdom is a Foreign Power: *Sue v Hill*' (1999–2000) 4(2) *Deakin Law Review* 151, 156.

[123] *Australia Act 1986*, ss 2, 10, 12. Section 1 of the Act states: 'No Act of the Parliament of the United Kingdom passed after the commencement of this Act shall extend, or be deemed to extend, to the Commonwealth, to a State or to a Territory as part of the law of the Commonwealth, of the State or of the Territory.'

[124] Zines (n 119 above) 439.

[125] See also Twomey, '*Rowe v Electoral Commissioner*' (n 51 above) 184–85.

power' and 'alien' indeed changed over time, their meanings stayed within the legally constituted camp. By contrast, the changed meaning of 'directly chosen by the people' switched categories from a legally constituted kind to a sociologically and politically constituted kind. The analogy is therefore weak.

(iv) Legal Certainty, Equality before the Law, Maintaining Constitutional Authority

Regardless of the desirability of the policy outcome, the protection of voting rights found in *Roach* and *Rowe* arguably relies on uncertain legal reasoning. The outcome may undermine advocacy for constitutional entrenchment of rights protections on the uncertain basis that such protections are already implied. Yet the protection offered may be transitory because, as Twomey notes, it 'rests upon implications drawn by the High Court which may change over time'.[126] There is little to prevent the High Court at some future stage going back to an originalist interpretation and diminishing implied voting rights. The approach leaves rights protection dependent upon High Court interpretational trends, rather than parliamentary trends – and the Court's changed approach to interpretation cannot be said to be an irreversible evolution. It also relies on citizens having the means to go to court to argue for their implied rights, which is a slow and costly process with demonstrably unpredictable outcomes. As a result, judicially implied voting rights protections have tended to emerge too late in the day – after decades of severe discrimination against Indigenous peoples. How is it just that a universal franchise was declared by the High Court to be constitutionally required only when it had already come into existence due to political evolution, but not decades ago when many Indigenous Australians and others were being denied the vote and thus were seriously in need of such protection? The relevant constitutional clauses have not changed in the meantime; only High Court interpretation of the *Constitution* has changed. The result creates a sense of temporal inequality under Australia's constitutional law. While the outcome may (on some arguments) be fairer for vulnerable citizens today, it makes more stark the unfairness of the past – yet those subject to past injustice suffered under the same *Constitution*.

On one hand, the approach employed in *Roach* and *Rowe* seems to overempower the High Court to subtly undertake constitutional reform through judicial interpretation. On the other hand, it in effect allows for constitutional reform via legislative change, and in doing so offers a way for legislators to bypass the requirements of section 128. As Twomey explains, the approach 'gives power to a Parliament effectively to bind future Parliaments by expanding participation in elections even further'.[127] This is troubling, because it is not just the end result of rights protection that is important: the system of rights

[126] Twomey, 'Obituary for s 25' (n 28 above) 138–39.
[127] Twomey, '*Rowe v Electoral Commissioner*' (n 51 above) 202.

protection is also important and should be consistent in the protection that it offers.[128] Professor George Winterton has pointed out the risks of judicial overuse of extra-constitutional notions, which in effect may enable covert constitutional amendment.[129] For Winterton, the rule of law depends not only on outcomes, but also on the means by which they are achieved: 'The rule of law and the integrity of judicial interpretation of the Constitution should not be sacrificed for anything – even a result which, on a particular occasion, may promote human or civil rights.'[130] To do so, Winterton warned, could undermine public confidence in the judiciary but also the *Constitution* as a source of knowable law, potentially weakening the *Constitution*'s ability to operate as an authoritative limit on government power.[131] These factors should be considered in determining the best approach to interpretation of the phrase 'directly chosen by the people'.

IV. WHAT DOES THIS MEAN FOR RESERVED INDIGENOUS SEATS?

In *Roach* and *Rowe*, the High Court demonstrated an inclination to interpret the phrase 'directly chosen by the people' in a way that protects voting rights, by incorporating the idea of an irreversible universal franchise. So how would the Court view a special legislative inclusion of Indigenous peoples through reserved Indigenous seats? Would the reserved Indigenous seats be considered sympathetically? This is hard to predict, but probably.

Under the *Constitution*, a new Indigenous power or the current Race Power would provide Parliament with authority to enact the Indigenous reserved seats law, subject to the *Constitution*. Absent a racial non-discrimination clause in the *Constitution*,[132] Parliament's power to legislate with respect to Indigenous people would remain broad. From a policy perspective, the law establishing Indigenous reserved seats could be presented as a special measure to ensure the full participation and enjoyment of human rights of a particularly disadvantaged group. Parliament could indicate that the legislation is intended as a special measure in the Act's preamble, as it did with the *Native Title Act 1993* (Cth).[133] But in the event of a challenge the court would consider constitutional limitations, including those arising under sections 7 and 24.

[128] George Winterton, 'Justice Kirby's Coda in *Durham*' (2002) 13(3) *Public Law Review* 165, 170.

[129] Winterton, 'Extra-constitutional Notions' (n 59) 238–39.

[130] Winterton, 'Justice Kirby's Coda' (n 128 above) 170.

[131] See also Nicholas Aroney, 'The Implied Rights Revolution: Balancing Means and Ends?' in HP Lee and Peter Gerangelos (eds), *Constitutional Advancement in a Frozen Continent: Essays in Honour of George Winterton* (The Federation Press 2009) 175.

[132] This reform option was discussed in Chapter 3 of this volume.

[133] The preamble to the *Native Title Act* states: 'The people of Australia intend: (a) to rectify the consequences of past injustices by the special measures contained in this Act, announced at the time of introduction of this Act into the Parliament, or agreed on by the Parliament from time to time, for securing the adequate advancement and protection of Aboriginal peoples and Torres Strait Islanders.'

Comments in *Rowe* suggest that the High Court will intervene to protect the right to vote over Parliament's constitutional imperative to legislate to determine electoral processes, where 'electoral laws effect change adverse to the exercise of the entitlement to vote'.[134] This probably means that the Court is less likely to intervene where a change *promotes* participation of a vulnerable group.[135] This view may be bolstered by the 2016 *Murphy* decision, where the Court distinguished *Roach* and *Rowe*. Gageler J explained the decision not to invalidate the electoral law in question as informed by the fact that there were no vulnerable 'minority interests' in need of protection:

> Unlike *Roach* and *Rowe*, this is not a case in which provisions impugned have expanded an exclusion from the franchise ... Extrinsic material in *Roach* showed that the new disqualification from voting of all persons serving any sentence of imprisonment for an offence could be foreseen to result in the disenfranchisement from time to time of perhaps up to 10,000 persons, many of them indigenous, who were serving short terms of imprisonment yet otherwise entitled to vote. The agreed facts in *Rowe* demonstrated that the new contraction of the cut-off for enrolment to the date of the issue of the writs resulted at the 2010 general election in disenfranchising about 100,000 persons ...
>
> The point of recalling those circumstances is not to dwell on the absolute numbers of those disenfranchised but rather to indicate the tendency of the disenfranchisement in each of *Roach* and *Rowe* to freeze out of the political process discrete minority interests. That tendency engaged to a significant degree the central concern underlying the constitutional tempering of the Parliament's wide and flexible authority to determine the qualification of electors and the method of election through insistence on a judicially enforceable core requirement that senators and members of the House of Representatives remain directly chosen by the people.[136]

It may be, therefore, that the High Court would not invalidate reserved seats legislation, because the law presents a proactive *inclusion* of a vulnerable minority, not an *exclusion*. According to Murray, *Murphy* may also indicate that 'the current High Court bench will be more deferential to Parliament's ability to legislate in the electoral context',[137] perhaps increasing the likelihood that the High Court will not intervene regarding reserved seats.

An interesting question would arise if Parliament decided that the reserved Indigenous seats were no longer needed, and a litigant challenged the amending legislation. It is uncertain whether the High Court would then intervene to protect the reserved seats, on the basis that they were an irreversible evolution. If special measures principles were applied, this would not be the case, so long as the legislative amendment did not disenfranchise Indigenous people in any way.

[134] *Rowe* (n 77 above) 19.

[135] Though it must also be remembered that a litigant may try to argue that non-Indigenous citizens are somehow discriminated against by the implementation of Indigenous reserved seats, and the strength of such an argument would depend on the details of the electoral reform.

[136] *Murphy* (n 84 above) 73 [105]–[107].

[137] Murray (n 41 above) 898.

A special measure is meant to be temporary; it is only supposed to last as long as the particular disadvantage being remedied persists.[138] But if voting rights principles were applied, it is uncertain whether the judiciary would intervene on the basis that the seats constituted an irreversible evolution.

V. CONCLUSION

There are various approaches which might be taken in implementing reserved seats. Michael Mansell argues for 12 Indigenous Senate seats.[139] Geoffrey Robertson QC suggests at least four.[140] Chesterman suggests five or six representatives would be proportionate and proposes various possible models, but recommends that the Indigenous reserved seats be allocated in the House of Representatives.[141] Any reform would need to comply with the relevant constitutional constraints, including the nexus requirement under section 24.[142] As well as negotiating the constitutional hurdles, the model would need to be politically palatable to be implemented.

Depending on which model was preferred and which method of constitutional construction predominates in the High Court, the legislation implementing the reserved seats may or may not survive a constitutional challenge. A certain way of ensuring legal validity would be to amend the *Constitution* through a referendum to establish Indigenous reserved seats. But then the seats would be inflexibly entrenched, which may not be desirable, unless the constitutional provision stated that the number of Indigenous seats could change according to population fluctuation, like in section 24. It is also questionable whether such a constitutional reform would be politically viable.

A strategic consideration is whether reserved Indigenous seats may unhelpfully confine Indigenous voices to the structures of party politics, dampening their independence and the extent to which Indigenous interests are fulsomely represented.[143] As Mansell notes, party loyalty is 'a dilemma for Aboriginal politicians … if they are members of a mainstream political party they are often

[138] *International Convention on the Elimination of All Forms of Racial Discrimination*, opened for signature 21 December 1965, 660 UNTS 195 (entered into force 4 January 1969) art 1(4) states: 'Special measures taken for the sole purpose of securing adequate advancement of certain racial or ethnic groups or individuals requiring such protection as may be necessary in order to ensure such groups or individuals equal enjoyment or exercise of human rights and fundamental freedoms shall not be deemed racial discrimination, provided, however, that such measures do not, as a consequence, lead to the maintenance of separate rights for different racial groups and that they shall not be continued after the objectives for which they were taken have been achieved.'

[139] Mansell (n 2 above) 35–41.

[140] ibid viii.

[141] Chesterman (n 4 above) 278–85. Models are also explored in Evans and Hill (n 3 above).

[142] Mansell (n 2 above) 37–38.

[143] Although note that, in New Zealand, the formation of the Māori Party has enabled Māori to wield increased political power.

silenced by party demands for solidarity'. Mansell warns that 'Designated seats may only shift the dilemma.'[144] Even if Indigenous reserved seats were one day implemented, therefore, it would still be useful to create a First Nations representative, consultative and advisory institution that is outside Parliament, so that Indigenous people can engage independently with Parliament and government on Indigenous affairs – including those decision-makers in the theoretical reserved seats. Reilley suggests that an Indigenous representative body external to Parliament may be more independent than reserved seats, because 'A representative body that exists outside the mainstream political institutions can question the legitimacy of the institution in making laws for Indigenous peoples. It can refuse legislative compromises and demand a better deal.'[145] Notably, New Zealand has both: reserved Māori seats and the Māori Council operating as an independent Māori voice outside Parliament.[146] For reasons of political viability and achievability, I do not advocate reserved Indigenous seats here. Implementation of reserved seats is a constitutionally complex question. It is not what the Referendum Council recommends, nor what advocates of the Uluru Statement are seeking.

My view is that a more targeted Indigenous participatory mechanism is preferable. After all, the problem is not just that Indigenous peoples should have greater political representation in general, though it is crucial that Parliament should more genuinely reflect the diversity of Australian society.[147] Proportionate representation is only part of the challenge and that issue is slowly being addressed: currently there are five Indigenous members of Parliament,[148] which is not far off three per cent of the 226 parliamentary seats. The more specific constitutional problem is that the First Nations do not have an adequate say in political decisions made specifically *about their own affairs*. Parliament necessarily has a special power under the *Constitution* to enact Indigenous-specific laws which give effect to Indigenous-specific rights and interests. Before 1967 the Race Power was never used, and after 1967 the power has only ever been used in relation to Indigenous people.[149] But being only three per cent of the population, Indigenous people can only ever have a three per cent say in the democratic exercise of the Indigenous-specific power, or any other powers being used in an Indigenous-specific way. This would be the case even with the

[144] Mansell (n 2 above) 39. See also discussion in Reilley (n 11 above) 95.

[145] Reilley (n 11 above) 97.

[146] See discussion in Chapter 4 of this volume.

[147] Indigenous under-representation is not the only challenge in this regard. As Tim Watts has pointed out, Asian-Australians are severely underrepresented in Parliament. Proportionately there should be about 30 Asian-Australian politicians, as they make up 13% of Australia's population. There are only five. See Tim Watts, *The Golden Country* (Text Publishing 2019) 132.

[148] Hannah Gobbett, 'Indigenous Parliamentarians, Federal and State: A Quick Guide' (Politics and Public Administration Section, Parliamentary Library, Research Paper Series 2017–18, 11 July 2017).

[149] For example, the power is said to support the *World Heritage Properties Conservation Act 1983* (Cth), the *Aboriginal and Torres Strait Islander Heritage Protection Act 1984* (Cth), the *Native Title Act 1993* (Cth), and the *Corporations (Aboriginal and Torres Strait Islander) Act 2006* (Cth).

theoretical implementation of Indigenous reserved seats to guarantee that Indigenous people make up three per cent of the Parliament (unless more Indigenous people sit in general seats), and the representatives in the Indigenous reserved seats would not have any *specific* required participation in relation to their Indigenous-specific matters – they would be having a say on all matters.

Regardless, the First Nations would still need mechanisms through which to engage more fairly and productively with the Australian government and Parliament – both its Indigenous and non-Indigenous representatives – in decision-making with respect to their distinct affairs. An approach that incorporates regional and localised First Nations empowerment would remain useful, so that when regional policy action is contemplated (like the Northern Territory Intervention or an alcohol ban in northern Western Australia)[150] those regional First Nations who are directly affected can be empowered to engage with Parliament on development of an appropriate and just policy response. With or without reserved Indigenous seats, Indigenous empowerment at the community, regional and national level is still needed to make this relationship fairer and more productive.[151]

A more targeted response, and arguably a more politically viable response, to this challenge would be to amend the *Constitution* to establish a First Nations voice to consult with and advise Parliament and government when it makes laws or policies relating to Indigenous matters, as recommended by the Referendum Council. Such a body would require a simpler constitutional amendment than Indigenous reserved seats, and the enacting legislation could ensure that regional and local communities were empowered to be heard in their local affairs. This would entail no constitutional change to sections 7, 24 or 29. It would also be simpler compared to the legislative implementation of reserved seats. The make-up of the Houses of Parliament would remain the same. There would be no change to electoral divisions. And it would not engage questions of uncertain and changeable constitutional interpretation of 'directly chosen by the people' under sections 7 and 24. The First Nations voice would serve a specific purpose: representing Indigenous views, enabling Indigenous participation, and advising and consulting on laws and policies with respect to Indigenous affairs. Such a body would leave the structure and function of Parliament and Australia's electoral law unchanged, while constitutionally guaranteeing that Indigenous people can actively participate in the political decisions made about them. The next chapter will make the case for a First Nations constitutional voice.

[150] See Paige Taylor, 'Police push for remote booze ban in WA', *The Australian* (2 January 2020).
[151] See Reilley (n 11 above) 97.

6

The Case for a First Nations Voice in the Constitution

I. INTRODUCTION

INDIGENOUS CONSTITUTIONAL RECOGNITION aims to reform the power relationship between Indigenous peoples and the Australian state, to ensure it is fairer than in the past. As discussed in Chapter two above, however, various obstacles complicate the task of constitutional reform in Australia: there is only a narrow window of political opportunity. While Indigenous support for any recognition proposal is both a moral and political prerequisite, Indigenous consensus alone is not enough to achieve constitutional change: under section 128, Parliament must initiate the reform and a 'double majority' referendum must be held, requiring widespread public approval.

The evident political difficulty often gives rise to the misguided assumption that only a symbolic, minimalistic constitutional amendment can succeed. This is the wrong approach, however – a merely symbolic proposal for a new preamble, which included a statement of Indigenous recognition, failed in 1999. Every successful change to the *Australian Constitution* has been practical and has solved practical problems – none has been merely symbolic. But while a purely symbolic or minimalistic insertion does not fit with Australia's practical *Constitution* and in my view cannot succeed (and in any case does not enjoy Indigenous support – so it should not succeed), at the other end of the spectrum, a new judicially adjudicated rights protection (see Chapter three) is similarly not the answer. As discussed in Chapter two, every past attempt at inserting a new rights guarantee into the *Australian Constitution* has proven unsuccessful. Such approaches do not comfortably cohere with Australia's 'Bill of rights'-free *Constitution*, which prefers political participation and federal power-sharing as the main mechanisms for rights protection. Most importantly, Indigenous Australians moved away from a racial non-discrimination guarantee in the Uluru Statement of 2017. Neither a symbolic insertion nor a racial non-discrimination clause adequately accords with Indigenous wishes, and neither adequately addresses concerns to uphold the *Constitution*: both introduce uncertain words which, through judicial interpretation, would enliven legal uncertainty and undermine parliamentary supremacy.

Given that mere symbolism cannot succeed, and given that a judicially adjudicated rights guarantee also cannot succeed, what is the practical and substantive constitutional amendment that can succeed? The Uluru Statement provides an intelligent and pragmatic answer to the complex challenge of Indigenous constitutional recognition. Followed up by the recommendations of the Referendum Council, the proposal calls for a constitutionally guaranteed First Nations voice – a representative and advisory body, to ensure that Indigenous people will always be heard in the laws and policies made about Indigenous affairs. A First Nations constitutional voice, properly formulated, argued, designed and implemented, is a proposal that fits with the *Constitution* and can succeed.

Building on arguments made in preceding chapters, this chapter re-caps the case for a First Nations constitutional voice, distilling seven key reasons why this proposal is a sensible way to achieve Indigenous constitutional recognition in Australia. It then moves on to questions of execution and implementation: I distinguish and draw lessons from the Inter-State Commission and the Aboriginal and Torres Strait Islander Commission (ATSIC), before discussing ideas for constitutional drafting and potential legislative design. The final part addresses common objections to the proposal for a First Nations constitutional voice.

II. RE-CAPPING THE CASE FOR CHANGE

There are at least seven key reasons why a constitutionally mandated Indigenous representative body is a sensible and viable proposal for constitutional recognition of Indigenous peoples in Australia:

1. It moves Australia from Indigenous constitutional exclusion, to inclusion.
2. It positively reforms the unfair power relationship between Indigenous peoples and the state.
3. It will help achieve improved practical outcomes in Indigenous affairs.
4. It upholds the *Constitution*.
5. It is a politically viable proposal.
6. It will assist in achieving human rights compliance in Indigenous affairs.
7. It draws constructively from international experience.

A. Moving from Indigenous Constitutional Exclusion, to Inclusion

A First Nations constitutional voice would move Australia from constitutional exclusion of Indigenous peoples, to constitutional inclusion. The continent of Australia was colonised by the British without Indigenous consent. This colonisation wrought dispossession, destruction and discrimination for Indigenous peoples, the effects of which are still being felt today. Indigenous peoples were omitted from the constitutional negotiations that gave rise to the Australian nation and were not afforded a fair place in the resulting constitutional compact. They were explicitly excluded from the *Constitution*, which has presided over extensive discrimination against them.

Indigenous advocates have for decades argued for a fair place in Australia's constitutional compact, through proactive inclusion, participation, empowerment and representation. The vast majority of this advocacy has called for inclusive forms of self-determination in their affairs. There have been numerous calls for reserved Indigenous seats in Parliament (discussed in Chapter five) and treaties. Similarly, there have been repeated requests for Indigenous representative and advisory bodies, most recently through the Uluru Statement, which called for a constitutionally guaranteed First Nations voice. This was the first time a national Indigenous consensus on constitutional reform had been achieved.

The history of discrimination and exclusion Indigenous people have suffered under the *Constitution* underpins and drives the consistent call for formal constitutional recognition and inclusion through a guaranteed voice in political decisions made about Indigenous affairs. This history demonstrates why such a reform is warranted and justified: a fairer say in such decisions would be political insurance against the repeat of past wrongs. A constitutional commitment to ongoing dialogue will help prevent unjust discrimination. By formally including the Indigenous political community in Australia's founding compact, the nation can make a fundamental step towards healing, inclusion and ultimately national unity. As noted in Chapter two, Australia's *Constitution* is in essence a treaty; a unity pact from which the First Nations were wrongfully omitted. The nation can now move from exclusion of Indigenous peoples from this unity pact, to formal Indigenous recognition, inclusion and ongoing empowered participation in the governance of their affairs.

Belatedly including Indigenous peoples in the perpetual dialogues set up by the *Constitution* would create ongoing constitutional conversations.[1] These continued conversations, consultations and dialogues would bring Australians closer together, building shared understanding, mutual respect and empathy: reconciliation in action. Though such conversations and collaborations would not make ancient animosities disappear, inclusive political dialogue over time can help foster trust, partnership, solidarity and cohesion. Through shared dialogue and engagement, the parties will be better placed to learn from each other, understand one another, create better policies and produce better outcomes together. The constitutionally mandated hearing of Indigenous voices would make for a wiser Parliament and government, and fairer laws and policies with respect to Indigenous affairs. It would help create a wiser, more united and more reconciled nation.

[1] James Tully, *Strange Multiplicity: Constitutionalism in the Age of Diversity* (Cambridge University Press 1995) 8. See also Jeremy Waldron, 'The Principle of Proximity' (Public Law & Legal Theory Research Paper Series, Working Paper No 11-08, 2011) 25.

B. Reforming an Unfair Power Relationship

As articulated in the Uluru Statement, Indigenous people seek constitutional recognition to address the 'torment of powerlessness' that besets their relationship with the Australian state.[2] The discrimination of the past was able to occur because Indigenous peoples in Australia occupy a position of constitutional disempowerment unlike any other group: Indigenous peoples are a uniquely vulnerable constitutional constituency with a special relationship with the state. No other group in Australia was dispossessed by British settlement. No other group was especially excluded by the constitutional arrangements of 1901.[3] No other group is subject to a special constitutional power which Parliament uses exclusively to make laws – both positive and adverse[4] – about Indigenous rights (as noted, the Race Power, section 51(xxvi), has only ever been used in relation to Indigenous peoples).[5] And no other group has rights and interests, recognised in legislation and common law, arising out of this unique constitutional relationship and history (eg, native title rights and Indigenous heritage protection laws).

Indigenous constitutional powerlessness is historically, politically and legally evident. It is evident in the history of discrimination, and in the text and operation of removed, amended and remaining constitutional clauses.[6] It is evident in the absence of any positive constitutional protections or recognition of Indigenous rights and interests. It is also evident in the laws,[7] policies and case law[8] that flow from this constitutional situation, which demonstrate the extreme vulnerability of Indigenous peoples, rights and interests in Australia's legal and political system.

[2] For a full discussion see Shireen Morris, 'The Torment of Our Powerlessness: Indigenous Constitutional Vulnerability and the Uluru Statement's call for a First Nations Voice' (2018) 41(3) *University of New South Wales Law Journal* 629. Note that this chapter is a considerably updated and expanded version of this article.

[3] See removed s 127 and amended s 51(xxvi).

[4] *Kartinyeri v The Commonwealth* (1998) 195 CLR 337.

[5] See *World Heritage Properties Conservation Act 1983* (Cth); *Aboriginal and Torres Strait Islander Heritage Protection Act 1984* (Cth); *Native Title Act 1993* (Cth); *Corporations (Aboriginal and Torres Strait Islander Act 2006* (Cth).

[6] See removed s 127, amended s 51(xxvi), and remaining s 25.

[7] For example, the *Northern Territory Emergency Response Act 2007* (Cth) provided in s 132: '(1) The provisions of this Act, and any acts done under or for the purposes of those provisions, are, for the purposes of the *Racial Discrimination Act 1975*, special measures. (2) The provisions of this Act, and any acts done under or for the purposes of those provisions, are excluded from the operation of Part II of the *Racial Discrimination Act 1975*. (3) In this section, a reference to any acts done includes a reference to any failure to do an act.' In 2009, operation of the *Racial Discrimination Act 1975* (Cth) (RDA) was reinstated.

[8] For eg, in *R v Maloney* (2014) 252 CLR 168, the Indigenous litigants argued that Alcohol Management Plans were not a valid special measure because they had not been implemented with proper consultation, but the High Court held that consultation is not a legal requirement of a special measure under Australian law.

Absent constitutional protection, legislated protections of Indigenous rights can be repealed or amended, either explicitly or impliedly by later inconsistent Acts.[9] While Parliament can use its power to legislatively recognise Indigenous rights, it can also legislate them away.[10] For example, the *Racial Discrimination Act 1975* (Cth) (RDA) has provided important protection of Indigenous rights; however, the RDA has been suspended several times in recent decades – each time only in relation to Indigenous people.[11] Further, the RDA's allowance of special measures,[12] while practically necessary to enable affirmative action and recognition of distinct Indigenous rights, can also enable laws which purport to advance Indigenous rights but which, in fact, may introduce adversely discriminatory measures[13] that Indigenous people may not agree with.[14] Another example is the legislative vulnerability of native title rights,[15] which provided important recognition of Indigenous property rights, but which were watered down under the Wik Ten-Point Plan in 1998.[16]

That Indigenous rights can be easily trampled by Parliament is a direct result of the constitutional vulnerability of Indigenous peoples and rights. This speaks to a problem inherent within the constitutional relationship and can only be

[9] Julie Taylor, 'Human Rights Protection in Australia and Parliamentary Supremacy' (2004) 32(1) *Federal Law Review* 57; Jeffrey Goldsworthy, *Parliamentary Sovereignty: Contemporary Debates* (Cambridge University Press 2010).

[10] See Darryl Cronin, 'Trapped by History: Democracy, Human Rights and Justice for Indigenous People in Australia' (2017) 23(2) *Australian Journal of Human Rights* 220.

[11] The *Hindmarsh Island Bridge Act 1997* (Cth) displaced the application of the RDA. See also, *Native Title Amendment Act 1998* (Cth); *Northern Territory Emergency Response Act 2007* (Cth) s 132.

[12] Article 1(4) of the *International Convention on the Elimination of All Forms of Racial Discrimination*, opened for signature 21 December 1965, 660 UNTS 195 (entered into force 4 January 1969) provides: 'Special measures taken for the sole purpose of securing adequate advancement of certain racial or ethnic groups or individuals requiring such protection as may be necessary in order to ensure such groups or individuals equal enjoyment or exercise of human rights and fundamental freedoms shall not be deemed racial discrimination'. In Australia, the RDA explicitly allows for 'special measures' in s 8.

[13] For more on the vulnerability of Indigenous rights and the subjectivity of special measures under the RDA, see Cronin (n 10 above) 230–35.

[14] The High Court in *Maloney* (n 8 above) found that consultation and consent are not legal requirements of special measures under the RDA. However, French CJ in *Maloney* noted that: '[I]t should be accepted, as a matter of common sense, that prior consultation with an affected community and its substantial acceptance of a proposed special measure is likely to be essential to the practical implementation of that measure. That is particularly so where … the measure … involves the imposition on the affected community of a restriction on some aspect of the freedoms otherwise enjoyed by its members': at 186.

[15] After the historic *Mabo* case (*Mabo v Queensland (No 2)* (1992) 175 CLR 1), the *Native Title Act 1993* (Cth) recognised native title in legislation.

[16] This was subsequent to the 1996 *Wik* case, which held that native title rights were not extinguished by pastoral leases and that native title rights could coexist with the rights of pastoralist leaseholders. See *Wik Peoples v Queensland* (1996) 187 CLR 1; Wik Ten-Point Plan: *Native Title Amendment Act 1998* (Cth). See also, Paul Keating, 'The 10-Point Plan that Undid the Good Done on Native Title', *Sydney Morning Herald* (1 June 2011) <https://www.smh.com.au/politics/federal/the-10-point-plan-that-undid-the-good-done-on-native-title-20110531-1feec.html> accessed 22 December 2019.

addressed through empowering constitutional reform.[17] The Uluru Statement calls for a constitutional promise that Indigenous voices will always be heard in political decisions made about them. Such a constitutional promise would fundamentally reform this relationship so it is fairer than in the past.[18]

(i) *Democratic Disempowerment: The 'Elephant and the Mouse' Problem*

Indigenous constitutional vulnerability is exacerbated by the relative size of the Indigenous population. Indigenous people make up only three per cent of Australians, which means they are an extreme minority, more so than other Indigenous populations in comparable democracies.[19] Indigenous Australians are therefore particularly democratically disempowered and face difficulty being heard in parliamentary majoritarian decisions about their unique minority rights and interests[20] – which increases the potential for political decisions which trample their rights. This dynamic has been described by Noel Pearson as the 'elephant and the mouse problem which characterises Indigenous affairs'.[21]

Because of their extreme minority status, Indigenous people are especially vulnerable to disregard of their rights. The *Constitution* affords Indigenous people no specific protections to which they can appeal through the courts in defence of their rights, nor any mechanisms to specifically influence the making of laws and policies about them – apart from normal election processes. As a three per cent minority, Indigenous Australians have a limited capacity to influence policy and law-making through ordinary democratic processes. When elected to Parliament, Indigenous people, like all politicians, are duty bound to represent the interests of all Australians who voted for them and their political parties.

While Australia's *Constitution* is founded in federal principles that ensure the historic political communities a fair say, the Indigenous historic community went unrecognised in the compact of 1901. Accordingly, the *Constitution* makes no provision for Indigenous voices to be specifically heard, even on matters

[17] As Harry Hobbs explains: 'As Australia's existing constitutional and political framework disempowers Aboriginal and Torres Strait Islander peoples, reform of those institutions is the primary vehicle through which their aspirations may be realised': Harry Hobbs, 'Constitutional Recognition and Reform: Developing an Inclusive Australian Citizenship through Treaty' (2018) 53(2) *Australian Journal of Political Science* 176, 176.

[18] See Shireen Morris, 'What Promise Will the Nation Make?' in Damien Freeman and Shireen Morris (eds), *The Forgotten People: Liberal and Conservative Approaches to Recognising Indigenous Peoples* (Melbourne University Press 2016).

[19] Contrast the Indigenous population in New Zealand where, as noted, Māori people are around 15% of the population: 'New Zealand Population 2019' (*World Population Review*, 28 August 2019) <http://worldpopulationreview.com/countries/new-zealand-population/> accessed 8 December 2019.

[20] Michael Mansell, *Treaty and Statehood: Aboriginal Self-Determination* (The Federation Press 2016) 15, 20–24.

[21] See Noel Pearson, 'Time to Bring Us into the Nation through Constitutional Recognition', *The Australian* (13 September 2014).

directly concerning their interests, and even when Parliament exercises its special power with respect to Indigenous affairs.[22] Yet the *Constitution* does provide constitutional mechanisms for other minority 'mice' to be heard by the might of the majority: section 7 guarantees even the smallest former colonies – like Tasmania – an equal voice in the Senate. There are more Indigenous Australians than Tasmanians.[23] If Tasmanians should be constitutionally guaranteed a voice in their affairs, arguably Indigenous peoples should be constitutionally guaranteed a voice in theirs too. Such a reform would be in keeping with the essential character of the Australian *Constitution*, which protects rights through political processes and by ensuring the historic political communities a fair voice in their affairs.

(ii) The Need for an Enduring Constitutional Guarantee

The extreme minority status of the Indigenous population underscores the need for a constitutional guarantee, and explains why constitutional stability and durability are at the heart of advocacy for Indigenous constitutional recognition.[24] Only the *Constitution* is capable of providing enduring and stable protection of rights and interests – it presents a more decisive and long-term solution to Indigenous constitutional vulnerability than mere legislation, which, as shown, can be easily changed, abolished or weakened by the laws of the majority.

A constitutionally guaranteed voice, as called for in the Uluru Statement, addresses the vulnerability of a merely legislated institutional voice. Indigenous people are right to be vigilant about this. ATSIC (the Aboriginal and Torres Strait Islander Commission) was a representative body implemented under a Labor government, then abolished under the Liberal Howard government.[25] The easy axing of ATSIC demonstrates why it is important that any new Indigenous body is underpinned by a constitutional guarantee.[26] Although it should be legislatively adaptable and flexible in its design details, the body should not be abolished the moment there are difficulties. When there are corrupt or incompetent politicians in Parliament, no one seriously calls for the institution of

[22] Section 51(xxvi) has only ever been used in relation to Indigenous peoples.

[23] In 2017, the Tasmanian population was 519,166: 'Population of Tasmania 2019', *Population Australia* <http://www.population.net.au/population-of-tasmania/> accessed 22 December 2019. The 2016 Census reported the Indigenous population as 649,200: Australian Bureau of Statistics, 'Census: Aboriginal and Torres Strait Islander Population' (Media Release 075/2017, 27 June 2017) <http://www.abs.gov.au/ausstats/abs@.nsf/MediaRealesesByCatalogue/02D50FAA9987D6B7CA25814800087E03?OpenDocument> accessed 22 December 2019.

[24] Patrick Dodson, 'Until the Chains are Broken' (*Vincent Lingiari Memorial Lecture*, Darwin, 8 September 1999).

[25] Though with Labor Party support. See Will Sanders, 'ATSIC's Achievements and Strengths: Implications for Institutional Reform' (Centre for Aboriginal Economic Policy Research, ANU College of Arts & Social Sciences, Vol 23(10), August 2004).

[26] Other past Indigenous bodies were also 'short-lived and unsecured'. See Mansell (n 20 above) 14.

Parliament to be abolished.[27] Indigenous institutions, like any institutions, must be adapted and improved over time: legislative flexibility in the details, processes and design of the body will allow for this evolution, but a constitutional guarantee provides stability and longevity.[28] A body with constitutional status would be intended as a permanent part of Australia's constitutional and institutional arrangements – guaranteeing that Indigenous peoples will always have a voice in their affairs.

C. Improving Practical Outcomes

A constitutionally guaranteed Indigenous voice in Indigenous affairs will help improve policy-making and thus outcomes. Addressing this is urgent. Indigenous people experience worse outcomes in life expectancy, incarceration, suicide, family violence, employment and education than other Australians.[29] This day-to-day vulnerability arising from extreme disadvantage is caused, exacerbated and perpetuated by Indigenous constitutional powerlessness.[30] Indigenous people, due to their extreme disadvantage, are more likely to be subject to special government interventions intended to address that disadvantage. This means there is greater scope for injustice and harm caused by state interventions – whether inadvertent or intended. Indigenous vulnerability experienced by individuals and communities in day-to-day life is therefore closely connected to Indigenous constitutional and structural vulnerability. The disempowerment is cyclical, systemic and embedded, resulting not only in discrimination and injustice, but also in policies and laws that are not as effective as they could be in addressing disadvantage, because Indigenous people are not structurally empowered to influence and improve laws and policies intended to assist them.[31] The effect is entrenched structural and systemic disempowerment that can seem intractable.

The Uluru Statement calls for a structural 'circuit-breaker' to effect a fundamental paradigm shift. The assertion is that Indigenous powerlessness must not only be addressed through policies, programmes, and services; it must be addressed constitutionally and structurally, for Indigenous disadvantage carries a

[27] As Sanders argues: 'To get rid of ATSIC as a way of pushing aside a particular chairperson is like abolishing Parliament to push aside a particular Prime Minister': Sanders (n 25 above) 6.

[28] Pearson has noted with respect to ATSIC that government bureaucracies and other industries were also responsible for ATSIC's deficiencies: Noel Pearson, 'Recent Indigenous Policy Failures Can't Be Pinned on Aborigines', *The Australian* (15 June 2013).

[29] See Australian Government, *Closing the Gap Report* (2019) 10 <https://ctgreport.niaa.gov.au/> accessed 22 December 2019.

[30] See discussion of the connection between historical and structural discrimination, and contemporary disadvantage in Darren Dick, on behalf of Tom Calma, 'Social Determinants and the Health of Indigenous Peoples in Australia: A Human Rights Based Approach' (*International Symposium on the Social Determinants of Indigenous Health*, Adelaide, 29–30 April 2007).

[31] See Noel Pearson, 'A Rightful Place: Race, Recognition and a More Complete Commonwealth' (2014) 55 *Quarterly Essay* 48; Mansell (n 20 above) 8–9.

constitutional and structural dimension. The call for a constitutionally guaranteed First Nations voice in their affairs is a call for constitutional empowerment – a circuit-breaking solution to Indigenous constitutional vulnerability and powerlessness. It is also an acknowledgement that current approaches to remedying Indigenous disadvantage are not working: despite significant spending and good intentions, the gap is not on track to close.[32] The proposal for a First Nations constitutional voice in their affairs is driven by a desire to improve policies and outcomes, propelled by the conviction that policies and outcomes will improve when Indigenous peoples are empowered to take charge of the problems that face them, in partnership with government.[33] The conviction is that genuine Indigenous involvement, collaboration and ownership in the development of Indigenous policies and laws will improve those policies and laws – making them less discriminatory, more just and more effective in achieving positive results.

An ongoing challenge in Indigenous affairs is discerning fair policy from unfair policy: who decides? Sometimes governments with good intentions, seeking to alleviate Indigenous disadvantage and suffering, nonetheless enact policies and laws that Indigenous people argue are discriminatory and unjust, or which are ineffective.[34] Other times, particularly historically, governments are deliberately discriminatory.[35] A constitutionally empowered Indigenous voice is an intelligent and nuanced solution to this subjectivity problem: it provides a way of combatting not only the hard racism of prejudiced policy, but also the well-meaning, benevolent policy that may be inadvertently discriminatory, paternalistic, or simply ineffective. This latter type of policy is what Pearson, borrowing the phrase coined by George W Bush, describes as 'the soft bigotry of low expectations'.[36] A First Nations voice would empower *Indigenous peoples themselves* to combat and prevent both kinds of oppressive and unjust policy through empowered, active, and vocal engagement with

[32] Only 2 out of 7 targets are on track to be met. See *Closing the Gap* (n 29 above) 10.

[33] See, eg, 'About Us', *The Harvard Project on American Indian Economic Development*, <https://hpaied.org/about> accessed 22 December 2019. See also comments on Indigenous empowerment and closing the gap outcomes in Victoria Tauli-Corpuz, 'End of Mission Statement by the United Nations Special Rapporteur on the Rights of Indigenous Peoples', United Nations Office of the High Commissioner for Human Rights <https://www.ohchr.org/EN/NewsEvents/Pages/DisplayNews.aspx?NewsID=21473&LangID=E> accessed 22 December 2019.

[34] For example, the Northern Territory intervention was implemented by government to address the challenge of child sexual abuse in Indigenous communities in the Northern Territory. But it initially suspended the RDA, and many Indigenous people complained that it was discriminatory, arguing that the 'top-down' approach was flawed. See Sarah Everingham, 'Northern Territory Emergency Response: Views on "Intervention" Differ 10 Years On', *ABC News* (21 June 2017).

[35] See, for example, the *Koowarta* case, where the Queensland government enacted a policy to prevent Indigenous people from buying land, which was subsequently struck down by the High Court as a breach of the RDA. See *Koowarta v Bjelke-Petersen* (1982) 153 CLR 168.

[36] Joshua Robertson, 'Noel Pearson Says "Soft Bigotry" of the Left the Biggest Challenge to Indigenous Reform', *The Guardian* (8 December 2016) <https://www.theguardian.com/australia-news/2016/dec/08/noel-pearson-says-soft-bigotry-of-the-left-the-biggest-challenge-to-indigenous-reform> accessed 22 December 2019. George W Bush, 'No Child Left Behind' speech to the NAACP 91st Annual Convention, July 2000.

the state – for Indigenous people are best placed to decipher good Indigenous policy from bad, and to help develop better policy solutions in their communities. They are arguably better placed to do so than either politicians in a Parliament or judges in a High Court. A First Nations constitutional voice is innovative in this regard, because it proposes a way of addressing Indigenous constitutional vulnerability that does not rely on a judicially adjudicated rights clause.[37] Rather, it seeks more active Indigenous involvement and empowerment in political decision-making with respect to Indigenous affairs.

D. Upholding the Constitution

The Referendum Council recommends a constitutionally mandated First Nations voice through a *political* constitutional guarantee, not a justiciable guarantee. The proposal would empower the First Nations with a fairer say in their affairs, but it is also deliberately respectful of parliamentary supremacy in its intent and design. In recommending a political, rather than justiciable, approach to constitutionally empowering Indigenous peoples, the proposal stays true to Australia's ingrained preference for political and procedural approaches to rights protection and fits coherently with Australian constitutional culture, history and design. The proposal takes on board concerns about legal uncertainty arising from judicial review (discussed in Chapter three) and deliberately excludes this potential.

A First Nations constitutional voice therefore fits with the central organising values of the *Australian Constitution*. The *Constitution*, in a fundamental sense, is all about voices. In creating the *Constitution*, the parties agreed on the best ways to regulate fair future relations and determined that the political process should take primacy over judicially adjudicated rights clauses.[38] They chose to predominantly protect citizens' rights through democratic procedures and federal power-sharing,[39] thus relying mainly on institutional mechanisms for rights protection.[40] Federalism sets up a 'check and balance' system[41] in

[37] See Shireen Morris, 'The Argument for a Constitutional Procedure for Parliament to Consult with Indigenous Peoples When Making Laws for Indigenous Affairs' (2015) 26(3) *Public Law Review* 166, 169–70.

[38] AV Dicey, *Introduction to the Study of the Law of the Constitution* (8th edn, Macmillan 1915) 196–99; Jeffrey Goldsworthy, 'Constitutional Cultures, Democracy and Unwritten Principles' [2012] (3) *University of Illinois Law Review* 683, 685–88; Jeffrey Goldsworthy, 'The Constitutional Protection of Rights in Australia' in Greg Craven (ed), *Australian Federation: Towards the Second Century* (Melbourne University Press 1992) 151, 151–57.

[39] Greg Craven, *Conversations with the Constitution: Not Just a Piece of Paper* (University of New South Wales Press 2004) 38–42.

[40] Jenina Boughey and Dan Meagher, 'Rights, Rhetoric and Reality: An Overview of Rights Protection in Australia' in Matthew Groves, Jenina Boughey and Dan Meagher (eds), *The Legal Protection of Rights in Australia* (Hart Publishing 2019) 4–7; Cheryl Saunders, 'The Australian Constitution and Our Rights' in Helen Sykes (ed), *Future Justice* (Future Leaders 2010) 117.

[41] *Wilson v Minister for Aboriginal Affairs* (1996) 189 CLR 1, 11 (Brennan CJ, Dawson, Toohey, McHugh and Gummow JJ).

which the Senate, as the house of review, tempers the power of the House of Representatives.[42]

In setting up this reciprocal arrangement, the *Constitution* recognises and represents the historic political communities, ensuring that even the most minimally populated States are guaranteed an equal voice in the Senate.[43] The *Constitution* thus creates a balanced web of political restraints and competing interests to ensure a tempering of majoritarian rule by recognised minority voices.[44] The system protects rights by ensuring these various voices are heard and through institutional arrangements requiring political dialogue and deliberation.[45] As argued in Chapter two, Australia's 'Bill of rights'-free *Constitution* adopts a Waldronian respect for parliamentary supremacy, which positions political participation as the 'right of rights'.[46]

The Indigenous historic political community, however, was wrongfully excluded from the power-sharing deal: they missed out on their rightful place and fair participation in the compact. So while the *Constitution* specifically empowers Parliament to make laws about the Indigenous minority,[47] it does not ensure Indigenous peoples meaningful input into those decisions. It does not require reciprocity, consultation or dialogue with Indigenous peoples. This exclusion goes against the spirit of the *Constitution* and the culture of comity and mutual respect it establishes. A First Nations constitutional voice would address this problem in a way that aligns with Australian constitutional culture – more so than the insertion of new judicially adjudicated rights guarantees, and more so than the insertion of poetic, symbolic statements into what is fundamentally a structural rulebook. The proposal would not impose a veto and would be drafted to be non-justiciable (explained further below), thus eliminating legal uncertainty and upholding parliamentary supremacy.

As Waldron argues in defence of political processes as the best means for resolving disagreements about rights, 'those who are to be required to comply with a decision are surely entitled to *some* sort of voice in that decision'.[48] There is a powerful moral argument that the First Nations should be ensured a

[42] Cheryl Saunders, 'The Constitutional, Legal and Institutional Foundations of Australian Federalism' in Robert Carling (ed), *Where To For Australian Federalism?* (Centre for Independent Studies 2008).

[43] Section 7 requires 'equal representation' of each Original State.

[44] JA La Nauze, 'The Inter-State Commission' (1937) 9(1) *The Australian Quarterly* 48, 48. For arguments on why recognition of Indigenous governance fits with Australian federalism, see Alexander Reilly, 'A Constitutional Framework for Indigenous Governance' (2006) 28(3) *Sydney Law Review* 403.

[45] Scott Stephenson, 'Deliberation as a Constitutional Value' in Rosalind Dixon (ed), *Australian Constitutional Values* (Hart Publishing 2018) 133–50.

[46] Jeremy Waldron, 'Participation: The Right of Rights' (1998) 98 *Proceedings of the Aristotelian Society* 307.

[47] Under s 51(xxvi).

[48] Jeremy Waldron, 'A Right-Based Critique of Constitutional Rights' (1993) 13(1) *Oxford Journal of Legal Studies* 18, 38.

specific say in the political decisions made about them and their rights. A non-justiciable, *political* constitutional requirement that Indigenous voices must be heard in the making of political decisions about Indigenous affairs would therefore achieve two important and compatible objectives: it would increase the fairness of political decision-making with respect to Indigenous affairs by empowering Indigenous peoples with a voice in such decisions, and it would do so in a way that upholds the *Australian Constitution*.

E. A Politically Viable Solution

A First Nations voice addresses ongoing Indigenous advocacy for substantive and empowering constitutional reform, yet as discussed above, it is also a fundamentally constitutionally conservative proposal. Indeed, it is the only proposal for Indigenous constitutional recognition that fulfils both of these criteria. For this reason, it is the most politically viable proposal and, in my view, the only proposal that can win a recognition referendum.[49]

As noted, a minimalist, purely symbolic model failed in 1999. It would fail again today, because it does not accord with Indigenous wishes for substantive reform. Australians are unlikely to vote 'yes' to a form of Indigenous recognition that Indigenous people themselves do not agree with. A symbolic insertion would likely also attract opposition from constitutional conservatives who view the *Constitution* as a rulebook – not the place for poetic clauses that may enliven uncertain judicial interpretation.[50] The republic debates of the 1990s demonstrated how habitual enemies can sometimes unite to defeat a proposal for constitutional change, although they may oppose it for different reasons.[51] In the Indigenous recognition debate, constitutional symbolism would become the common enemy of Indigenous advocates, who want substantive constitutional reform over symbolic gestures, and constitutional conservatives seeking to protect the *Constitution* from legal uncertainty. With resistance from Indigenous Australians and constitutional conservatives alike, a minimalist, merely symbolic, form of recognition cannot succeed. This approach would repeat the failure of 1999. Yet a judicially adjudicated rights guarantee will also struggle. As discussed in Chapter two, in the Australian history of constitutional reform, no attempt to insert new rights guarantees into the *Constitution* has eventuated. This is perhaps because reforms that transfer significant power to the High

[49] See also Shireen Morris and Noel Pearson, 'Indigenous Constitutional Recognition: Paths to Failure and Possible Paths to Success' (2017) 91(5) *Australian Law Journal* 350.

[50] See, eg, Julian Leeser, 'Uphold and Recognise' in Damien Freeman and Shireen Morris (eds), *The Forgotten People: Liberal and Conservative Approaches to Recognising Indigenous Peoples* (Melbourne University Press 2016).

[51] During the constitutional conventions, the direct electionists joined forced with the monarchists to defeat constitutional reform for a republic. See also Glenn Patmore, *Choosing the Republic* (UNSW Press 2009) 25; Morris and Pearson (n 49 above) 356.

Court are an incongruent fit with Australian constitutional and political character, which favours Parliament as the best defender, balancer and adjudicator of rights. It is also a practical reality that Parliament, as the initiator and thus the gatekeeper of constitutional reform, is unlikely to put forward and champion proposals that diminish its own power.

A First Nations constitutional voice is the middle ground, 'radical centre' reform proposal that can succeed. It responds to Indigenous advocacy for empowering constitutional reform, while also responding to constitutionally conservative concerns to uphold the *Constitution*. It is the only proposal for constitutional recognition that genuinely aligns with Australian constitutional culture and history, as well as Indigenous aspirations for empowering and substantive change. Assessing the political parameters and the lessons of the history of Australian constitutional reform, a First Nations constitutional voice is the only proposal that can win a recognition referendum.

F. Human Rights Compliance in Indigenous Affairs

Implementation of a First Nations constitutional voice would support Australia's human rights compliance. Australia endorsed the UN Declaration on the Rights of Indigenous Peoples (DRIP)[52] in 2009, but its principles are yet to be domestically implemented.[53] As noted in Chapter four above, Articles 18 and 19 of DRIP focus on the importance of Indigenous participation and consultation in political decisions affecting Indigenous rights. Article 18 provides:

> Indigenous peoples have the right to participate in decision-making in matters which would affect their rights, through representatives chosen by themselves in accordance with their own procedures, as well as to maintain and develop their own indigenous decision-making institutions.

Article 19 similarly requires:

> States shall consult and cooperate in good faith with the indigenous peoples concerned through their own representative institutions in order to obtain their free, prior and informed consent before adopting and implementing legislative or administrative measures that may affect them.

Measures for consultation and participation facilitate the Indigenous right to self-determination.[54] DRIP thus makes provision for Indigenous peoples to

[52] *United Nations Declaration on the Rights of Indigenous Peoples*, GA Res 61/295, UN Doc A/RES/61/295 (2 October 2007, adopted 13 September 2007).

[53] For more on the status of Indigenous peoples in international law, see Patrick Macklem, 'Indigenous Recognition in International Law: Theoretical Observations' (2008) 30(1) *Michigan Journal of International Law* 177.

[54] See Article 3 provides that: 'Indigenous peoples have the right to self-determination. By virtue of that right they freely determine their political status and freely pursue their economic, social

represent their interests through dedicated institutions within the state, as well as to participate as equal citizens in ordinary democratic processes. The approach is one of inclusive participation, rather than separatism and fragmentation.

But Australia is not living up to its human rights obligations under DRIP. Like all international human rights instruments, DRIP is not legally enforceable until implemented domestically through Australian legislation.[55] Mechanisms for genuine Indigenous consultation and participation in Indigenous affairs have not been legislated, and are therefore not legally required.[56] The Parliamentary Joint Committee on Human Rights (PJCHR) – the parliamentary committee tasked with scrutinising Bills for international human rights compliance[57] – has emphasised that genuine Indigenous participation and engagement is crucial to safeguarding Indigenous rights and ensuring that special measures are effective and fair,[58] but observes that this is often not occurring in the development of key Indigenous policies.[59] Similarly, the UN Special Rapporteur on the Rights of Indigenous Peoples in 2017 noted that:

> While Australia has adopted numerous policies aiming to address Aboriginal and Torres Strait socioeconomic disadvantage, the failure to respect the right to self-determination and the right to full and effective participation in these is alarming. The compounded effect of these policies has contributed to the failure to deliver on the targets in the areas of health, education and employment in the Closing the Gap strategy and has contributed to aggravating the escalating incarceration and child removal rates of Aboriginal and Torres Strait Islanders.[60]

If Australia were to implement a constitutionally guaranteed First Nations voice, this would be a significant and important step towards human rights compliance

and cultural development.' The right of all peoples to self-determination is also recognised in the common Art 1 of both the *International Covenant on Civil and Political Rights*, opened for signature 16 December 1966, 999 UNTS 171 (entered into force 23 March 1976) and the *International Covenant on Economic, Social and Cultural Rights*, opened for signature 16 December 1966, 993 UNTS 3 (entered into force 3 January 1976).

[55] *Dietrich v The Queen* (1992) 177 CLR 292 (Mason CJ and Hugh J); *Kioa v West* (1985) 159 CLR 550, 570 (Gibbs CJ).

[56] The High Court found in *Maloney* that consultation is not a legal requirement of a special measure under the *Racial Discrimination Act 1975*, as it is not required specifically under domestic law: *Maloney* (n 8 above) 185–86.

[57] See Shireen Morris, 'Parliamentary Scrutiny and Insights for a First Nations Voice to Parliament' in Laura Grenfell and Julie Debeljak (eds), *Law Making and Human Rights* (Thomson Reuters 2020).

[58] Parliamentary Joint Committee on Human Rights, *Stronger Futures in the Northern Territory Act 2012 and related legislation* (11th Report of 2013, June 2013) 34 [1.122]. This was also emphasised by Brennan J in *Gerhardy v Brown* (1985) 159 CLR 70, 135: 'The wishes of the beneficiaries for the measure are of great importance (perhaps essential) in determining whether a measure is taken for the purpose of securing their advancement. The dignity of the beneficiaries is impaired and they are not advanced by having an unwanted material benefit foisted on them.'

[59] PJCHR, *Stronger Futures* (n 58 above) 75 [1.275]. See also Parliamentary Joint Committee on Human Rights, *2016 Review of Stronger Futures Measures* (March 2016) 60 [4.95].

[60] Tauli-Corpuz (Special Rapporteur), 'End of Mission Statement' (n 33 above).

under DRIP. Ensuring Indigenous input into Indigenous policy would also help Australia close the gap on Indigenous disparity – because empowered Indigenous involvement in laws and policies made about them will improve those policies, and thus outcomes.

Rather than reactively enabling Indigenous people to go to the High Court to challenge discriminatory laws already enacted, a First Nations voice would ensure Indigenous political involvement and participation right at the start, when relevant laws and policies are being devised and enacted – hopefully preventing discrimination. The proposal has therefore been described by some Indigenous advocates as a proactive 'sword', whereas a racial non-discrimination guarantee would be a reactive 'shield',[61] because political participation, in contrast to perpetual litigation, creates an increased sense of Indigenous peoples as self-determining political actors in the governance systems of the nation – which is, for many, an attractive and empowering prospect. This self-determinative approach to Indigenous constitutional recognition will assist Australia in meeting its international human rights obligations.

G. International Precedent Supports the Reform

As discussed in Chapter four, comparable democracies with minority Indigenous populations – like New Zealand, Canada, and the Scandinavian countries of Norway, Sweden, and Finland – have implemented reforms to empower the Indigenous peoples of those nations with a voice in their affairs. Each nation does this in different ways. New Zealand has the Māori Council and reserved Māori seats in Parliament. Canada has a court-enforced duty to consult with Indigenous peoples, arising from section 35 of the *Constitution* which recognises and protects Aboriginal and treaty rights. Norway, Sweden and Finland each have Sámi Parliaments which are consultative and advisory Indigenous bodies. Each of these countries utilises forms of Indigenous constitutional recognition that empower Indigenous people with a voice in their affairs. Each has an Indigenous representative structure operating within the nation. Australia stands apart from these nations as lacking any institutional mechanisms which enable Indigenous peoples to engage productively with the state.

These international examples show that Indigenous representative institutions, and mechanisms to empower Indigenous peoples with a dedicated voice within states, are not novel. Australia can learn from these international examples to implement its own version of a First Nations voice, appropriate to Australian First Nations and suitable to Australian constitutional and political culture.

[61] Aboriginal Provisional Government, Press Release, 8 July 2015.

III. DISTINGUISHING THE INTER-STATE COMMISSION AND ATSIC

The proposal for a First Nations constitutional voice is a concept that works through the political process, not the courts. It is not an Indigenous veto. The constitutional amendment is intended to be non-justiciable (discussed further below). Thus, the First Nations voice will carry political and indeed constitutional authority, but the effectiveness of the institution will also depend on its design, the persuasiveness of its members, the political will and culture that allow it to function effectively, and the spirit with which the parties engage.

Two historical bodies are relevant to the discussion of a First Nations constitutional voice. First, the Inter-State Commission (the Commission) was mandated by the *Constitution* but failed to operate for most of Australia's history. The Commission may be relevant to assessing the effectiveness of constitutional guarantees requiring the existence of institutions. Second, ATSIC was a legislated Indigenous representative body which was eventually abolished. Consideration of ATSIC is relevant because the present proposal seeks to fill the representative gap left by the abolition of ATSIC, while also improving upon the characteristics that, on some views, undermined ATSIC's effectiveness. It is important to draw lessons from the intent, design and eventual demise of these two institutions.

A. The Inter-State Commission

Section 101 of the *Constitution* requires the existence of an Inter-State Commission with adjudicatory powers,[62] but despite the constitutional imperative, no Inter-State Commission has existed for most of Australia's history.[63] Although the *Constitution* came into force in 1901, the Commission was not successfully legislated until 1912 and did not start operating until 1913.[64]

The Commission was intended as a piece of 'constitutional and economic machinery'[65] to regulate inter-State relations,[66] prevent inter-State discrimination,[67] and encourage federal free trade. The Commission was to be

[62] Sections 73, 101, 102, and 103 of the *Constitution* also deal with the Inter-State Commission.

[63] Bell says that the Commission's non-existence is 'a somewhat remarkable fact' given 'the mandatory language of s 101': Andrew Bell, 'The Missing Constitutional Cog: The Omission of the Inter-State Commission' [2009–2010] (Summer) *Bar News* 59 <http://www.austlii.edu.au/au/journals/NSWBarAssocNews/2009/63.pdf>.

[64] Ian Radbone, 'The Inter-State Commission' (1982) 41(4) *Australian Journal of Public Administration* 323, 324; Michael Coper, 'The Second Coming of the Fourth Arm: The Role and Functions of the Inter-State Commission' (1989) 63(11) *Australian Law Journal* 731, 733.

[65] Bell (n 63 above) 59.

[66] Particularly in relation to railways and rivers: La Nauze (n 44 above) 48.

[67] See s 102 of the *Constitution*.

a constitutional watchdog[68] of section 92,[69] an 'independent critic',[70] or 'policing body', to help manage inter-State rivalry as well as promote economic prosperity.[71] It was supposed to be a constitutional check on Commonwealth and State power;[72] designed as a non-judicial and non-parliamentary compromise solution to trade regulation.[73] Some considered it the intended 'fourth arm' (a combined administrative and adjudicatory arm)[74] of Australian government.[75] In some ways, it was a constitutional innovation – a deviation from the simplistic three arms.[76]

The Commission's utility waned after the 1915 *Wheat Case*,[77] which concerned whether the Commission could exercise judicial power. This case was a key reason for the Commission's failure.[78] The establishing Act allocated the Commission many judicial-sounding powers,[79] but the High Court decided that the powers conferred on the Commission by the *Constitution* were not of a judicial nature – despite the adjudicatory language of section 101.[80] Stripped of its key functions, the Commission became 'merely a body of inquiry without any

[68] Bell (n 63 above) 70.

[69] Section 92 provides that 'intercourse among the States, whether by means of internal carriage or ocean navigation, shall be absolutely free'.

[70] Quoting Mr Hughes, introducing the Bill in 1909: La Nauze (n 44 above) 50.

[71] Coper (n 64 above) 746; Bell (n 63 above) 70.

[72] For example, under s 102, the Commonwealth had the power to forbid discriminatory State railway laws, but only if the Commission found that such laws were 'undue and unreasonable'.

[73] Coper (n 64 above) 733.

[74] DJ Cremean, 'The Inter-State Commission: Rethinking the Wheat Case' (2009) 83(11) *Australian Law Journal* 765, 765.

[75] Coper (n 64 above) 731–33.

[76] Stephen Gageler, 'The Inter-State Commission and the Regulation of Trade and Commerce under the Australian Constitution' (2017) 28(3) *Public Law Review* 205, 205–6.

[77] *New South Wales v Commonwealth* (1915) 20 CLR 54 (the *Wheat Case*).

[78] Bell (n 63 above) 68; Coper (n 64 above) 734.

[79] For eg, 'it could hear and determine complaints, award damages, inflict heavy fines for disobedience of its order and commit to prison for failure to pay. It could compel witnesses to attend and examine them on oath': La Nauze (n 44 above) 209. See *Inter-State Commission Act 1912* (Cth).

[80] Bell argues that: 'Isaacs [J]'s conclusion was totally at odds with not only the express reference to "adjudication" in s 101 but also with the constitutional commentary of Quick and Garran to the effect that s 101 "clearly enables part of the actual judicial power of the Commonwealth to be vested in the Inter-State Commission". … The net effect of this decision coincided with aspirations Isaacs expressed some eighteen years previously as a young Victorian delegate in the Melbourne Convention Debates: "I want to eliminate the constitutional creation of the Inter-State Commission. I think it a great mistake that we should erect this body – a fourth branch of Government"': Bell (n 63 above) 68. Stephen Gageler also notes that Isaacs was one of the Commission's 'main detractors' because he saw it as usurping the power of Parliament and the Courts: Gageler (n 76 above) 208. Cremean similarly contends that the case 'could well have been decided differently. The minority view could well have prevailed, in the face of the *Constitution*'s provisions': Cremean (n 74 above) 765. In Zines' view, the decision read s 101 narrowly in order to apply the 'important and fundamental' implications from Chapter III of the Constitution, relating to the separation of powers. 'The judgement of Isaacs J is more rigid and dogmatic in its application of the doctrine of the separation of powers and it is obvious that it was not merely the textual arrangement that influenced him': Leslie Zines, *The High Court and the Constitution* (5th edn, Federation Press 2008) 209–11. See also La Nauze (n 44 above) 55.

power of enforcing its decisions',[81] and operated only from 1913 until 1920. The Commission started operating again in 1984,[82] but not for long.[83]

Given that the existence of the Commission was constitutionally mandated, how was this able to occur? While constitutionally required, the Commission depended 'for its existence and practical operation on legislative definition of its powers and executive action in relation to appointments'. As Coper explains, 'the peremptory command in s 101 ... that there "shall be" an Inter-State Commission is not self-executing and no doubt is unenforceable, at least to bring a non-existent Commission into being'.[84] Some have suggested that the story of the Inter-State Commission demonstrates the potential ineffectiveness of constitutional clauses requiring the existence of institutions. In 2015, Professor George Williams pointed to the Commission to query the usefulness of a constitutionally mandated First Nations body, arguing that a judicially adjudicated racial non-discrimination guarantee would be needed to improve its operation and effectiveness.[85] In my view, however, there are several reasons to be optimistic about the operation of the proposed Indigenous body, as well as differentiating factors in relation to the Inter-State Commission. The proposal for a First Nations constitutional voice is distinguishable from the Commission on at least four grounds.

First, the story of the Inter-State Commission does not present a general lesson about the ineffectiveness of constitutional provisions requiring the existence of institutions; rather, it presents a lesson about the risks associated with *justiciable* constitutional imperatives or guarantees. It is true that constitutional clauses do not always guarantee that Parliament will follow the rules contained in them, just as the existence of a constitution does not always entail the existence of the institutions mandated by it. Constitutions, institutions and the authority of constitutional provisions depend on political will, public support and respect for the rule of law, sometimes along with judicial enforcement (although the existence and authority of the High Court itself depends on political will and respect for the rule of law). The same, of course, can be said for judicially adjudicated constitutional rights guarantees: declarations of rights in a constitution do not guarantee that such rights will be respected;[86] nor do justiciable constitutional guarantees ensure that the High Court will interpret the words of those

[81] La Nauze (n 44 above) 55.

[82] Coper (n 64 above) 731.

[83] Cremean (n 74 above) 765; Bell (n 63 above) 71.

[84] Coper (n 64 above) 733, 738.

[85] George Williams, 'Constitutional Recognition by Way of an Indigenous Advisory Body' (2015) 8(18) *Indigenous Law Bulletin* 12, 13, 15–16.

[86] See Suri Ratnapala, 'Bills of Rights in Functioning Parliamentary Democracies: Kantian, Consequentialist and Institutionalist Scepticisms' (2010) 34(2) *Melbourne University Law Review* 592, 609. Similarly, Goldsworthy argues that Australia's human rights record, while 'far from perfect', is at least 'as meritorious as that of the United States', where a constitutional Bill of rights has been in operation: see Goldsworthy, 'Constitutional Cultures' (n 38 above) 687.

clauses in the ways that advocates for the rights of the vulnerable might predict or hope.[87]

Many important institutions are required by Australia's *Constitution* and most operate effectively. As the Centre for Comparative Constitutional Studies (CCCS) explained in a 2018 submission:

> It would be wrong to assume that a judicially adjudicated constitutional amendment would automatically carry more authority and weight than a non-justiciable amendment. Many integral institutions of the Australian constitutional order, such as the Senate in s 7, the House of Representatives in s 24 and the High Court in s 71, maintain their existence and legitimacy only through *popular and political support*.[88]

The non-justiciability of the proposed First Nations voice does not automatically mean its power will be diminished.[89] As the CCCS explains, judicial oversight of itself would provide 'no guarantee that the Voice to Parliament will be maintained'.[90] Indeed, the story of the Inter-State Commission demonstrates the corollary point: that institution suffered and faded *as a result* of judicial intervention. As noted, the *Wheat Case* controversy was a primary reason for the Commission's demise.[91] Key driving factors were the Commission's role as a watchdog of section 92 – a justiciable provision guaranteeing freedom of inter-State trade – as well as the need for judicial adjudication of section 101. Justiciability did not work in the Commission's favour. In contrast to the Commission, the clause requiring the establishment of a First Nations voice is intended to be non-justiciable and is not intended to be connected to any justiciable guarantees.[92]

The argument that justiciability automatically equals effectiveness needs to be questioned. In Chapter four above, reflecting on section 35 and the justiciable duty to consult in Canada, I noted the risk that courts may read down and narrow broad constitutional rights protections in favour of Crown power. The story of the Inter-State Commission similarly demonstrates why connecting the First Nations voice to a racial non-discrimination guarantee, to give it 'something in the Constitution to advise on',[93] may be ill-advised. This suggestion also undermines the intent of a First Nations constitutional voice as a

[87] See discussion of s 35 of the *Canadian Constitution* in Chapter 4 of this volume.

[88] Centre for Comparative Constitutional Studies, *Submission 289 to the Joint Select Committee Inquiry into Constitutional Recognition Relating to Aboriginal and Torres Strait Islander Peoples* (15 June 2018) 14, available at: <https://www.aph.gov.au/Parliamentary_Business/Committees/Joint/Former_Committees/Constitutional_Recognition_2018/ConstRecognition/Submissions> accessed 23 December 2019 (I was a joint-author of this publication).

[89] For concerns about non-justiciability, see Megan Davis and Rosalind Dixon, 'Constitutional Recognition through a (Justiciable) Duty to Consult? Towards Entrenched and Judicially Enforceable Norms of Indigenous Consultation' (2016) 27(4) *Public Law Review* 249, 258.

[90] CCCS, Submission 289 (n 88 above) 14.

[91] La Nauze (n 44 above) 57; Gageler (n 76 above) 215–16.

[92] *Final Report of the Referendum Council* (30 June 2017) 38.

[93] Williams, 'Constitutional Recognition' (n 85 above) 16.

non-justiciable alternative to a racial non-discrimination guarantee. The demise of the Inter-State Commission demonstrates that justiciability comes with its own risks. Through non-justiciability, a First Nations voice avoids the judicially-driven uncertainties that ultimately hampered the Inter-State Commission. A First Nations constitutional voice is intended to operate through politics, not the courts.[94] It would thus 'be the responsibility of all parliamentarians, and all Australians, to ensure the Voice operates effectively'.[95] The non-justiciability of the proposed institution fundamentally distinguishes this proposal from the Inter-State Commission.

Second, part of the problem with the Inter-State Commission was its wide conferred powers, including adjudicatory powers under section 101, which meant other institutional authorities (including the High Court) were threatened by the Commission's existence.[96] A similar attitude was demonstrated by Parliament's 'unappreciative and, at times, hostile reception' of Commission reports, revealing 'resentment at the apparent erosion of a staple parliamentary function'.[97] Even the States seemed to be threatened.[98] The Commission's intended role as a 'fourth arm' of government therefore may not have been politically viable due to 'possible opposition from State governments, interest groups, elements within the Federal government itself and possibly the High Court'.[99] It seems that the only interest group lobbying to keep the Commission were the Commissioners, and their voices were evidently not politically strong enough – they did not represent a genuine interest group or political constituency.

A First Nations voice would be fundamentally different. The institution is not intended to be adjudicatory; therefore its operation would not be complicated by separation of powers issues. Further, Indigenous people are a real interest group and a distinct political and constitutional constituency; and the proposed Indigenous body would provide a political voice into political decision-making. While there is bound to be oppositional tension from other

[94] See below for discussion of how non-justiciable constitutional provisions could be drafted.

[95] CCCS, Submission 289 (n 88 above) 14.

[96] 'That the Inter-State Commission was a threat, real or perceived, to other established power bases, either because of its wide constitutional jurisdiction or its guaranteed independence, is perfectly plain. The enormous grant of power in s 101 of the Constitution, reflecting the important role the Inter-State Commission was intended to play in the federal compact, was paradoxically responsible for its weakness. … the High Court's decision in the *Wheat Case* is susceptible of an interpretation of institutional rivalry and a concern on the part of the majority of the High Court to prevent an encroachment into its jurisdiction': Bell (n 63 above) 70–71.

[97] ibid 70. An important related lesson is that a body can become useless if the Parliament never implements its recommendations: at 68.

[98] '[T]he Commission's rebirth in 1984 received a rather lukewarm reaction from the States: perhaps they saw little to gain and much to lose from the potential impact of a national perspective on local interests, especially when that perspective would be taken by a body over which the States had no direct control': Coper (n 64 above) 740. The 'States … originally had little or no interest in its creation': La Nauze (n 44 above) 49.

[99] Radbone (n 64 above) 324.

interests (the same productive tension on which any check and balance system is based), Indigenous Australians would be the constituency politically driving and lobbying for the body's existence – hopefully supported by all Australians who would have voted for constitutional recognition of this institution through a successful referendum.

Third, following the *Wheat Case*, the Commission was stripped of its key powers and thus prevented from exercising its constitutional functions.[100] The 'constitutional vacuum'[101] this created was over time legislatively filled. The Commission's functions were 'taken over by specialist statutory bodies created for the task', including the Tariff Board, the Grants Commission,[102] the Trade Practices Commission, and others.[103] But unlike the Commission whose role was eventually filled by other legislative bodies, there currently exists no national Indigenous representative body with a legal mandate to formally engage and consult with Parliament. There is the government's Indigenous Advisory Council (IAC), but that is a non-representative advisory body, comprising government-appointed advisors[104] – it is not an Indigenous representative voice to Parliament and government. Notably the IAC was not even consulted before the Turnbull Government's decision to reject the Uluru Statement, demonstrating a lack of productive engagement from government with the IAC on key Indigenous matters.[105] The Congress of Australia's First Peoples (Congress), before it was defunded, was a national Indigenous representative body; it was not a statutory body, but a private corporation.[106] While the Congress website stated it did not 'depend upon the good will of parliament or the government of the day',[107] in practical terms it was heavily reliant on government funding.[108] There was no legal requirement for Congress to be supported by government, and no constitutional (or any weaker, legislative) imperative for Congress to

[100] Bell (n 63 above) 68–69.
[101] ibid 68.
[102] La Nauze (n 44 above) 57.
[103] Radbone (n 64 above) 333.
[104] Australian Government, 'Prime Minister's Indigenous Advisory Council', *National Indigenous Australians Agency* <https://www.niaa.gov.au/indigenous-affairs/prime-ministers-indigenous-advisory-council> accessed 23 December 2019.
[105] Stephen Fitzpatrick, 'Closing the Gap: Reconciling a Policy Mess', *The Australian* (5 September 2018).
[106] National Congress of Australia's First Peoples, *The National Congress of Australia's First Peoples* <https://web.archive.org/web/20190310003710/http://nationalcongress.com.au/about-us/> accessed 23 December 2019.
[107] ibid.
[108] In June 2019, Congress went into voluntary administration: Douglas Smith, 'Australia's Largest Indigenous Organisation May Be Forced to Close', *NITV* (13 June 2019) <https://www.sbs.com.au/nitv/article/2019/06/13/australias-largest-indigenous-organisation-may-be-forced-close> accessed 23 December 2019. See also Heath Aston, 'Social Services Scraps Funding for Homeless and Housing Groups', *Sydney Morning Herald* (22 December 2014) <https://www.smh.com.au/politics/federal/social-services-scraps-funding-for-homeless-and-housing-groups-20141222-12cf67.html> accessed 23 December 2019.

advise Parliament in its policy- and law-making for Indigenous affairs.[109] By contrast, the proposed First Nations constitutional voice is intended to be part of the public institutional and parliamentary machinery of the nation. It would be both constitutionally guaranteed and legislatively articulated, and there should be mandated mechanisms for productive engagement with government on Indigenous affairs.

There is a further political lesson here. That legislated bodies overtook the Commission's role, removing any need for its existence, demonstrates the risks associated with legislating for a First Nations voice before it is constitutionalised.[110] If a First Nations voice is legislated and put into action without the constitutional guarantee called for by the Uluru Statement, this may diminish the political urgency and momentum driving the campaign for a First Nations *constitutional* voice, because the constitutional vacuum may ostensibly have been legislatively filled. Opponents of the proposal may then point to the legislated institution to argue on the one hand that no constitutional reform is needed because an Indigenous voice already exists; on the other hand, they may point to imperfections in the institution (for no institution composed of imperfect humans can be perfect) to contend that it is not worthy of constitutional recognition. Despite having a legislated voice, Indigenous people will remain vulnerable to the legislation being struck down at any time, as occurred in the past, and efforts at constitutionalisation may also be undermined. Further, lacking constitutional authority, a merely legislated voice is less likely to carry the political weight needed to ensure it is effective. For these reasons, it may be preferable to hold a referendum to insert the constitutional provision requiring a First Nations voice, before legislating it into action. If needed, however, the legislation could be co-designed with Indigenous peoples and even drafted, if desired, before the referendum.

Fourth, the proposed constitutional institution is likely to carry a more powerful and specific popular endorsement than the Inter-State Commission, if the proposal succeeds at a referendum. The Commission was just one part of the 1901 *Constitution* which, as a whole, was endorsed by the people. While the 1901 *Constitution* mandated the existence of the Commission, the Commission did not operate until 12 years later. Arguably, this was able to happen because there was no special or particular popular endorsement directed at the Commission.

109 Congress often complained of lack of serious engagement from political leaders. See Anna Henderson, 'Prime Minister's Office Confirms Plans to Meet with Indigenous Congress, After Accusations of Bias', *ABC News* (15 March 2016) <https://www.abc.net.au/news/2016-03-15/pm-confirms-plans-to-meet-with-indigenous-congress/7247170> accessed 23 December 2019.

110 See Frank Brennan, 'Walking Together for a Better Future', *Eureka Street* (1 October 2018) <http://www.eurekastreet.com.au/article.aspx?aeid=56783> accessed 23 December 2019. For a response to this argument, see Gemma McKinnon, 'Trialling an Indigenous Voice Before a Referendum is Like Forcing Us to Audition', *The Guardian* (4 October 2018) <https://www.theguardian.com/commentisfree/2018/oct/04/trialling-an-indigenous-voice-before-a-referendum-is-like-forcing-us-to-audition> accessed 23 December 2019.

A contemporary Indigenous recognition referendum would be fundamentally different. If the Australian people vote to amend the *Constitution* to establish a First Nations voice, there will be a highly specific, political mandate from the Australian people for the Indigenous body to function and operate effectively. This would place an onerous responsibility on the Parliament to follow the constitutional requirement, as directed by the Australian people through a contemporary, single-issue referendum. As the CCCS argues:

> It would be *unthinkable* that Parliament would ignore this powerful political, moral and constitutional imperative, as reflected in the constitutional amendment. Yet should this occur, Indigenous Australians would demand the constitutional imperative be respected and the institution operate. Additionally, the Australian people would demand Parliament adhere to their popular will, as expressed through the constitutional mandate.[111]

B. Learning from ATSIC

In designing an Indigenous body, it will be important to learn from the strengths and weaknesses of ATSIC. While usually remembered for its weaknesses rather than its strengths,[112] ATSIC was a representative institution and consultative body that allowed Indigenous people to exercise a voice in Indigenous affairs. The idea of such a body was based on principles of self-determination and, as Kingsley Palmer explains, 'the right of Indigenous peoples to achieve some form of autonomy within an overall system of mainstream government'.[113]

Some have pointed to ATSIC's wide mandate and the tension within its competing dual roles as a key weakness. It was both an administrative body and a representative body, at once tasked with administrating programmes and being an independent national Indigenous voice. This meant that its representative role may have been compromised; a problem which was compounded by the fact that ATSIC's elected representatives were 'dependent upon the government for funding and … subject to the sensitivities of the Commonwealth in

[111] CCCS, Submission 289 (n 88 above) 15.

[112] Sanders (n 25 above). It may also be appropriate to take lessons from the design of Congress, but given that Congress is a private corporation rather than a public institution, it is not explored here. See, however, Sam Muir, 'A New Representative Body for Aboriginal and Torres Strait Islander People: Just One Step' (2010) 14(1) *Australian Indigenous Law Review* 86.

[113] Kingsley Palmer, 'ATSIC: Origins and Issues for the Future – A Critical Review of Public Domain Research and Other Materials' (AIATSIS Research Discussion Paper No 12, 2004) 10. See also, Aboriginal and Torres Strait Islander Commission, *Review of the Operation of the ATSIC Act: Report to the Minister for ATSI Affairs* (1989); Angela Pratt, 'Make or Break? A Background to the ATSIC Changes and the ATSIC Review' (Social Policy Group, Parliamentary Library, *Current Issues Brief No 29 2002–03*, 26 May 2003); Aboriginal and Torres Strait Islander Social Justice Commissioner, Human Rights and Equal Opportunity Commission, *Submission to the Review of ATSIC* (20 August 2003); Sanders (n 25 above).

relation to spending on Indigenous peoples'.[114] It was therefore ultimately answerable to the government of the day, rather than the Indigenous people that it represented.[115] It may have been that ATSIC carried too wide a spectrum of roles, which complicated its purpose. There are similarities here with the Inter-State Commission which, according to Bell, was 'overburdened with a veritable miscellany of tasks' and so, perhaps, could excel at none.[116] Others have argued that ATSIC may have been too far removed in its accountability structures from Indigenous people at the regional level.[117] Similarly, ATSIC was intended to be a national Indigenous representative body to influence government policy, but there were few formal structures for productive interaction with government.[118] While ATSIC was intended to be a 'corner-stone of national Indigenous representation and the source of advice to government', this was 'neither mandated nor facilitated by required process'. In Palmer's view, 'a more robust system needs to be designed to effect the desired outcome'.[119]

There are several ways that a First Nations constitutional voice could improve upon the ATSIC experience. Unlike ATSIC, the proposed Indigenous body, as currently construed, is aimed at facilitating Indigenous political participation rather than creating an unwieldy administrative bureaucracy. The proposed structure could thus work in a way that is supportive of, and complementary to, other connecting reforms which would seek to improve programme delivery on the ground. These include the proposed Empowered Communities (EC) style reforms, developed by Indigenous leaders from eight regions around Australia, which aim to enable increased Indigenous authority in Indigenous relationships with government at the bureaucratic and service delivery level, through greater transparency and increased local Indigenous choice and empowerment in funding and programme delivery arrangements.[120] While the First Nations voice can be a representative and advisory voice to Parliament and the Executive at the policy- and law-making level, the EC proposed structural reforms are more concerned with making Indigenous affairs at the bureaucratic and service delivery level work in a way that is conducive to Indigenous empowerment.[121] The design challenge will be to properly connect a national First Nations voice to regional and local structures for Indigenous empowerment, in ways that ensure efficiency, transparency and appropriate accountability to local and regional

[114] Palmer (n 113 above) 11. See also John Chesterman, 'National Policy-Making in Indigenous Affairs: Blueprint for an Indigenous Review Council' (2008) 67(4) *Journal of Public Administration* 419, 422.

[115] Palmer (n 113 above) 5–6, 22.

[116] Bell (n 63 above) 70.

[117] Palmer (n 113 above) 22–23.

[118] ibid 5–6, 23.

[119] ibid.

[120] Empowered Communities, *Empowered Peoples Design Report* (Wunan Foundation 2015).

[121] See Noel Pearson, 'Empowered Communities have Spoken: Time for Action', *The Australian* (30 January 2016).

Indigenous communities. Further, in terms of the delivery of advice to government and Parliament, while the First Nations voice should be empowered to advise on broad matters if it wishes, its members will need to exercise acuity and discretion by focusing on the proposed policy and legislation that is most important to Indigenous interests, so they do not become overloaded with too many tasks.[122]

The institutional design of a First Nations voice can learn from the ATSIC experience by ensuring the devolution and decentralisation of power. ATSIC was made up of regional bodies but was also centralised in its structure. A review into ATSIC found that the body would have benefitted from greater control at the regional level.[123] Others suggest there could have been 'better representation of community views'.[124] The design of a First Nations voice can learn from this feedback by ensuring that it is closely connected and accountable to Indigenous people at a local level.[125] If it is to utilise old ATSIC boundaries, the design of the structure could vest power at the bottom – in the regions and the communities – rather than the top. The structure could give voice to the First Nations of Australia, by building upon and connecting with existing and developing representative mechanisms, including Native Title Representative Bodies (NTRBs) within native title structures.[126] At the same time, the structure can ensure that Indigenous Australians who do not or cannot win native title recognition, perhaps due to a legal finding of loss of cultural connection,[127] can also be represented.[128] The system could enable Indigenous people living in remote, regional or urban areas to have a voice in the Indigenous law- and policy-making that affects them, whether or not they are culturally connected with their traditional lands in a way that satisfies native title legal requirements.[129] Where a legislative or policy action only affects one area, as was the case with the Northern Territory Intervention, it would make sense for the structure to enable Indigenous people and representatives in that particular region to be specifically consulted and express their views to Parliament and government. Design principles of this kind can be articulated in the legislation setting up the structure.[130]

[122] The issue of scope will be discussed further below.

[123] See John Hannaford, Jackie Huggins and John Collins, *In the Hands of the Regions: A New ATSIC – Report of the Review of the Aboriginal and Torres Strait Islander Commission* (November 2003).

[124] See Palmer (n 113 above) 11, 22–23; Sanders (n 25 above) 10.

[125] Marion Scrymgour, 'Looking Back and Looking Forward After the Intervention', *Nugget Coombs Memorial Lecture* (Charles Darwin University, 8 October 2014); HC Coombs also argued that 'any organisation designed to give Aborigines an effective influence on government policies must be firmly based on, derive its authority from, and be accountable to, local groups and communities and their organisations': HC Coombs, *Aboriginal Autonomy* (Cambridge University Press 1994) 141–42.

[126] Noel Pearson, 'In Pursuit of a Regional, Reciprocal Responsibility Settlement for Cape York' (*National Native Title Conference*, Port Douglas, 18 June 2015).

[127] See, eg, *Members of the Yorta Yorta Aboriginal Community v Victoria* (2002) 214 CLR 422.

[128] The Māori Council approach could be adapted. See *Māori Community Development Act 1962* (NZ) s 19.

[129] See *Native Title Act 1993* (Cth), s 223.

[130] Further insights for structural design are discussed further below.

Importantly, a First Nations voice could operate under a constitutional requirement, further articulated in legislation, for the Indigenous body to engage with Parliament and government – something ATSIC did not have. This would address the concern that ATSIC did not have clear, mandated procedures for effective government engagement and dialogue. Similarly, the easy axing of ATSIC demonstrates why it is important that this institution has a constitutional anchor. The body should not be abolished the moment there are difficulties. All institutions are made up of, run and designed by, imperfect human beings who inevitably make mistakes and must learn and improve over time. Institutions themselves are imperfect and must evolve. The details of the Indigenous body or institution would be articulated in legislation (although its existence will be required by the *Constitution*). There would thus be flexibility to evolve and improve the institution over time as needed. This flexibility is important. But when problems do arise, there should be a constitutional imperative for Parliament and government to sort out the design issues in partnership with Indigenous people. The success of the Indigenous body will depend not only on its Indigenous members; it will also depend on how well it is supported and respected by the arms of government.[131]

Since ATSIC was abolished, nothing has filled the institutional gap to give Indigenous Australians a genuine voice in national affairs. As journalist Nicholas Rothwell notes, addressing Indigenous disadvantage requires power to be returned to Indigenous peoples, 'by giving them the reins, and asking them to have a hand in shaping their own fate'[132] – thereby enabling Indigenous self-determination. The proposed constitutional voice seeks to enable Indigenous peoples to exercise leadership, agency and influence in their affairs. Indigenous peoples would be able to exert political pressure, with a constitutional mandate, to ensure that the body exists and operates effectively. This would be a vast improvement on the current situation.

IV. ASSESSING OPTIONS FOR CONSTITUTIONAL AMENDMENTS

How might a First Nations constitutional voice be achieved? What could the constitutional amendment look like? In the lead up to the Uluru Statement and the Referendum Council's report, a number of draft constitutional amendments were put forward by Indigenous leaders and constitutional experts to progress discussion of a constitutionally guaranteed Indigenous

[131] As Pearson has noted with respect to ATSIC, government bureaucracies and other industries were also responsible for ATSIC's deficiencies: Pearson, 'Recent Indigenous Policy Failures' (n 28 above).

[132] Nicholas Rothwell, 'A Decade After ATSIC was Axed, Aborigines Still Have Little Say', *The Australian* (27 September 2014).

voice in Indigenous affairs.[133] Here I briefly outline the Referendum Council's directional recommendations for constitutional drafting.[134] In light of these recommendations, I assess some drafting options against principles of constitutional suitability and responsiveness to concerns about parliamentary supremacy, legal uncertainty and political viability, and attempt to refine the drafting according to these principles where possible. I also offer some alternative approaches to constitutional drafting that may not yet have been considered.

A. The Referendum Council's Recommendations

With respect to constitutional reform, the Referendum Council recommended:

> That a referendum be held to provide in the Australian Constitution for a representative body that gives Aboriginal and Torres Strait Islander First Nations a Voice to the Commonwealth Parliament. One of the specific functions of such a body, to be set out in legislation outside the Constitution, should include the function of monitoring the use of the heads of power in section 51 (xxvi) and section 122. The body will recognise the status of Aboriginal and Torres Strait Islander peoples as the first peoples of Australia.[135]

The Referendum Council explained that Parliament would need to formulate the precise form of the constitutional amendment, noting the importance of continued Indigenous agreement and consultation on such details going forward. The Council also set out some constitutional principles that should guide the drafting.

First, while the existence of the body should be constitutionally guaranteed, the proposed body should be set up in legislation enacted by Parliament. Legislation should set out the details, processes and design, including 'how the body is to be given an appropriately representative character and how it can properly and most usefully discharge its advisory functions'.[136] Such details need not be included in the *Constitution*. Second, the Council was clear that the body should not have 'any kind of veto power'[137] – it is intended to be advisory in nature and cannot give binding advice. The Referendum Council further stated that the proposed voice must not 'interfere with parliamentary supremacy' and

[133] See Anne Twomey, 'Putting Words to the Tune of Indigenous Constitutional Recognition', *The Conversation* (20 May 2015); Allens Linklaters, *Submission 97 to Joint Select Committee on Constitutional Recognition of Aboriginal and Torres Strait Islander Peoples*, Inquiry into Constitutional Recognition of Aboriginal and Torres Strait Islander Peoples (30 January 2015); Warren Mundine, 'Practical Recognition from the Mobs' Perspective: Enabling Our Mobs to Speak for Country' (Uphold & Recognise Monograph Series 2017); Davis and Dixon (n 89 above).

[134] *Final Report of the Referendum Council* (n 92 above).

[135] ibid, Recommendations.

[136] ibid 36.

[137] ibid.

would therefore 'not be justiciable'.[138] Third, it was suggested that the constitutional amendment should describe 'the function of the body and its relationship to the parliamentary process', noting that 'the concept of providing advice on certain matters requires definition of the relevant matters'. The Council therefore acknowledged that it 'would not be realistic' for the body

> to provide advice on all matters 'affecting' Aboriginal and Torres Strait Islander peoples because most laws of general application affect such peoples. On the other hand, it may be too narrow to limit the subject matters to laws with respect to Aboriginal and Torres Strait Islander peoples because some laws of general application have particular impact on or significance to such peoples.[139]

It was therefore proposed that a balance must be struck, with the focus being on laws and policies directed at, or significantly or especially impacting, Indigenous people.

Fourth, the Council noted that in recommending a constitutional voice, it was taking on board political objections to a racial non-discrimination clause, as proposed by previous reports.[140] It noted that the preference for a constitutional voice

> took account of the objections raised against the alternative substantive constitutional amendment option: the insertion of some form of non-discrimination protection into the Constitution. The objections to a non-discrimination provision which would render parliamentary legislation justiciable under the jurisdiction of the High Court, may be appropriate or inappropriate – but that is not the point. The point is that such a non-discrimination provision has strong objections and objectors, which the Council believes will see it fail at a referendum. The choice of an institutional alternative – a Voice to the Parliament – is therefore a highly reasonable proposal, put forward at Uluru and supported by our Council.[141]

The Referendum Council's reasoning and justifications provide broad principles by which constitutional drafting should be assessed. The constitutional drafting giving effect to a First Nations voice should be responsive to previously articulated concerns about parliamentary supremacy and legal uncertainty (by not constituting a veto, by being non-justiciable, and by leaving institutional details to Parliament), so that it can broadly be considered politically viable. To this I would add a further, though related, lens through which to evaluate constitutional suitability: any drafting should cohere and align with Australian constitutional culture and design. The following sections evaluate and, in some cases, attempt to refine options for constitutional drafting with these issues in mind.

[138] ibid 38.

[139] ibid 36.

[140] These objections are explained in Shireen Morris, 'Undemocratic, Uncertain and Politically Unviable? An Analysis of and Response to Objections to a Proposed Racial Non-Discrimination Clause as Part of Constitutional Reforms for Indigenous Recognition' (2014) 40(2) *Monash University Law Review* 488. See also Chapter 3 of this volume.

[141] *Final Report of the Referendum Council* (n 92 above) 38.

B. A Constitutionally Guaranteed Indigenous Advisory Body: A Non-Justiciable Guarantee

The Referendum Council is correct that, in order to properly take on board parliamentary supremacy and legal uncertainty concerns, the constitutional amendment for a First Nations voice should not establish a veto and should be drafted to be non-justiciable. Non-justiciable constitutional clauses generally arise in relation to the internal workings of Parliament and mean that Parliament is immune to judicial review in respect of its internal procedures and choices to exercise its powers. This is what makes constitutional clauses relating to 'proposed laws' non-justiciable. Non-justiciability is a way of recognising 'the primacy of the political process and the subsidiary role of the judiciary',[142] thus avoiding the uncertainty of judicial interpretation. It is a way of respecting parliamentary supremacy and the separation of powers. In Chapter four, I discussed the issues that have arisen with a justiciable duty to consult in Canada. Above (in section III) I noted the problems that arose with the Inter-State Commission. By ensuring that the First Nations voice operates under a non-justiciable constitutional amendment, the uncertainties of High Court interpretation can be avoided.

In the Indigenous constitutional recognition debate, the concern to avoid legal uncertainty and maintain parliamentary supremacy has regularly been expressed through the inclusion of 'no legal effect clauses' in State constitutions that have symbolically recognised Indigenous peoples in preambles or specific clauses.[143] However, it has been previously established that 'no legal effect' clauses would not be supported by Indigenous people.[144] Fortuitously, there are non-justiciable provisions in the *Australian Constitution*[145] which can be emulated.[146] These clauses do not include explicit 'non-justiciable' or 'no legal

[142] Henry Burmester, 'Locus Standi in Constitutional Litigation' in HP Lee and George Winterton (eds), *Australian Constitutional Perspectives* (Law Book Company Ltd 1992) 178.

[143] eg, the *Constitution Act 1975* (Vic) recognises Indigenous peoples in s 1A, and s 1A(3) provides that: 'The Parliament does not intend by this section – (a) to create in any person any legal right or give rise to any civil cause of action; or (b) to affect in any way the interpretation of this Act or of any other law in force in Victoria.' The *Constitution Act 1902* (NSW) recognises Indigenous peoples in s 2, and s 2(3) provides that: 'Nothing in this section creates any legal right or liability, or gives rise to or affects any civil cause of action or right to review an administrative action, or affects the interpretation of any Act or law in force in New South Wales.' The *Constitution of Queensland 2001* (Qld) recognises Indigenous peoples in its preamble, providing a 'no legal effect clause' in relation to the preamble in s 3A. The *Constitution Act 1934* (SA) recognises Indigenous peoples in s 2, and s 2(3) provides a 'no legal effect' clause. Western Australia and Tasmania are the only States to have recognised Indigenous peoples in the preambles to their constitutions without a 'no legal effect' clause. See *Constitution Act 1889* (WA) and *Constitution Act 1934* (Tas).

[144] The Expert Panel on Constitutional Recognition of Indigenous Australians, *Recognising Aboriginal and Torres Strait Islander Peoples in the Constitution* (2012) 113–15.

[145] See, eg, ss 53, 54, and 56.

[146] Tarunabh Khaitan notes that approximately 37 international state constitutions feature non-justiciable thick moral commitments ('constitutional directives') which are not enforced by courts, but 'help shape the discourse over a state's constitutional identity', and 'are a key tool to realise a morally-committed conception of political constitutionalism'. See Tarunabh Khaitan, 'Constitutional Directives: Morally-Committed Political Constitutionalism' (2019) 82(4) *Modern Law Review* 603.

effect' specifications, but are nonetheless generally treated by the High Court as non-justiciable.[147] Both the drafters of the *Constitution*[148] and the High Court have viewed these sections as non-justiciable[149] because the provisions refer to 'proposed laws', indicating that they are internal rules to govern Parliament's law-making.[150] The High Court stays out of such matters, because the judiciary's role is to deal 'with what is law rather than proposals to make law'.[151] The non-justiciability of such clauses reflects the fact that, in the words of McTiernan J: 'Parliament is master in its own household.'[152] But, as discussed above, it should not be assumed that non-justiciable constitutional clauses carry less authority or force. They are still constitutional law: constitutional laws that are adjudicated and enforced by Parliament, not the courts. Non-justiciability does not diminish their constitutional authority. As former Chief Justice Murray Gleeson has noted, 'the rule of law does not require all possible disputes to be justiciable, or all grievances to be resolved by litigation'.[153] Indeed, as discussed in Chapter four in relation to section 35 of the *Canadian Constitution*, as well as in relation to the Inter-State Commission above, there may be benefit for Indigenous Australians in leaving the courts out of the constitutional dialogue created between the First Nations and the Australian state.

In 2015, Professor Anne Twomey intelligently emulated existing non-justiciable constitutional clauses to develop constitutional drafting to give effect

[147] See Anne Twomey, 'An Indigenous Advisory Body: Addressing Concerns about Justiciability and Parliamentary Sovereignty' (2015) 8(19) *Indigenous Law Bulletin* 6.

[148] *Official Record of the Debates of the Australasian Federal Convention* (Adelaide, 13 April 1897) 473 (Edmund Barton).

[149] The non-justiciable character of s 53 was discussed in *Osborne v Commonwealth* (1911) 12 CLR 321, 336, 339; *Western Australia v Commonwealth* (1995) 183 CLR 373, 482. Geoffrey Lindell, 'The Justiciability of Political Questions: Recent Developments' in HP Lee and George Winterton (eds), *Australian Constitutional Perspectives* (The Law Book Co 1991) 180–81; Gabrielle Appleby and Andrew Webster, 'Parliament's Role in Constitutional Interpretation' (2013) 37(2) *Melbourne University Law Review* 255, 272; JA Thompson, 'The Judicial Branch: Non-justiciability and the Australian Constitution' in Michael Coper and George Williams (eds), *Power, Parliament and the People* (The Federation Press 1997) 57.

[150] With respect to s 53, Sir Samuel Griffith explained: 'Secs 53 and 54 deal with "proposed laws" – that is, Bills or projects of law still under consideration and not assented to – and they lay down rules to be observed with respect to proposed laws at that stage. Whatever obligations are imposed by these sections are directed to the Houses of Parliament whose conduct of their internal affairs is not subject to review by a Court of law': *Osborne* (n 149 above) 336, 339. See also, *Western Australia v Commonwealth* (n 149 above) 482.

[151] See Glenn Worthington, 'How Far Do Sections 53 and 56 of the Australian Constitution Secure a Financial Initiative of the Executive?' (Parliamentary Studies Paper 12, Australian National University) 4.

[152] *Victoria v Commonwealth* (1975) 134 CLR 81, 138. See Kirsty Magarey, 'Alcopops Makes the House See Double: "The Proposed Law" in Section 57 of the Constitution' (Law and Bills Digest Section, Parliamentary Library, Research Paper No 32 2008–09). For a discussion of how non-justiciability can be achieved in the constitutional drafting, see Morris, 'The Argument for a Constitutional Procedure' (n 37 above) 179–86; Morris, 'The Torment of Our Powerlessness' (n 2 above) 653–65.

[153] Murray Gleeson, 'Courts and the Rule of Law' (*The Rule of Law Series*, Melbourne University, 7 November 2001) <http://www.hcourt.gov.au/assets/publications/speeches/former-justices/gleesoncj/cj_ruleoflaw.htm> accessed 24 December 2019.

to the proposal for a constitutionally mandated Indigenous body to advise Parliament on laws and policies with respect to Indigenous affairs. Twomey's proposed new Chapter 1A of the *Constitution* would read:

> 60A(1) There shall be an Aboriginal and Torres Strait Islander body, to be called the [insert appropriate name, perhaps drawn from an Aboriginal or Torres Strait Islander language], which shall have the function of providing advice to the Parliament and the Executive Government on matters relating to Aboriginal and Torres Strait Islander peoples.
>
> (2) The Parliament shall, subject to this Constitution, have power to make laws with respect to the composition, roles, powers and procedures of the [body].
>
> (3) The Prime Minister [or the Speaker/President of the Senate] shall cause a copy of the [body's] advice to be tabled in each House of Parliament as soon as practicable after receiving it.
>
> (4) The House of Representatives and the Senate shall give consideration to the tabled advice of the [body] in debating proposed laws with respect to Aboriginal and Torres Strait Islander peoples.

In Twomey's 2015 amendment, sub-section 60A(1) requires Parliament to establish an Indigenous body through legislation. An enabling Act would set up the mechanisms for how its representatives are to be chosen, the body's powers, functions and processes. Sub-section 60A(1) gives the body its main function: providing advice to the Parliament and the Executive Government on matters relating to Aboriginal and Torres Strait Islander peoples. The proposed draft thus constitutionally empowers the body to advise both the Parliament and the Executive – enabling Indigenous input into law- and policy-making.

While section 60A(4) spells out only Parliament's constitutional obligation to consider the body's advice with respect to proposed laws debated in the Parliament, section 60A(1) would also give the body constitutional authority to advise the Executive. Legislation or internal parliamentary practice could set in place further processes, timelines, and procedures for the body to engage with government on Indigenous policy development, and these processes would, in an important sense, be underpinned by the constitutional right of the body to provide its views.

The tabling of the advice is an important element in Twomey's draft constitutional procedure, which speaks to the Referendum Council's point about the importance of the engagement and advice function in the *Constitution*: it provides the formal mechanism for engagement between the Indigenous body and the Parliament. As Twomey explains, ensuring that the advice is tabled

> provides a permanent public record of that advice; it gives the advice the status of a privileged document … and it provides a direct channel from the Indigenous body into the parliament, providing a constitutional means for Aboriginal people and Torres Strait Islanders to have a voice in parliamentary proceedings concerning their affairs.[154]

[154] Twomey, 'Putting Words to the Tune' (n 133 above).

Once tabled, the Houses of Parliament would have a constitutional duty under section 60A(4) to consider the advice in the debating of proposed laws with respect to Aboriginal and Torres Strait Islander peoples, but this obligation would be non-justiciable.[155]

Twomey's amendment is deliberately drafted to provide a non-justiciable constitutional guarantee of the Indigenous voice in Indigenous affairs,[156] thus aligning with the Referendum Council's principles. The amendment uses the language of 'proposed laws', which indicates that the clause is to be adjudicated and enforced by Parliament, not the High Court. The High Court is constitutionally empowered to adjudicate with respect to enacted laws, not proposed laws, under the principle of the separation of powers. Twomey explains that, although the requirement for Parliament to consider advice is non-justiciable, it would operate as a 'political and moral obligation upon members of parliament to fulfil their constitutional role in giving consideration to such advice, but it would be for the houses, not the courts, to ensure that this obligation is met'.[157] I would go further than this: the obligation would be a constitutional requirement. It would not be justiciable, because Parliament is immune to judicial review of its internal procedures. But Parliament would be bound by the law of the *Constitution* to fulfil this requirement, and the requirement would be enforced and adjudicated by Parliament, rather than the judiciary.

The procedure is designed so it cannot delay Parliament if no advice is received from the body: 'Hence, the responsibility is on the Indigenous body to provide advice if it wants it considered. Failure to provide advice cannot hold up the process.'[158] This is important, because it means that the procedure cannot operate as a veto by inaction. This means that this amendment is fully respectful of parliamentary supremacy, in line with the strong parliamentary supremacy established by the *Constitution*. It cannot be considered a radical proposed change and aligns with the Referendum Council's intention in this regard.

Twomey's proposed section 60A(2) also delegates power to Parliament to legislate for the composition and design of the Indigenous body, rather than articulating such details in the *Constitution*:

> It is not appropriate to set out in the Constitution the detail of how such a body is to be chosen. Just as the Constitution leaves it substantially to legislation to determine how members of parliament are elected and the powers and procedures of the

[155] For a full discussion of Twomey's drafting and the issue of non-justiciability, see Morris, 'The Argument for a Constitutional Procedure' (n 37 above) 179–83.

[156] Twomey, 'An Indigenous Advisory Body' (n 147 above). It should be noted here that there is a difference between the potential for constitutional justiciability discussed in this chapter, which can result in laws being struck down by the High Court, thus giving rise to concerns about parliamentary supremacy, and justiciability arising under legislation created by Parliament, which does not give rise to laws being invalidated by the courts, and thus does not create legal uncertainty in the same way – Parliament remains in charge of this justiciability.

[157] Twomey, 'Putting Words to the Tune' (n 133 above).

[158] ibid.

> parliament, so too this amendment would leave such matters to the parliament to determine, in collaboration with Aboriginal and Torres Strait Islander people.[159]

This, too, is in line with the Referendum Council's broad direction that it is not appropriate to put all the details of the proposed body in the *Constitution*. As Professor Rosalind Dixon has noted, such deferral is common in Australia's constitutional law which leaves many institutional and democratic matters to Parliament, and this too shows respect for the supremacy of Parliament.[160] The design and method of election of the body are matters that Indigenous Australians should decide and negotiate with Parliament. Further details can then be articulated in legislation, ultimately subject to parliamentary will.

Twomey's proposal is balanced because it empowers Indigenous peoples with a constitutional voice, without the downsides and legal uncertainty created by justiciable, High Court adjudicated guarantees. This eliminates the risk of laws being struck down, which is often cited as a concern for parliamentarians anxious to retain their power in this constitutional relationship.[161] It also strikes a balance between the need for constitutional flexibility in body design, and the Indigenous desire for the security and stability of a constitutional guarantee – the Twomey approach provides both. The approach is also balanced in its handling of the issue of scope, in line with the Referendum Council's suggested approach: ie, what matters the body can advise on. Section 60A(1) provides that the body may advise on matters 'relating to' Indigenous peoples – creating a broad scope – the body would need to use discretion on which matters it wishes to advise on. This broad scope is justifiable, because there is no veto and the mechanism cannot delay Parliament: if there is no advice provided, nothing need be tabled and there is nothing for parliamentarians to consider. Further, parliamentarians, under section 60A(4), must only consider advice on matters that are 'with respect to' Indigenous peoples, which seems to indicate a very narrow range of issues under section 51(xxvi). This provides a narrow obligation to consider advice 'with respect to' Indigenous peoples, and additionally, the obligation is non-justiciable.

An obvious reality of this proposal is that, because there is no veto, the advice can be ignored by the state. This accords with the Referendum Council's direction which, in my view, is justifiable. It is unlikely that a veto would be practically workable, let alone politically accepted: a constitutionalised veto would probably be opposed by many on the grounds that it undermines parliamentary supremacy. As noted, this proposal is a radical centre, noble compromise. As the Referendum Council notes, it is intended to achieve Indigenous aspirations as articulated in the Uluru Statement, but also to address concerns about

[159] ibid.

[160] Rosalind Dixon, 'Let's Give Indigenous People a Voice in Parliament', *The Australian* (21 July 2017).

[161] See full discussion of objections to a racial non-discrimination clause, as proposed by the Expert Panel, in Morris, 'Undemocratic, Uncertain and Politically Unviable?' (n 140 above).

parliamentary supremacy and legal uncertainty. Thus, the aim should be an authoritative but non-binding Indigenous voice in political decisions about Indigenous rights and interests. After all, the Uluru Statement is a request 'to be heard', not a demand to command. It asks for a voice, not a veto. Although the requirement of consultation and advice is weaker than free, prior and informed consent, this can be justified on the grounds of practical workability and political viability.[162] It would arguably be unworkable to give the three per cent Indigenous minority a constitutional veto over the decisions of the majority,[163] and this would probably not be politically sellable. Thus, the reality of this non-justiciable constitutional amendment is that there would be no recourse to the High Court where it was felt that advice was not properly considered by Parliament, or if the advice was rejected.[164] Nonetheless, a constitutional voice would carry special authority.[165] There are a variety of mechanisms that can be built legislatively into the design and processes of the body that can support its impact and effectiveness in influencing policy and legislative decisions with respect to Indigenous affairs, as examined further below.

On balance, Twomey's proposal for a constitutionally guaranteed Indigenous advisory body provides a modest and constitutionally conservative way of achieving the Uluru Statement's aspirations for constitutional recognition, which aligns with the Referendum Council's broad guidelines. It is an amendment that coheres with Australia's political process-driven constitutional culture and accords with Australia's strong parliamentary supremacy. It is thus arguably politically viable.

C. Omitting the Tabling of Advice Function

A similar though simpler constitutional approach was put forward by Allens Linklater law firm in 2015,[166] which proposed drafting along the following lines:

> There shall be a First Peoples Council established by Parliament and with such powers as may be determined by Parliament from time to time. Parliament shall consult with and seek advice from the First Peoples Council on legislation relating to Aboriginal and Torres Strait Islander peoples.

This drafting would create a constitutional obligation on Parliament to 'consult with and seek advice from' the body on legislation relating to Indigenous

162 Russell A Miller, 'Collective Discursive Democracy as the Indigenous Right to Self-Determination' (2007) 31(2) *American Indian Law Review* 341, 369, 371.

163 Even where such political decisions appear only to affect Indigenous interests, the vast majority of such decisions are about resources and land – and so involve competing interests.

164 This is pointed out by Davis and Dixon (n 89 above), discussed further below.

165 Fergal Davis, 'The Problem of Authority and the Proposal for an Indigenous Advisory Body' (2015) 8(19) *Indigenous Law Bulletin* 23.

166 Allens Linklaters, *Submission* 97 (n 133 above).

peoples. One difference with the Twomey approach is that this version does not mention the Executive, and so does not require consultation on policy, which may be a weakness.[167]

The drafting is less sophisticated than Twomey's approach in its consideration and implementation of non-justiciability. While the Allens Linklater submission intends that 'the power to advise and consult, and the extent and nature of that interaction with the legislative branch would be determined by the Parliament', and the 'precise remit and the mechanics of its operation must be outlined by the legislature',[168] this is not necessarily clear in the proposed constitutional drafting. On the text, it is uncertain whether the obligation to consult would be justiciable. There is no use of 'proposed laws' unlike in the Twomey approach and so the High Court may not interpret this as a non-justiciable clause. It is not clear that Parliament is to determine the consultation procedures, so this may also be left open for judicial intervention, whereby the High Court may decide what 'advise and consult' means. It is also unclear whether legislation could be invalidated if the Parliament is found by the High Court to have failed to consult. Similarly, the High Court may also be left to resolve which matters are 'relating to' Indigenous people or not, to clarify when the duty to consult arises.

The Allens Linklater submission states that its proposal is aimed at adhering to the policy intent of the drafting as articulated by Cape York Institute.[169] This means respecting parliamentary supremacy and eliminating legal uncertainty. The drafting can be improved to better fulfil its stated aims by amending it to read as follows:

> There shall be a First Peoples Council established by Parliament to advise Parliament and the Executive on proposed laws and other matters relating to Aboriginal and Torres Strait Islander peoples, under procedures to be determined by Parliament, and with such powers, processes and functions as may be determined by Parliament.

This revised amendment would be non-justiciable due to its focus on 'proposed laws', thus avoiding the risk of laws being struck down by the High Court due to a failure to consult, whilst upholding parliamentary supremacy. It would constitutionally empower Indigenous peoples with a voice in their affairs in a significant and meaningful way, as requested by the Uluru Statement. The revised version also refers to advising the Executive, which means Indigenous input would address policies as well as laws. The addition of 'under procedures to be

[167] This criticism was inaccurately raised by Professor George Williams in relation to Twomey's amendment, which empowers the body to advise the Executive as well as Parliament, but is accurately applicable to the Allens Linklaters' amendment. See George Williams, 'Pearson Proposal at Odds with Reality', *Sydney Morning Herald* (14 June 2015) < https://www.smh.com.au/opinion/pearson-proposal-at-odds-with-reality-20150614-ghngc3.html> accessed 24 December 2019.

[168] Allens Linklaters, *Submission 97* (n 133 above) 18.

[169] Cape York Institute, *Submission 38.2 to Joint Select Committee on Constitutional Recognition of Aboriginal and Torres Strait Islander Peoples*, Inquiry into Constitutional Recognition of Aboriginal and Torres Strait Islander Peoples (January 2015).

determined by Parliament' clarifies that Parliament must articulate the rules and processes for consultation and advice, as well as the issue of scope of advice. The Allens Linklaters' approach is more modest than the Twomey amendment, because it omits requirements for tabling advice or a specific obligation for parliamentarians to consider advice, and it may be politically attractive for its comparative simplicity. With the refinements suggested, it would fulfil the Referendum Council's guidelines and is an amendment that coheres with Australia's process-driven constitutional culture and strong parliamentary supremacy.

An even simpler version of this approach could emulate article 153 of the *Singapore Constitution*, which requires the establishment of an advisory council.[170] An Australian emulation requiring the establishment of a First Nations voice to advise on Indigenous affairs could read:

> Parliament shall by law make provision for constituting a First Nations body to advise Parliament and the Executive on proposed laws and other matters relating to Aboriginal and Torres Strait Islander affairs.

Such a clause would be succinct, non-justiciable and politically achievable.

D. Constitutionally Recognising Local and Regional First Nations Voices

In 2017, in the lead up to the Uluru convention, Indigenous leader Warren Mundine made a proposal for establishing local bodies rather than a national body, drawing on Twomey's work.[171] Mundine's intent was to put forward examples of constitutional guarantees to require Parliament to establish local Indigenous bodies, rather than a national body. Mundine argues that the focus on local First Nations better aligns with how the First Nations culturally recognise and organise themselves. It is also more in step with the principle of subsidiarity and the idea that local people should have a say over their local matters – a principle that is arguably infused within Australia's federal constitutional culture.[172] Mundine's first suggested amendment would read as follows:

> The Parliament shall, subject to this Constitution, have power to make laws for the peace, order, and good government of the Commonwealth with respect to:
>
> (1) Aboriginal and Torres Strait Islander heritage, cultures and languages and the relationship of Aboriginal and Torres Strait Islander peoples with their traditional lands and waters; and

[170] See also Khaitan (n 146 above) 613.

[171] Mundine, 'Practical Recognition' (n 133 above) 12. This proposal has been specifically supported by Liberal Senator, Andrew Bragg. Sarah Martin, 'Liberal Senator to Outline a Model for an Indigenous voice to Parliament', *The Guardian* (1 October 2019) <https://www.theguardian.com/australia-news/2019/oct/01/liberal-senator-to-outline-a-model-for-an-indigenous-voice-to-parliament> accessed 24 December 2019.

[172] For more on subsidiarity and federalism, see Nicholas Aroney, 'Subsidiarity: European Lessons for Australia's Federal Balance?' (2011) 39(2) *Federal Law Review* 31.

(2) the establishment, composition, roles, powers and procedures of local Aboriginal and Torres Strait Islander bodies which shall be established to manage and utilize native title lands and waters and other lands and sites, preserve local cultures and languages and advance the welfare of the local Aboriginal or Torres Strait Islander peoples.

Leaving to one side Mundine's proposed characterisation of the Indigenous head of power,[173] this proposal is an interesting flipping of the idea of a First Nations constitutional voice – it instead focuses on local voices.

The use of 'shall' in paragraph (2) would constitutionally require Parliament to establish the local First Nations bodies. It also determines some of their functions: to manage native title land, preserve culture and language, and advance Indigenous welfare – and these constitutional functions could be added to in legislation. There is no constitutionally mandated engagement or expressly stated advisory role to Parliament, however, which may be a weakness – the Referendum Council indicated that such engagement was important. The drafting can be adjusted to accommodate this, however.

Mundine also proposes a more modest approach that completely leaves Parliament to decide what functions to give these bodies and retains a broader plenary power for Indigenous affairs. This version reads:

> The Parliament shall, subject to this Constitution, have power to make laws for the peace, order, and good government of the Commonwealth with respect to Aboriginal and Torres Strait Islander affairs, and the Parliament shall establish bodies for each of the Aboriginal and Torres Strait Islander peoples, the composition, roles, powers and procedures of which bodies shall be determined by the Parliament.

This version through the use of 'shall' would require Parliament to establish the local bodies, but there is no constitutionally mandated engagement or expressly stated advisory role to Parliament. On the one hand, this is logical, given that the focus is on local bodies. It would not make sense for all local bodies across the country to advise Parliament (unless, for example, a particular law or policy was locally focused).[174] But there may be ways to refine the drafting to refer to an advice function, which the Referendum Council noted was important, while leaving Parliament to determine the appropriate mechanisms for this advice to be filtered through and delivered in an efficient and workable way.

Again, leaving aside the issue of the characterisation of the replacement Indigenous affairs power, there are several comments that can be made regarding the provisions requiring Parliament to establish local Indigenous bodies, so as to give them authority and responsibility over their local affairs. First, the idea of

[173] Amendment of the Race Power was not endorsed at the Uluru Convention and is not advocated here. Also, it may be unwise for the power to be narrowed in this way, as it could lead to legal uncertainty. For more on characterisation of the power, see Anne Twomey, 'A Revised Proposal for Indigenous Recognition' (2014) 36(3) *Sydney Law Review* 381.

[174] For example, where a law or policy is directed at a particular region, it would make sense for the design of this body to enable those local First Nations to provide advice on the law or policy.

any Indigenous constitutional voice being focused on local First Nations, being 'bottom-up, not top-down', and representing grass-roots, local voices, is a suggestion that resonated in all the First Nations dialogues.[175] Notably, however, this is predominantly a legislative design question: Twomey's constitutional amendment could also refer to a national Indigenous advisory body that is drawn from and focuses on local First Nations voices – if the body is legislated to facilitate local and regional empowerment. Yet Mundine's approach is interesting because it takes the constitutional focus to the local instead of the national. This may be desirable, if Indigenous people and politicians prefer this approach.[176]

One element missing in Mundine's proposals is an explicit constitutional requirement for First Nations engagement with Parliament on Indigenous affairs. On one view, this may not matter, as Indigenous people and Parliament may wish to leave this to be articulated in legislation, rather than in the *Constitution* as in Twomey's version. On the other hand, if the engagement with Parliament and government is thought important enough to be expressly required or at least indicated in the *Constitution*, as the Referendum Council suggests, Mundine's proposals can be adjusted to include this. Another consideration is non-justiciability. It would appear that Mundine's proposals would be non-justiciable, but non-justiciability can be confirmed through the added use of the 'proposed laws' device, along with the clarification that these local bodies would have an important role in engaging with Parliament and government with respect to their local Indigenous affairs. The amendment could thus be adjusted to read as follows:

> There shall be local First Nations bodies, with such composition, roles, powers and functions as may be determined by Parliament, and which shall include the functions of managing and utilising native title lands and waters and other lands and sites, preserving local First Nations languages, advancing the welfare of the local Aboriginal or Torres Strait Islander peoples, and advising Parliament and the Executive on proposed laws and other issues relating to these matters, under procedures to be determined by Parliament.

This version has the benefit of constitutionally clarifying the scope of any advice given, which, as the Referendum Council notes, is sometimes raised as a concern (although this scope issue can also be addressed in the legislation): advice can be related to land and sacred sites, culture and language, and Indigenous welfare. The words 'under procedures to be determined by Parliament' clarify that Parliament can legislate to set out appropriate mechanisms for advice on laws and policies to be given. An appropriate system[177] can be established for

[175] See Cape York Institute for Policy and Leadership, *A First Nations Voice in the Constitution: Design Issues – Report to the Referendum Council* (June 2017) 9–12.

[176] Martin (n 171 above). Note that the CYI Design Issues Report argued that the body should focus on empowering First Nations local voices. See Cape York Institute, *A First Nations Voice* (n 175 above).

[177] Perhaps a collegiate system.

engagement with the various levels of government and Parliament in the Federation, as appropriate and workable.

Similarly, a more succinct version could read:

> There shall be local bodies for each of the Aboriginal and Torres Strait Islander peoples, the composition, roles and powers of which shall be determined by Parliament, and which shall include procedures for Aboriginal and Torres Strait Islander peoples to provide advice to Parliament and the Executive on proposed laws and other matters relating to Aboriginal and Torres Strait Islander affairs.

This version of the drafting is simpler, shorter and thus perhaps more desirable; however, it omits clarification of the scope of the advice, eg on matters relating to land, culture and welfare. In other respects, this version, like Mundine's more complex example, would also fulfil the stated criteria: it would be non-justiciable, there would be no veto, relevant details would be legislated by Parliament; thus it respects parliamentary supremacy and minimises legal uncertainty. These clauses also provide for a constitutional guarantee and recognition for local First Nations bodies, in a way that may align with expressed Indigenous preferences for local voices being heard. The adjusted Mundine proposals would be another way of achieving the aspirations of the Uluru Statement, in a way that coheres with Australia's process-driven constitutional culture and strong parliamentary supremacy. Arguably these approaches would also be politically viable.

An even shorter, and in my view, better version of the bottom-up approach could read:

> Parliament shall by law recognise local First Nations bodies and enact procedures for Aboriginal and Torres Strait Islander peoples to advise Parliament and the Executive on proposed laws and others matters relating to Aboriginal and Torres Strait Islander affairs.

Such a clause would be succinct, non-justiciable and politically achievable.

E. A Justiciable Duty to Consult?

Professors Megan Davis and Rosalind Dixon have critiqued the Twomey model's non-justiciability, arguing that it may be too weak to constitute meaningful constitutional recognition. 'The problem with this procedural "solution" to the current impasse in constitutional recognition debates is that it is designed to be non-justiciable; the Parliament can ignore the advice and ATSI peoples have no recourse', Davis and Dixon observe.[178] Indeed, advice can be ignored because no veto is proposed. The non-justiciable guarantees discussed above are constitutionally modest solutions to the problem of Indigenous constitutional powerlessness. They are responses that aim to recalibrate and reform – but not

[178] Davis and Dixon (n 89 above) 258.

totally flip – the constitutional relationship. The constitutional relationship would therefore remain unequal, although it will have shifted from a purely top-down dynamic, towards a reciprocal partnership dynamic where consultation, dialogue and engagement are constitutionally mandated. This is a constitutionally 'modest yet profound' proposal, intended to be a politically viable, noble compromise between competing concerns.

In highlighting the risks associated with this constitutional modesty, Davis and Dixon identify two possibilities for how Twomey's tabling of advice procedure may work in practice – spanning optimistic to pessimistic potentials. One is that 'executive practice could quite quickly establish an informal political norm or understanding that the government must follow the advice of the committee, or at least offer a clear public justification for declining to do so', which gradually may 'then even harden into something like a true constitutional convention'.[179] This would be a good outcome. Alternatively, they raise the concern that

> government might disregard the advice of the committee in early cases, and that this might then create an informal understanding that true attention to the advice of such a committee is purely optional for Parliament, and not required as part of a commitment to consultation with and the empowerment of Indigenous Australians in processes of democratic self-government.[180]

This would be a poor outcome. As a response to this latter concern, Davis and Dixon propose a justiciable Indigenous consultation guarantee in the *Constitution*, through a clause that would provide recourse to the High Court, under tentative drafting along the following lines:

> In exercising its power to make laws under s 51(xxvi), and in all other cases in which laws have a significant or disproportionate impact on Indigenous peoples, the Commonwealth Parliament shall consult with Indigenous peoples in good faith, and through appropriate procedures.[181]

They explain that this constitutional amendment 'could provide a legal basis for Indigenous Australians to challenge the legislation ultimately enacted by Parliament before the High Court', and that 'the failure to follow appropriate procedures for consultation could itself also provide a potentially powerful basis for affected ATSI peoples to challenge the validity of relevant legislation'.[182]

The proposed amendment would provide a justiciable guarantee of the Indigenous voice in Indigenous affairs, but its justiciability enlivens detracting factors as previously discussed. Chapter four above discussed the potential down-sides of a justiciable duty to consult as it operates in Canada. The proposed justiciable amendment also does not respond to the legal uncertainty and parliamentary

[179] ibid.
[180] ibid.
[181] Note that, in the Davis and Dixon article, s 51(xxxvi) is cited, but I presume that this is an error, and that it should read s 51(xxvi).
[182] Davis and Dixon (n 89 above) 259.

supremacy objections that were raised in relation to a racial non-discrimination clause, as proposed by the Expert Panel. Rather, this amendment attracts the same criticisms: it would transfer power to the High Court to invalidate Parliament's laws. It therefore does not move the debate towards the establishment of greater common ground, as the Referendum Council suggests should be the aim.[183] Rather, it re-enlivens the original core disagreement with respect to further empowering the High Court at the expense of parliamentary supremacy, leaving this concern unresolved. While the reality of judicial intervention is embraced in this proposal,[184] it means the approach may not be conducive to political consensus.

Non-justiciability will be key to consensus on a First Nations constitutional voice. In my view, the Twomey approach, along with the revised Mundine approaches (or variations of these approaches), would be constitutionally modest options that align with the principles stated by the Referendum Council and Australian constitutional culture. These proposals are politically viable and should now be further explored and refined through discussions between Indigenous leaders, constitutional experts and political representatives.

V. LEGISLATIVE MECHANISMS TO ENHANCE IMPACT

The discussion above raises a crucial point about the risk that a First Nations constitutional voice may at times be ignored – a reality that must be honestly considered. This should be a persuasive and authoritative voice; it should operate through moral and political and indeed constitutional force, but it should not be a veto. It must strike the appropriate balance. What mechanisms might be put in place to foster such aims, empowering Indigenous people with a voice in their affairs, and guaranteeing that they are heard in political decision-making with respect to their rights, while upholding parliamentary supremacy?

At the constitutional level, a constitutional requirement with respect to a First Nations voice would carry constitutional authority in the same way that other non-justiciable sections carry authority, despite non-justiciability, as part of Australia's constitutional law (and perhaps more so, given the political reality of a recent successful referendum, were this proposal to be implemented). The constitutional amendment, however, would need an Act of Parliament to bring the First Nations voice to life. Further empowering mechanisms could be considered and incorporated into the enabling legislation to support the authority and effectiveness of the First Nations voice. Any design must ultimately be decided by Parliament, which will legislate to bring the institution to life, but Indigenous peoples must own and drive the design in partnership with government if the

[183] Notably, this article was published before the Referendum Council report, as is the case for all these proposals.

[184] Davis and Dixon (n 89 above) 259.

structure is to be legitimate and effective.[185] The following suggestions may be useful in design conversations.

A. A First Nations Voice should be Independent and Advice should be Public

To be an effective voice informing government and Parliament on Indigenous affairs, it must be independent. The Referendum Council made clear that a First Nations voice should have its representatives chosen by Indigenous peoples, not by government.[186] This is crucial. Indigenous people have repeatedly emphasised the importance of representative legitimacy in the design of a First Nations voice.[187] This principle is also embedded in the idea of Indigenous empowerment and self-determination, as articulated in DRIP.[188] Ensuring that the First Nations voice carries the legitimacy of having members chosen by Indigenous people will ensure that its views carry political and moral authority. It will also support genuine dialogue: this is not government conversing with self-appointed advisers; it would be government conversing and engaging with individuals chosen by Indigenous people themselves to represent First Nations communities.

Just as representative legitimacy can enhance productive political and moral authority, so too will transparency and publicity increase political impact. This is a proposal that operates through politics; and political dynamics are shaped by public scrutiny and opinion. When the First Nations voice delivers advice to government and Parliament, the advice should, insofar as practicable, be public. Likewise, there should be mechanisms for verbal, as well as written, dialogue between the First Nations voice and the state, discussed further below.

B. Dialogue should Start Early in the Policy Process

If a First Nations voice works as intended, the ensuing dialogue should not only propel productive deliberation and debate, but also collaboration and partnership. Robust contestation of ideas is important in generating better policy, but this should also enliven early co-operation. This too can help improve policy outcomes. There are lessons which can be taken from existing parliamentary committee systems in this respect. As shown in the parliamentary human rights scrutiny process and other parliamentary committees, early collaboration and

[185] Notably, the 2018 Joint Select Committee recommended a process of co-design to flesh out the details of a First Nations voice. See Joint Select Committee on Constitutional Recognition relating to Aboriginal and Torres Strait Islander Peoples, *Final Report* (November 2018). This co-design process is now beginning.

[186] *Final Report of the Referendum Council* (n 92 above) 30, 166.

[187] Each of the First Nations dialogues reiterated the importance of representatives being chosen by Indigenous people (ibid).

[188] See art 18 (section II.F above).

co-operation in policy development helps shape policy direction and decisions and can help avoid disagreements at the legislative stage. As noted with respect to the PJCHR, legislative influence is best when there are strong relationships with government departments, enabling effective early engagement.[189] In one sense, early engagement will happen naturally. For example, if there is a constitutional or legislative requirement that advice be tabled in Parliament, one can imagine the parties would begin their communication early so that advice on the proposed law is more likely to be supportive. A First Nations voice could similarly develop such relationships, but early engagement can also be required in legislation setting up the First Nations voice.

As recommended by the Aboriginal and Torres Strait Islander Social Justice Commissioner and endorsed by the PJCHR, the state's engagement with Indigenous peoples regarding laws and policies made about them should 'be in the nature of negotiations'.[190] Engagement should be more than mere consultation: it should be true dialogue, collaboration and negotiation. As Grenfell and Moulds observe in relation to the PJCHR, 'the Commonwealth experience suggests that creating a committee environment where the major political actors feel comfortable negotiating over the detail of a proposed law may play a significant role in legislative success'.[191] Similarly, early collaboration and negotiation regarding policy detail would enhance the impact and influence of a First Nations voice. A partnership approach is crucial and must begin right from the early stages of policy development.

There are many procedures available to facilitate this kind of early dialogue. Departments could produce Indigenous Impact Statements, akin to Regulatory Impact Statements and Family Impact Statements,[192] which alert the First Nations voice when a policy entails a special or significant impact on Indigenous people, and thus requires their input. Work on all new and amended policies by the Minister or the Department of Indigenous affairs should automatically trigger such notifications – as all their policies relate to Indigenous affairs. For other departments, an assessment should be made about whether a particular policy has special or disproportionate impact on Indigenous people.[193] Where it does, a notification should be issued so that collaboration can begin. Existing governmental procedures and processes can thus be adapted to enable the First Nations voice to provide input into relevant policies in development.

[189] For a full analysis of lessons from the PJCHR for a First Nations voice, see Morris, 'Parliamentary Scrutiny' (n 57 above).

[190] Aboriginal and Torres Strait Islander Social Justice Commissioner, Australian Human Rights Commission, *Native Title Report* (2010). PJCHR, *Stronger Futures* (n 58 above) 33–34 [1.121]–[1.123].

[191] Laura Grenfell and Sarah Moulds, 'The Role of Committees in Rights Protection in Federal and State Parliaments in Australia' (2018) 41(1) *University of New South Wales Law Journal* 40, 72.

[192] See explanation in Simon Evans, 'Improving Human Rights Analysis in the Legislative and Policy Process' (2005) 29(3) *Melbourne University Law Review* 665, 680–82, 685–86.

[193] This enlivens the issue of scope – what matters a First Nations voice should advise on. This will be discussed further below.

Consideration should also be given to the incorporation of First Nations policy committees as part of the First Nations voice, to support the development of policy solutions devised and led by the First Nations, and to facilitate focused engagement with the state on a particular issue. Such committees could enable a cross-section of First Nations representatives to have input into policy development on particular subject areas important to their communities,[194] focusing on issues including land rights and economic development, culture and language, health, education or suicide prevention. Where useful, the committees could be place-based. For example, if a First Nations voice had operated before the NT Intervention was instigated, the government might have collaborated with a Northern Territory First Nations Empowerment Committee – a committee of First Nations representatives, focused on leading policy solutions and partnering with government to address the problems of child suffering, disadvantage and violence in the Aboriginal communities of the Northern Territory. If this had occurred, the NT Intervention might have been better accepted by communities, less discriminatory and potentially more effective in achieving its aims. Through such mechanisms, the state could engage in direct, proactive and place-based dialogue with Indigenous peoples.

C. Structure should Facilitate Dynamic Dialogue at All Levels of the Federation

A First Nations voice could enable efficient consultation, dialogue and engagement with Indigenous people at all levels: the federal level, the State/Territory level, as well as regionally and locally. Australia's *Constitution* operates via a federal system, and a First Nations voice must accordingly engage at all levels of the Federation. Many laws and policies impacting Indigenous people, and many of the services administering Indigenous communities, are enacted and implemented by State and Territory Parliaments and governments. While federal legislation will be required to give effect to a constitutional guarantee requiring the establishment of a First Nations voice, it would make sense for the States and Territories to enact complementary legislation, to ensure their Parliaments and governments can also interact productively with the corresponding State and Territory elements of the First Nations voice.

As well as enabling early input into policy development, the legislation establishing the First Nations voice could set out processes for productive dialogue with Parliament in law-making processes.[195] The Act could emulate the procedures in existing pieces of legislation requiring consultation and engagement in

[194] The Sámi Parliaments in Scandinavia incorporate Sámi policy offices; eg, a Language Office and an Education Office.

[195] These processes could be emulated at all levels of the federal system, as appropriate, facilitated through an inter-governmental agreement.

law-making processes, building on what already works.[196] By way of example, the legislation could provide for:

1. Statements of Advice to accompany proposed laws with respect to Indigenous affairs or significantly or especially impacting Indigenous peoples (like Statements of Compatibility in sections 8 and 9 of the *Human Rights (Parliamentary Scrutiny) Act 2011* (Cth)).
2. A non-justiciable duty for rule-makers to consult with the First Nations voice before making a rule with respect to Indigenous affairs (as in section 17 of the *Legislation Act 2003* (Cth)).
3. A Parliamentary Joint Committee to enable direct verbal and written dialogue.
4. Verbally addressing Parliament on matters of special significance.
5. Provision of reasons where advice is not followed.

(i) Statements of Advice

The *Human Rights (Parliamentary Scrutiny) Act 2011* (Cth) (*Scrutiny Act*) establishes mechanisms for non-binding Statements of Compatibility on human rights compliance with respect to proposed laws to be tabled in Parliament. The legislation setting up the First Nations voice could similarly enable Statements of Advice with respect to Indigenous affairs to be prepared by the First Nations voice and tabled in Parliament. The legislation could emulate section 8 of the *Scrutiny Act*, as follows:

> Statements of Advice in relation to Bills with respect to Aboriginal and Torres Strait Islander affairs
>
> (1) A member of Parliament who proposes to introduce a Bill for an Act with respect to Aboriginal and/or Torres Strait Islander affairs, or a Bill for an Act that significantly or especially impacts on Aboriginal and/or Torres Strait Islander peoples, into a House of the Parliament, must request a statement of advice to be prepared by the First Nations Voice in respect of that Bill.
>
> (2) A member of Parliament who introduces a Bill for an Act with respect to Aboriginal and/or Torres Strait Islander affairs, or a Bill for an Act that significantly or especially impacts on Aboriginal and/or Torres Strait Islander peoples, into a House of the Parliament, or another member acting on his or her behalf, must cause a statement of advice prepared under subsection (1) to be presented to the House.
>
> (3) A statement of advice must include an assessment of whether the Bill is beneficial or detrimental to Aboriginal and/or Torres Strait Islander peoples and may include suggestions for how the Bill can be improved.

[196] Note, many of these ideas are advocated in Cape York Institute, *A First Nations Voice* (n 175 above) 47–50, which was drafted by Shireen Morris when working at Cape York Institute, under the leadership of Noel Pearson. Some of the ideas are also discussed in Morris, 'Parliamentary Scrutiny' (n 57 above).

(4) A statement of advice prepared under subsection (1) is not binding on any court or tribunal.

(5) A failure to comply with this section in relation to a Bill that becomes an Act does not affect the validity, operation or enforcement of the Act or any other provision of a law of the Commonwealth.

Like the PJCHR, a First Nations voice should also be able to advise on regulations with respect to Indigenous affairs. An example of a duty to consult, emulating section 9 of the *Scrutiny Act*, could be as follows:

Statements of Advice in relation to legislative instruments with respect to Aboriginal and Torres Strait Islander affairs

(1) The rule-maker in relation to a legislative instrument with respect to Aboriginal and/or Torres Strait Islander affairs, or a legislative instrument that significantly or especially impacts on Aboriginal and/or Torres Strait Islander peoples, must request a statement of advice to be prepared in respect of that legislative instrument.

(2) The statement of advice must be included in the explanatory statement relating to the legislative instrument (see section 15J of the *Legislation Act 2003*).

(3) A statement of advice must include an assessment of whether the legislative instrument is beneficial or detrimental to Aboriginal and/or Torres Strait Islander peoples and may include suggestions for how the Bill can be improved.

(4) A statement of advice prepared under subsection (1) is not binding on any court or tribunal.

(5) A failure to comply with this section in relation to a legislative instrument does not affect the validity, operation or enforcement of the instrument or any other provision of a law of the Commonwealth.

The Statements of Advice delivered by the First Nations voice could be coupled with the Second Reading Speeches of relevant Bills, as occurs with Statements of Compatibility, or included in the Explanatory Memorandum.

At the legislative stage, the First Nations voice could engage with a Joint Parliamentary Committee on Indigenous Affairs (see discussion below). The Committee could consider advice from the First Nations voice and hold public hearings to enable verbal dialogue that would be on the public record. The Committee could report its findings from this dialogue to Parliament, with recommendations for amending legislation where necessary or appropriate.[197]

In this legislative engagement, it is important to establish appropriate timelines. Early collaboration should prevent legislation from being rushed through without advice from the First Nations voice, should allow adequate time for dialogue, consideration, and collaboration, while also avoiding undue disruption to the parliamentary process. Williams and Reynolds, advising on a Human Rights Act for Queensland, observe that the PJCHR was hampered

[197] This would not preclude the PJCHR from also engaging with the First Nations voice, to help them ascertain whether proposed laws are compatible with Indigenous human rights.

in its effectiveness by insufficient time to advise.[198] They note, however, that the parliamentary scrutiny process of the Australian Capital Territory (ACT) utilises 'a requirement that no bill proceed to debate until the Committee has reported', which might help 'ensure that the relevant parliamentary committee has the time it needs to conduct its analysis'.[199] This does not seem a good fit for a First Nations voice at the federal level. A legislative requirement that the Commonwealth Parliament cannot pass a law until the First Nations voice has advised would likely be a constitutionally invalid attempt by the Commonwealth Parliament to bind itself.[200] While theoretically, despite constitutional invalidity, such a requirement may nonetheless be politically persuasive,[201] its inclusion may be unattractive to the parliamentarians who would need to implement it. Rather, appropriate timelines (with appropriate mechanisms for extensions) should be developed by government in negotiation with the First Nations, as part of designing a First Nations voice.

(ii) A Non-Justiciable Duty to Consult

The *Legislation Act 2003* (Cth) requires rule-makers to consult before making legislative instruments. The legislation establishing the First Nations voice could similarly require law-makers or rule-makers with respect to Indigenous affairs, or with respect to proposed laws or policies significantly or especially impacting Indigenous people, to properly consult with the First Nations voice. In keeping with the logic of this proposal, any duty to consult articulated in legislation should be non-justiciable. An example of a duty to consult, emulating section 17 of the *Legislation Act*, follows:

> Rule-makers should consult with the First Nations Voice before making legislative instruments with respect to Aboriginal and Torres Strait Islander affairs
>
> (1) Before the making of a legislative instrument with respect to Aboriginal and/or Torres Strait Islander affairs, or a legislative instrument that significantly or especially impacts on Aboriginal and/or Torres Strait Islander peoples, the rule-maker must be satisfied that there has been undertaken any consultation with the First Nations Voice that is:
>
> (a) considered by the rule-maker to be appropriate; and
> (b) reasonably practicable to undertake.

[198] George Williams and Daniel Reynolds, 'A Human Rights Act for Queensland? Lessons from Recent Australian Experience' (2016) 41(2) *Alternative Law Journal* 81, 84.

[199] ibid.

[200] In practice, this could also amount to a veto by inaction – if the First Nations voice wanted to block the legislation, it could just withhold advice – this would not be politically workable.

[201] Note that such a requirement is not without precedent. The *Flags Act* provides that the national flag can only be altered (and therefore the *Flags Act* can only be altered) through a popular vote by a majority of electors (*Flags Act 1953* (Cth) s 3). While this may operate to politically restrain hasty flag changes, this manner and form clause is legally ineffective, as the Commonwealth Parliament lacks power under the *Constitution* to bind itself in this manner. Similarly, national Goods and Services Tax legislation purports to prevent the Commonwealth from altering the GST rate 'unless

(2) In determining whether any consultation that was undertaken is appropriate, the rule-maker may have regard to any relevant matter including the extent to which the consultation:

(a) drew on the knowledge of the First Nations Voice; and

(b) ensured that the First Nations Voice had an adequate opportunity to comment on its proposed content.

(3) Without limiting, by implication, the form that consultation referred to in subsection (1) might take, such consultation could involve notification of the First Nations Voice. Such notification could invite input to be offered by a specified date or might invite participation in Parliamentary Committee hearings to be held concerning the proposed instrument.

(4) The fact that consultation does not occur does not affect the validity or enforceability of a legislative instrument.

(5) The fact that consultation does not occur may be a matter for further investigation by Parliament.

Note: An explanatory statement relating to a legislative instrument with respect to Aboriginal and/or Torres Strait Islander affairs, or a legislative instrument that significantly or especially impacts on Aboriginal and/or Torres Strait Islander peoples, must include a description of the consultation undertaken, or if there was no consultation, an explanation for the lack of consultation and an indication of the First Nations Voice's views in relation to the legislative instrument.

These examples show that existing practices can be emulated to ensure ordered processes for productive interaction and dialogue between a First Nations voice and Parliament.

(iii) A Parliamentary Joint Committee Interface

It may be said that a voice needs an ear, so it can be heard. It is one thing for the First Nations to be empowered to have a fairer say in their affairs, but it is another thing for Parliament to be properly equipped to listen. In her submission to the 2018 Joint Select Committee on Constitutional Recognition, Professor Anne Twomey suggested that:

> To ensure that what was said was heard, there could be a parliamentary committee that would be responsible for reviewing that advice, in a similar way to the manner in which the Joint Standing Committee on Treaties reviews all treaties that Australia proposes to ratify. It could alert Parliament to the issues raised in that advice, as is done by the Senate Standing Committee on Regulations and Ordinances.[202]

each State agrees to the change'. *A New Tax System (Commonwealth-State Financial Arrangements) Act 1999* (Cth) s 11. See Anne Twomey, 'Manner and Form' (*Gilbert + Tobin Public Law Conference*, University of NSW, 18 February 2005) 2.

[202] Anne Twomey, Supplementary Submission 57.1 to Joint Select Committee on the Constitutional Recognition of Aboriginal and Torres Strait Islander Peoples, Inquiry into Constitutional Recognition of Aboriginal and Torres Strait Islander Peoples Submission 57.1 (September 2018).

A Joint Parliamentary Committee on Indigenous Affairs could enable verbal, as well as written, dialogue with the First Nations voice. Interactions could emulate the ACT model. The ACT Elected Body was established under the *Aboriginal and Torres Strait Islander Elected Body Act 2008* (ACT) to enable First Nations in the ACT to have an elected voice. One of its functions is to monitor the ACT government's policy success by reviewing programmes and services being delivered. The ACT Elected Body has developed a system in negotiation with Treasury for giving guidance on expenditure and efficiencies in Indigenous affairs. A system of Senate Estimate-style hearings is used to engage with politicians.[203] Hearings are held annually and transcripts are available on Hansard.[204] A report is then submitted to the Minister and the government responds, creating ongoing dialogue between the ACT Elected Body and the ACT government. A First Nations voice at the Commonwealth level could undertake this detailed work with government, and then report back to the Joint Parliamentary Committee on Indigenous Affairs to enable parliamentarians to give focused attention to advice received and to enable verbal dialogue through hearings.

(iv) Addressing Parliament on Matters of Special Significance

Similarly, to assist in generating political force and public attention, First Nations representatives could be authorised to address Parliament and answer questions from Parliament with respect to advice in matters of special importance.[205] This would be a matter of privilege to be dealt with under section 49 of the *Constitution*, which enables Parliament to enact House Rules and standing orders. Parliament could enact House Rules to enable Indigenous representatives to address Parliament. The rules could set out the particular circumstances and processes to allow this to occur, including the seeking of leave from the Speaker or the Minister for Indigenous Affairs, or on invitation. In the past, international dignitaries and heads of state have been invited by the Speaker onto the floor of the House to address Parliament. For example, a delegation from the UK House of Commons was invited to address the House in 1951, and in 2020, the Indonesian President, Joko Widodo, addressed a joint sitting of the Australian Parliament.[206] If it is acceptable for dignitaries of foreign nations to

[203] Along with the development of Indigenous Expenditure Reports to examine expenditure against outcomes and challenge the decision-making and priorities adopted by government.

[204] 'Fact Sheet', *ACT/ATSIEB* (3 July 2013) <http://atsieb.com.au/wp-content/uploads/2016/07/Estimate-Hearings-and-process.pdf> accessed 24 December 2019.

[205] As Indigenous advocates have argued in the past: 'Representatives of indigenous peoples, including ATSIC, should have legally enforceable speaking rights in legislatures and in Local Government councils on issues relating to indigenous peoples. The Chairperson of ATSIC should be entitled to address the Parliament annually to report on the state of indigenous affairs': ATSIC, *Review of the Operation of the ATSIC Act* (n 113 above) 4.31.

[206] *House of Representative Practice* (6th edn, 2012) ch 4: 'Parliament House and access to proceedings'; 'Joko Widodo uses historic speech to call for greater action to tackle climate change', *ABC News* (10 February 2020) <https://www.abc.net.au/news/2020-02-10/joko-widodo-indonesian-president-addresses-australian-parliament/11948604> accessed 11 February 2020.

be invited to address the House, then it should also be acceptable for the formal representatives of the First Nations to be invited to address Parliament regarding special and relevant matters.

Constitutional recognition of the kind proposed would require significant reform of the relationship between Indigenous peoples and the Australian state. This important shift should also be appropriately reflected in legislation, House Rules and parliamentary custom. Such mechanisms would ensure the dialogue, verbal and written, is public and imbued with appropriate political weight.

(v) Provision of Reasons

John Chesterman has argued that where the Parliament does *not* follow an Indigenous advisory body's advice on proposed laws, the responsible Minister should state why the Parliament is proceeding contrary to its recommendations.[207] The Parliament in legislation or in its House Rules could also require itself to state the approval or disapproval of the body in the preamble to relevant Indigenous Acts. These would be forms of 'self-embracing' procedural requirements, compatible with parliamentary supremacy, because they specify the ways in which Parliament should exercise its power, rather than imposing substantive limits on that power.[208] These types of self-imposed rules and procedures could increase public scrutiny and political pressure so that Parliament gives the body's advice appropriate weight; however, like all these suggestions, their implementation is obviously reliant on political will.

D. Empowering Local and Regional First Nations Voices

It is suggested that the structure of the First Nations voice should empower local people to participate in political and policy decisions regarding their local interests. In formulating advice to the Commonwealth Parliament and government (or to State or Territory Parliaments and governments), the First Nations voice should therefore be appropriately informed by its State and Territory representatives, as well as its regional and local connections. For the structure to be truly empowering and to have greatest impact, it should be closely connected to local and regional First Nations voices. The structure could be powered from the bottom up, not top down, for it is local people who are best placed to understand the challenges that their communities face and assess how well particular policies are working or will work on the ground. What success means in one community or region may be different to what success means in another. The benchmarks of success should therefore be developed by communities themselves.

[207] Chesterman (n 114 above) 424.
[208] Goldsworthy, 'Constitutional Protection of Rights' (n 38 above) 175–76.

In line with an approach that respects local and regional voices and differences, the design of the First Nations voice should facilitate national and regional engagement between the First Nations voice and Parliament and government. There should be scope for regions to liaise directly with government on matters concerning them, just as there should be scope for the First Nations to act collectively and provide unanimous advice where appropriate. In-built flexibility and choice will be crucial in ensuring that the structure of the First Nations voice enables empowerment and self-determination. For example, as noted, if a First Nations voice had existed when the NT Intervention was being devised, it would have made sense for the First Nations of the Northern Territory to engage with government to develop that policy in direct partnership. For an amendment to the *Native Title Act* that applies nationally, however, the First Nations voice may wish to work with the regions across States and Territories to develop unanimous advice, if possible. The structure should thus flexibly facilitate national engagement, State and Territory engagement, as well as regional and local engagement.

E. There should be Discretion and Flexibility as to Scope of Advice

A First Nations voice should be flexible in the matters for which engagement is required. The Referendum Council noted that the scope of matters on which a First Nations voice should be empowered to provide advice should not be too broad, but nor too narrow.[209] Rather, it should be for Parliament to determine the appropriate balance in the legislation establishing the First Nations voice, in consultation with Indigenous people.

The legislation could specify that law-makers and policy-makers use their discretion in deciding which measures are 'with respect to Indigenous affairs', or which measures 'significantly or especially impact on Indigenous people', and therefore whether to issue the appropriate notification requesting engagement with the First Nations voice. The Minister could issue regulations or guidelines for the kinds of measures which are with respect to Indigenous affairs, or which significantly or especially impact on Indigenous people, by nominating certain areas or topics of regulation, or listing factors to be taken into account in so assessing.

A First Nations voice should also be able to initiate its own advice within the agreed parameters – it should be proactive, not just reactive to government requests for advice. In the spirit of true partnership and dialogue, it should be free to propose its own policy and legislative reform ideas for government consideration, thereby addressing government and legislative action *and inaction*. To be effective and worthwhile, the body should be able to advise on a wide

[209] *Final Report of the Referendum Council* (n 92 above) 36.

range of subject matters that the First Nations *themselves* consider important, whether or not government has requested engagement. To significantly restrict this discretion would diminish effectiveness and utility.

The First Nations voice should have discretion to advise on matters ranging from Native Title and cultural heritage laws, to 'closing the gap' and economic development policies, and matters that may especially impact Indigenous people in unexpected or unintended ways. For example, climate change or tree-felling policy may have distinct economic development implications for under-developed Aboriginal land, and advice in relation to this issue may be valuable to Parliament in promoting development in remote communities. Tax reform policy may have a particular impact on the efficiency of Indigenous corporations that may be subject to different corporate rules – advice on these issues may enable refinement of such laws. A policy in relation to alcohol licensing may have an unintended impact on vulnerable First Nations communities, to which the First Nations wish to alert government – advice on this could potentially minimise unintended harm or exacerbation of alcohol abuse in Indigenous communities. Development of a national suicide prevention scheme may benefit from advice on how to best tackle the especially high rates of suicide in Indigenous communities. These are examples of proposed laws and policies for which a First Nations voice may sensibly wish to provide advice, to make Parliament and government aware of a particular, special or unexpected impact on Indigenous people, and to help improve policy outcomes in Indigenous affairs. To summarise, any guidelines adopted should enable advice on a broad range of matters, including:

- native title and land rights;
- Indigenous heritage, culture and languages;
- economic development;
- closing the gap issues – measures addressing social and economic disadvantage;
- Indigenous affairs funding and budget issues; and
- other measures which indirectly impact Indigenous people or communities in a distinct or special way.

The First Nations voice itself should have flexibility and discretion as to which matters it advises on. Just as it should be able to initiate its own proposals and advice for government consideration, it should equally be empowered to decline to give advice even when requested by government if it so chooses.[210] This will enable the representatives on the First Nations voice to prioritise the issues of most importance to them, without being inundated by too much work.

[210] The ability to decline to give advice if it so chooses further demonstrates why a strict requirement that legislation cannot proceed unless advice from the First Nations voice is received may be too onerous.

VI. ADDRESSING POLITICAL OBJECTIONS

In the sections above I made the case for a First Nations constitutional voice and canvassed some ideas for how this proposal might be practically achieved, in the hopes of stimulating discussion. There now must be negotiation between Indigenous people and government to settle the words of the constitutional amendment, as well as collaboration on the appropriate legislative design of the institutional structure. All that requires political will and leadership.

I now turn to common objections to the idea of a First Nations constitutional voice. These objections tend to disagree with the concept on principle and are generally made on six grounds. I address each in turn.

A. The 'Third Chamber' Objection

In his statement rejecting the Uluru Statement in 2017, former Prime Minister Malcolm Turnbull argued:

> Our democracy is built on the foundation of all Australian citizens having equal civic rights – all being able to vote for, stand for and serve in either of the two chambers of our national parliament – the House of Representatives and the Senate.
>
> A constitutionally enshrined additional representative assembly which only Indigenous Australians could vote for or serve in is inconsistent with this fundamental principle.
>
> It would inevitably become seen as a third chamber of Parliament ...[211]

This statement reflects a fundamental misinterpretation of the Uluru Statement and the Referendum Council's recommendations, which call for a First Nations voice *to* Parliament, not an 'additional representative assembly' within Parliament. As made clear in the Referendum Council's report, the proposed Indigenous body would sit outside Parliament: it would be constituted by Parliament through legislation and is specifically intended to respect parliamentary supremacy. The proposal presents no change to the way parliamentarians are voted in or to Australia's electoral system, and it would not in any way alter the make-up of Parliament. No veto is proposed, and the body would not have power to vote in the making of legislation – only to provide non-binding advice on proposed legislation and policy. Thus, the First Nations voice cannot accurately be characterised as an 'additional representative assembly' within Parliament or a new 'third chamber' of Parliament. Notably, the 'third chamber

[211] Australian Government, Department of the Prime Minister and Cabinet, 'Response to Referendum Council's Report on Constitutional Recognition' (Media Release, 26 October 2017) <https://ministers.pmc.gov.au/scullion/2017/response-referendum-councils-report-constitutional-recognition> accessed 24 December 2019.

of Parliament' phrase was coined by former National Party leader, Barnaby Joyce, who has since admitted this characterisation was incorrect and has apologised unreservedly.[212]

The claim in the former Prime Minister's statement that a First Nations voice would 'become seen' as a third chamber, rather than actually *being* a third chamber, warrants closer scrutiny. It appears that the language is a distancing device that encourages an incorrect interpretation of the proposal, even while subtly acknowledging that such an interpretation is not accurate. The language blames *others* for adopting the incorrect interpretation, while doing nothing to correct it – indeed the Prime Minister's statement repeated and exacerbated the 'third chamber' misrepresentation. When political leaders make arguments of this kind, they are intending to defeat a proposal rather than honestly discuss it. As Barnaby Joyce has shown, however, Australian political leaders need not adhere to this approach. They can shift gears and lead an honest discussion.

Advocates for constitutional reform can also assist by trying to understand the concerns underlying the 'third chamber' misnomer. While it is clear the Referendum Council did not propose a third chamber of Parliament, it is now open to all parties to work together to address each other's concerns to try to find consensus. Constitutional amendment and legislative design conversations going forward should constructively take on board the concerns of government, as well as Indigenous aspirations, to design a constitutional and legislative approach that works for all stakeholders. Contrary to common reflexes, the appropriate solution will not be a resort to minimalism or mere symbolism, which Indigenous people have repeatedly rejected and which will fail at referendum. Rather, it will mean working together to design a constitutional amendment and legislative structure for a First Nations voice that fulfils Indigenous expectations of empowerment, but which also alleviates and addresses misguided 'third chamber' concerns. With good faith collaboration, careful listening by all parties, and intelligent constitutional drafting and legislative design that is alive to the political dynamics, this is possible.

Part of the answer will be refinement of the issue of scope. The 'third chamber' worry is partly driven by the concern that the proposed Indigenous body will be required to advise on all laws, because all laws impact Indigenous people. On the television panel discussion programme, *Q & A*, Malcolm Turnbull argued that the First Nations voice 'would be effectively a third chamber' because:

> If … it's to advise the Parliament on laws that affect Aboriginal and Torres Strait Islander people, do you know what that means? That means every law affects Aboriginal and Torres Strait Islander people. Every single law that goes through the Parliament, whether it's tax, whether it's defence, whether it's social security, whether

[212] Amy Remeikis, 'Barnaby Joyce "Apologises" for Calling Indigenous Voice a Third Chamber of Parliament', *The Guardian* (18 July 2019) <https://www.theguardian.com/australia-news/2019/jul/18/barnaby-joyce-apologises-for-calling-indigenous-voice-a-third-chamber-of-parliament> accessed 8 December 2019.

> it's health, they all affect Aboriginal and Torres Strait Islander people because they're part of the Australian community. And that would mean that that assembly would have the right, if it chose, to examine every piece of legislation, it would be, in effect, a third chamber.[213]

This concern can be addressed by discussing and defining the issue of scope (examined above). The legislation can articulate appropriate rules to determine which measures the First Nations voice should be able to advise on. As noted, the body should be able to advise on matters directly impacting Indigenous affairs, as well as matters that have a special, significant or different impact on Indigenous people. The Indigenous members of the body will need to exercise discretion in this respect – they will likely have neither the capacity nor desire to advise on every single law. These concerns can therefore be alleviated through sensible design discussions. There must be give and take on both sides, but if the First Nations voice is too restricted in scope, its utility will be diminished. Part of its benefit will be in alerting government to unforeseen Indigenous impacts in proposed laws and policies. In order to fulfil that function, the body needs some discretion and flexibility as to what it advises on, within agreed parameters.

The 'third chamber' concern can also be addressed in structural design, by demonstrating that this need not be a top-down assembly, but a bottom-up conduit for grass-roots First Nations views to be conveyed to Parliament and government. This is about empowering local and regional Indigenous communities to be heard in their affairs. Bottom-up approaches to the constitutional amendment and the legislative design could productively be incorporated into co-design conversations, and this may help address misguided 'third chamber' concerns.

B. The Equality Objection

The other prolific objection expressed in the statement above is that the proposal for a First Nations constitutional voice would undermine 'equal civic rights' in Australian democracy. The assertion seems to be that affording Indigenous people a constitutionally guaranteed, non-binding say in laws and policies made about Indigenous affairs would be contrary to the principle of equality. This argument must be refuted on a number of grounds.[214]

First, there is no principle of individual equality in Australia's constitutional arrangements. The High Court has declined to read in any guarantee of equality before the law under Australia's *Constitution*, because discriminatory

[213] 'PM Malcolm Turnbull on Q&A, *Q&A* (Australian Broadcasting Corporation, 11 December 2017) <http://www.abc.net.au/tv/qanda/txt/s4758471.htm> accessed 24 December 2019.

[214] See also Shireen Morris, 'False Equality' in Shireen Morris (ed), *A Rightful Place: A Roadmap to Recognition* (Black Inc 2017).

provisions and its discriminatory history demonstrate clear *in*equality before the law.[215] The *Constitution* contains provisions demonstrating inequality on the basis of 'race'[216] – an inequality that has had direct and painful implications for Indigenous peoples. As former Chief Justice Gleeson has observed: 'The race power, by its very existence, calls into question the assumption of equality.'[217] Similarly, Heydon J, supported by the majority in *Kruger v Commonwealth* in 1997, explained that, '[g]uarantees of equality before the law … were specifically rejected' in the drafting of the Constitution,[218] and 'the Constitution is in many respects inconsistent with a doctrine of legal equality'.[219] As noted in Chapter two, unlike most other democracies, the Australian *Constitution* contains no bill of rights and no constitutional guarantee of equality before the law. Past pushes to insert a racial non-discrimination guarantee into the *Constitution* have been unsuccessful. Given there is no equality before the law under Australia's constitutional arrangements, the argument that a First Nations voice would undermine such equality is unpersuasive.

The claim that a First Nations voice is contrary to Australia's 'equal civic rights' is also unpersuasive, and the extent to which such civic rights exist is highly questionable.[220] The *Constitution* does not adhere to the principle of equality in its approach to democratic representation. In Chapter two above, I explained that Australia's federal system does not adopt strict, individualistic equality in its democratic arrangements. Instead, Australia's federal *Constitution* recognises the historic political communities within the national majority – it affords these historic communities *constitutional recognition* and a guaranteed equal voice in the system. In doing so, the *Constitution* compromises strict majoritarianism and tempers individual equality in favour of ensuring that the historic political communities (now the States) are heard in their affairs.[221] Importantly, the *Constitution* recognises the equality of these historic political communities more than it recognises the equality of individuals. As Gleeson explains: 'Under the Constitution, about half a million Tasmanians are represented by the same number of Senators as about seven and a half million people of New South Wales.'[222] That Tasmanians are proportionately more powerfully represented

[215] See *Leeth v Commonwealth* (1992) 174 CLR 455; *Kruger v Commonwealth* (1997) 190 CLR 1; Sarah Joseph, '*Kruger v Commonwealth*: Constitutional Rights and the Stolen Generation' (1998) 24(2) *Monash University Law Review* 486, 491–92.

[216] See ss 25 and 51(xxvi).

[217] Murray Gleeson, 'Recognition in Keeping with the Constitution: A Worthwhile Project' (Gilbert & Tobin, Sydney, 18 July 2019) 15.

[218] *Kruger* (n 215 above) 65.

[219] ibid 64.

[220] See Chapter 5 of this volume for my argument on why the implied constitutional protection of equal voting rights is dubious.

[221] Nicholas Aroney, 'Reasonable Disagreement, Democracy and the Judicial Safeguards of Federalism' (2008) 27(1) *University of Queensland Law Journal* 129, 139–40.

[222] According to Gleeson, this reality demonstrates the weakness of simplistic equality objections to Indigenous recognition: Gleeson, 'Keeping with the Constitution' (n 217 above) 15.

in the Senate is a readily accepted fact of the Australian federal *Constitution*, which guarantees a fair voice to the pre-existing political communities – even the very small ones. A constitutionally guaranteed First Nations voice in Indigenous affairs, to ensure that the Indigenous minority is heard, is thus particularly suited to Australia's essential constitutional character. It would not in any way alter the way in which elections are conducted or the way parliamentarians are voted in. It would, however, ensure that the First Nations have a constitutionally guaranteed advisory voice in their affairs, helping to ensure that the injustices and exclusions of the past are less likely to be repeated. This would not be a 'radical change', as has been incorrectly suggested,[223] but a constitutionally congruent one.

The argument that a First Nations voice would undermine principles of equality is further weakened by the fact that Indigenous peoples are already treated in a different and unequal way. This too is a feature of Australia's colonial and contemporary history, as well as its legal and political reality. As noted, Indigenous peoples in Australia are the only group that was dispossessed by British settlement. They are the only group that was especially excluded from the constitutional arrangements of 1901, particularly as noted, through sections 127 and 51(xxvi). They are the only group that have particular rights and interests arising out of this history. These rights and interests are recognised at common law[224] and in legislation – there is legislation recognising Indigenous native title rights[225] and Indigenous cultural heritage.[226] Further, Indigenous peoples are the only group for whom the Commonwealth makes such special laws, and the only group for whom the Commonwealth requires a special constitutional head of power to do so – section 51(xxvi) has only ever been used with respect to Indigenous peoples.[227] It is clear, therefore, that the *Constitution* already works in a way that applies differently to Indigenous people than to other Australians. The Commonwealth Parliament necessarily makes laws recognising distinct Indigenous rights, which apply to Indigenous people in a way that is not relevant to other Australians. Indigenous peoples are therefore a demonstrably distinct constitutional constituency with a special relationship with Australian governments under the *Constitution*.[228] Indigenous

[223] In its statement, the Government stated: '[T]he Government does not believe such a radical change to our constitution's representative institutions has any realistic prospect of being supported by a majority of Australians in a majority of States: Australian Government, 'Response to Referendum Council's Report' (n 211 above).

[224] See, eg, *Mabo* (n 15 above).

[225] eg, *Native Title Act 1993*.

[226] eg, *Aboriginal and Torres Strait Islander Heritage Protection Act 1984* (Cth).

[227] eg, *World Heritage Properties Conservation Act 1983* (Cth); *Aboriginal and Torres Strait Islander Heritage Protection Act 1984* (Cth); *Native Title Act 1993* (Cth); *Corporations (Aboriginal and Torres Strait Islander) Act 2006* (Cth). Before the 1967 amendments, the Race Power was never used.

[228] In some other jurisdictions, like Canada and New Zealand, the special relationship between Indigenous peoples and the settler state has been characterised as akin to a fiduciary relationship, giving rise to principles of partnership. See *Te Runanga o Wharekauri Rekohu Inc v Attorney-General* [1993] 2 NZLR 301, 304, 306; *New Zealand Maori Council v Attorney-General* [1987]

constitutional recognition through a First Nations voice seeks to reform and reset this relationship to make it fairer than it has been in the past – by guaranteeing that Indigenous people will be heard in political decision-making about them and their rights.

Inserting a constitutional provision requiring that Indigenous peoples are heard in laws and policies made about them would not undermine equality under Australia's *Constitution* – rather it would enhance the fairness of its operation. It would be a way of ensuring that Parliament's specific powers with respect to Indigenous affairs (and other powers when used in an Indigenous-specific way) are wielded with Indigenous input and participation. This would help improve policies and prevent unjust discrimination and poor outcomes, ultimately enhancing equality, not undermining it. Notably, former Prime Minister Turnbull, before rejecting the Uluru Statement, often promised to adopt a consultative approach to Indigenous policy, with a collaborative slogan vowing to 'do things *with* rather than *to*' Indigenous people.[229] The uncontroversial proposition that Indigenous people should have a say in laws and policies made specifically about them – native title, Indigenous heritage, closing the gap, and so on – is no more contrary to principles of equality than the Prime Minister's Indigenous advisory council (albeit government-appointed) which already exists and operates.[230] The repeated political promise of better consultation with Indigenous peoples in policy-making about them, along with the appointment of Indigenous advisers to inform Indigenous policy, demonstrate that a First Nations voice is not only sensible, but crucial to making good Indigenous affairs policy and closing the gap on Indigenous disparity.

The ideological equality arguments wielded in relation to a First Nations voice are therefore puzzling, given that most agree – at least at the rhetorical level – that government should consult more with Indigenous peoples, but mechanisms do not exist to ensure this happens effectively. A First Nations constitutional voice would address this through a constitutional promise.

1 NZLR 641, 664; *R v Sparrow* [1990] 1 SCR 1075, 1108. These fiduciary duties tend to arise out of the treaty relationships now recognised in the *Canadian Constitution*, and in legislative incorporation of the Treaty of Waitangi into New Zealand law. Such arguments have not been recognised in Australia, where there is no treaty, and where Indigenous rights are not constitutionally recognised. Note, however, that Toohey J in *Mabo* suggested that fiduciary duties may arise in state relationships with Indigenous peoples, because of the vulnerable nature of native title rights and the power of the Crown to extinguish such rights. See *Mabo* (n 15 above) 203–4. See also Kirsty Gover, 'The Honour of the Crowns: State–Indigenous Fiduciary Relationships and Australian Exceptionalism' (2016) 38(3) *Sydney Law Review* 339. Although a fiduciary duty has not been recognised, the history and law nonetheless demonstrate that some kind of special relationship between the Indigenous peoples and the state in Australia exists.

[229] Malcolm Turnbull, 'Speech to Parliament on the 2016 Closing the Gap Report' (10 February 2016) <https://www.malcolmturnbull.com.au/media/speech-to-parliament-on-the-2016-closing-the-gap-report> accessed 24 December 2019.

[230] Australian Government, 'Prime Minister's Indigenous Advisory Council' (n 104 above).

C. The 'Virtual Veto' Objection

The *constitutional* element to a First Nations voice seems to give rise to anxiety among some commentators. Perhaps the true concern is that a First Nations voice with constitutional status may be authoritative and effective, and government would not easily be able to get rid of it – because it will be in the *Constitution*. Sadly, resistance may sometimes arise because government may prefer not to have to contend with Indigenous opinions when making Indigenous policy. This depressing attitude can be seen in the 'virtual veto' objection.

Journalist Janet Albrechtsen, echoing others,[231] has made the exaggerated claim that, although proponents of a First Nations voice 'say there will be no veto power over legislation, the likelihood is a de facto veto power because no government will be brave enough to say no to the voice'.[232] This idea of a de facto or virtual veto seems based on a fear that the Indigenous body will be *effective* in influencing Indigenous policy – which is precisely its intended aim. That some commentators do not want this outcome is telling, but in order to conjure fear that might prevent a situation where Indigenous voices will be heard in Indigenous affairs, the argument strategically overstates the case. It de-emphasises the legal and political reality that an advisory body's advice will, at times, be ignored by government, in favour of the exaggerated scenario of an advisory body somehow terrifying the state into subservience to its will. On this argument, the majority 'elephant', the Australian government, would cower before the advisory powers of the three per cent 'mouse' – notwithstanding the lack of legal veto. The argument is implausible.

Ironically, while the 'virtual veto' objection – the idea that a First Nations voice will be *too* politically persuasive – is commonly put from the political right, the reciprocal objection from detractors on the progressive side of politics is that the body may be too weak, because it lacks a veto power and therefore its advice will at times not be followed.[233] On balance, such objections on both sides lend weight to the argument that this is a middle-ground, noble compromise proposal. It is impossible to please everybody, but this proposal is modest, yet profound.

D. The 'Not Enough Detail' Objection

Another objection sometimes raised is that the proposal lacks sufficient detail to be put forward to a referendum. Attorney-General, Christian Porter, says he

[231] See also Paul Kelly's comments in Shireen Morris, *Radical Heart: Three Stories Make Us One* (Melbourne University Press 2018) 221.

[232] Janet Albrechtsen, 'Shouted Down by the Crusading Voice of Division', *The Australian* (5 June 2019).

[233] eg, Sarah Maddison, 'It's Time for Indigenous Nationhood to Replace a Failing Colonial Authority', *The Conversation* (5 April 2019) <https://theconversation.com/its-time-for-indigenous-nationhood-to-replace-a-failing-colonial-authority-114088> accessed 24 December 2019.

must see the 'precise words' of the constitutional amendment before it can be supported.[234] Conversely, the 2018 Joint Select Committee complained that there were too many ('no fewer than 18 different versions') examples of precise words being offered up to government, making it difficult for the Committee to narrow down options.[235] As discussed in this chapter, much work has been undertaken by experts to progress options for constitutional drafting. The next step is for government representatives and experts to come to the table with Indigenous leaders to determine what precise words should be put to a referendum. This is not something external experts or Indigenous leaders can decide independently without government collaboration and leadership. Parliament must initiate any constitutional reform. This work therefore requires government leadership.

Turnbull's rejection of the Uluru Statement similarly complained that the Referendum Council had 'provided no guidance as to how this new representative assembly would be elected or how the diversity of Indigenous circumstance and experience could be fairly or democratically represented'.[236] This objection posits that the proposal cannot be pursued because the body's design and operation has not been sufficiently developed. Given that the proposal defers to Parliament to determine in collaboration with Indigenous people the details and operation of the institution as a way of explicitly respecting parliamentary supremacy, this objection seems a premature shirking of political responsibility. Parliament and government need to take the initiative in partnership with Indigenous people to determine the details of the proposed body – it is unhelpful for government to complain that the work has not already been done.[237]

The fact that the proposed constitutional amendments leave institutional design details to Parliament to determine under legislation is a *strength* of this proposal, underlining its respect for parliamentary supremacy. Deferral of institutional details to subsequent legislation is in keeping with the Australian constitutional approach to institutional design. As Dixon has noted, such deferral is common in Australia's constitutional law which leaves many institutional and democratic matters to Parliament.[238] In Chapter five, I explained that the *Constitution* leaves most of the details of electoral arrangements and political institutions to Parliament to decide.[239] The *Constitution* gives Parliament the power to create federal courts[240] and, as discussed above, the Inter-State Commission. These are all institutions required by the *Constitution* but detailed

[234] Michael Pelly, 'Public Won't "Buy" Uluru Statement, Claims AG', *Financial Review* (21 June 2019). Many constitutional experts have drafted versions of how this amendment could be worded.

[235] JSC on Constitutional Recognition, *Final Report* (n 185 above) ix.

[236] Australian Government, 'Response to Referendum Council's Report' (n 211 above).

[237] Although, notably, organisations like Cape York Institute and Uphold & Recognise have done considerable work on potential design details.

[238] Dixon, 'Let's Give Indigenous People a Voice' (n 160 above).

[239] See, eg, ss 7, 24, 30.

[240] See s 71.

by Parliament in subsequent legislation. The proposal for a First Nations voice in the *Constitution* is in keeping with this approach. Deferral of such detail shows respect for the authority of Parliament in determining appropriate political arrangements in consultation with Indigenous people. It is not a weakness of the proposal, but a strength.

Acknowledging the need for government to collaborate with Indigenous people to flesh out design details of the First Nations voice, the 2018 Joint Select Committee recommended a co-design process.[241] In 2019, it was announced that this process would be chaired by Professors Marcia Langton and Tom Calma.[242] This is a positive step forward, though the process should also determine the details of a constitutional amendment.

E. The 'Practical Action Over Symbolism' Objection

Policy short-term-ism, and a failure to see the links between constitutional and structural reform and definitively addressing Indigenous disadvantage, were contributing factors in the former Prime Minister Malcolm Turnbull's 2017 rejection of the Uluru Statement's call for a First Nations constitutional voice in their affairs.[243] This lack of understanding of the necessity of structural reform for improved policy outcomes was perpetuated in 2019, when Prime Minister Scott Morrison suggested that while a First Nations voice may be important, he was more concerned with practical matters, like addressing Indigenous youth suicide.[244] Neither leader seemed to properly grasp the connection between the two objectives: the Uluru Statement seeks empowering structural reform through a guaranteed voice in their affairs, precisely because Indigenous advocates want to see long-term practical improvement in policy areas like Indigenous incarceration, poverty and child removal.[245] Indigenous advocates call for constitutional and structural reform because they want fairer and better policy-making, to improve policy results, and close the gap on Indigenous disadvantage. Indigenous advocates, too, want practical action: that is why they reject merely

[241] JSC on Constitutional Recognition, *Final Report* (n 185 above).

[242] Katherine Murphy, 'Marcia Langton and Tom Calma to Lead Indigenous Voice Advisory Group', *The Guardian* (30 October 2019) <https://www.theguardian.com/australia-news/2019/oct/30/marcia-langton-and-tom-calma-to-lead-indigenous-voice-advisory-group> accessed 24 December 2019.

[243] Australian Government, 'Response to Referendum Council's Report' (n 211 above).

[244] Lorena Allam, '"Unfinished Business": What the Parties Offer Indigenous Voters in the 2019 Election', *The Guardian* (20 April 2019) <https://www.theguardian.com/australia-news/2019/apr/20/unfinished-business-what-the-parties-offer-indigenous-voters-in-the-2019-election> accessed 24 December 2019. On the Indigenous youth suicide epidemic, see Brooke Fryer, 'Indigenous Youth Suicide at Crisis Point', *NITV News* (15 January 2019) <https://www.sbs.com.au/nitv/article/2019/01/15/indigenous-youth-suicide-crisis-point> accessed 24 December 2019.

[245] *Uluru Statement from the Heart* (2017) <https://www.referendumcouncil.org.au/final-report.html#toc-anchor-ulurustatement-from-the-heart>.

symbolic constitutional recognition – because it would do nothing to improve such outcomes. Accordingly, the political preference for practical action should be the basis for agreement with Indigenous people – yet it is not. To the contrary, the government seems to prefer a merely symbolic constitutional amendment: this is why it tends to reject substantive proposals, whether in the form of a racial non-discrimination clause or a First Nations voice.

How might the political preference for practical action on the one hand, but constitutional symbolism on the other hand, be explained? The best interpretation is that the government wants practical *policy* approaches, but not practical or structural or substantive constitutional reform to change the way such political and policy decisions are made. The government thus far has sought to maintain the structural and constitutional status quo. The persuasive response to this preference – which is at odds with stated Indigenous preferences – lies in the fact that current structures and systems are not working to produce good policy results in Indigenous affairs.[246] This is evidence of the need for structural reform.

Australian policy approaches are failing to seriously address Indigenous social and economic disparity. More of the same will not close the gap on Indigenous disadvantage, because one short-term policy or another cannot fix deep and ingrained Indigenous disadvantage that carries structural and historical, intergenerational dimensions. Because historic and structural causes are entwined with more proximate causes of Indigenous disadvantage, short-term policy solutions that do not address fundamental structural problems are unlikely to be sufficient to effect real improvement in outcomes. Until persisting power imbalances are addressed through Indigenous structural empowerment, Indigenous disadvantage is unlikely to be rectified. Structural reform is needed to empower Indigenous peoples to have genuine input in and ownership of policies made about them.[247]

F. The 'Political Unviability' Objection

In justifying the preference for a merely symbolic approach, opponents of a First Nations constitutional voice often assert that the proposal is not politically viable. For example, Malcolm Turnbull's rejection in 2017 stated that 'the Government does not believe such a radical change to our constitution's representative institutions has any realistic prospect of being supported by a majority of Australians in a majority of States'.[248] This assertion must be questioned.

[246] Only 2 out of 7 targets are on track to be met. See *Closing the Gap* (n 29) 10.
[247] See full discussion in Chapter 2.
[248] Australian Government, 'Response to Referendum Council's Report' (n 211 above).

A 2017 Omnipoll showed that 61 per cent of Australians would vote 'yes' to a First Nations voice in the Constitution,[249] and a February 2018 Newspoll showed 57 per cent support.[250] By July 2019, research showed support at 66 per cent,[251] despite sustained Government negativity about the proposal. For the purposes of comparison, in 2017, the Australian people voted 61 per cent 'yes' in a postal survey in support of reform to enable same sex couples to marry[252] – and this result was achieved with the leadership of a Prime Minister (Turnbull) making the positive case for reform. In the Indigenous constitutional recognition debate, polls show up to 66 per cent support, even in the face of sustained government opposition. The political unviability objection is therefore unpersuasive. While it is true that the proposal cannot succeed without government leadership (for Parliament must initiate any constitutional reform), it is inaccurate and misleading to blame the Australian people. It appears to be the politicians blocking progress, not the people.

For reasons discussed above, I argue that the proposal for a First Nations voice is the most politically viable constitutional recognition model currently on the table. It is more viable than a racial non-discrimination clause, or variations thereof, which elicit objections on the basis of judicial review. It is more viable than the insertion of a symbolic statement, which already failed in 1999, does not enjoy Indigenous support, and will also attract constitutionally conservative opposition. A First Nations voice is a constitutionally congruent, practical and empowering, yet modest proposal that can win a recognition referendum. The proposal represents the 'radical centre' in the recognition debate. With political will and leadership, and with good faith collaboration, this proposal can succeed.

VII. CONCLUSION

Indigenous constitutional recognition is about setting in place fairer rules to improve the relationship between Indigenous peoples and the Australian state.

[249] Calla Wahlquist, 'Most Australians Would Support Indigenous Voice to Parliament Plan that Turnbull Rejected', *The Guardian* (30 October 2017) <https://www.theguardian.com/australia-news/2017/oct/30/most-australians-support-indigenous-voice-to-parliament-plan-that-turnbull-rejected> accessed 24 December 2019.

[250] Simon Benson, 'Bill Shorten Raising Voice a Winner with Voters: Newspoll', *The Australian* (20 February 2018).

[251] Katherine Murphy, 'Essential Poll: Majority of Australians want Indigenous Recognition and Voice to Parliament', *The Guardian* (12 July 2019) <https://www.theguardian.com/australia-news/2019/jul/12/essential-poll-majority-of-australians-want-indigenous-recognition-and-voice-to-parliament> accessed 24 December 2019. Earlier, in May 2019, research showed 64% support: Isabella Higgins and Sarah Collard, 'Federal Election 2019: Vote Compass Finds Australians Are Ready to Back Indigenous "Voice to Parliament"', *ABC News* (3 May 2019) <https://www.abc.net.au/news/2019-05-03/vote-compass-federal-election-voice-to-parliament/11071384> accessed 24 December 2019.

[252] See results on Australian Bureau of Statistics, '1800.0 – Australian Marriage Law Postal Survey 2017' (15 November 2017) <https://www.abs.gov.au/ausstats/abs@.nsf/mf/1800.0> accessed 24 December 2019.

It is fundamentally geared at constitutional inclusion, not separatism. Australia's *Constitution* recognises and represents the voices of the pre-existing political communities, or constitutional constituencies – even the very small ones. Given that the *Constitution* confers upon Parliament a necessary power to make laws with respect to Indigenous affairs, it should also guarantee Indigenous peoples a fairer say in the exercise of that power, and other powers when exercised in relation to Indigenous matters. This would shift the constitutional relationship between Indigenous peoples and the state from a top-down power dynamic, towards a reciprocal partnership dynamic. It would not institute a veto. Such a reform would be modest yet profound in nature, and would belatedly include the First Nations within the constitutional compact from which they were wrongfully excluded in 1901. The ensuing dialogue, consultation and collaboration between Indigenous peoples and the Australian state could help build trust, cohesion and mutual understanding. Such ongoing partnership and dialogue would be reconciliation in action.

Properly drafted, a constitutional amendment of this kind would be a neat fit with the *Australian Constitution*. As constitutional conservative, Julian Leeser MP, has described in relation to Twomey's draft amendment, this is the kind of clause that 'Griffith, Barton and their colleagues might have drafted, had they turned their minds to it'.[253] Indeed, had First Nations representatives been included at the negotiating table when the constitutional compact was being created, perhaps they would have negotiated themselves something along these lines. There is more work to be done and debate to be had, but the proposal for a First Nations voice sets us on the right path to reconciliation and constitutional justice.

[253] Leeser (n 50 above) 87.

7

Conclusion

THE DEBATE ABOUT Indigenous constitutional recognition in Australia has moved on from discussion about judicially adjudicated rights guarantees, to how best to achieve First Nations empowerment through a constitutionally guaranteed voice as called for by the Uluru Statement. This is a good shift, both in terms of constitutional congruence and political viability, but also in terms of Indigenous self-determination. Indigenous peoples have for decades advocated for a fairer say, better engagement and more active participation in their affairs. Successive governments have failed to ensure Indigenous empowerment in Indigenous policy-making, and policy outcomes in Indigenous affairs have been poor. A constitutional guarantee is needed to decisively shift this relationship from a top-down, unilateral approach, to a reciprocal, partnership and dialogue approach. This cannot happen through policy and legislation alone. A constitutional imprimatur is needed to ensure real and long-lasting change to the way governments do business with Indigenous peoples.

Despite the government's rejection of the Uluru Statement in 2017, the Joint Select Committee of 2018 identified a First Nations voice as the only viable pathway forward for Indigenous constitutional recognition, and recommended a co-design process to elucidate the design details of the proposed structure.[1] Though the government dishonestly dismissed the proposal as a 'third chamber' early in the debate, some of the key proponents of that misnomer have since admitted the mischaracterisation.[2] And despite government negativity about the concept, public positivity about the Uluru Statement's proposed reform remains high.[3] If there was strong political leadership, public support would be higher.

[1] Joint Select Committee on Constitutional Recognition relating to Aboriginal and Torres Strait Islander Peoples, *Final Report* (November 2018).

[2] Amy Remeikis, 'Barnaby Joyce "Apologises" for Calling Indigenous Voice a Third Chamber of Parliament', *The Guardian* (18 July 2019) <https://www.theguardian.com/australia-news/2019/jul/18/barnaby-joyce-apologises-for-calling-indigenous-voice-a-third-chamber-of-parliament> accessed 8 December 2019.

[3] Katherine Murphy, 'Essential Poll: Majority of Australians want Indigenous Recognition and Voice to Parliament', *The Guardian* (12 July 2019) <https://www.theguardian.com/australia-news/2019/jul/12/essential-poll-majority-of-australians-want-indigenous-recognition-and-voice-to-parliament> accessed 8 December 2019. Earlier, in May 2019, research showed 64% support: Isabella Higgins and Sarah Collard, 'Federal Election 2019: Vote Compass Finds Australians Are Ready to Back Indigenous "Voice to Parliament"', *ABC News* (3 May 2019): <https://www.abc.net.au/news/2019-05-03/vote-compass-federal-election-voice-to-parliament/11071384> accessed 8 December 2019.

This is a debate in which people can go on an intellectual journey and change their minds. Such re-evaluation is to be encouraged. Australians cannot stop having the conversation. In this book, I have tried to share something of my own intellectual journey over the last nine or more years. Over these years, I also changed my mind.

I had to start by asking: what problem does Indigenous constitutional recognition seek to solve? Examining the history of Indigenous advocacy, I came to the conclusion that constitutional recognition seeks much more than just a static, symbolic statement with no practical or operational effect. Indigenous constitutional recognition seeks to reform the working relationship between Indigenous peoples and the Australian state, to ensure that it is fairer than in the past. It seeks a constitutional promise or guarantee that the discrimination of our history will not be repeated – that things will happen in a fairer way.

At a high level, there are two types of substantive constitutional promises that could be made. Australia could adopt a justiciable constitutional guarantee: perhaps a guarantee of non-discrimination as proposed by the Expert Panel, or a guarantee of Indigenous rights as adopted in Canada. Such guarantees would be brought to life through litigation. Alternatively, Australia could adopt a non-justiciable, political – but nonetheless constitutional – guarantee that Indigenous voices will always be heard in the making of political decisions about their affairs. This is the approach called for by the Uluru Statement and the Referendum Council, and the approach advocated in this book. Such a guarantee would be brought to life through legislated structures, politics and political dialogue.

The latter approach is constitutionally innovative, yet also constitutionally conservative. Australia's *Constitution* protects rights not through a judicially adjudicated Bill of rights, but through political processes and institutions and by ensuring that historic political communities have a fair say. Australia's federal system tempers the might of the majority by incorporating recognised minority voices. This is why the smallest former colony, Tasmania, has an equal voice in the Senate, equivalent in power to any of the more populous former colonies – like Victoria or New South Wales. That these historic political communities deserve to have their voices heard is an accepted fact of Australia's federal constitutional system, which affords the historic political communities *constitutional recognition*. The call for a First Nations constitutional voice is profoundly consistent with Australia's constitutional history, culture and design, which positions political participation as 'the right of rights'.

The First Nations missed out on the culture of reciprocity, comity and mutual respect established by the *Constitution*. When the founding fathers negotiated the compact that would unite the colonies as a single Commonwealth, no First Nations representatives were included. They did not participate in the discussions and so could not negotiate a fair place in the resulting unity pact. Indigenous constitutional recognition seeks to correct this omission. The Uluru Statement presents an authoritative Indigenous consensus view on how this should be done: constitutional recognition should occur through inclusion of a First Nations constitutional voice. It now incumbent upon political leaders, Indigenous leaders and constitutional scholars to work together to flesh out the details of how this will be achieved. What constitutional words should give effect to the constitutional guarantee? What should the legislation giving life to the constitutional guarantee look like? How should this work in practice?

These are questions that must be resolved through respectful political negotiation. In undertaking such collaborative conversations, all sides should listen to the concerns of the others. The proposal for a First Nations constitutional voice would not have arisen without striving to understand and accommodate opposing views to forge collaborative, synthesis solutions.[4] Now political leaders should hear Indigenous concerns as expressed in the Uluru Statement in that same spirit, and Indigenous people reciprocally should hear political concerns being expressed in relation to the proposals being put forward. It is my firm belief that the parties can work together to address each other's concerns. A consensus view can be reached on how best to achieve the Uluru Statement.

I urge all parties not to be close-minded on possible ways forward. This will be a process. Just as there were multiple ways to achieve Indigenous constitutional recognition, which the Uluru Statement through the First Nations dialogues has now narrowed down, there are also multiple ways to achieve a constitutionally guaranteed First Nations voice. These various possibilities must now also be narrowed down through dialogue between Indigenous peoples, government and legal experts. The options are many. There are justiciable and non-justiciable options – here I have argued that non-justiciable amendments are to be preferred. There are wordier and more succinct options – succinctness is preferable. There are top-down and bottom-up options: do we constitutionally guarantee a national Indigenous representative and advisory body, or do we constitutionally guarantee First Nations local and regional bodies that will no doubt affiliate into a national voice? Either way, the local and regional must connect to the national.

Discussions going forward will require creative thinking, careful constitutional drafting and dynamic legislative design to ensure that the concerns of all stakeholders are addressed. Indigenous voices must be central in this process – it would be unconscionable for any constitutional recognition, and any form of First Nations voice, to go ahead without Indigenous ownership and endorsement. But this must necessarily be a two-way conversation between Indigenous peoples and the state, for this is the relationship being reformed and only Parliament can initiate constitutional reform. Genuine negotiation and dialogue is now needed to settle the details of the model. But Australia can and must have this conversation.

[4] For the journey of the development of this proposal, see Shireen Morris, *Radical Heart: Three Stories Make Us One* (Melbourne University Press 2018).

It is a conversation of crucial importance for the nation. I have argued that Indigenous constitutional recognition is fundamentally about Indigenous constitutional inclusion, not separatism. There is a real sense in which the *Australian Constitution* is not yet adequately owned by Indigenous Australians. It is not yet theirs; therefore is it not yet all of ours. How can we expect all Australians to truly share a sense of national unity, and cohesion, when they – the group that was here long before any other – remain excluded from the constitutional compact that created the Australian nation? Despite past bloodshed and conflict, the broken promises and unresolved ruptures of history, Indigenous and non-Indigenous Australians live on this continent, side by side, in close proximity. Yet the relationship still lacks trust, understanding and empathy. We are not yet reconciled.

Properly understood, the Uluru Statement is a request to talk more constructively, to consult, to get to know one another. An ongoing political dialogue of the kind requested could build trust and mutual respect. Such a reform would belatedly include Indigenous peoples in the constitutional compact from which they were excluded in 1901. More than that, it would bring Australians closer together, such that we might better hear and learn from each other, understand one another, create better policies and produce better outcomes together. The constitutionally mandated hearing of Indigenous voices would make for a wiser Parliament and government, and fairer laws and policies with respect to Indigenous affairs. It would help create a more united and more reconciled nation.

Index

www.ingramcontent.com/pod-product-compliance
Lightning Source LLC
Chambersburg PA
CBHW071303180926
51613CB00001B/114